PARANOIA
PUBLISHING

Power told is power lost.
Zuni Proverb

To Keith,
and to
conspiracy,
Joan d'arc

Paranoia Publishing
P.O. Box 1041
Providence, RI 02901
www.paranoiamagazine.com

PARANOIA: The Conspiracy Reader, Volume 1

ISBN 978-0-615-29995-2

April 2010

Please send article submissions of 3000 to 5000 words with list of sources to:
conspiracyreader@gmail.com

Disclaimer

The statements and opinions expressed herein are not necessarily endorsed or held by Paranoia Publishing, its agents, employees, or assigns. No claim is made as to the accuracy, currency, and reliability of material provided. We do not knowingly publish disinformation, but sometimes it's hard to tell.

PARANOIA
The Conspiracy Reader™

Volume 1

Compiled and Edited by
Joan d'Arc and Al Hidell
co-editors of *PARANOIA* Magazine
www.paranoiamagazine.com

Contents

Introduction

Well, it's 2010 and the world is falling apart. But don't say we didn't warn you.

The economy, which supposedly hit bottom last year, is still in freefall. The unemployment rate, say economists who are not afraid to say so, is actually twice the official number. Even after the recession ends, it could take ten years for the unemployment rate to return to pre-recession levels. This last warning comes from that bastion of radical economics, the Federal Reserve Bank of Kansas City.

But nothing surprises *PARANOIA* readers anymore, does it?

PARANOIA: The Conspiracy Reader grew in 1992 out of material collected by a group called The Providence Conspiracy League, which met in a small bookstore in Providence, Rhode Island, called Newspeak. The first issue was photocopied at Kinko's. The print run was a few hundred copies.

Through the 90s and into the new millenium, the cryptocracy's agenda became undeniable: from the Ruby Ridge FBI fiasco, to the Waco massacre, the OKC bombing and 9/11, *PARANOIA* was there connecting the dots. In hindsight, *PARANOIA* was a time capsule, capturing the first decade of an America in decline.

Careening into 2008, the economy screeched to a halt, and well over 500 magazines and newspapers "stopped the presses," permanently. *PARANOIA* magazine was not immune to the forces that were pummeling the print media. By 2009, over half the magazines we were paying to print were being destroyed by the retailers, unsold. This magazine "consignment" paradigm was clearly unsustainable in the new internet economy.

Was *PARANOIA* doomed to become a collection of virtual bytes that could only be read on a computer screen? We found a middle path, "print on demand" technology that allows publishers to print in small quantities, as needed. The idea hadn't yet caught on in the ad-driven magazine industry, where mass-production and mass-circulation are a necessity.

Welcome to *PARANOIA*, the magazine that became a book. What you're holding in your hands is volume one of *PARANOIA: The Conspiracy Reader* in book format. It contains the same kind of content as the magazine did, and you can buy it in the same places you used to buy the magazine—only on the book shelf rather than the magazine rack.

In keeping with PARANOIA's peculiar fusion of conspiracy and kook, this volume contains a few vintage interviews from back issues, including the late great grandfather of the Apollo hoax, Ralph René; ancient secret society researcher, William Bramley; eminent dot connector, David McGowan; and ukulele crooner, Tiny Tim. We've also packed in several new interviews, including self-proclaimed JFK "witness," Roderick A. MacKenzie, III; astrotheologist, Acharya S; Apollo hoax videographer, Jarrah White; 9/11 scholar, David Ray Griffin; and secret society historian, Craig Heimbichner.

We're also proud to present several articles by the best conspiracy and paranormal researchers in the business; all the writers and interviewees in this volume are appreciated beyond measure. We'd like to thank contributing artists, Lee Harvey Roswell, Saint John, James Quigley, Iona Miller, John David Moore and Ned Sonntag. We'd also like to thank our two editorial assistants, Liz Lee and Mark Elliott, for their editing and proofreading assistance on this volume.

In other exciting news, in early 2009 *PARANOIA* was approached by an archivist at Baylor University in Waco, Texas, offering space in their Poage Political Archives, which focuses on JFK assassination research and other fringe political materials. This means you can now take a road trip to Waco to visit all 51 original issues of *PARANOIA* at Poage Legislative Library, Baylor University, 201 Baylor Avenue in Waco, Texas. For directions or information call 254.710.3540.

The whole set of back issues has also been archived at the University of Rhode Island in Kingston, Rhode Island. The Robert L. Carothers Library, located in the center of campus, was founded in 1892 and houses 1.4 million volumes. In 2009, the *PARANOIA* collection was updated, replenished, and moved to the Special Collections Unit located on the second floor of the Library. For directions to the URI campus, go to *www.uri.edu*.

Last but not least, due to a high demand for sold-out back issues, you can now download PDFs of select vintage issues of *PARANOIA* for FREE at *www.paranoiamagazine.com*. And of course, there are back issues of *PARANOIA* still in print—we have included a list at the end of this volume. You can purchase back issues by mail or on the PARANOIA website, where you can do some free reading as well.

So to our new readers in the book world, welcome to *PARANOIA*! To our old magazine format readers, we hope you like our new, more sustainable book format. Thank you for making this great leap with us.

Al Hidell and Joan d'Arc

Illustrations by Saint John, *inkshadows.com, myspace.com/inkshadows*

The *Necronomicon*

How Lovecraft's Creation Grew a Tale

by Dan Harms

A recent list of the top ten grimoires—books of magic—included a book called the *Necronomicon*. Not too bad for a work that started as a literary in-joke. How did the *Necronomicon* make the leap from fiction to occult notoriety? Let's look at the story.

One century ago, a young man named Howard Phillips Lovecraft was living in Providence, Rhode Island. Having left high school due to illness before graduating, he was unable to fulfill his dream of going to Brown University. His once-wealthy family was slipping into genteel poverty, but he was nonetheless expected to uphold the lifestyle of a gentleman of leisure. Lovecraft must have found negotiating these expectations and hopes a difficult situation.

He found an answer in writing. At first he wrote essays on political and cultural topics, but soon he found his true strength: short stories of monsters and tortured souls, written in the style of Edgar Allan Poe. In 1923, he submitted these works to the pulp magazine *Weird Tales*, where he found himself gaining some success—and a little money on the side.

As Lovecraft continued to write, he sought his own voice, creating a series of fictional props to express his philosophy and aesthetics. The most notable of these creations, the dread *Necronomicon*, appeared for the first time in his story "The Hound," written in 1922. This tale centers around two graverobbers who take a magical talisman from a corpse, causing them to be pursued by a horrible undead monster. In their desperation, they consult the *Necronomicon* for more information on the topic—but it does not tell them how to stop the beast.

In "The Hound," Lovecraft mentions "Abdul Alhazred" as the book's author. Alhazred was actually a childhood name of Lovecraft's during a period when he was fascinated with *The Arabian Nights*. In a previous story, Lovecraft had even composed a piece of poetry by Alhazred:

That is not dead which can eternal lie,
And with strange aeons even death may die.

This poem was to become the leitmotif of Lovecraft's fiction. Humanity, according to Lovecraft's cosmology, is but a transitory phenomenon on this planet. Beyond the realm of everyday consciousness are older forces—magic, monsters, lost civilizations, and other mysteries of the universe. The protagonists in his tales are usually men driven to explore the past due to curiosity or compulsion. The horrific—or awe-inspiring—revelations they uncover leave the narrators shaken, missing, or insane.

Throughout these works, the *Necronomicon* continued to appear. At different times, it was a collection of lore regarding the dead, a book of spells, or a history of the pre-human aliens who inhabited our planet. As Lovecraft continued to write and submit his stories for publication, these references to the *Necronomicon* showed up more often in *Weird Tales*.

Lovecraft's creations were destined for greater things, however. As he wrote, Lovecraft developed a circle of friends with whom he often exchanged stories before publication. In addition, he sometimes revised the stories of others for publication, usually at a minimal fee, which were then published under his clients' names. These behind-the-scenes relationships became mirrored in his stories, with monsters and books—including the *Necronomicon*—mentioned by one author appearing in stories by another.

One incident will illustrate how this process worked. Lovecraft's young protégé Frank Belknap Long composed a quote from the *Necronomicon* for his short story, "The Space-Eaters." Long claimed that his particular quote came from the English translation made by the real-life Elizabethan wizard John Dee, a famous figure in occult history. Lovecraft himself inserted John Dee's translation of the *Necronomicon* into his story "The Dunwich Horror." When publishing Long's story, an editor cut the original quote from John Dee. Thus, Dee's translation of the *Necronomicon* appeared through Lovecraft, even though Long actually created it.

If this is hard for us to follow, imagine the reaction of the pulp magazine readers. If the *Necronomicon* appeared in tales by multiple authors, could the book be real? Both *Weird Tales* and Lovecraft himself received letters asking if the book really existed. Both told the inquirers that it was Lovecraft's invention, but the letters continued.

Lovecraft passed away in 1937 from a combination of cancer of the intestine and Bright's disease. He had never received top billing in *Weird Tales*, but soon he was recognized as a giant in his field. His fiction was republished and read throughout the burgeoning fandom in what would soon be known as science fiction.

As Lovecraft's fame grew, so did that of the *Necronomicon*. Fans of Lovecraft wrote stories in their small-press magazines that featured the infamous book. As time went on, the first *Necronomicon* hoaxes appeared. Booksellers published tongue-in-cheek ads seeking or selling the book, and entries for the book appeared in the card catalogs of many libraries. This low-grade hoaxing only spread the fame of the book further.

The *Necronomicon* Explosion

The Sixties counterculture encouraged people to seek out new realities beyond the commonplace and everyday, whether through escapist fiction or new philosophies. As a result, Lovecraft's stories were converted into movies for the first time, with films such as *The Haunted Palace* (1963) and *The Dunwich Horror* (1970) bringing distorted retellings of his vision to broader audiences. Lovecraft's stories, along with classic fantasy and science fiction works, were re-discovered and reprinted for these new audiences. In addition, past writings by occult explorers such as Israel Regardie, Gerald Gardner, and Aleister Crowley found popularity once again. All of this led to an atmosphere ripe for the resurgence of Lovecraft—and the *Necronomicon*.

The first major *Necronomicon* hoax to appear was the *Al Azif*, published by the science fiction publisher Owlswick Press in 1973. Its owner, George Scithers, commissioned artist Robert Dills to draw page upon page of Arabic-like calligraphy. Author L. Sprague de Camp then wrote up a description of how he had bought the book on a trip to Iraq, after three scholars of ancient languages had disappeared while attempting to decipher it. The book had a limited run of 348 copies, but it soon became a collector's item purchased or given to many libraries. Occasionally someone runs across this book in a special collections department and gets a thrill out of it.

The Owlswick book's text was indecipherable, but its circulation through the fan community nonetheless inspired two other *Necronomicon* hoaxes that are still with us today. One of these *Necronomicons* was assembled at the behest of the British publisher Neville Spearman. Robert Turner, head of the Order of the Cubic Stone, used his deep knowledge of ceremonial magic to assemble a grimoire with ornate magical tools and intensive, complicated rituals requiring long preparations and mystical substances. David Langford claimed that this grimoire had emerged from a computer analysis of Liber Loagaeth, a set of mystical tables of letters created by John Dee, who we've seen mentioned before.

If the reader was to believe this, however, it was necessary to find out how Lovecraft could have uncovered the mysterious book without contact with Dee's manuscripts or a convenient computer decipherment. Occult author Colin Wilson spun a story about Lovecraft's father being a Freemason who owned the *Necronomicon* as part of his lodge activities. Though Lovecraft's maternal grandfather was the head of a Masonic lodge, no evidence that he or anyone else possessed the *Necronomicon* has ever emerged. Wilson also spoke of L. Sprague de Camp's *Al Azif* as if it were an actual book. Nonetheless, all of this made for an entertaining new *Necronomicon*. Wilson and his compatriots even published a sequel to this book—the *R'lyeh Text*, named after another book of forbidden lore created by Lovecraft correspondent August Derleth.

The other work has been so influential—and not always in a positive manner—that it deserves its own section.

The Simon *Necronomicon*

Across the Atlantic, another *Necronomicon* was being written. We know relatively little about its ultimate genesis, save for rumors that it emerged from a particularly wild party held at or near the Warlock Shop, a magical supply company in Brooklyn. Nonetheless, it might be possible to reconstruct a large part of the story.

Central to this scheme was Simon, a supposed priest of an Eastern Orthodox denomination. Speculation has been rife as to the man's real identity. The most likely candidate, identified as such by both author Alan Cabal and the U. S. Copyright Office, is noted conspiracy author Peter Levenda, best known for his book *Unholy Alliance* on Nazi occultism.

In 1973, two monks of a questionable Eastern Orthodox denomination were caught attempting to steal numerous books from libraries and private collections across the country. According to Simon, these men found a ninth-century Greek manuscript which made its way to him. He commissioned three translators to decipher the book and then returned it to his sources—just in time for the evidence of these crimes to be conveniently destroyed. The only person's word we have for any of this is that of Simon himself.

Simon's first articles, appearing in the pages of *Earth Religion News*, the Warlock Shop's newsletter, reveal a likely motivation for the hoax. At the time, the Warlock Shop had two major groups of customers. On one hand were the Pagans, who possessed an earth-based spirituality and performed simple rituals drawing on the moon and the goddess. On the other were the ceremonial magicians, who practiced magic from ancient manuscripts that was formalized and Judeo-Christian in content. Simon wrote a series of articles attempting to bring together both Paganism and ceremonial magic in a new synthesis, based on the beliefs and practices of the ancient Sumerian civilization.

Another likely source for the book was the Owlswick Press hoax. An ad in *Earth Religion News* from 1973—the same year as the Owlswick edition's release—lists a *Necronomicon* in the "original script" for $25 at the Warlock Shop. At the same time, it promises a "forthcoming"

English translation selling for $10. One individual I talked to mentioned seeing the *Al Azif* prominently displayed in the store. Oddly—or perhaps not—Simon has never mentioned this book or its presence at the Warlock Shop.

The Simon *Necronomicon* presents a dualistic cosmology in which the "Elder Gods," or the deities of the ancient Sumerian civilization, must be approached to save us from the "Ancient Gods," similar to the alien monsters from Lovecraft's fiction. To contact the Elder Gods and gain their power, the magician must walk through seven "gates" corresponding with each of the classic planets (Mercury through Saturn, plus the Moon and Sun) and particular colors and metals. In doing so, they become capable of using various spells, calling up the dead, and invoking the "Fifty Names" of the Babylonian god Marduk, so that they might protect the world when the Ancient Ones returned.

To sell this book, Simon marketed it to a wide variety of belief systems. His introduction is a tour de force of marketing. Not content with simply covering ceremonial magicians and pagans, he also included sections appealing to Satanists, science fiction readers, and fans of *The Exorcist*.

This rampant commercialism did take a turn toward white supremacist ideology. Many of the etymologies from the *Necronomicon* are taken from L. A. Waddell's dubious *Sumer-Aryan Dictionary* (1927), a work claiming that all ancient civilizations, including that of the Sumerians, were founded by fair-haired men. This might have been an effort to sell the book to the followers of National Renaissance Party founder James Madole. Madole was known for his fascist leanings, his love of science fiction and the occult, and—according to one source—a deep familiarity with the works of Lovecraft and other associated authors. He spent much time at the Warlock Shop and advised Levenda, who was working on a book on neo-Nazism.

The month after Madole's passing, Levenda traveled to Colonia Dignidad, a supposed Nazi colony in Chile. The experience left him shaken, and he left the New York City occult scene shortly thereafter—but not before Avon Books had offered a contract for the publication of the *Necronomicon* in paperback.

Paradoxically, the *Necronomicon* became both highly influential and largely disregarded in the years to come. Its sales in chain bookstores across the country made it one of the top-selling books on magic of its time, and many teenage practitioners learned about occultism for the first time in its pages. At the same time, most practitioners with a few years of experience found the book's combination of disparate doctrines with fiction to be distasteful or humorous. As such, the *Necronomicon* has had little impact on Western magic outside of those who practice the system on their own.

The Simon *Necronomicon* inspired a number of books on how to work its system more effectively. The first of these, the *Report on the Necronomicon* or *Necronomicon Spellbook* by Simon, appeared in 1981. This work provided simple instructions for dealing with the "names of Marduk." A few other unauthorized books on working with the *Necronomicon* appeared over the years. In 2006, Simon issued the long-awaited *Gates of the Necronomicon*, which described in great detail the procedure for walking the Gates.

Simon also made another contribution to the *Necronomicon* controversy in 2006, which he issued a book called *Dead Names* refining his previous story of how the *Necronomicon* came into being. His justifications of the book's authenticity are clumsy, largely built upon selective quotes from reference books, random and unverified Internet articles, and invective at "so-called" occultists—a label that seems to be based on whether someone disagrees with him. Simon has appeared repeatedly since then, giving at least three contradictory stories as to why he must remain anonymous and thereby turning his dramatic tale into an ongoing farce. It is telling that no associate from the Warlock Shop has emerged to validate his account.

Another Shot at the Title

A more recent addition to the ranks of the *Necronomicons* was the edition written by Donald Tyson and published by Llewellyn. Ironically, this book began with *The Necronomicon Files*, a book I co-wrote with John Wisdom Gonce on what we called the "*Necronomicon* phenomenon." We asked

Tyson to write a foreword to the book, and, to our deep appreciation, he did so.

Afterward, Tyson contacted me with a new project. Our book had inspired him to delve further into Lovecraft and the *Necronomicon* myth. He wanted to create a new *Necronomicon*, a work of fiction completely faithful to Lovecraft's vision of the book. I thought it was a great plan, and I happily made some comments on his draft as he continued. In the end, Tyson's *Necronomicon: The Wanderings of Alhazred* (2004) went into the publisher's marketing division as fiction and emerged as non-fiction, thus adding me to the ranks of *Necronomicon* hoaxers! I should add that I bear Tyson no animosity over this, as he has always dealt fairly with me.

Since then, Tyson's *Necronomicon* has become an occult publishing phenomenon, giving inspiration to a novel (*Alhazred*), a Tarot deck, and a workbook (*Grimoire of the Necronomicon*). Until recently, however, most accepted the book itself as a recent creation. Nonetheless, recently an aura of mystery has begun to build around the book. The latest rumor is that I am working with Donald Tyson in a Lovecraftian magical order bent on discrediting the Simon *Necronomicon* to gain power for ourselves!

The Evolving *Necronomicon*

In recent years, the legend of the *Necronomicon* has grown. Its appearances in media have become more prevalent, as the book turns up in novels, comic books, movies, television shows, and games. One notable appearance has been the *Evil Dead* franchise, in which the smart-mouthed department store clerk, Ash, battles zombies and demons he accidentally freed from incantations in the black book. In fact, mentions of the *Necronomicon* have been so prevalent in the horror genre that director Guillermo del Toro decided not to quote the book at the beginning of the first *Hellboy* movie because he felt it had been overused.

With the ubiquity of the Internet, it is unsurprising that the book has become part of online folklore. Rumors and tales of the book can circulate more quickly now. Believers in the book's reality quote as gospel articles such as Colin Low's "*Necronomicon* Anti-FAQ" and Ryan Parker's "*Necronomicon* Info Source," both of which were early Internet jokes. One of my friends, while in a feverish state one afternoon, wrote his own *Necronomicon*, entitling it the *Grimoirium Imperium*. This has turned up on numerous sites thereafter, with at least one person insisting it was the magical equivalent of a nuclear weapon.

Numerous permutations of the various classic *Necronomicons*—de Camp, Hay, and Simon—continue to appear online. Some of these are straight reprints, while others include warnings and clarifications of those who have edited, worked with, or otherwise touched these books. Simon has even publicly complained about the theft of his work—an odd attitude for a man who supposedly received his book from thieves!

To further muddy the waters is the appearance, over the last few years, of live action role-playing games, or LARPs, in which people play out genre adventures using props and costumes. Among these creations have been prop *Necronomicons*, the product of desktop publishing software and long hours of painstaking labor by their creators. These are often quite impressive, including leather bindings, archaic fonts, and texts taken from Lovecraft, published *Necronomicons*, and the authors' own imaginations.

In this manner, *Necronomicon* rumors and texts continue to appear, recombine, and reappear, like a mystical kaleidoscope. One wonders whether Lovecraft would have laughed or stared in horror at the whole affair.

Nonetheless, some of you might insist on looking for the *Necronomicon* yourself. I encourage you to do so, and not merely to take my word for it. After all, given the dark rumors that surround me, I cannot be trusted on such matters. All such seekers should beware, lest the revelations you encounter drive you mad!

About the Author

Dan Harms is the author of *The Necronomicon Files*. He is a librarian and writer living in upstate New York. He has written two books, *The Cthulhu Mythos Encyclopedia* (Elder Signs Press) and *The Necronomicon Files* with John Wisdom Gonce (Weiser). You can read more of his writing and contact him via his blog, "Papers Falling from an Attic Window," at *http://danharms.wordpress.com.*

Crimson Shadows

Freemasonry, the OTO and the CIA

Joan d'Arc Interviews
Craig Heimbichner

Craig Heimbichner is the author of *Blood on the Altar: The Secret History of the World's Most Dangerous Secret Society*, which among other topics covers the relationship between Freemasonic groups, the OTO, the CIA and the military. In this interview, Craig discusses a few of the controversial subjects of his book—blood sacrifice, the homunculus ritual, legal loopholes of the Talmud, Aleister Crowley, Alfred Kinsey, and James Shelby Downard.

Joan: In your book, Blood on the Altar, *you talk about the "Invisible Government" as an "amorphous grouping of individuals and agencies." Who are these individuals and agencies, what type of 'glue' coheres them, and what, do you surmise, is the origin of this group or these groups? Are they largely made up of patriarchal Freemasonic groups? What do they wish to accomplish?*

Craig: These groups comprise the true power-brokers behind the scenes. As Benjamin Disraeli writes in *Coningsby*, "the world is governed by very different personages from what is imagined by those who are not behind the scenes."

To give some examples, let's start with the CIA. Clearly the CIA has operated in the shadows from its inception and has planned major events with world-shaking impact, including assassinations. Officially, where are they in the 'civics course' version of government? Where are they in the Constitution? But they exist, and have had great power—from the shadow side, as part of the "Invisible Government." Just because a group is 'known,' as the CIA is, doesn't mean that its activities are transparent. The CIA retains great power in spite of occasional forays into oversight, real or feigned, from Congress.

We could also bring up financial and military organizations, but I think your question is aiming at a shadow-level behind those groups. That level really gets to the back room, the realm of the dealmakers. The glue that binds them tends to be partly ideological and goal-driven, but there is more to it than that. You mention patriarchal Freemasonic groups, and this is starting to touch on the "glue," which is actually a larger, sprawling network of fraternal organizations and secret societies. These groups, which have a long and complex history, usually have a large base of well-meaning and clueless members, but the organizations are also perfect covers for those who wish to plot and cut deals, with agendas that can include criminal activities or shady power grabs.

One example of a Masonic group that is usually overlooked would be the National Sojourners—the military organization for Freemasons. I've written about this group in my article, "Brotherhood of the Gun," in the recently published *Secret and Suppressed II* (Feral House, 2009). Goals of the elites in these various fraternal orgs and secret societies center on the usual—power and money—but there's a layer past all of that, and domination of the Group Mind is at the heart of their core ego-maniacal dreams: the creation of a zombie level of patsies who feed the upper structure of power.

Joan: Tell me more about the National Sojourners. How does this group stay so secretive? One website (masonicworld.com) states that the group "formally brings together Masonic leaders

of the uniformed services of the U.S. to further the National Defense, and works to oppose any influence calculated to weaken our National Security." So this is a surprising claim. What might that include?

Craig: It might include practically anything, if the past eight years under George W. Bush is any indication of what gets pulled off in the name of "National Security." And it hasn't ended with Obama, by the way. The problem here is that we are not only dealing with the already secretive world of military decisions, but another layer as well. Goethe (himself a Freemason) famously criticized the Lodge for being a "government within a government." The danger of a group like the National Sojourners is that we can be dealing with a military within the military, a secretive group of decision-makers within the already protected war-structure that decides to drop bombs and invade countries.

Joan: We've noticed here in Providence that the Freemasons have started overt membership campaigns via radio ads. What is the nature of the Freemasonic belief system and why do most people believe Freemasons to be a benign (hamburger-eating) order?

Craig: If you mention a "Freemasonic belief system" the Masons will immediately object that they have no dogmas or creed. Formally that's true, but there are also common rituals and purposes that hold them together, and a large body of Masonic writing which in its upper echelons veers into the occult. This level of esoteric Freemasonry tends to view the initiatory system as a continuation of ancient occult mysteries, including a veneration of Sirius symbolized by the pentagram or "blazing star" and the two pillars within the Lodge itself, Jachin and Boaz. At a deeper level this binary star and these two columns are a symbol of the dualistic system or Double Mind that has fascinated humanity for thousands of years—whether symbolized as Janus, yin and yang, Shiva and Shakti, or the two pillars of the kabbalistic Tree of Life—and which have served as a blueprint for psychological control for unscrupulous power-lords or adepts. The modern reflection is the two-party system in this country, which keeps the herd bouncing between two phony alternatives while the elites retain control.

Most Freemasons are indeed of the "knife and fork" variety, and many can be fine individuals, without question. The charitable work of the well-intentioned gives a cover for the few who use the ties of the organization for less honorable purposes, whether we are speaking of the murder of Captain William Morgan in 1826 or, if you accept the Downard thesis, the assassination of JFK, an event filled with Masonic symbolism, whatever the organizations or individuals immediately responsible.

Joan: So, not to give away the secret of your book, but what is the relationship between the Freemasons and the Ordo Templi Orientis (OTO)?

Craig: The OTO itself is less well known. Getting back to esoteric Freemasonry, the OTO originally claimed to be an *academia masonica* or Masonic academy—a sort of graduate school for Freemasons. Today they function as an occult 'fringe-masonic' Order—one of the organizations which uses a Masonic structure but is officially denied 'status' by the Grand Lodge. James Shelby Downard considered these relationships part of the Masonic "hoodwink"—a system set up to ensure informal relationships when desirable and also to give "plausible deniability" when convenient. And it is a fact that there are overlapping high members in the Grand Lodge, the Scottish Rite and the OTO.

The OTO has a long history and involves many groups. The current OTO is much smaller than the Masonic Lodge but carries members involved in esoteric purposes which can range from sex magick to rather fascist-sounding aims, such as those I've quoted in my book from official OTO documents, where we learn that one of the OTO dreams is that the "slaves shall serve," and that the "slaves" deserve that fate. Most lower OTO members (technically "MMM" or Mysteria Mystica Maxima, those from 0° to VII°) refuse to take official OTO documents literally, and think they are involved in a freewheeling experiment in liberty. In my opinion, it's just one more Masonic jest.

Joan: You write that Crowley also calls for "the blood of the child" in rituals. Do you believe Crowley meant literally the blood of children should be sacrificed in OTO rituals, and do you believe this group has ever or continues to sacrifice children in blood rituals?

Craig: These passages have several layers to them. First, the OTO will claim that Crowley is referencing sex magick in a code. I don't have a problem with allegory in a religious worldview, and prefer it to literal interpretations which are barbaric, so I'm willing to concede that viewpoint to those members who read it that way. However, Crowley did literally condone instances of bloody sacrifice, such as his famous ritual in which he baptized a toad as Jesus and then crucified it. Granted, that's not a child, but most people would see it as a fairly sick form of cruelty, and ask what it's all about. In fact, I received a copy of an email from someone within OTO who did this ritual and was joking about it—and he alleges he is a "practicing Episcopalian."

Blood does in fact drip around the OTO. Take the "Mass of the Phoenix," for example, in which the member does extract his own blood. It's a bit of self-vampirism if you will. A friend of mine was thrown down and had a cross carved on his chest during his OTO initiation at a higher level—and he's Jewish. Beyond such examples, there's a whole level of obsession with menstrual blood in the OTO. No getting away from it: blood is part of the landscape of the OTO.

Does it pass beyond that to actual child sacrifice? Officially, of course not. However, there have been those who have allegedly used the frequent images and apparent recommendations of human sacrifice in the OTO literature as an inspiration to commit atrocities. Matthew Murray, the Colorado Springs 2007 killer, had been part of the local OTO scene and carried the OTO's red *Book of the Law*. The OTO will always quickly point out that these types of actions are those of deranged types and not officially sanctioned (they quickly distanced themselves from Murray). Granted. But does the OTO's blood-soaked (literal or metaphorical) mindset of their writings and rituals play a role as a foreseeable catalyst, and is their role in propagating such material irresponsible, to say the least? That's a fair question, and it likely won't go away.

Beyond those like Murray, there are still occasional tales of ritual abuse, and while many victims have been discredited, can we discredit them all? The CIA tortures people without qualms; MK-ULTRA is a documented fact: is there any intersection between government torture and ritual abuse, and how much does all of this intersect with the inspiration of blood-sacrifice and torture language and ritual in esoteric Orders?

James Shelby Downard claims to have witnessed an OTO-CIA intersection; the important

Crowley follower Marcelo Motta claimed the CIA and one branch of the OTO conspired against him. Motta also claimed that he learned through his contacts that Oscar Schlag was in the employ of the psychological warfare section of the Shin Bet and also the CIA. Besides being an associate of the famed psychologist Dr. Carl Jung, Schlag moved in high OTO circles (with Jane Wolfe, Karl Germer, and Felix Pinkus, "spiritual father" of OTO leader Hermann Metzger). Such questions of intersection with intelligence agencies and psy-ops will always haunt groups like the OTO, and until they purge themselves of the language of blood sacrifice, fascist and/or cultic mind-control tendencies, and their recurring focus on blood, we might say they have it coming.

Joan: What was the OTO-CIA connection claimed by James Shelby Downard? Can you tell me more about that?

Craig: Downard claimed there was a definite OSS-CIA tie-in to sex magick, which is the basis of the OTO. As you know, he made a lot of amazing claims—meeting "Wild Bill" Donovan (and there are claims of Donovan's involvement in the OTO, but I've never verified it). Downard claimed that the CIA drugged and wired his beautiful wife Anne to perform sex magickal rituals with them. His story: he followed her and caught them in the act with FBI personnel and other secret service intel types, holding these rituals while immersed in light from the star Sirius in the constellation *Canis Major*, beamed through the 200-inch Palomar telescope. As I mentioned, Sirius, the dual star, symbolizes a great deal in esoteric masonry, including the Double Mind, further symbolized as the androgynous Baphomet or Goat of Mendes, something about which Lodges routinely joke ("riding the goat") with initiates.

Downard isn't the only one to claim an OTO-CIA connection. As I mentioned, one of the key OTO leaders, Marcelo Motta of Brazil, lost control of the rights of the OTO in the U.S. courts to William Breeze, the current leader of its main body, and claimed the whole operation was a sort of courtroom Masonic kangaroo coup engineered by the CIA. Motta apparently felt that the powers didn't see him as a "player."

Joan: What do you mean that Marcelo Motta lost control of the rights of the OTO? Can you tell me more about this court case?

Craig: Motta saw himself as a legitimate head of the OTO, coming from the lineage of Karl Germer, Crowley's OTO rep in Germany and, allegedly, his successor as Outer Head of the Order (OHO). When Grady McMurty (a.k.a. "Hymenaeus Alpha") kick-started the OTO again in 1969, Motta did not agree with McMurty's assumed leadership. Motta, for example, wanted rights to publish Crowley's works, and the whole case fell into the U.S. Courts. Motta lost, and the tendency for the "court-approved" OTO to rely on lawyers has only increased, which is very interesting, given the freewheeling image promoted in its recruitment literature.

Joan: In Blood on the Altar *you write that the roots of pedophilia actually go back to the Talmud where "genital contact" with a child below a certain age is not considered sexual. Is this a loophole in Talmudic law? Where does the Talmud get this mentality? Is it essentially legalese for pedophiles?*

Craig: After I wrote about this topic, Swiss OTO historian Peter Koenig explored the issue in a subsequent German publication of his own. Of course there are famous Jewish critics of Talmudic fundamentalism, including the late Professor Israel Shahak of Hebrew University, Jerusalem—and in all fairness, Reform Judaism would have an entirely different approach to the Talmud from the strict, Orthodox interpretation.

The entire subject is highly controversial. I'm sometimes misunderstood. It's not a Jewish or anti-Jewish thing: but one might wonder, why write about the Talmud, when the roots of the OTO are kabbalistic? But the OTO on the inside loses its flavor of the Kabbalah; it reflects (especially today) a legalistic mentality. On the outside, it looks magically kabbalistic; on the inside, it feels, ironically, fundamentalist and lawyerish—particularly if you buck their authority. Legal shysterism is not exclusive to any one religion, of course, and reflects a type of fundamentalist mentality, which, ironically, appears to be dominant within the current OTO itself. That's highly ironic because many are attracted to it as a rebellion against fundamentalism, and years down the road wind up finding the new house rather all too familiar—only darker.

The "loophole" mentality which Israel Shahak attacked comes more from the dialectic of legalese, and in a broader sense is reflected in the maze of cover stories and "blinds" which populate any initiatory system such as the OTO. The Talmud—an enormous dialectical work—does include this passage, and if taken literally implies shocking attitudes toward child victimization. Currently some religions are media-propaganda targets, and such headlines serve the wars and distractions necessary for the Cryptocracy to advance its agenda. Islam, for example, has any number of books plumbing its Hadith for horrors, real or imagined. The Catholic priest-pedophilia connection is another famous case. But such Talmudic rationalizations are unknown and shocking to hear about.

The relevance has to do with the fact that the OTO is a product of the West (in spite of its homage to the "Orient" in its title), and the culture in which it grew was planted in soil tilled by two religions: Judaism and Christianity. The OTO chose to style itself a Gnostic or heretical variety of Christianity, but acknowledged its debt to the former by claiming the Kabbalah to be its basis. And in actual fact, you can't truly separate the Kabbalah from the Talmud. Within the OTO it's an outer-inner irony as I pointed out; outside it looks magical, and inside you meet the lawyers and autocrats.

The mentality behind justifying pedophilia is, of course, older than the OTO, the Talmud or any major surviving religious structure or document; it's inherent in the rationalizing tendency of the human psyche when faced with desires it would hide or reject. Mystery religions could be viewed as one of the ancient sources of sanction for these desires in that initiatory structures were set up to safeguard such practices from scrutiny. It is only to be expected that once a cloak of secrecy is drawn, some of the goings-on behind that cloak will include the abominable—including pedophilia.

Joan: In Blood on the Altar *you talk about Alfred Kinsey, author of* Sexual Behavior in the Human Male and Sexual Behavior in the Human Female *(in the late 1940s and early 1950s), as being one of the first people to lift the social stigma of pedophilia. His research likened sex with children to "sexual liberation"? What's the real story with Kinsey?*

Craig: Another reworked fraud known by myth today rather than fact. Judith Reisman uncovered his massive research involving sexual abuse of at least 317 infants and young boys in the name of "science." Kinsey had a soundproof laboratory built to his specifications at Indiana University where horrendous experiments were performed, which became the basis for a lot of today's sex education. Should we be surprised to learn that he was enamored of Aleister Crowley, who also advocated lifting the taboo against sex with children? Crowley writes in his *Commentary on the Book of the Law* that "incest, adultery, and paederasty" should be openly practiced and that "all children shall be accustomed from infancy to witness every type of sexual act..."

Kinsey made a pilgrimage to Crowley's Abbey of Thelema in Cefalù, Sicily, to pay homage to the "Great Beast." Doc Kinsey also tried to acquire the "Magical Diaries" of Crowley for the Kinsey Institute. Under the cloak of secrecy, children have always been abused, but this time it was done not in the name of ritual, but of science. Charles Fort held that modern science is largely a replacement of magical ritual anyway, so perhaps Kinsey is really a modern priest, an occult shaman in the modern garb of the new priesthood: the lab coat.

Joan: You write of Hollywood's connection to the OTO, and that the film Rosemary's Baby *could be considered a "symbolic enactment of a homunculus ritual." Can you explain what a homunculus ritual is and what it's designed to do?*

Craig: The details are in the advanced rituals of the OTO, and they reflect very old, key alchemical goals. A homunculus or "Moonchild" ritual aims to create a man, or to animate or possess a body, under control of the magician; it relates to the legend of the Golem or the Frankenstein monster. Crowley's rituals were attempted in the "Babalon Working" by Jack Parsons and L. Ron Hubbard with Marjorie Cameron in an attempt to create a "possessed baby" bringing the spirit of Babalon the Great Whore into the world.

Downard claimed the ultimate techno-occult homunculus attempt was carried out at Trinity Site in New Mexico on July 16, 1945 with the first atomic bomb blast. Nearby was a huge steel "bottle" code-named "Jumbo" which weighed nearly one-half million pounds. Twenty-five feet long and twelve feet in diameter, it had been custom-made at an eastern steel mill and shipped by a 64-wheel trailer to the site—never explained in any reasonable sense by the government. Downard held that a "mannikin" (or homunuculus, subject of a poem by Crowley recited by Parsons before each rocket launch) was inside, and that the occult purpose of the atomic detonation was at least in part to perform the ultimate homunuculus ritual.

Our government involved in the occult? For the curious, I recommend *Sex and Rockets* and *Dark Mission* (Feral House) to get some background on the Masons-on-the-moon, mind-blowing occult tie-ins.

Joan: There were stories floating around about the strange death of David Carradine, who had been investigating secret societies while on a film shoot in Thailand. Initially the news reported autoerotic asphyxiation or suicide. Was there any indication that this was a ritual murder?

Craig: Possibly. David's father John Carradine attended events at the Agape Lodge in Pasadena, California, and appears in a group photograph taken outside the Lodge in 1934, according to an OTO source. Then we have David's daughter's and his own apparent involvement with the Thelemic "cousin," the Church of Scientology (the *Los Angeles Times* posted blog photos of David reading to the crowd at the Church's 2008 Christmas party). So it would appear that secret society involvement of one sort or another ran in his family.

The first allegations, however, were that David was investigating martial arts secret societies. I find this a stretch, if not a cover or deflection: groups like the Triads in my opinion would not have killed him in a manner so suggestive of sexual ritual.

On the other hand, from the photograph leaked to the press it *does* appear that he was murdered and could not have killed himself. Some have suggested hookers, but they would have been picked up on hotel cameras, and why would the police protect them? Fortean colleague Loren Coleman explored the surrounding locale and Bangkok is permeated with sexual symbolism, making it a synchronous place for a ritual murder. Was David Carradine investigating a secret society, more occult and sex magical than martial arts-oriented—and did he get dirt on the wrong people? It's a question worth pursuing, but I think the ball has been dropped—or buried.

Joan: You have mentioned to me that you're a follower of the Medieval Catholic mystic, Meister Eckhart, who contended that the "absolute cause" (God) is pure intellect and not being. How was Eckhart's thinking considered heretical at the time?

Craig: I'm not sure "follower" is the right descriptor; my approach to life resonates with his, and his writings inspire me with their depth, perception, and paradoxical insight. For example, he said, "Truth is something so noble that if God could turn aside from it, I could keep to the truth and let God go." I'm driven by the same feeling for truth. I'm also not sure of the quote which you paraphrase as his. A lot was done in his name which scholars are still trying to clear up. He saw the divine as pure existence or being, in the present moment or eternal now, which wasn't actually heretical or original in that sense. Boethius wrote about it from a prison in the 6th century, and Augustine said virtually the same thing, but people had forgotten his radical side. Eckhart loved paradox and, in effect, blasted the complacent Group Mind of his time, which naturally got him into trouble.

Anyone hard to classify is usually declared a heretic by somebody. I'm sure I'm somebody's heretic: I'm a real-time mixture of the rationalist and the mystic, the profane and the sacred, the skeptic and the spiritual or Catholic. I'm not comfortable with being preachy, although I've been squeezed into the role at times, sometimes by an editor, publisher (not you), or host, and usually regret it. I'm always rethinking conclusions, since we all have to put our chips on some number in life (even the lack of position is a position), and I like to recalculate all my bets. The last thing I want to do is what Mark Twain called picking a viewpoint and "putting up shingles to protect it from the weather." So I suppose that makes me something of a perpetual revisionist. I think Eckhart was a revisionist as well, a spiritual revisionist. That doesn't mean he wasn't orthodox, at least in his own mind. He just wanted truth, and wanted to experience it himself, in the present moment. I'm the same.

Speaking of resonance, I could add that as a pianist I also deeply relate to the music of the pianistic wizard Franz Liszt. He was another paradoxical dynamo, who felt the pull of things eternal (he almost became a priest) but left a trail of babies across Europe (I can't compete there). I feel the tensions of life in a dynamic tapestry and usually relate to others who do, including my son who is on his own quest with his edgy band *The Cosmonauts*. He and his band members study Wing Chun kung fu from me, which keeps us all grounded in reality.

When we laugh and lift our eyes from the nightmarish and mind-controlled, cultish world of the OTO, with its dark obsessions with blood, power, and death—or the landscape of zombies in this country supporting whatever psychic vomit the media happens to spew at them—we wind up right where we are: in the "sacrament of the present moment" extolled by Meister Eckhart, in a world of divine beauty in which the Masonic glue dissipates, and thought-programming is deleted by the master key of sympathetic awareness.

About the Interviewee

Craig Heimbichner is the author of the popular book, *Blood on the Altar: The Secret History of the World's Most Dangerous Secret Society*, published by Independent History and Research (2005) *www.revisionisthistory.org*. Craig is a freelance writer, lecturer and researcher. He lives in California with his family.

The Mystery of Albert Pike

Saint or Satanist?

by Robert Guffey

The enigma of Albert Pike is a persistent one. Certain facts are known about him, facts that detractors and supporters alike can both agree upon. He's a little-known figure whose impact upon American history far exceeds his notoriety. He founded the Scottish Rite and single-handedly created the higher degrees of Freemasonry (degrees 4 through 33). He was Sovereign Grand Commander of the Southern Jurisdiction of Scottish Rite Freemasonry from 1859 to 1891, the year of his death. He was a Confederate General during the American Civil War. He was a powerful attorney in his day. He was also a prominent poet, whose literary works have been forgotten except by a small handful of devotees. He is the author of the most important work on Masonic ritual, philosophy and symbolism, i.e., *Morals and Dogma.*

On these facts, everyone can agree. It's the interpretation of these facts that begins to grow a bit misty.

Pike is a polarizing figure. There seems to be very little objective analysis of his impact on history. Mainstream historians rarely, if ever, refer to him. Therefore, we are left with volumes of questionable interpretations that often draw upon half-truths, rumors, innuendoes, misinterpretations, and outright forgeries. Pick up any book that contains even a minor reference to the man and you will find that the interpretation of the author falls into one of two categories: 1) Pike was a genius and a saint whose very touch turned men's souls into alchemical gold, or 2) Pike was a Satan worshipper whose noxious acts still stain the very heart of the United States of America—indeed, the very world itself.

There is no middle ground among these "researchers." Pike was either good or evil. Of course, the world would be much simpler if anyone was wholly good or wholly evil. Zen Buddhist Alan Watts once wrote a book entitled *The Book: On the Taboo Against Knowing Who You Are* in which he advised his readers to drop that dialectic way of thinking, what he called "the game of Black-versus-White" (Watts 30). It only causes confusion because it is a model that does not reflect reality. Human beings are far more complicated than that, and this includes Pike.

With most historical figures, the latter statement could normally go unsaid, but strange as it is to say, a very small minority of pundits have indeed implied that Albert Pike was not human at all (he was really a shape-shifting reptilian in disguise). I'm going to immediately crawl out on a limb, right here in the fifth paragraph, and propose we eliminate that theory for lack of evidence. I hope to now move on to more pressing matters....

But first, picture a scene for me, if you will. Picture an underground train depot, a twisted set of metal tracks sunk about ten feet into the concrete. On either side of the tracks people are yelling at each other: men, women, children... all races, all creeds. Strangely, some of the people who are shouting the loudest have no faces at all. A giant bronze bust of Pike is sitting in the middle of the tracks. In the distance, a train is barreling down upon this immense monument. The train is so loud, nobody can hear what anyone else is saying.

Let's slow this scene for a moment, turn the volume down on the train, and turn up the volume only on certain individuals... just one at a time. There's no preferred order amidst this chaos. We'll select our speakers at random....

Ralph Epperson, a Fundamentalist Christian and author of the book *The New World Order*, has concluded that Albert Pike was a Satanist whose secret goal was to stamp out all organized religions in the world. (But isn't Satanism itself an organized religion? Oh, wait, sorry about that. Let's leave aside editorial intrusions for a moment and just examine the claims.) Here's Epperson in his own words:

> ...Pike considers Lucifer to be the God that is good, and the God of the Bible is the devil, the god of evil. That is what [Pike's] statement about 'that which is Below is as that which is Above' means. That means that the God in the heavens is the god that is below, and the god who is below is the god in the heavens.
>
> So the Masons do believe in a god: it is in the fallen lightbearer, Lucifer. There can be no other reasonable explanation of what Mr. Pike just wrote (Epperson 159).

No other reasonable explanation? This is a common belief among Christians, particularly the Southern Baptists, many of whom are very concerned about the ongoing "threat" of Freemasonry. Most people reading this publication will already be aware of the fact that the hermetic dictum "As above, so below" is a common phrase among the ancient practitioners of alchemy and does not refer in any way to either God or Satan. In fact, the belief systems associated with alchemy no doubt existed long before the Christian religion came into being. But when one is viewing the world through a limited framework, the amount of information one has to draw upon will be equally limited; and thus may lead to numerous misperceptions, like the one we've just heard.

Now let's pan over to the other side of the tracks, shall we?

Manly P. Hall, a 33rd Degree Scottish Rite Freemason who wrote scores of books attempting to illuminate the esoteric meanings of Masonic symbolism (*The Secret Teachings of All Ages* being the most exhaustive) seems to have an endless supply of adoring adjectives to describe Albert Pike. He variously refers to Pike as "the Plato of Freemasonry," "this Masonic Prometheus," "the Homer of America," "the Master Builder," "the Real Master of the Veils," "the Oracle of Freemasonry," and (perhaps most confusing) "the Zoroaster of modern Asia" (Hall 37-8). And that's just scraping the surface.

Hall chooses to introduce Pike in his illustrated review of occultism and Philosophy, *The Phoenix*, with the following anonymous tribute:

> Albert Pike was a king among men by the divine right of merit. A giant in body, in brain, in heart and in soul. So majestic in appearance that whenever he moved on highway or byway, the wide world over, every passer-by turned to gaze upon him and admire him. Six feet, two inches, with the proportions of a Hercules and the grace of an Apollo. A face and head massive and leonine, recalling in every feature some sculptor's dream of a Grecian god.... (Hall 37).

Hall does not mention who wrote the preceding tribute or where it was originally published. It's hard to imagine what sort of prostrate position the writer was in when these words flowed from his (or her) pen. Perhaps Pike himself wrote it. Or maybe even Manly P. Hall. When it comes to attribution in Hall's writing, everything is in doubt. He had a bad habit of being rather too lackadaisical about citing his sources—a habit he shared with Pike himself. For this reason alone much of his writing is considered useless by mainstream historians, and I understand their dismissal of him on those grounds. But it could be that Hall didn't *want* his work to be useful to historians. Like Pike himself, Hall was interested in history only on his own terms, and those terms involved the practice and explication of metaphysics. Every aspect of the mundane world somehow related back to the big Masonic "G"—whether that G stood for the initial letter of the Hebrew alphabet, "Geparaith," "God," "Geometry," or "the generative principle" is entirely open to interpretation. Pike cites them all as possible candidates. (On pp. 780, 640, 40, and 632 of *Morals and Dogma*, respectively.)

Hall saw himself reflected in Pike and came to admire him accordingly. They were both preeminent scholars of the arcanum, perhaps the *most* knowledgeable of their respective centuries who chose to compile their occult knowledge in encyclopedic works, and therefore it might be no surprise that Hall would place Pike on a such a lofty pedestal. And here we come to an important point about the enigma of Albert Pike: Because so much of Pike's real life and career is shrouded in mystery, it's easy for him to become a polymorphous Rorschach blot upon which people with an intense interest in the esoteric can project their own highest hopes or darkest fears.

To Anton Chaitkin, author of *Treason in America*, Albert Pike is nothing more than...

> ...one of the most physically and morally repulsive individuals in American history. Horribly obese—easily 300 lbs. or more—Pike was known in his adopted state of Arkansas as a practitioner of Satanism. His reported sexual proclivities included sitting astride a phallic throne in the woods, accompanied by a gang of prostitutes. He would bring to his revels one or more wagon-loads of food and liquor, most of which he would consume over a period of perhaps 48 hours, until he passed into a stupor.
>
> Pike was thrilled at the chance he got to kill Spanish-Americans in the Mexican War; he pushed himself forward in Arkansas politics with noisy anti-Negro and pro-slavery rhetoric; and in the 1850s he became the leading Southern organizer and boss of the American Party or 'Know-Nothings'—the third-party grouping based on hatred and fear of immigrants (Chaitkin, *Treason in America*, 234-35).

Where Chaitkin is getting some of his information, particularly the bit about the prostitutes in the woods and the phallic throne (what *is* a phallic throne?), I have no idea. He doesn't cite a source for these allegations.

In a Labor Day lecture delivered to the Schiller Institute in Washington, D.C., Chaitkin later attempted to delineate what he called "the Scottish Rite's KKK Project" by attempting to connect Pike to the founding of the Ku Klux Klan. He said, "The Knights of the Ku Klux Klan was a terrorist counterattack, beginning in Tennessee, designed to block Reconstruction and reverse the outcome of the Civil War. *The Klan and the Scottish Rite were one and the same enterprise*, continuing the imperial effort behind the slave owners' rebellion." (emphasis added) (Chaitkin)

Albert Pike (Library of Congress)

But to James T. Tresner II, author of the anecdotal biography *Albert Pike: The Man Beyond the Monument*, Pike is nothing less than...

> ...one of the most amazing men who has ever lived. During his long life, he was a teacher, an explorer of the American frontier, a poet, a newspaper editor, a lawyer—in fact he is still regarded as one of the outstanding legal scholars of the 1800s—a short-story writer, a linguist, a worker for reform in both education and the criminal justice system, an active advocate for the rights of women and the rights of Native Americans, an orator whose speeches are still reprinted in collections of Southern literature, a general in the Civil War, and a philosopher.
>
> He made and gave away fortunes. He built the finest home in Little Rock, Arkansas. The society columns of the Washington, D.C. newspapers spoke of him as one of the most graceful dancers, cordial hosts, and knowledgeable connoisseurs of food in

> the capital city. He always had a joke to tell his legion of friends, and his hearty laugh was famous.
>
> When, in the last years of his life, he moved to an apartment in the House of the Temple, his personal library contained thousands of books. He was a profound student of religion and philosophy (Tresner 39).

Could this possibly be the same person under discussion here? The preceding two examples were chosen almost at random, by simply dropping books about Albert Pike on the floor and letting the pages fall open where they may. Other examples of this extreme dichotomy could be reprinted here, but I think you get the point by now.

When researching this article, I decided to give Pike the benefit of the doubt. I wondered if writers like Epperson and Chaitkin might have given Pike short shrift; after all, facts can always be misinterpreted to bring about a negative conclusion. My first goal, therefore, was to visit the library established by Manly P. Hall at the Philosophical Research Society in Los Angeles, one of the largest repositories of occult texts in the United States. Since Manly P. Hall was one of Pike's most ardent admirers, I concluded that this might be the best place to go in order to get a more positive view of Pike and his work.

The librarian at the Philosophical Research Society is Maja D'Aoust, who has lectured frequently over the years on the subject of alchemy, and has recently co-authored a book on hermeticism entitled *The Secret Source*. I asked Ms. D'Aoust to comment on Pike and his contributions to Freemasonry, as well as on the study of the occult in general:

* * *

Guffey: Do you know anything about Pike's life?

D'Aoust: Not a lot. Albert Pike was a member of the Ku Klux Klan. He was a Grand Wizard. And, of course, I read *Morals and Dogma*.

Guffey: I'd like to talk about the KKK angle in a minute, but first let's talk about Morals and Dogma. You've read the entire book?

D'Aoust: Oh, yeah.

Guffey: Would you say it's a mélange of different sources?

D'Aoust: Oh, he takes stuff from *everywhere*.

Guffey: What do you mean? Just straight-out rips off another text?

D'Aoust: Completely.

Guffey [Laughs]: He uses the cut-up technique?

D'Aoust: Cut-and-paste, is more like it.

Guffey: Is he upfront about that?

D'Aoust: Oh, no, no, no. No![1] [Laughs] And not that that's a bad thing. I mean, we all do the same thing in our lives, right? We're taking bits and pieces from everywhere we go. Pike's main source was this gentleman by the name of Eliphas Levi, and Arthur Edward Waite. Those are the two main people Albert Pike is reading when he makes his *Morals and Dogma*. And almost all Masons base their information on that book by Pike. So the first thing that I would think to do is ask, where did Albert Pike get his information? He's getting it from Eliphas Levi, whose information is all coming from hermeticism and Kabala... and Arthur Waite, who gets all *his* information from hermeticism and Kabala. Albert Pike did it so that he could amass a text which then people could use to get the information from, right? Instead of having to read twenty bazillion books to get it from, he made this nice encyclopedic volume that, from then on, any Mason who needed the information could just look in that book and there it would be. Same with [Madame] Blavatsky. [Her book] *The Secret Doctrine* is also meant to be an encyclopedic volume.

Guffey: Would you say that Blavatsky was like Pike? In that she had a lot of contradictions in her personality?

D'Aoust [Laughs]: She was a mess of a person. First of all, she was so fat before she died she had to be wheeled around in a cart by, like, three men. And meanwhile she's writing about all these disciplines that take a lot of will power. If you see what happens to her physical body....

Guffey: Are you saying she wasn't practicing what she was preaching?

D'Aoust: There's a lot of different levels of practice. Some people can be astral projection masters but they can't get out of bed to go to the bathroom, so... there are so many different levels of "practice," who knows?

Guffey: Well, in terms of not practicing what you preach... when you mention the thing about

Albert Pike and the KKK, that's something I've actually been trying to research and pin down. Anton Chaitkin was the first person I ever read who mentioned Pike's supposed KKK connection. Pike's a very elusive fellow. If you read a book by a Freemason, Pike's a wonderful guy who was against slavery and . . .

D'Aoust: Of course. Sure! And if you read a book about Hitler by a Nazi, they'll say the same thing.

Guffey: Oddly enough, you can easily find another book about Pike in which you'll have the exact opposite information, but both stories will seem equally plausible somehow.

D'Aoust: They probably are both true, because he had different faces for different parts of the community. There are bridges and elementary schools built to him in his home town because he was such a helpful member of the community, and to that part of the community he *was* very helpful. He was *very* helpful to many people, but not to—you know, unfortunately—the black Americans who he probably strung from a tree.

* * *

After the interview Ms. D'Aoust referred me to Paul Austad, the Director of Technology at the Philosophical Research Society. Mr. Austad provided several valuable sources that dealt with Pike's involvement in the Ku Klux Klan.

The 1905 book *Ku Klux Klan: Its Origin, Growth and Disbandment* by J. C. Lester and D. L. Wilson contains an introduction by Dr. Walter L. Fleming, who was a professor of History at West Virginia University and held a Ph.D. in History from Columbia University. In his introduction he lists "[s]ome well-known members of the Klan" and states, "General Albert Pike, who stood high in the Masonic order, was the chief judicial officer of the Klan" (Lester 24).

The 1924 book *Authentic History, Ku Klux Klan, 1865-1877* by Susan Lawrence Davis contains an oil portrait of General Pike given to the author by Pike's own son (Yvon Pike of Leesburg, Virginia) for the specific purpose of including it in her book. In Chapter XVIII, entitled "Arkansas," Davis reports:

> General Pike organized the Ku Klux Klan in Arkansas after General [Nathan] Forrest appointed him Grand Dragon of that Realm at the convention at Nashville, Tenn. He was also appointed at that time Chief Judicial Officer of The Invisible Empire. He advised in this capacity that the Ku Klux Klan memorize their Ritual and to never make it public....
>
> General Pike appointed Mr. Henry Fielding and Mr. Eppie Fielding of Fayetteville, Arkansas, to assist him in organizing Dens in that state. They were members of the Athens, Ala., Klan from its beginning and went to Arkansas, to live in 1867. They were Confederate soldiers, and gave me much information about the powerful influence General Pike had over the people of Arkansas during the dark days of reconstruction.
>
> In 1872 Arkansas had two governments operating at one time and civil war was threatened and great excitement prevailed against the Washington Government. General Pike called a mass meeting at Little Rock, Ark., in the Capitol building and appealed to the people to be patient until better times would come and assured them that he would go to Washington and intercede for them, which he did many times.
>
> At this meeting General Pike unfurled the Stars and Stripes and in a most beautiful manner, asked the people to follow it, which thousands of them did, promising him to be patient until the Ku Klux Klan could redeem the state (Davis 276-77).

In his 1929 book *The Tragic Era: The Revolution After Lincoln,* a former Ambassador to Spain and Chile named Claude G. Bowers writes, "In the earliest phase [of the Klan] only men of the highest order were in control." He lists the leaders in each of the Southern states in which the Klan had lowered their roots including Alabama, Mississippi, North Carolina, Texas, and Georgia—leaders such as "[i]n Arkansas, General Albert Pike, poet and journalist, scholar and jurist, solider and explorer, and a commanding figure in Masonry for half a century..." (Bowers 310).

Far more recently, Wyn Craig Wade's 1987 overview of the White Supremacy movement, *The Fiery Cross: The Ku Klux Klan in America*, identifies Pike as having served as the Grand Dragon of Arkansas during the early days of the Klan's inception. But Wade also adds this clarification:

> [T]he leadership of these men, originally appointed by Memphis officials, was usually in name only and nowhere lasted longer than 1869; such experienced veterans quickly realized the impossi-

> bility of governing *in secret* such widespread bands of young hellions and wanted no responsibility for it (Wade 58).

In a very rare book, *History and Evolution of Freemasonry*, written in 1954 by a Freemason named Delmar D. Darrah, Pike's own words seem to further clarify his sympathies. Regarding the establishment of the Prince Hall Masonic Lodges for African-Americans, Pike wrote a letter in 1875 in which he stated, "I took my obligations from white men, not from negroes. When I have to accept negroes as brothers or leave masonry, I shall leave it" (Darrah 329). He goes on to declare that he is dedicated to keeping "the Ancient and Accepted Rite uncontaminated, in *our* country at least, by the leprosy of negro association" (Upton 215). Some Masons claim these quotes are being taken out of context. Interested readers, however, can see the entire text in Appendix 12 of William H. Upton's 1902 study entitled *Negro Masonry: Being a Critical Examination of Objections to the Legitimacy of the Masonry Existing Among the Negroes of America*, a book written by a Freemason. (The entire letter can be read at this pro-Masonic website: *www.masonicinfo.com/pikesracism.htm*. Feel free to judge for yourselves.)

Pike's *Morals and Dogma*

Even earlier, in 1868, Pike published an editorial in his own newspaper named the *Daily Appeal* in which he wrote:

> With negroes for witnesses and jurors, the administration of justice becomes a blasphemous mockery. A Loyal League of negroes can cause any white man to be arrested, and can prove any charges it chooses to have made against him [...]. The disenfranchised people of the South [...] can find no protection for property, liberty or life, except in secret association [...]. We would unite every white man in the South, who is opposed to negro suffrage, into one great Order of Southern Brotherhood, with an organization complete, active, vigorous, in which a few should execute the concentrated will of all, and whose very existence should be concealed from all but its members.[2]

There are still more voices to be heard amidst the turmoil: The Grand Lodge of British Columbia and Yukon has published a lengthy essay on its website entitled "Albert Pike Did Not Found the Ku Klux Klan," which countered the claims that Albert Pike had any connection to the Ku Klux Klan.[3] This title is, in fact, a true statement: Albert Pike did *not* found the Ku Klux Klan. During the American Civil War, he founded a secret society called the Knights of the Golden Circle, which later *transformed* into the Ku Klux Klan.

The Knights of the Golden Circle is the X factor in this debate. What *was* the Knights of the Golden Circle? What was Albert Pike's intention in forming it? Was it an esoteric secret society with a benign interest in hermetic rites that was then later *twisted* into what we now know as the Ku Klux Klan? In 2003 journalist Warren Getler published a fascinating history of the Knights of the Golden Circle, *Shadow of the Sentinel*, a book that's been sadly overlooked despite the fact that it's a highly readable, true-to-life detective story. Getler claims that the main purpose of the Knights of the Golden Circle was to overcome the North on the battlefield and prepare for a contingency plan to continue the war underground, secretly, in the event that the South was defeated. This book is the best and most comprehensive analysis of Pike's involvement with both the Knights of the Golden Circle and the Ku Klux Klan. (I've written more extensively about the Knights of the Golden Circle's involvement in the Civil War in an article entitled "The History of Unknown Men" published in *New Dawn Magazine's Special Issue* #3 in the Spring/Summer of 2007.)

There's no doubt that Pike was involved in these secret societies. The question is, why? Let's now turn up the volume on another member of the crowd, shall we?

James Tresner II, who's a 33rd Degree Scottish Rite Freemason, attempts to defend Pike's connection to the Knights of the Golden Circle by putting the following words in his mouth in a strange videotape produced by the Scottish Rite Research Society in which Tresner dresses up like Pike and answers questions from a contemporary Mason who's sent back in time into Pike's library for a late night chat (yes, that really is the plot of the video). Here is what Tresner, in the role of Pike, has to say about the American Civil War:

> Have the people of your time reduced the terrible and complex issues of the war to a simple-minded belief that the North wanted to free the slaves and the South wanted to impose slavery? [...] Oh, sir. No, no. I knew no one personally who argued that slavery was a good thing, though there may have been such people. But how do you end it? Decree, in a day, that the slaves are free? No, I believed that the only way to end slavery was to make it unnecessary economically. And I hoped for better conditions in the South than in the North; for there were slaves there, too—women and children who worked in the manufactories for so low a wage that they starved to death even as they worked. To that end, I worked and argued to increase shipping and manufacturing in the South.
>
> When the Southern Convention met in 1856 and introduced a resolution in favor of resuming the slave trade, I took the floor and spoke against it. I ended that speech by saying that I looked forward to the day when ALL men would be free. And for that I was booed off the floor, my character was attacked, and I was threatened with physical assault.
>
> No, sir, I was no lover of slavery. But to me, and to many of us, that was not the issue of the war. The issue was whether the states or the federal government was to control. I feared the despotism of a large government, and I believed in my heart that the states were better suited to governing the citizens and protecting their interests (Tresner 60).

Some of these statements strike me as plausible. Indeed, the central issue of the American Civil War was *not* the abolition of slavery, though high school history books have encapsulated the war as such in order to make it more easily digestible by students whose knowledge of American history has been bastardized by years of just such oversimplification. Other statements strike me as outright dissimulation, particularly the notion that Pike never once came into personal contact with a single person in the antebellum South who argued "that slavery was a good thing." In complex technical language, this statement could be categorized as "a shuck and a jive." Quite frankly, for me, that comment alone strains the credibility of the rest of Tresner's statement.

Let's return to what can be documented: not Tresner's words, but Pike's. How do we reconcile Pike's incendiary, overtly racist comments with his own magnum opus, the apex of Masonic philosophy, *Morals and Dogma*? Let's turn the volume up on Pike's own words at the moment. Is *Morals and Dogma* the work of a man who advocates slavery or violence in any form? Let's allow the monument to speak for himself at last....

> Might, in an army wielded by tyranny, is the enormous sum total of utter weakness; and so Humanity wages war against Humanity, in despite of Humanity. So a people willingly submits to despotism, and its workmen submit to be despised, and its soldiers to be whipped; therefore it is that battles lost by a nation are often progress attained. Less glory is more liberty. When the drum is silent, reason sometimes speaks.
>
> Tyrants use the force of the people to chain and subjugate—that is, *enyoke* the people. Then they plough with them as men do with oxen yoked. Thus the spirit of liberty and innovation is reduced by bayonets, and principles struck dumb by cannon-shot. (*Morals and Dogma* 3)
>
> * * *
>
> ...[I]t is one of the fatalities of Humanity to be condemned to eternal struggle with phantoms, with superstitions, bigotries, hypocrisies, prejudices and the pleas of tyranny. Despotisms, seen in the past, become respectable, as the mountain, bristling with volcanic rock, rugged and horrid, seen through the haze of distance is blue and beautiful. The sight of a single dungeon of tyranny is worth more, to dispel illusions and create holy hatred of despotism, to direct FORCE aright than the most eloquent volumes. The French should have preserved the Bastile as a perpetual lesson; Italy

should not destroy the dungeons of the Inquisition (*Morals and Dogma* 4).

* * *

[The Mason] labors equally to defend and to improve the people [...]. He knows that the safety of every free government, and its continuance and perpetuity depend upon the virtue and intelligence of the common people; and that, unless their liberty is of such a kind as arms can neither procure nor take away; unless it is the fruit of manly courage, of justice, temperance, and generous virtue—unless, being such, it has taken deep root in the minds and hearts of the people at large, there will not long be wanting those who will snatch from them by treachery what they have acquired by arms or institutions.

He knows that if, after being released from the toils of war, the people neglect the arts of peace; if their peace and liberty be a state of warfare; if war be their only virtue, and the summit of their praise, they will soon find peace the most adverse to their interests. It will be only a more distressing war; and that which they imagined liberty will be the worst slavery. For, unless by the means of knowledge and morality, not frothy and loquacious, but genuine, unadulterated, and sincere, they clear the horizon of the mind from those mists of error and passion which arise from ignorance and vice, they will always have those who will bend their necks to the yoke as if they were brutes; who, notwithstanding all their triumphs, will put them up to the highest bidder, as if they were mere booty made in war; and find an exuberant source of wealth and power, in the people's ignorance, prejudice, and passions (*Morals and Dogma* 177).

* * *

To honor the Deity, to regard all men as our Brethren, as children, equally dear to Him, of the Supreme Creator of the Universe, and to make himself useful to society and himself by his labor, are [Freemasonry's] teachings to its Initiates in all the Degrees (*Morals and Dogma* 329).

* * *

Quotes such as these are often used by Freemasons to "prove" that Pike could not have been a racist or a supporter of slavery. The Freemasons are right: these are *not* the words of a man who supports either racism or slavery. These words have as much relevance today, perhaps even more so, as they did when Pike first wrote them. Does that mean that the man who wrote them was not a racist?

No, it doesn't. No one can know, at this late date, exactly what Pike was like in his private life. This would not be the first time in the fields of philosophy, religion, or literature when the words a man penned were far nobler than his actions. Do a man's actions invalidate a man's work? Does the fact that Ezra Pound was a fascist anti-Semite lessen the artistic quality of his *Cantos*? Does the fact that Lewis Carroll had a penchant for taking nude photographs of prepubescent children invalidate *Alice in Wonderland* as a classic in British literature? Does the fact that William S. Burroughs shot and killed his wife cancel out his status as one of the great innovators in American literature in the 20th century?

Perhaps.

And perhaps the fact that neither Ezra Pound, Lewis Carroll, nor William S. Burroughs ever deigned to pen a 1,086-page didactic tome entitled *Morals and Dogma* should be taken into consideration here as well.

If so, it should also be kept in mind that the words inscribed in the Declaration of Independence are clearly not those of men who support the slavery of fellow human beings... and yet, nonetheless, most of the learned gentleman who signed that auspicious document did indeed own slaves and continued to own them once their tidy revolution was complete.

Listen to the clamor growing: these are the arguments of the crowd still milling around in that underground depot, cut off from the rest of society. Few people today, above ground, care whether or not Albert Pike was a member of the Ku Klux Klan. Few people today even know what Freemasonry is, and far less have ever heard the words "Knights of the Golden Circle." Quite frankly, it's not something they really need to know in order to pursue their daily lives.

But still, here in the dusty underground, the war continues to wage as if there were never a better war worth fighting. The masses can barely hear each other over the noise of the oncoming train, the apocalyptic clamor of a bronze statue being shattered into tiny shards. The masses stand agape, staring dumbly as the train whizzes past.

Would these paralyzed fellows be shocked to see who's driving this train, the very same coal-black engine that just reduced Pike's larger-than-life-sized monument into copper-colored dust? Look closely through the front window and you can almost make out the engineer's bedraggled, wizened features: it's him all right, the one person who went the farthest to encourage all this mystery and obfuscation in the first place: Grand Commander Albert Pike, Confederate General and Master of the Royal Secret... yes, the "Zoroaster of modern Asia" himself.

There's no doubt in my mind Pike would be pleased to learn that his *mystery*, at the very least, still persists even as the amount of people in the world who actually read his cryptic words dwindle ever further into non-existence.

After all, there's something to be said for *mystery*... one notion with which everyone huddled in this underground depot can agree.

References

Bowers, Claude G. *The Tragic Era: The Revolution After Lincoln*. New York: Blue Ribbon, 1929.

Chaitkin, Anton. "The Scottish Rite's KKK Project," a speech to the Schiller Institute. <*www.theforbiddenknowledge.com/hardtruth/scottishriteproject.htm*>.

Chaitkin, Anton. *Treason in America: From Aarron Burr to Averell Harriman*. 1985. Washington, D.C.: Executive Intelligence Review, 1999.

Darrah, Delmar D. *History and Evolution of Freemasonry*. Chicago: C. T. Powner, 1954.

Davis, Susan Lawrence. *Authentic History, Ku Klux Klan, 1865-1877*. New York: American Library Service, 1924.

Epperson, A. Ralph. *The New World Order*. Tucson, AZ: Publius P, 1990.

Getler, Warren and Bob Brewer. *Shadow of the Sentinel*. New York: Simon & Schuster, 2003.

Hall, Manly P. *The Phoenix: An Illustrated Review of Occultism and Philosophy*. 1956. Los Angeles: The Philosophical Research Society, 1995.

Lester, J.C. and D.L. Wilson. *Ku Klux Klan: Its Origin, Growth and Disbandment*. New York: Neale P, 1905.

Pike, Albert. *Morals and Dogma*. 1871. Richmond, VA: L.H. Jenkins, 1956.

Tresner II, James T. "A Visit with General Albert Pike." *Heredom* 10 (2002): 39-62.

Upton, William H. *Negro Masonry: Being a Critical Examination of Objections to the Legitimacy of the Masonry Existing Among the Negroes of America*. 1902. New York: AMS P, 1975.

Wade, Wyn Craig. *The Fiery Cross*. 1987. New York: Oxford University Press, 1998.

Watts, Alan. *The Book: On the Taboo Against Knowing Who You Are*. New York: Collier, 1967.

Endotes

1. In all fairness to Pike, D'Aoust's interpretation here is not exactly accurate. In the preface to *Morals and Dogma*, Pike couldn't be more upfront about his intentions:

"In preparing this work, the Grand Commander has been about equally Author and Compiler; since he has extracted quite half its contents from the works of the best writers and most philosophic or eloquent thinkers. Perhaps it would have been better and more acceptable if he had extracted more and written less.

"Still, perhaps half of it is his own; and, in incorporating here the thoughts and words of others, he has continually changed and added to the language, often intermingling, in the same sentences, his own words with theirs. It not being intended for the world at large, he has felt at liberty to make, from all accessible sources, a Compendium of the Morals and Dogma of the Rite, to re-mould sentences, change and add to words and phrases, combine them with his own, and use them as if they *were* his own, to be dealt with at his pleasure and so availed of as to make the whole most valuable for the purposes intended. He claims, therefore, little of the merit of authorship, and has not cared to distinguish his own from that which he has taken from other sources, being quite willing that every portion of the book, in turn, may be regarded as borrowed from some old and better writer" (iii-iv).

2. See, Chaitkin, Anton, *www.theforbiddenknowledge.com/hardtruth/scottishriteproject.htm*.

3. Website: *http://freemasonry.bcy.ca/anti-masonry/kkk.html*.

About the Author

Robert Guffey's short stories, articles and interviews have appeared in such magazines and anthologies as Jeremy Lassen's *After Shocks*, *Alien Skin*, *The Chiron Review*, Rudy Rucker's *Flurb*, *The Fortean Times*, *HunterGatheress Journal*, *Like Water Burning*, W.H. Horner's *Modern Magic: Tales of Fantasy & Horror*, *New Dawn*, *The New York Review of Science Fiction*, *Paranoia*, *The Pedestal*, *Steamshovel Press*, and *The Third Alternative*. Further stories are scheduled to appear in Allen Ashley's forthcoming PS Publishing anthology *Catastrophia*, Mike Philbin's *Chimeraworld 6: New World Disorder*, *Dark Jesters* edited by Nick Cato and L.L. Soares, and *Escape Clause* edited by Clélie Rich. He is currently teaching English at CSU Long Beach and can be contacted at rguffey@hotmail.com.

2012

Odyssey of Time

by Philip Coppens

Does 2012 signal the end of the world, or the dawning of a new age? Is it just another empty media frenzy, a genuine evolutionary opportunity, or the legacy of an ancient civilisation that we are only just beginning to understand?

At the end of the 20th century, many predicted the advent of doom—or the return of Christ. In the 16th century, French prophet Nostradamus spoke of the solar eclipse that would occur on August 11, 1999. Was this a sign? Was the turn of the century destined to be the end of an era?

In recent years, doomsday theorists and New Age cultists alike have postponed the new end date—our meeting with destiny—until December 21, 2012. So exactly what is meant to happen on this date? Climate change, devastating hurricanes and increasingly violent earthquakes are an ever-present force in modern-day news media. Are these natural disasters simply the result of global warming or are they indicative of something greater? Some claim that there are strange things happening to the Sun itself. Some scientists even hold the Sun responsible for climate change, noting that global warming is not only happening on this planet, but all throughout the solar system. But if the end truly is nigh, can it be pinpointed to one day in time?

The fact is that December 21, 2012 is indeed the end of the Long Count calendar, a calendrical system used by the ancient Mayan civilisation of Central America. On that day, the thirteenth b'ak'tun cycle will be completed. Some Mesoamerican historical texts name our era as the Fifth Age, or the fifth cycle of creation. According to these texts, the next age, set to begin in 2012, will be that of the Sixth Age. The Fifth Age started on August 11, 3114 BC—but if this date didn't mark the beginning of the world, why should 2012 be considered the end of the world, or the birth of a new one for that matter?

Harmonic Convergence

As we highlight in the DVD, *2012: Odyssey of Time*, amongst those to first popularise the 2012 theory was Jose Arguelles, who hosted the Harmonic Convergence, a series of worldwide esoteric religious events that took place on August 16 and 17, 1987. The event was celebrated at a number of "sacred" places throughout the world, from Stonehenge to the Golden Gate Bridge, where individuals, many referring to themselves as "light beings," gathered to usher in a new era.

To concoct his Harmonic Convergence theory, Arguelles used information gathered from the ancient Aztec and Mayan calendars, New Age spiritualism, and a classical Chinese text called the *I Ching*. To him, August 16, 1987 was important, as it marked the end of a Mayan time cycle, specifically nine "hell" cycles, which had begun in 1519 AD. The Harmonic Convergence then signalled the final 26-year countdown to the end of the Mayan Long Count calendar in 2012, which would be the "end of history" and the beginning of a new 5,125-year cycle in which all the evils of the modern world—war, materialism, violence, injustice, governmental abuses of power, etc.—would end with the birth of the Sixth Sun from the Fifth World on December 21, 2012.

Many changes have taken place in the world since 1987. The Iron Curtain has come down and the Cold War has ended. But it's obvious enough that it would require nothing short of a miracle to end such forces as violence, war and political corruption by January 1, 2013. While the concept of instant world salvation is popular among certain sects of Christianity, most other philosophical doctrines, religious and otherwise, acknowledge that creating heaven on earth is a slow, and human, task.

TimeWave Zero

Arguelles was not the first to focus the attention of the world on the year 2012. A decade before Arguelles published his ideas in *The Mayan Factor*, Terence McKenna and his brother Dennis authored *The Invisible Landscape*, announcing 2012 as the year that humankind's accelerating technological impact would reach a climax and tip everything into another dimension. McKenna's model is known as "TimeWave Zero," and is part of his "Novelty Theory," which attempted to calculate the ebb and flow of novelty—new things—in the universe as an inherent quality of time. The fractal waveform, the TimeWave, is simply a wave that maps the amount of novelty that manifests in the universe. Within the quantum universe in which we live, "new things," in essence, means that any new conscious decision made by each of us is a decision that breaks a pattern, and thus has a direct impact on reality. And according to McKenna, this simple, scientific, yet little known fact might hold the key to a brighter future.

McKenna recruited mathematicians Leon Taylor and Royce Kelley to generate a number set from the King Wen sequence of the *I Ching*, as part of his quest to scientifically study the TimeWave. Unlike a normal graph, the wave goes down rather than up, since the Novelty Theory presumes there is a maximum novelty value, and this is represented by the baseline of the graph. The line goes up towards habit—events that occur repeatedly, without conscious intervention, and down towards novelty—when conscious decisions lead to "new things" being introduced into the daily life of the universe.

The graph hits the baseline and signifies a maximum novelty state only twice—at the start and end of the graph—the beginning and end of time. Maximum novelty value is therefore zero, which is why the original Timewave was called Timewave Zero.

Having produced the wave, McKenna was determined to somehow correlate it to history, in order to determine where we are on the wave. The explosion of the atomic bomb at Hiroshima in 1945, for instance, was interpreted as a massive ingression of novelty and equated with a large spike near the end of the Timewave. After this correlation was made, it was found that the wave hit the baseline exactly sixty-four 13-month lunar years later, on November 17, 2012. When McKenna learned that this was very close to the Mayan Long Count Calendar end-date, further study and adjustments had him thinking that December 21, 2012 might indeed be "the" day when time as we know it becomes a thing of the past, so to speak. Time, after all, is something that everyone experiences, but has never been fully explained by science.

McKenna labelled the end of the wave a "singularity," which in astronomical terms is where density is infinite—like at the center of a black hole. A singularity is exactly what author Peter Russell has called the centre of his accelerating time spiral, which he refers to as the "White Hole in Time." Russell realized that there are ten thousand million, or ten to the power of ten atoms, in a neuron and the same number of neurons in the human cortex of the brain. We are now at a population level of well over ten to the power of nine, approaching the critical number of ten to the ten. Could we, as Russell suggests, soon see this shift, where individual units link and become functioning parts of a larger organ—the global brain?

The writer-philosopher Robert Anton Wilson touched on this subject after conducting a study on the concept of "Information Doubling"—the idea that information continues to double faster all the time—and updated it over a period of eight years. French economist Georges Anderla did the groundwork for the study in 1973, and Wilson built on it, starting with the first appearance of *Homo sapiens* in 40,000 BC. According to Wilson, it took 40,000 years for information to build to a significant level in the Bronze Age around 3,000 BC—neatly coinciding with the beginning of the Mayan Long Count calendar.

The study claims that the next doubling took 3,000 years, occurring during the Roman Empire in the year 1 AD and, according to Wilson, when he began the study in 1982, information was doubling once every three years. In 1990, after another installment of the study had been completed, he theorized the doubling rate to be once every eighteen months. When Wilson graphed the process, the figures produced a chart that shows a gradual build leading up to a sudden acceleration of information doubling occurring in the 20th century, and the graph goes vertical shortly after the year 2000—in fact, right around 2012.

The Long Count

Is it possible that the Mayans knew all of this? In our DVD *2012: Odyssey of Time*, we point out the fact that December 21, 2012 is indeed an important date in their calendar. The Long Count date of the start point in 3114 BC is written as the completion of 13 Baktuns, with zero katuns, zero tuns, zero uinals, zero days. On the winter solstice of 2012, the same date is repeated for the first time in a span of around 5,125 solar years.

The question is, will a new cycle simply begin on this date—just as our clocks keep ticking every year on the first of January—or will something more profound happen? Unfortunately, the creators of the Long Count aren't around to answer that question for us. At the end of the Classic era, six hundred years before the Spanish conquered Central America, the Long Count calendar fell out of use. The people who worked the mathematical Long Count and tracked it were the priestly elite, and they were all long dead before the arrival of the Conquistadors. It is only over the last hundred years that the Long Count calendar has been reconstructed and mapped on the Gregorian calendar to December 21, 2012.

There is an incomplete inscription on Monument 6 in Tortuguero, a Mayan archaeological site in Mexico, which records this 13th b'ak'tun "end date." This is the only known inscription that mentions 2012. This end date is also carved on the walls of the Temple of Inscriptions in Palenque, as well as on the so-called Creation monument at Quirigua, but it is the end date of 3114 BC—the Fourth Age of creation—while 2012 is the completion of the Fifth Age of creation.

The Tortuguero inscription says that when the completion of 13 baktuns occurs on 4 ahau 3 kankin, December 21 2012, "it will occur—it will be the descent of the Bolon Yokte K'uh (Nine Support Gods) to the ---." It's tempting to imagine that the missing word is "Earth," but the outline of the glyph is visible and a search in the Maya glyph dictionary doesn't find a match for Earth or World. However, the "it" that will occur is semi-visible and looks like the glyph for darkness.

There is support for this interpretation in the Chilam Balam, or "Jaguar Priest" texts. These are disparate Mayan texts that include both pre-Spanish and colonial writings. Maud Makemson, who translated the Chilam Balam of Tizimin, found evidence that some of these texts specifically dealt with the 13-baktun cycle. Although they are applied to a short-term 13-katun calendar of 256 years (which was in use when the Spanish arrived), it is quite probable that the prophecies were simply kept and re-applied to the 13-katun cycle or Short Count when the Long Count fell out of use.

In the Chilam Balam of Chumayel, it says that in katun 4 Ahau (which is the katun from April 1993 to December 2012) the feathered serpent god, Kukulcan, will return. This god originated with the Toltecs as "Quetzalcoatl," and it is now known that the original Quetzalcoatl religion was about raising a serpent-like energy up the spine—a concept very similar to the Hindu concept of Kundalini. In the Aztec myth, Quetzalcoatl sacrifices himself, spends eight days in the underworld, and reappears as Venus. According to this myth, he is expected to return at some point between Venus transits, and we are now between the Venus transit of June 2004 and the next one in June 2012. As a consequence, the followers of John Major Jenkins, author of *Tzolkin: Visionary Perspectives and Calendar Studies*, and *Maya Cosmogenesis 2012*, expect that from within the Mayan world a new political leader might stand up during this time, and will be identified with Quetzalcoatl. Though most expect he will consequently be "sacrificed"—after all, all religious leaders, whether Osiris, Odin or Jesus, have been sacrificed—perhaps the time of sacrifice will become, like our concept of time, a thing of the past.

The big question nevertheless remains, and it appears that no one is around to answer it. But perhaps that is precisely the point; maybe we are here to define what comes next. This is the key message we aim to bring out in our *2012* DVD: that 2012 does not have to be about doom and gloom. After all, with massive novelty being predicted by the Timewave Zero theorem, does this not seem an appropriate time for us to think outside of the box and imagine our own future?

According to the Mayan civilisation, 2012 is meant to be a milestone, the end of an age. Within this context, we are approaching a point at which we can shift from the descending phase of a cycle, to an ascending phase. And if nothing else, perhaps this means that the Western imperialistic mindset will fully acknowledge that ancient civilisations knew far more about astronomy, and perhaps even more about the universe, than what science knows today.

For several decades, there have been loud voices arguing that human beings should leave materialism behind, become more "spiritual" and care for the Earth. But approaching our current situation with a broader perspective could prove beneficial. The time frame we need to assess in 2012 is not the one from 1980 to 2012, but rather from 3114 BC to 2012 AD. And it's clear that we'll call this the "Age of Civilisation," though that's perhaps not the best name for it. The global focus on the exchange of goods has started to become the end, rather than the means, of living. But especially now, during this time of economic crisis, that way of life may very well be expiring. And if the world has become increasingly smaller with communications between distant parts of the world happening in a matter of seconds, then the possibility of "one global mind" is within reach—if not already occurring.

The Fifth Age has been one in which human beings have stopped being largely nomadic, and decided to settle. With that have come many wonderful developments but, at the same time, a new dichotomy has arisen; we have stopped caring about those parts of the world we haven't settled, places like the Amazon, Siberia, and vast parts of Africa and Central Australia. These are the regions where we still encounter the old shamans of the previous Age—if not Ages. It is in this type of environment that McKenna had his insights and, to a large extent, where the Maya have survived and live today.

That we even consider that the world will end in 2012 is another sign of our Age. We have chosen to interpret these prophecies literally, and this is in sharp contrast with the ways in which shamans foresee future events. Modern religions tend to focus on dogma and preaching; shamanism is a technique centred on more direct contact with spiritual entities, and seldom relies on dogmatic texts.

So perhaps another positive outcome of the events of 2012 will be a mass realisation that institutionalised religions could benefit from becoming more spiritual and less narrow—a lesson that can be learned from the Maya. And if this alone would happen post-2012, the global impact would indeed be profound.

At the start of a New Age, the Sixth Sun, the Mayan creation mythology states that a new vision quest is required. We have come a tremendously long way, for better or for worse, since the days of our Mayan ancestors. But if we want to reach the centre of our galaxy, and learn about the cradle of life, we have an even longer voyage ahead of us. And 2012 may only be the beginning.

References

Arguelles, Jose, *The Mayan Factor: Path Beyond Technology*, Bear & Co., 1987.

Jenkins, John Major, *Maya Cosmogenesis 2012*, Bear & Co., 1998.

McKenna, Terence and Dennis, *The Invisible Landscape*, HarperOne, 1994.

Stray, Geoff. *Beyond 2012: Catastrophe or Ecstasy: A Complete Guide to End-of-Time Predictions*, Vital Signs Publishing, 2005.

Wilson, Robert Anton, *Cosmic Trigger Volume II: Down to Earth*, New Falcon, 1996.

About the Author

Philip Coppens is an author and investigative journalist in subjects ranging from the world of politics to ancient history and mysteries. He is the former editor-in-chief of the Dutch magazine *Frontier*. Since 1995, he has lectured extensively around the world. He is the author of *The Stone Puzzle of Rosslyn Chapel*, *The Canopus Revelation*, *Land of the Gods*, *The New Pyramid Age* and *Servants of the Grail*. His website is *www.philipcoppens.com*. Please visit his site to read more about the books. The DVD, *2012: Odyssey of Time: Mayan Prophecy and the Shift of the Ages* is produced by Reality Entertainment, and may be purchased at: *www.reality-entertainment.com*.

Deep Secrets of a UFO Think Tank

RAND, Battelle and "Memory Metal"

by Anthony Bragalia

Since the 1940's the U.S. government has quietly engaged one of its key defense and intelligence agency contractors as a secret UFO "think tank." New investigation reveals that the esteemed RAND Corporation has given far more than a passing thought to things extraterrestrial. RAND's hidden history of UFO involvement has been discovered to include work in policy analysis, evaluation of evidence, and in advising on the potential technological advantages achieved from UFO study. Telling connections have also been found between RAND and the Roswell crash event of 1947.

Who is RAND?

RAND Corporation was established in 1946 by the U.S Army Air Force as Project RAND ("Research ANd Development") and is today registered as a nonprofit organization. It is funded through government contracts, university collaborators and "private donors." RAND's primary agency clients include the CIA and the Defense Advanced Research Projects Agency (DARPA). Headquartered in Santa Monica, California, the think tank maintains branches worldwide. RAND's stated mission is to "help to improve policy and decision making through objective research and analysis." Its work is officially conducted "for the public welfare and security of the United States of America."

Over thirty Nobel Prize winners have been employed by RAND. From physics to economics, the 2,000-person think tank provides high-level information and evaluation to the U.S. government. Deeper review shows that RAND has conducted studies in such areas as weapons development, intelligence gathering and analysis, and the design of sensitive underground installations for the U.S. Air Force. Far more concealed is RAND's intimate involvement in highly-classified UFO study for the U.S. government.

From its very inception, the men of RAND knew much about saucers. RAND was conceived by Donald Douglas, CEO of Douglas Aircraft (protégé of Dr. Jerome Hunsaker at MIT) along with two military officer luminaries who carried with them significant "UFO histories": Major General Curtis LeMay (the U.S. Air Force's Chief of Development) and General Hap Arnold (considered the "father" of the modern U.S. Air Force).

In May of 1948, RAND was separated from Douglas Aircraft and became its own operating entity. Among RAND's earliest government reports was the release of the enigmatically titled, "Preliminary Design of an Experimental World-Circling Spaceship."

General Curtis LeMay

Curtis LeMay expressed deep interest and concern about flying saucer phenomena. More than this, LeMay himself was a keeper of the purported 1947 Roswell UFO crash debris. This was revealed in a stunningly candid interview with the late U.S. Senator Barry Goldwater. Goldwater (a former U.S. Presidential Candidate, Major General and

Command Pilot) was General LeMay's professional associate and close friend. LeMay's UFO involvement was related by Goldwater in a live worldwide broadcast with CNN's Larry King in 1994. The USAF had just issued its report that debunked the Roswell crash of 1947 as a Mogul balloon. Goldwater (who died just a few years later) informed King that he knew the truth to be far different.

He knew this, he explained, because in the 1960's he had approached LeMay about the crashed UFO issue. Goldwater—who no doubt held the highest security clearances—told Larry King: "I think at Wright-Patterson, if you could get into certain places, you'll find what the Air Force and the government knows about UFOs. Reportedly, a spaceship landed. It was all hushed up. I called Curtis LeMay and I said, 'General, I know we have a room at Wright-Patterson where you put all of this secret stuff. Could I go in there?' I've never heard General LeMay get mad, but he got madder than hell at me, cussed me out and said, 'Don't ever ask me that question again!'" Goldwater never did.

LeMay was very well acquainted with Roswell Army Air Field Base Commander Butch Blanchard. Blanchard oversaw the base at the time of the Roswell crash event in 1947. It is believed that Blanchard helped issue the original press release on the crash, which prompted the famous headline, "RAAF Captures Flying Saucer on Ranch in Roswell Region." Blanchard's former wife and daughter say that he was visibly upset by the event. He repeated only, "those Russians have some amazing things."

Roswell mayor William Brainerd says that Blanchard told him, "What I saw was the damndest thing I've ever seen!" To Art McQuiddy, editor of the *Roswell Morning Dispatch* in 1947, Blanchard said, "I'll tell you this and nothing more, the stuff I saw I'd never seen anyplace else in my life." Pilot Ben Games related in interviews (with this author and to reporter Billy Cox) that he had flown General Laurence Craigie (Director of the Air Force's R&D) to Roswell Army Air Field after the Roswell crash.

In LeMay's 1965 biography, *Mission with LeMay*, he speaks sparingly about the UFO subject. LeMay of course discounts a government cover-up about UFOs, but belies this with a brief and telling statement, "There is not a question about it: these were things which we could not tie in with any natural phenomena known to our investigators."

General Hap Arnold

As early as 1943, this fabled Five Star General was investigating unidentified flying objects. Found in Box 166 of General Arnold's papers (at AFHRC, Maxwell AFB) is a detailed analysis from 1943 that assessed a number of sightings of "small, luminous, silvery discs" reported by B-17 pilots. "Foo fighters" were an anomalous aerial "ball-of-light" phenomena reported and photographed by pilots during combat in Europe in the 1940s. Hap Arnold was intimately involved in the study of the baffling phenomena.

In November of 1945, an Adjutant from Hap Arnold's office delivered a packet of sealed documents relating to analysis of the mysterious "foo fighters" to Arnold's friend, Jo Chamberlin of *American Legion Magazine*. In a 1991 interview with researcher Jeffrey A. Lindell (USAF retired Electronic Warfare Systems Analyst) Chamberlin said he retained these foo fighter documents from Arnold and had never opened them after reading them in 1945. At the time of the interview, Chamberlin said he had promised Arnold he would never circulate them. General Arnold was closely associated with Colonel William "Butch" Blanchard, the Commanding Officer of the 509th bombing wing and the Roswell Base Commander at the time of the 1947 crash.

On July 7, 1947 (just days after the Roswell crash) Arnold was quoted in a UP story that, "General H.H. (Hap) Arnold, head of the army air forces during WWII, said today the discs could be a development of United States scientists not yet perfected." Of course, during the period immediately following the Roswell crash, U.S. military were obfuscating by giving the public various explanations on the nature of the discs. But Arnold knew the discs had been seen by his own pilots operating in the European theater.

RAND'S Early UFO Involvement

An official Air Force memorandum written on October 12, 1948 has been located by the historical research group Project 1947. Project 1947 is operated by respected researcher Jan Aldrich, supported by the civilian UFO research organization CUFOS and is known for its expertise in Freedom of Information Act (FOIA) requests. This 1948 document is very instructive about RAND and the early study of the troubling UFO phenomena.

The subject header of the document is "Request for Study by RAND Project"[1] and is directed to the U.S. Air Force Chief of Staff. The author of the document is Col. W.R. Clingerman, the Acting Chief of Intelligence. Clingerman was associated with Project Sign, the official USAF study of the UFO phenomena. Clingerman seeks the approval of the USAF Chief of Staff: "It is requested that the special study, described in the enclosure, be approved and that the RAND Corporation be authorized to establish a study of priority, consistent in scope and degree of treatment with the described requirements."

In a later paragraph of the document, Clingerman explains that he wishes RAND to: "Assist in the collection of information relating to unidentified aerial objects that may possibly represent spaceships or spaceship test craft and the technical information that includes the distinguishing design and performance parameters for spaceships is considered necessary." He adds, "It would be valuable to this Command" to have RAND provide "further scientific clues that may assist in their detection and identification by RAND scientific personnel."

Clingerman writes that RAND is an organization considered ideal for initiation of work on the UFO phenomena. He suggests that the "spaceships" have "distinguishing characteristics" about which RAND personnel would be uniquely suited to provide technical information, and that they could find "further scientific clues" about the "unidentified aerial objects." RAND is to be "monitored" by Air Materiel Command, in conformance with an "Air Corps Letter" dated one year after the Roswell crash (Air Corps Letter 80-10, 21, July, 1948).

RAND and UFO Photo Analysis

Brief mention in extant literature notes that in 1966 RAND Corporation coordinated the photographic analysis of alleged UFO photos. The "Zanesville, OH UFO" photos of November 13, 1966 were taken by local barber Ralph Ditter. Widely circulated at the time, the two photos appear to show a large saucer above the Ditter home. The RAND photo analysis determined that the object was a model only 3-4 inches in diameter and only 3-4 feet from the camera. The analysis was correct and Ditter later confessed the hoax as a way to please his curious daughter. Interestingly, most such analysis was officially conducted by the National GeoSpatial Intelligence Agency (formerly the National Photographic Interpretation Center.) RAND apparently had such capability as well, and has applied this capability to the UFO phenomena.

While working for RAND, senior analyst Dr. James E. Lipp wrote one of two scientific reports for the USAF's official UFO study known as Project Sign. It was completed in February of 1949 and was classified. In the report Lipp makes an extraordinarily astute observation. He notes that by the spring of the previous year there had been a total of five atomic bomb explosions. Lipp believed that these explosions could have served as interstellar 'smoke signals', and that they would be a potential source of extraterrestrial interest. Even skeptic Curtis Peebles noted that Lipp's evaluation might represent, "the first U.S. government sponsored study of non-human life in the universe."

Lipp added, "visits from outer space are believed possible." Ultimately though, Lipp seemed to cautiously conclude that he did not consider most reported UFO events as described to be evidence of such visits because they made "no logical sense."

Stephen H. Dole, scientist at the RAND Corporation, authored the intriguingly titled "Habitable Planets for Man" in 1964. Based on his analysis while at RAND, Dole believed that the existence of extraterrestrial intelligence was extremely high, even probable. In other reports he estimated the number of life-bearing planets (based on available information at the time) at 640 million.

It appears that RAND not only analyzed the UFO problem, but also evaluated the larger cosmological issues of our place in the universe, the likelihood of ET, and how to determine and quantify the extent of cosmic life.

The Report They Didn't Want Us to See

RAND analyst George Kocher authored an assessment report entitled, "UFOs: What to Do?" dated November 27, 1968.[2] Kocher's paper was stamped "For RAND Use Only." It further instructs on its cover page: "Do not quote or cite in external publications or correspondence." Though known by the UFO research community for some years, it was only in 2000 that RAND was forced to officially acknowledge the paper's existence and authenticity. Today RAND counters that it was an "internal draft" that was never formally considered. It is easy to understand why RAND would want us to think this is the case.

From a summary of this report we learn the author's conclusions about the phenomena: "Since WWII there seems to have been a drastic increase in sightings. We have enough data to know that the phenomena is unambiguously extraordinary and clearly inexplicable in modern terms." Chapters in the previously restricted document include, "UFOs: Historical Aspects" "UFOs: Astronomical Aspects" "Phenomenological Aspects" and its conclusion, "UFOs: How to Proceed and Why."

We know based on the above-mentioned 1948 Air Force document that RAND was engaged in official research. In 1968, two decades later, RAND was still engaged in such analysis. And they likely continue this work today.

Keeping It All in the Family

RAND's Executive Vice President is Michael D. Rich. Mr. Rich is also Director of RAND National Security Research. A family man, Mr. Rich's own family history is very telling. His father was aviation genius Benjamin Rich. Ben helped to lead aerospace giant Lockheed Martin as President of Lockheed Advanced Aeronautics. He oversaw the ultra-secret Lockheed "Skunk Works" division, where he spearheaded the development of the Stealth bomber. Rich Sr. is universally acknowledged as "the father of Stealth technology."

Ben Rich stated some extremely revealing things about the reality and nature of UFOs before he passed. In a letter to his friend and associate John Andrews he replied to Andrew's observations about the UFO phenomenon. Andrews had written a letter to Rich in which he wrote, "I believe with certainty in manmade UFOs. I am tending to believe there are also extraterrestrial UFOs."

Rich, in a handwritten letter, replied to Andrews, "Yes, I am a believer in both categories." Andrews was a forensic illustrator and aviation model-maker. Before his own death, Andrews related that Rich went further in privately explaining that, "there are two types of UFOs, the ones we build and the ones 'they' build." Rich told Andrews of his concern that the public should not be told. But Rich told Andrews he had recently changed his mind on this and that those "involved in dealing with the 'subject' could represent a bigger problem to citizens than knowledge of the visitors themselves." Just before he died, Andrews says that Rich confirmed to him that "items" were recovered at the crash at Roswell in 1947. Rich also told associate Jeff Goodall, "we have things at Area 51 that you and the best minds in the world won't even be able to conceive for the next 30-40 years." (YouTube, Search: "Lockheed Skunk Works Chief Ben Rich remark to Jim Goodall")

In fact, Rich gave numerous clues and hints about the alien reality to several before he passed. The father of Stealth, who is also the father of RAND's current Director, gave his gift of truth to history before he died. He confirmed official government study of the UFO reality and the crash of an extraterrestrial vehicle to earth.

RAND-Battelle Connection to UFOs

Prior articles by this author (available on the UFO Iconoclasts website http://ufocon.blogspot.com, and in the book *Witness to Roswell*) have shown that, like RAND, Battelle Memorial Institute was heavily engaged by the U.S. government to study UFOs. It now appears that Battelle metallurgists likely analyzed the memory metal retrieved from Roswell. That conclusion was drawn from a "reverse engineering of information" of the literature on shape recovery metal, the statements of two U.S. Generals, the confession of a senior Battelle scientist, and by establishing other connections.

Perhaps the most interesting of these telling connections is this: The Director of Battelle at the time of the Roswell crash, Clyde E. Williams, simultaneously sat on the Board of Trustees of the RAND Corporation. Williams directed RAND and Battelle's activities at a time when both organizations were highly engaged in UFO study. Clyde Williams was installed as Trustee of RAND in 1948 (the year after Roswell) and remained a RAND trustee until 1963. Battelle is also known to have supported analysis of UFO sightings for the Air Force's Project Blue Book during William's tenure.

The line between "public" and "private" sectors is blurred when it comes to things UFO. Such fuzzy, "quasi-public" organizations were of grave concern to a wise President and military icon. Dwight Eisenhower was instructive in his farewell to the nation. He warned that we should beware of the unchecked powers of the "military-industrial complex." And the Five Star General was right, for it is in military-industrial complexes like Battelle and RAND that the alien truth resides, unchecked. Until now.

The Roswell Debris

Newly discovered documents reveal that in the months immediately following the purported 1947 UFO crash at Roswell, secret government studies began on a material that was previously unknown to science. The "memory metal" that was studied precisely matches some of the debris material reported by several witnesses to the crash. Evidence shows that, under military direction, these unique metal studies were undertaken by a contracted laboratory that possessed advanced technical capabilities that the U.S. government itself did not have at the time. A former high-level scientist employed by the laboratory has offered a confession that he was tasked to study the crashed UFO material. Information provided by two U.S. Air Force Generals also offers direct support for this discovery.

The documents suggest that after the crash, the U.S. government attempted to develop a unique material that is today referred to as memory metal. This shape-recovery alloy was reported by several witnesses to the Roswell crash in the summer of 1947. The lightweight "morphing" material was able to be crumpled or deformed and then return itself instantly and seamlessly to its original state. The metallurgical discoveries that resulted from these studies were then "seeded" for further technology development to other government agencies (including NASA) and through a series of military contracts to universities and industry.

The laboratory contracted by Wright-Patterson to perform these studies was Battelle Memorial Institute in Columbus, Ohio. It has been credibly reported that Wright-Patterson was the very base where the Roswell UFO debris was flown after the crash. Recently obtained documents reveal that these studies were conducted at Battelle under the direction of Dr. Howard C. Cross. In the late 1940's, H.C Cross was Battelle's expert scientist in exotic metallurgy and Titanium alloy research.

Curiously, although he was a research metallurgist, Cross was also Battelle's "point person" in later studies on UFOs that Battelle conducted in the early 1950's for the U.S. Air Force's official UFO study, Project Bluebook. Cross is likely an author of Project Bluebook's still-missing Report Number 13. He is also the author of a strange letter from Battelle to Wright-Patterson known as "The Pentacle" memo.

Founded in 1929, Battelle is engaged in research, development and commercialization of technological innovation. They specialize in materials science and engineering, life sciences, energy science and national security. Battelle operates many of our country's National Laboratories, including some of the U.S.'s most sensitive installations such as Oak Ridge, Lawrence Livermore and Brookhaven Laboratories. Battelle is headquartered in proximity to Wright-Patterson and remains one of the nation's leading defense contractors. Their metallurgical capabilities and technical talent continue to be recognized as world-class.

Nitinol Memory Metal

The direct connection between the Roswell debris and Battelle studies is revealed in a material known as Nitinol. Nitinol is a specially processed combination of Nickel and Titanium, or NiTi. It displays many of the very same properties and physical characteristics as some of the crash debris materials that were reported at Roswell. Both are memory metals that "remember" their original shape and both are extremely lightweight. The materials are reported to have similar color, possess a high fatigue strength and are able to withstand extreme heat.

Today Nitinol is incorporated in items as far-ranging as medical implants and bendable eyeglass frames. It is produced in many forms including sheet, wire and coil. Newer "intelligent metal" systems are being studied by NASA in the creation of bendable or flappable wings, as self-actuators and as a "self-healing" outer hull "skin" for spacecraft. It is believed that the memory metal found at Roswell came from the outer structures of a downed extraterrestrial spacecraft.

The earliest known combination of Titanium and Nickel reported in the scientific literature was in 1939 by two Europeans. However, this crude sample was a "by-product" of research entirely unrelated to the study of Nitinol. Its "memory metal" potential was not sought or noted. The scientists would have been unable to purify Titanium to sufficient levels at that time, and would not have known about the energy requirement needed to create the "morphing" effect.

The next time the unique combination of Titanium and Nickel emerged was at the U.S. Naval Ordnance Lab. It was there that Nitinol was "officially" created in the early 1960s. But Nitinol's "official" history, including the date and reasons for discovery, is conflicting. Recently gained information suggests that it was, in fact, Battelle's metallurgist and UFO researcher, Dr. Howard Cross, who "fed" the U.S. Navy information (including the "phase diagram" and details on Titanium processing) that is required to create Nitinol.

Research by this author has confirmed that Nitinol studies actually began at Battelle immediately after the Roswell crash and not in the early 1960's, and that it was Wright-Patterson (the base where the crash material was flown) that contracted the secret work. Confirmation is given in a brief footnote found in a study by one of Nitinol's "official" inventors at the U.S. Naval Lab. In that military report on Nitinol, the author footnotes a 1949 Battelle study that clearly pertains to the refinement of Titanium and Nickel. The citation relates to a "phase diagram" that examines states of matter and how the two metals could be successfully alloyed. If processed in the right way, the result is Nitinol memory metal. It is possible that the "official" co-inventors of Nitinol were unaware that the memory metal's origin was to be found in the study of the Roswell debris.

Only three other references to this Titanium and Nickel memory metal report by Battelle have ever been found. In each case, they appear only as buried footnotes, and only in metals studies conducted under U.S. military auspices. In one case this included having a "Project Monitor" present from Wright-Patterson Air Force Base.

A historical analysis of the scientific literature shows that no other alloys had ever been studied by the U.S. military as a potential "memory metal" prior to this late 1940's timeframe and Battelle's Wright-Patterson study contract. Wright-Patterson needed Battelle to accomplish this work. Much of the reason for this is because Battelle had something that Wright-Patterson did not—an advanced arc furnace that was capable of melting and refining Titanium to the purity required to make memory metal.

The history of Titanium (which is required to make Nitinol) is itself also revealing. According to *Encyclopedia Britannica*: "After 1947, Titanium changed from a laboratory curiosity to an important structural metal." According to the Industrial Arts Index, the number of science abstracts published on Titanium spiked dramatically after 1947. In RAND Corporation's 1962 abstract "The Titanium Decade" we learn that: "A far larger Titanium industry arose from the point of view of production capacity than was needed to produce the material that was actually used in aircraft. The time period of 1948-1958 involved virtually all of the costs." An astonishing $2.5 billion (in today's dollars) was spent on Titanium research by the U.S. government in the years immediately following 1947.

The Battelle memory metal report is titled "Second Progress Report on Contract AF33 (038)-3736" and was completed for Wright-Patterson Air Force Base in 1949. It is authored by C.M. Craighead, F. Fawn and L.W. Eastwood. It appears to be part of a series of such contracts conducted through the early 1950's. Interestingly, the scientists who authored the report were very closely associated with Battelle's chief Titanium metallurgist (and later, Battelle's UFO researcher for Project Bluebook) Dr. Howard Cross, previously mentioned. The scientists went on to author reports on exotic metallurgy that related to such areas as "metal and superplasticity," "metal transformation," and "metal microstructures."

Based on the sections of the studies that were found that reference this Battelle report, we know that this "progress report" offers the first "phase diagram" ever produced to attempt to successfully alloy Titanium and Nickel. This would be required to make memory metal. We can also infer that it examined refinement of Titanium to high purity levels required to create the shape-recovery effect.

No references have ever been located to something that must surely exist: Battelle's "First Progress Report" on the memory metal. While the Second Progress Report (completed in 1949) refers to techniques to process the alloy, the First Progress Report (authored in 1947 or 1948) probably relates to the actual analysis of "Roswellian" memory metal. Although Nitinol is not identical to the Roswell debris material, it represents our best attempts at re-creation of the found memory metal. The impetus for this "shape-recovery" metallurgical research has to be the crash debris discovered at Roswell in the summer of 1947.

Missing Battelle Reports

A year-long effort was made by this author to locate Battelle's First and Second Progress Reports on memory metal. Though footnotes have been located to the reports in military sponsored studies on memory metal, access to the actual reports remains impossible.

Battelle's own Historian/Librarian was unable to locate the documents. In a later follow-up call to Battelle, *Sarasota Herald Tribune* reporter Billy Cox was told that Battelle is still unable to find the report and that it remains a "mystery." Likewise, Wright-Patterson Air Force Base's own Archivist and Manager of its Special Collections was unable to locate the documents. Both librarians from each organization worked together to find them. They are baffled and suggest that it may mean that the reports were destroyed (though there is no record of this) or that they may remain highly classified.

The U.S. DOD's Defense Technical Information Center (DTIC) is the master repository of our nation's military-sponsored technical reports and studies. Their database also fails to locate the Battelle reports. Finally, with the guidance of reporter Billy Cox, a Freedom of Information Act (FOIA) request to the Secretary of the Air Force/WPAFB was filed by this author. Information has yet to be provided that is responsive to this request.

It is hoped that the Second Progress Report will one day be located. If it contains "phase diagrams" for the alloying of Nickel and Titanium, it will confirm the work on memory metal. It would strongly suggest that shape-recovery alloys were precisely what Battelle was attempting to create for the military in the time period directly after the Roswell crash. The likelihood that the First Progress Report by Battelle on memory metal will ever be found is even more remote.

Confirmation By Air Force Generals

In an interview conducted in the 1990's, former Wright-Patterson Air Force Base Brigadier General Arthur Exon confirmed the existence of the Roswell metal reports. Exon, the Base Commander of Wright-Patterson in the 1960s, related that he was privy to some of the details on the composition of the crash debris and the variety of tests that were performed on it. Astonishingly, Exon stated of the debris: "It was Titanium and some other metal they knew about, and the processing was somehow different." Of course, special "processing" of Titanium and the "other metal" that "they knew about" (Nickel) is required to create Nitinol.

Exon added tellingly, "And it wouldn't surprise me if the material wasn't still around, certainly the reports are." Exon was likely referring to the Battelle Progress Reports on memory metal done for Wright-Patterson in the late 1940's.

Air Force General George Schulgen (who led Intelligence at the Pentagon at the time of the Roswell incident) authored a previously "secret" draft memo on the flying saucer issue on October 30, 1947, about four months after the crash. In the verified version of this memo is found a section entitled "Items of Construction." Schulgen instructs his officers to be aware of flying objects and their materials of construction. He specifically notes the "unusual fabrication methods to achieve extreme lightweight," and that the material is of a "composite construction ... using various combinations of metals."

Schulgen is describing precisely some of the very characteristics of Nitinol. Just like the Roswell debris material, it is an "extreme lightweight" intermetallic alloy. As a novel "composite construction," it is created by an "unusual fabrication" method that "uses a combination of metals," perhaps like Titanium and Nickel.

Battelle Scientist Confesses

Battelle scientist Elroy John Center has stated that he analyzed metal from a crashed UFO when he was employed by the Institute. Center was a Senior Research Chemist who worked for Battelle for nearly two decades, from 1939 to 1957. This has been confirmed by both his University of Michigan alumni files and by the location of scientific papers that he authored during his employment at Battelle.

A graduate Chemical Engineer, Center authored papers that appeared in highly technical journals. His areas of research included the chemical testing of metals; the microdetermination of metals in alloys; and the spectroscopic analysis of unique materials. Center was likely involved in early analysis of the Roswell debris. A groundbreaking metals analysis technique that Center developed has been found cited in studies related to the "polygraphic determination of Titanium" in alloys. Specially-selected Titanium is required to create the Roswell-like "memory metal" Nitinol.

Center's family members confirm that he had an intense interest in UFOs and the extraterrestrial. In May of 1992, noted historical researcher Dr. Irena Scott of Columbus, OH (a former Battelle scientist) interviewed a close professional associate of Elroy Center for the Ohio MUFON Journal. Center had privately related to him in June of 1960 that while he was employed at Battelle he had been involved in a very strange laboratory project.[3]

Center said he had been tasked by his superiors to assist on a highly-classified Battelle study that was contracted by the government to work on a very unusual material. He understood that this debris material was retrieved by the U.S. government from the earlier crash of a UFO. He referred to the item he studied as a "piece." He explained that this "piece" was not something with which anyone was familiar. He also said that the debris had been inscribed with strange symbols that he called "glyphics." Similar markings have been reported by some of the witnesses to the Roswell crash debris. Center stopped short of providing any further details. The Battelle scientist passed away in 1991.

References

1. "Request for Study by RAND Project," Col. W.R. Clingerman, (October 12, 1948) is available at *www.project1947.com/gr/48randufostudy.htm.*

2. The RAND document "UFOs: What to Do?" (November 27, 1968) is posted in PDF format at *www.nicap.org/docs/rand/randdoc681127.pdf*.

3. Telephone conversation between the author and Dr. Irena Scott.

About the Author

Anthony Bragalia writes for the UFO Iconoclasts website at *http://ufocon.blogspot.com*. The full story of the Roswell-Battelle connection is relayed in the newly published sequel book *Witness to Roswell* (Revised, 2009) by Tom Carey and Don Schmitt, in chapter contributions made by this author. Scientific citations, references and report images are also included in the updated edition.

Messages from Space

Long Delayed Echoes and Other Intelligent Contact

by Joan d'Arc

In the midst of the Great Depression of the 1930s, American radio engineer Karl Jansky discovered radio waves emanating from the Milky Way. With the development of RADAR during World War II, the military began using large radio telescopes to listen to the chatter of the stars. The first official crib monitor was erected in 1960, and was called Project Ozma after Frank Baum's *Wizard of Oz*. The plan was hatched by then-Director of the National Radio Astronomy Observatory (NRAO), Frank Drake.

After four weeks of aiming their rotating antenna at the constellations of Tau Ceti and Epsilon Eridani, both over ten light years away from Green Bank, West Virginia, Project Ozma ended in apparent frustration, like many similar Search for Extraterrestrial Intelligence (SETI) projects. To this day, writes Michael Theroux in his paper, "Detecting Biodynamic Signals," no signals have been found by "standard radio-astronomical methods" (Theroux).

The major difficulty with conventional interstellar communications based on radio-astronomy, says Theroux, is that it "assumes that an extraterrestrial civilisation's technology is comparable to, and has evolved to a state equal to our own." This is an anthropocentric assumption, as technological R&D can never be assumed to follow a parallel trajectory. Indeed, some fringe scientists have suggested that intelligent messages might even be emanating from *inside* the solar system.

Why Not Send a Messenger Probe?

Many scientists had reasoned that the signal from an extraterrestrial intelligence (ETI) would consist of a string of prime numbers, so the receiver might be able to discriminate intelligent signals from the noise of natural background radiation. However, in his 1974 book, *The Galactic Club*, Ronald Bracewell concluded otherwise; expecting instead "a little poetry or art," and, perhaps, "a program that would rivet our attention" (Bracewell 52). He wrote of the hypothetical message we should perhaps be expecting: "messages might be nested within messages—short items, frequently repeated, sandwiched between episodes of a longer story repeated less frequently, all of which is contained within an even longer communication" (Bracewell 52-53).

After considering the "anticlimactic" slowness of interstellar communication, Bracewell was the first to propose, in 1960, the idea that a highly technological civilization might send a messenger probe into circular orbit of a star in the mid-point of that star's habitable zone. He proposed that the hypothetical robot probe (now known as a "Bracewell probe") would contain radio equipment for use in communicating with another advanced technological society. He expanded on the idea:

> This need not be an individual of their race, although their biological engineering may well have proceeded to the point where a sub race of interstellar messengers has been bred. It would

> be completely unacceptable to us, but perhaps not to them, to breed brains in bottles, with eyes and arms but not bodies or legs; possibly one can do the equivalent with solid-state devices. One way or another, it is clearly possible in principle to pack an enormous amount of information into a modest interstellar probe, and to send it into the vicinity of a likely star (Bracewell 70).

Bracewell believed that a dispatch of such messenger probes would be undertaken by a "Class 2" civilization, and "would already have been followed by some of the 10 million communities more advanced than we, which are distributed, albeit thinly, throughout the galaxy." He proffered, "possibly such a program is currently being engaged in by our nearest superior community," from 30 to 300 light-years away. He gave this hypothetical advanced civilization the name *Superon* (Bracewell 71).

Continuing his hypothetical dialogue, Bracewell wrote, "After settling into the approximate orbit where the inhabited planet should be, the probe begins a program of investigation, supplementing its internal power source with stellar power." He speculated: "It is quite possible that a probe arrived in our solar system when our radio transmissions had not yet begun .... the earth could have been the target of a messenger probe as recently as a few decades ago, but even then we did not have commercial broadcast transmitters in operation" (Bracewell 70-72).

All that would be needed to tune into such broadcasts, he said, was a simple radio receiver with a knob. He further speculated, "If an alien probe near the earth picks up a terrestrial broadcast from a radio transmitter that you are listening to and then amplifies and retransmits it, you will hear first the direct transmission followed by a repeat equal to the time taken to travel out to the probe and back. The general effect will be like an echo" (Bracewell 73). This now widely documented phenomenon, under research for the past several decades, is known as Long Delayed Echoes (LDEs).

During the years 1899-1924, three scientists independently observed identical radio phenomena suggestive of interplanetary communications. A paper presented at the 17th annual meeting of the American Rocket Society in November of 1962 explained in detail the experiments of Nikola Tesla, Guglielmo Marconi, and Dr. David Todd (Jackson & Hohmann).

Tesla's Experiments in High Frequency

In 1899, inventor Nikola Tesla began conducting experiments at Colorado Springs in an attempt to identify the "frequency" of the planet. In effect, Tesla theorized, "the planet Earth has a circuit identification, a signature of its own, and, given the proper equipment, he could broadcast this identity wholesale to the universe." Indeed, his Colorado laboratory "was designed in keeping with Tesla's plans to make the terrestrial globe a propagation device for the transmission of energy" (Jackson).

Tesla's earliest attempts at communication could have been detected by such an extraterrestrial probe in the solar system. In fact, the "multi-million volt surges of radio noise" he transmitted were intended to produce electrical waves "of such magnitude that, without the slightest doubt, the effect will be perceptible on some of our nearer planets."

On or about July 28, 1899, using an invention he called a Magnifying Transmitter, Tesla reportedly received coherent radio signals from space. Tesla claimed, during a pause in experiments he was surprised by a series of incoming signals of periodicity, number, and order, traceable to no cause known to him. In a *Collier's Weekly* article in March 1901, Tesla wrote:

> It was sometime afterward when the thought flashed upon my mind that the disturbances I had observed might be due to an intelligent control. Although I could not decipher their meaning, it was impossible for me to think of them as having been entirely accidental. The feeling is constantly growing on me that I had been the first to hear the greeting of one planet to another.

Tesla continued to believe he had received intelligent messages from space. He became increasingly reluctant to discuss the subject with the media, since he had been ridiculed in the press for believing the signals came from Mars. On July 11, 1937, the *New York Times* reported on Tesla's pronouncement that he had perfected a certain compact apparatus that could transmit energy through space "to any distance without the slightest dispersion." It was later revealed that the name of this device was the "Teslascope."

According to Tesla's assistant, Arthur Matthews, Tesla had two massive magnifying transmitters built in Canada. Matthews claimed Tesla invented the Teslascope "to communicate with beings on other planets." Matthews' book, *The Wall of Light*, contains a diagram of the Teslascope, explaining, "In principle, it takes in cosmic ray signals.... Eventually the signals are stepped down to audio.... Speak into one end, and the signal goes out the other end as a cosmic ray emitter." Yet, the existence of the Teslascope has never been confirmed (Nelson).

The Experiments of Marconi

On March 27, 1899, inventor Guglielmo Marconi was concluding his first experiments in wireless transmission across the English Channel, having successfully transmitted the Marconi-code letter "V" from France to England, a distance of 50 miles.[1] On December 12, 1901, Marconi successfully transmitted the code-letter "S" from Cornwall, England to St. Johns, Newfoundland, a distance of 1800 miles.

In September of 1921, 22-years after these first experiments, while conducting atmospheric experiments in the Mediterranean on his floating laboratory, the 220 foot yacht, the Elettra, Marconi detected what he later described as an interplanetary communication. Marconi reported that the signals registered high in the meter band, but were not electrical disturbances. The pulses were regular and apparently consisted of an unfamiliar code. The only signal he recognized was the letter "V" from his own code: the Marconi code. He believed the signals had originated in outer space. Was Marconi's own "V" signal being repeated by intelligent receivers?

Marc Seifer, in "Confessions of a Tesla Nerd," suggests Tesla may have heard Marconi's transmissions and somehow did not place them as terrestrial (presumably because they were in Marconi code and not Morse code). Granted, the two radio pioneers were likely the only possible terrestrial senders, but since there was a four-month delay between Marconi's transmission of his own "V" signal on March 27, 1899 and Tesla's receipt of unidentifiable signals on or about July 28, 1899, it is possible that Tesla could have intercepted an intelligent extraterrestrial reply to Marconi's transmission.

Marconi continued to receive anomalous transmissions in 1921, although pulsars, quasars and other natural phenomena have not been ruled out (Seifer).

In his discussion of the signals in a *New York Times* article on September 3, 1921, Marconi stated that he would expect interplanetary communications to take the form of "transmission of pictures accompanied by a simple code." This statement anticipated the following "listening experiment" of Dr. David Todd three years later.

National Radio Silence Day

According to the theories of astronomer Frank Drake, an advanced civilization would "send out pulses in clusters, a series of pulses, followed by a pause ... the number of signals in each pulse could stand for intensity of light or dark, and we could build up a picture on the basis of the information received" (Jackson).

On August 22, 1924, with the close approach of Mars, David Todd, professor of Astronomy at Amherst College in Massachusetts, began what he called a listening experiment. Todd asked the U.S. government to request, through diplomatic channels, that all countries with high-power transmitters turn off their equipment for five minutes every hour during a 24-hour period.

Incoming radio signals during the test period, called National Radio Silence Day, were recorded on a radiophoto message device called a Jenkins Radio Camera, attached to a receiver, which was set to a wavelength of 6,000 meters. The radio signals were converted to light signals, which were then printed on a five-inch wide reel of photosensitive tape. Any radio signals that were within the limits of the wavelength would cause a tiny lamp to flash and the flashes would expose the light-sensitive strip. The strip was developed on a motion picture film rack, which had recorded sixteen frames of pulses in clusters, each frame separated by a 30-minute pause. Todd also received the Morse code "S" plus other codes (Jackson).

A paper delivered to the American Rocket Society in 1962 by C.D. Jackson and R.E. Hohmann, entitled "An Historic Report on Life in Space: Tesla, Marconi, Todd," took specific note of the response time between the transmission of the Marconi code "V" in March, 1899 and the incoming code "V" recognized by Marconi in September, 1921, a cycle of 22 years. The consistency held true for the transmission of the Morse code "S" by Tesla in December, 1901, and the monitoring of the Morse code "S" plus additional codes by Todd in August, 1924, a cycle of 22 years.

If we were to consider the monitored signals as an intelligent response to those sent by Tesla and Marconi, the 22-year response time places the distance of the sender at approximately 10.8 to 11.8 light years away, which is the vicinity of Epsilon / Eridani / Tau Ceti (Jackson).

The Eindhoven Radio Experiments

In 1927, radio telegraph engineer, Jorgan Hals, and physicist, Professor Carl Störmer, both of Oslö, began a discussion of curious radio echo phenomena received on both sides of the Atlantic. While normal radio echoes took one-seventh of a second to circle the entire Earth, Hals had documented echoes from his own pulsed Morse code transmissions with a three second delay. The two were well aware that the Earth's ionosphere reflected radio waves, and that reflections from the Moon can bounce back in 2.7 seconds. However, in this case, the echoes were of a longer delay than could be explained by such reflections. It was as though someone were recording the transmissions and retransmitting them. In his 1955 book, *The Polar Aurora*, Störmer wrote that Hals believed the echoes were coming from the vicinity of the Moon.

Americans, A.H. Taylor and L.C. Young, had reported a similar anomaly, but their echoes had been received within a few hundredths of a second. Taylor and Young published their findings in the *Proceedings of the Institute of Radio Engineers* in May of 1928. Their research indicated that the echoes were coming apparently from a region 2,900 to 10,000 kilometers overhead (Lunan, 223). Today we would associate this distance with the inner Van Allen radiation belt, discovered in 1958. It has been noted that this would be a likely spot for an intelligent "self-replicating" space probe (von Neumann probe), since the belt is made up of a huge amount of natural building materials for astro-engineering projects (d'Arc, *Space Travelers*).

Störmer and Hals began a series of experimental signal-pulse transmissions from Eindhoven, Norway, to test the hypothesis that the long-delayed echoes were of artificial origin. The first anomalous echoes were received on April 14, 1927 and again in October of 1927. Suspecting the echoes were not being properly identified, the team altered the program, spacing the pulses at twenty-second intervals instead of five-second intervals. Hals began to send groups of three dots (representing the Morse code letter S), at intervals of two seconds. The received echoes consisted mostly of a Morse *dash*, "as if the three dots had been blurred together." The duration of the dash was of the same duration as the transmitted signal. The signal frequency also remained the same. The delay time between the transmitted signal and the received echo was consistently three seconds (Lunan 224).

On September 25, 1928, Hals and Störmer transmitted, and received echoes sixteen days later, on October 11. These echoes began to vary from three seconds to fifteen seconds. Radio pioneer, B. van der Pol, repeated the experiment the same evening at the behest of Störmer and Hals, increasing the time interval to thirty seconds. The echo pulses came in at intervals ranging from three seconds to fifteen seconds. Following this experiment, van der Pol continued his transmissions at consistent intervals of thirty seconds. There was silence for thirteen days, then on October 24 the echoes commenced at intervals varying from three seconds to thirty seconds. Van der Pol published his findings in the journal *Nature* in 1928.

Contact with Epsilon Boötes

Scottish space enthusiast and science fiction writer Duncan Lunan, author of *Interstellar Contact* (1973), suggested the probe was intelligently adapting its communications to those it had received (Lunan 224). Lunan, a member of Association in Scotland to Research into Astronautics (ASTRA), formed in 1953, argued that communication by delay time might be more effective than picture-sending systems, where "zero symbols" have to be transmitted along with "picture-element pulses."

In 1973, using the careful records of the 1927-1929 Norwegian experiments, Lunan plotted the echo delay patterns on a simple L-shaped graph to see whether they might apply to any known star maps. He plotted the delay times, in seconds, each represented by a black dot along the x-axis. When he connected the dots he noted, "The main figure of the diagram has a striking but incomplete resemblance to the constellation Boötes, the Herdsman." He wrote fancifully: "It would seem that Epsilon Boötes was the star the probe came from, and had we returned the completed map to it, it would have 'known' it had contacted intelligent beings" (Lunan 226).

Yet, there was one problem with Lunan's hypothesis, as he saw it. Relative to an Earth observer today, the dot that represented the star Arcturus, the Alpha star in the constellation Boötes, was plotted well above and to the left of its true position in the skies. After much study Lunan arrived at a solution, and wrote, "The probe could have arrived here thousands of years ago, compiled its maps, and then ceased operations until we invented radio on Earth." Lunan reasoned, "We can't date the arrival accurately by Arcturus because the star's motion in the heavens is not regular ... a seven degree displacement would correspond to an interval of 12,600 years."

Lunan more closely approximated the time of the arrival of the probe after plotting the next LDE event in the records of the Norwegian radio pioneers, noting, "The next map received strongly suggests a figure of about 13,000 years." Lunan then found that if he rotated his star map diagram slightly to allow for the curvature of the heavens the star points were finally brought into line (Lunan 229). He hypothesized that the probe from Epsilon Boötes lay in either the L4 or L5 "Lagrange point" in the Moon's orbit around the Earth, a place of equilibrium of the gravity of the two bodies.

Duncan Lunan's Star Maps

Hals and others continued to hear anomalous long-delayed echoes in experiments conducted at Eindhoven between February and May of 1929, and Andreas Kleve, a radio operator at Bödo, near the Arctic Circle, documented five 12 to 13-second echoes during a thirty-minute transmission from Eindhoven (Appleton). Yet, perhaps one of the most fascinating events in radio history occurred in May of 1929, when two French naval vessels were sent to Indo-China to study the effects of an eclipse of the Sun on radio propagation, specifically on the phenomenon of long-delayed echoes (Lunan 234).

On May 8, 1929, using a 500-watt transmitter, the two ships transmitted signals for the first ten minutes of every half-hour. On May 9, the day of the eclipse, the same signals were sent again: "Two dots were sent every thirty seconds on a 25-meter wavelength, varying in a fixed musical sequence to aid correct identification and timing of the echoes." As reported in *L'Onde Electrique*, large numbers of echoes were recorded as weak or strong, with delay times ranging from one to thirty-two seconds. The marked intensity of the strong echoes was "too great for natural reflection at such apparent distances," but this point was apparently missed at the time (Lunan 234).

The full report on the French expedition, published in *L'Onde Electrique* in 1930, detailed a complex pattern of echoes difficult to transcribe. Writing in 1975, Lunan concluded the message had eluded them, suggesting, "the May 9 signals might be an attempt to communicate complex information in the form of visual puzzles, in hopes to arouse the interest of a culture more advanced than ours" (Lunan 236).

Lunan Solves the Big Puzzle?

As Ronald Bracewell had proposed, "messages might be nested within messages—short items, frequently repeated, sandwiched between episodes of a longer story." This inspired Lunan to transcribe the complicated sequence by first separating it into what appeared to be natural "panels." Following is a brief version of Lunan's explanation of the complex diagrams found in his 1973 book, *Interstellar Contact*:

Panel 1 – The probe is launched from Epsilon Boötes, a two sun system, by boosting it past the minor sun against the star's orbital motion, giving it a gravitational slingshot effect. The probe moves from left to right and is captured by the Earth-Moon system, begins its retrofire and slows down enough to be captured by the Sun.

Panel 2 – Confirms the probe is in a stable position in the leading equilateral position left of the Moon as seen from the northern hemisphere. The remaining puzzle in panel 2 shows a body orbiting the Earth at about 164,300 miles. That orbit is not stable; the Moon would perturb anything positioned there.

Panel 3 – Tells us that the probe placed another body in orbit; perhaps another probe (a "von Neumann probe" or self-replicating "probot"?). Accepting the data in panel 2 to be correct, the second orbiter's distance is 164,300 miles and the time it takes to circle the Earth is 15.73 days.

Panel 4 – Provides a "key" to panel 5, showing the retrofire approach through the solar system.

Panel 5 – Compares the Epsilon Boötes planetary system with the solar system, and shows the probe's entry into the solar system, identified by rows of nine dots. The probe began its retrofire at the orbit of Uranus, but its capture by the Sun was achieved in its swing around Jupiter. Lunan notes, "At times the star map shows Neptune as the outer planet, perhaps it was at the time the probe arrived."

Panel 6 – Shows the entry trajectory of the probe as it swings around Jupiter, compares our Sun with its two suns, and shows their planetary system has seven planets. Located between panels 5 and 7, panel 6 is an artistic representation of those two panels, containing the same information.

Panel 7 – Is "intellectually beautiful because of its logical clarity." It is so prominent that perhaps

we were expected to crack it first, which Lunan did. Panel 7 can be read as follows:

AB – start here
BC – our home is Epsilon Boötes
CDE – which is a double star
FG, GH – we live on the sixth planet of seven, check that, the sixth of seven
EM – counting outwards from our sun
FEG, GN – which is the larger of the two
HO, OP – our sixth planet has one moon, our fourth planet has three, and our first and third planets each have one
GQ, QR – our probe is in the orbit of your moon
ST – updates the earlier position of Arcturus.

Lunan further suggested, "ST tells us that by May 1929 the probe had more systems on-line, including visual sensors, and had updated its previous star maps. It couldn't correct the map without redrawing the whole of panel 7." He wrote, "If we had had the capability in 1929, we might have found the probe ready to communicate by laser." Considering the planet's close proximity to its sun, Lunan concluded, "we can guess that the sixth planet was not the probe-makers' original home." Strangely, Lunan alluded to the fact that if this planet were their original home, the probe makers would be "giants" (Lunan 237-39).

Contact with Ursa Major

Dr. L.G. Lawrence proposed that advanced civilizations might use a form of biological communication using patterns to complete an eidoform, or eidetic picture, which would be nearly instantaneous. On October 29, 1971, while conducting "remote biological sensing" experiments in Riverside County, CA, Dr. Lawrence, field manager of the Ecola Institute, intercepted a train of apparently intelligent communication signals. As reported in *Borderlands* (Vol. 1, 1996), during a short rest period, Lawrence's field equipment, an "organic transducer complex," had accidentally remained pointed at the constellation Ursa Major. Lawrence reported that the pulses were tightly spaced and were received at discrete intervals for over 33 minutes (Nelson).

On April 10, 1972, Lawrence documented a similar phenomenon. This time the signals grew weaker, and "appeared to be transmitted at great intervals ranging from weeks to months, possibly years." He noted a "faint, coherent, binary-type phenomenon ... at intervals between rapid series of pulse trains ranged from ... 3 to 10 minutes." In his paper entitled, "Communication by Accident," Lawrence described the pulses as "a short, incremental series of deep, harmonious oscillations resembling nonsense chatter or background modulations," containing "an intelligent character ... discrete spacing patterns, apparent repetitions of sequences, and highly attenuated Gaussian noise" (Nelson).

As reported in *Borderlands* (Vol. 1, 1996), Lawrence's experiment was replicated in 1995 by Michael Theroux and Michael Elsey at the Joshua Tree National Park in southern California. Theroux has no doubt that he received a biodynamic signal from the direction of the constellation Ursa Major, and caught it on audiotape.

The Wow! Signal

On August 15, 1977, the Big Ear radio telescope at Ohio State University picked up a signal that occurred once and was never detected again. Known as "the Wow! signal," in reference to the word "Wow!" scribbled in the margin of the computer printout by Dr. Jerry Ehman, the signal remains unexplained. Says Ehman, "At first, I thought it was an earth signal reflected from space debris, but after I studied it further, I found that couldn't be the case."

Researchers have analyzed the Wow! Signal and have found that the source was moving with the background stars. In addition, terrestrial interference, such as telecommunications equipment, aircraft and spacecraft, has been ruled out. Judging from the antenna coordinates, the signal was not coming from any known nearby stars. More than one hundred searches of the same region of the sky have been made, and the signal has never been repeated ("Wow! Signal Page").

Greg Radio

In the 1980s, electrical engineer Greg Hodowanec experimented with his "gravity wave detector," which detects "coherent modulations" in the microwave radiation. According to his Theory of Rhysmonic Cosmology, radio waves travel at the speed of light, but gravitational signals are "instantaneous." Hodowanec insisted the gravitational technique was superior because of the simplicity of the instrumentation. He published his first report "SETI with Gravitational Signals" in April of 1986 in *Radio Astronomy*, noting that the tone-like signals appeared to come from the Auriga and Perseus region of the galaxy.

In a letter to the editor of *Radio-Electronics* magazine dated July 23, 1988, Hodowanec told of his contact with an apparently extraterrestrial communicator, explaining that he had recorded Morse code-like pulses. By August of 1988, he began to notice digital-type communication: dots and dashes, or ones and zeros. Similar to International Morse code symbols in pulse form, he found the most persistent symbol to be "SE."

Hodowanec believed the signals "came from either the Auriga-Perseus region near my zenith or the Boötes region under my Earth position" (Nelson).

On August 26, 1988, Hodowanec sent the message "Greg Radio" during a local gravity signal transmission test. The signals he received following this contained the letters G and D. Two days later, Hodowanec received a strong, repeated message of "Greg Radio," ending with a series of "SE" codes. On October 11, 1988, Hodowanec sent a series of "Greg Radio" messages at normal code speed of five words per minute, followed by a series of "KKTT." The same series was later received at a slower speed, followed by "KKTT."

On October 12, 1988, Hodowanec sent a series of A's and R's, with "Greg Radio" occasionally inserted, followed by "Greg Radio" sent as a series of five repetitions of each letter (example: Greg was sent as GGGGGRRRRREEEEEGGGGG.) He wrote, "Sufficient messages have now been received to indicate that perhaps a serious attempt to contact this writer was being made by some unknown communicator. ... While some apparently Morse code signals are being used, the communicator is not familiar with such usage, other than recognizing the coherent nature of the signals."

Since the messages were received at a specific hour, Hodowanec believed they were coming from "the general direction of the constellation Andromeda, but not necessarily the Galaxy there." By 1989, Hodowanec's communications had become more peculiar. He described conversations with several ETs using tones and what appeared to be "guttural voices" (Nelson).

Object 1991VG

In April of 1995, the British journal, *The Observatory*, published an article entitled, "SETA and 1991VG" [Search for Extraterrestrial Artifacts, specifically probes] by Duncan Steel of the University of Adelaide in Australia. Author of *Rogue Asteroids and Doomsday Comets*, Steel reported on a ten-meter object in orbit around the Sun, which had been initially discovered in November of 1991 by the Spacewatch Telescope at Kitt Peak. He noted that in 1991 the object had passed just 300,000 miles from the Earth, a little over the distance between the Earth and the Moon. The object, now known as 1991VG, was observed again in April 1992 by a larger telescope at Kitt Peak, and Steel believed it could be a candidate for an ETI probe ("Epilogue: Earth Probe").

Steel's conclusion was based on the two rather unnatural characteristics of the object. First, it was highly reflective, with "rapid variations in brightness," a characteristic of artificial satellites which rotate for stability. Second, it had an Earth-like orbit, "low eccentricity and inclination, and an orbital size slightly larger than that of the Earth." He argued against the object being an asteroid due to both its close orbit and its Earth-like orbit, which would cause it to be unstable.

Steel also observed that 1991VG had "made its close approach to Earth in 1991, sixteen years earlier in 1975 and sixteen years earlier in 1959." Noting that the object had a periodicity of sixteen years, he calculated that the object would have made a close approach in 1943 and in 1927. Interestingly, the latter is the year in which LDEs were first studied extensively.

LDEs and Space Probes: Hidden or Hypothetical History?

Although not conclusive evidence, these little-known examples of potential intelligent radio contact are certainly intriguing. If anything, in the case of Duncan Lunan's star maps, there is now a hypothetical scenario that might serve as a guide if such a message were ever received. In fact, Lunan's story is taken to its fullest import in Carl Sagan's book and film, *Contact*, where the embedded message is decoded to find instructions for building a wormhole through space. Although Lunan now wonders whether he construed his "visual puzzle" correctly, he does not doubt the LDEs of 1927-29 were of intelligent design.

As Jackson & Hohmann wrote in 1962, "The signals monitored by Tesla in 1899, by Marconi in 1921, and by Hals, Stormer, and van der Pol in 1927, are characteristically simple. They are basically a 'response in kind,' repeating the original transmission, although on a higher frequency, and performing, at least in part, a recognition function." As discussed in this article, it is possible the long delayed echoes of the 1920s were an intelligent extraterrestrial response to Tesla's 1899 high-frequency experiments.

After careful research of the LDE data observed in 1927-28, a study by Budden and Yates concluded in 1952 that the LDE phenomena were the result of "planar reflections from a system fixed in space relative to the earth and moving [in orbit] permanently with the earth." If this describes the Moon, any delayed echoes longer than 2.7 seconds are anomalous.

Robert Freitas has suggested the Earth-Moon libration or "halo" orbits might be "the most universally convenient meeting places for alien spacecraft exploring arbitrary stellar systems." Freitas suggests that such orbits could be "the best places to begin a search for evidence of ancient spacecraft parked in the Earth-Moon system."

A preliminary search was undertaken in 1979 at Leuschner Observatory for artificial objects in the libration orbits, under various conditions, with a visual limit of about 14th magnitude. Freitas reported in *Icarus* (1980) that, "no ancient space-craft, or other object of reflectivity greater than lunar albedo, having the size of Skylab or larger, is parked at L4, L5, or in any of the predicted halo orbits in the Earth-Moon system." He recom-mended that a long-term program be founded upon a search for such artificial objects (Freitas).

Did Duncan Lunan crack the first code from an ETI civilization, or was it simply an exercise in cosmic communication; a dry run, so to speak? Was it a program of "poetry and art" sent by an ETI probe, as Bracewell had anticipated, or was it the pure poetry and art of a science fiction geek carried away with SF futurism? If real, the broadcast certainly didn't "rivet our attention" as Bracewell had proposed. Could this be the result of our overriding skepticism concerning extrater-restrial intelligence?

In June 1998, an article by Lunan appeared in *Analog* magazine. He continued to believe the LDE communications were of intelligent design, but updated his translation of the message. Lunan suggested the ETs weren't from Boötes, but were using it as a navigational marker. He believed the space probe may have moved in the 1970s, and may have taken position in orbit as object 1991VG.

References

Appleton, E.V. "Wireless Echoes of Long Delay." *World Radio*. May 11, 1934.

Bracewell, Ronald N. *The Galactic Club: Intelligent Life in Outer Space*. The Portable Stanford: 1974.

Bracewell, Ronald N. "Communications from Superior Galactic Communities." *Nature*, Vol. 186. 1960.

Budden, K. G. and G. G. Yates. "A Search for Radio Echoes of Long Delay," *Journal of Atmospheric and Terrestrial Physics*, 1952, Vol. 2, 272-281, Pergamon Press, London.

d'Arc, Joan. *Space Travelers and the Genesis of the Human Form*, www.thebooktree.com

Freitas, Robert. "A Search for Natural or Artificial Objects Located at the Earth-Moon Libration Points," *Icarus* 42, 442-447, 1980. (www.rfreitas.com/Astro/SearchIcarus1980.htm)

Hodowanec, Gregory: *Rhysmonic Cosmology*, Rex Research, P.O. Box 19250, Jean NV 89019; (www.rexresearch.com/hodowane/rhysmo~1.htm)

Jackson, C.D. and R.E. Hohmann. "An Historic Report on Life in Space: Tesla, Marconi, Todd," American Rocket Society, Nov. 13, 1962. www.virtuallystrange.net/ufo/updates/1998/nov/m23-015.shtml.

Lawrence, L.G. "Interstellar Communications Signals," *Borderlands* 1996: 52(1):27-29

Lunan, Duncan. *Interstellar Contact*. Henry Regnery Company: Chicago, IL. 1975.

Nelson, Robert. "Communicating with Mars: The Experiments of Tesla & Hodowanec." Borderland Science. (www.borderlands.com/archives)

Seifer, Marc "Confessions of a Tesla Nerd." (www.netsense.net/tesla/article1.html).

Theroux, Michael, "Detecting Biodynamic Signals: Interstellar Communication." (explorationscience.org/Articles/icomm.htm)

"WOW! Signal Page" (www.seds.org/~rme/wow.htm)

About the Author

Joan d'Arc receives preferably intelligent transmis-sions at huntergatheress@gmail. Be advised there may be silence for several days before your pulse clusters are echoed, followed by coherent or not so coherent strings of alphanumeric codes. She is the author of *Space Travelers and the Genesis of the Hu-man Form* and *Phenomenal World*, published by The Book Tree *(thebooktree.com)*. She is the co-founder of *PARANOIA* (*paranoiamagazine.com*), and the pub-lisher of the infrequently transmitted *HunterGather-ess Journal* (*huntergatheress.com*).

A longer version of this article, with diagrams, was published in *PARANOIA*, Issue 34 (2004).

Forbidden Archeology

And the Extraterrestrial Hypothesis

by Michael A. Cremo

Some researchers in the UFO field explain the origin of the human species through extraterrestrial contacts. Generally, the proposed scenarios involve accepting the standard evolutionary account of hominid evolution, with a relatively late extraterrestrial intervention giving rise to anatomically modern human beings within the past few hundred thousand years. It is not my purpose here to directly discuss specific theories of human origins involving extraterrestrial intervention. Instead, I will offer a general caution that such theories should take into account the actual physical evidence for human antiquity.

According to standard ideas, the human line branched off from the ancestors of the modern chimpanzees about 5 million years ago. The first hominids, or humanlike primates, were the australopithecines. Further developments led to *Homo habilis* and *Homo erectus*. Finally, at about 100,000 years ago, anatomically modern humans like ourselves appeared.

Scientists say the factual evidence supports this view and no other. But my research into the history of archeology reveals that archeologists have found much evidence showing that anatomically modern humans have been present on this planet for hundreds of millions of years. These results were reported in *Forbidden Archeology* (Cremo and Thompson 1993) and its abridged popular version *The Hidden History of the Human Race*. These books provoked shockwaves among mainstream archeologists and anthropologists, as documented in *Forbidden Archeology's Impact* (Cremo 1995).

Before moving on to examples of evidence for extreme human antiquity, let me explain why I undertook this research effort. As a member of the Bhaktivedanta Institute, which is the science studies branch of the International Society for Krishna Consciousness, I have deeply studied the ancient Sanskrit writings of India for almost thirty years. Among these writings are the *Puranas*, or histories. The *Puranas* contain accounts of human civilizations existing on this planet for hundreds of millions of years. During this time, according to these accounts, human beings like ourselves coexisted with intelligent races of apelike creatures.

As I mentioned in a paper that I presented at the World Archeological Congress (Cremo 1999), one can from the Puranic histories make two predictions about the archeological record. The first prediction is that one should expect to find a bewildering mixture of human fossils and artifacts, some appearing quite advanced and others appearing quite primitive, going back hundreds of millions of years. And in truth, one does find this.

The second prediction is that the archeological evidence for coexistence of humans and more apelike creatures will be edited by establishment scientists to conform to their linear progressive concept of time and evolution, with simple forms existing earlier and more complex forms later. And in fact, one also does find this. Scientists have indeed selectively suppressed the abundant evidence for the extreme antiquity of anatomically "modern" humans. This suppression has taken place by a process of knowledge filtration, whereby reports conforming to certain preconceived notions are preserved in scientific discourse and reports not conforming to these preconceived notions are dropped from scientific discourse. UFO researchers are well aware of how this knowledge filtration process operates in suppressing evidence in their field of research.

So what kind of evidence are we talking about? Let's begin with one example, which is typical of many others documented in *Forbidden Archeology*. In the year 1852, the journal *Scientific American* (June 5) carried an intriguing report of a metallic vase blasted out of solid rock at Dorchester, Massachusetts, near the city of Boston. Describing the vase, which was about 4.5 inches high, the report said: "The body of this vessel resembles zinc in color, or a composition metal in which there is a considerable portion of silver. On the side there are six figures of a flower or bouquet beautifully inlaid with silver, and around the lower part of the vessel, a vine, or wreath, also inlaid with silver." The vase came from fifteen feet deep in a layer of rock called "pudding stone." The "pudding stone" is now known to geologists as the Roxbury Conglomerate, and according to the United States Geological Survey this rock is of Precambrian age, over 600 million years old.

The process of knowledge filtration in the study of human origins has been going on systematically for about 150 years. In 1849, gold was discovered in California. Miners rushed there to extract it, digging mineshafts into the sides of mountains. Many such mines were opened at Table Mountain in Tuolumne County. The deposits at Table Mountain are covered by hundreds of feet of solid basalt, preventing objects from entering from above. The gold-bearing gravels near the bedrock are said by modern geologists to be from 33 to 55 million years old (Slemmons 1966). Miners recovered human artifacts and human skeletal remains from mineshafts at this level. Such artifacts and fossils were also found in gravels from the higher sub-basaltic gravels, which are at least 9 million years old.

These objects were found not only at Table Mountain, but at many other locations in the same region. Among the artifacts discovered in the mines were obsidian spear points and stone mortars and pestles, such as the stone mortar and pestle recovered by J. H. Neale 1,500 feet inside the Montezuma Tunnel mineshaft at Table Mountain. This specimen, found in the gravels near the bedrock, would thus be between 33 and 55 million years old. All of these discoveries were collected and reported to the scientific world by Dr. J. D. Whitney (1880), the state geologist of California, in a book published by Harvard University's Peabody Museum of Natural History.

So what happened to these very well documented discoveries, which placed human beings in California up to 55 million years ago? William H. Holmes, a very powerful anthropologist working at the Smithsonian Institution in Washington, DC used his prestige and influence to discredit Dr. Whitney and his discoveries. Holmes (1899, p. 424) wrote: "Perhaps if Professor Whitney had fully appreciated the story of human evolution as it is understood today, he would have hesitated to announce the conclusions formulated, notwithstanding the imposing array of testimony with which he was confronted." In other words, if the facts do not conform to the favored theory, then the facts, even an imposing array of them, must be set aside.

Someone might argue that such things may have happened in the 19th century but not today. Not true. In February 1996 the California gold mine discoveries and other interesting cases from my book *Forbidden Archeology* were featured on an NBC television special called *The Mysterious Origins of Man*. It was produced and directed by Bill Cote and his associates at BC Video. During the filming of *The Mysterious Origins of Man*, I told the producers to contact officials at the Phoebe Hearst Natural History Museum at the University of California in Berkeley for permission to film the artifacts stored there. Permission was denied.

Although we were not able to get the new video images we wanted, we were able to use published photographs taken of the objects in the 19th century. When broadcast, the show was very popular, and NBC decided to air it again. Establishment scientists, taken by surprise and outraged at the first showing, attempted to prevent the program from being rebroadcast. When they failed, they tried to get the U.S. government to take action against NBC (Cremo 1998, pp. 467-534).

On June 17, 1996, Dr. Allison R. Palmer, president of the Institute for Cambrian Studies, wrote to the Federal Communications Commission, the government agency that grants licenses to television broadcasting companies: "At the very least NBC should be required to make substantial prime-time apologies to their viewing audience for a sufficient period of time so that the audience clearly gets the message that they were duped. In addition, NBC should perhaps be fined sufficiently so that a major fund for public science education can be established" (Cremo 1998, pp. 533-534). Palmer's attempt to get the FCC to punish NBC failed, but the very fact that such an attempt was made should tell us something. It is worth noting that copies of Palmer's letter were sent to the executives of NBC and were widely distributed on the internet to scientists, who were invited to send their own letters of support to the FCC.

In the 1970s, Virginia Steen-McIntyre was a young geologist working for the U.S. Geological Survey. She took part in the dating of an archeological site in Mexico at Hueyatlaco near the city of Puebla. Anthropologist Cynthia Irwin-Williams had recovered advanced stone tools from this site. Tools of this level of sophistication are normally attributed to anatomically modern humans. Using four different methods (uranium series, tephra hydration, fission track, and stratigraphy), Viriginia Steen-McIntyre and her colleagues obtained dates of over 250,000 years for the Hueyatlaco site (Steen-McIntyre *et al.* 1981). This was unexpected for two reasons. According to standard views, human beings did not enter North America until about 25,000 years ago, at most, with conservative scientists favoring an entry time of 12,000 years. Furthermore, human beings capable of making such tools did not come into existence until about 100,000 years ago. The principal anthropologist at the site was quite unhappy with the dates obtained by Steen-McIntyre and her colleagues. She wanted a date of 25,000 or less! Steen-McIntyre, however, remained firm in her conviction that the age of 250,000 years was correct, but she paid a considerable price for her conviction. She found it difficult to get her report published, she was labeled a publicity seeker within her profession, she lost a teaching position she held at an American university, and found that her career as a geologist was blocked.

Describing her experience with the knowledge filtration process, Steen-McIntyre wrote in a letter (March 30, 1981) to Estella Leopold, associate editor of *Quaternary Research:*

> The problem as I see it is much bigger than Hueyatlaco. It concerns the manipulation of scientific thought through the suppression of 'Enigmatic Data,' data that challenges the prevailing mode of thinking. Hueyatlaco certainly does that! Not being an anthropologist, I didn't realize the full significance of our dates back in 1973, nor how deeply woven into our thought the current theory of human evolution has become. Our work at Hueyatlaco has been rejected by most archaeologists because it contradicts that theory, period. (Cremo and Thompson 1993, pp. 364-365).

The case of Steen-McIntyre shows the suppression of evidence by very direct means. In other cases, the process of knowledge filtration is more subtle. It can take the form of inability to properly evaluate evidence because of strongly held theoretical preconceptions. For example, in 1979 researchers in Tanzania found sets of footprints in volcanic ash deposits about 3.6 million years old. According to Mary Leakey (1979) and other scientists, these footprints are indistinguishable from modern human footprints. The usual explanation is that the footprints were made by *Australopithecus*, the apeman of that period. But careful study shows that none of the fossil foot bones of *Australopithecus* fit the Laetoli prints (Tuttle 1985).

Among other things, *Australopithecus* had toes much longer than those of modern human beings. As of today, the only creatures known to science that could make the Laetoli prints are human beings like ourselves. But most scientists would not even dream of considering this possibility. They are absolutely convinced that anatomically modern human beings evolved about 100,000 years ago and could not possibly have been present 3.6 million years ago in Africa.

One might ask if there are any human skeletal remains of that age, and the answer is yes. Such fossils occur at Castenedolo, in northern Italy. There the Italian geologist Giuseppe Ragazzoni (1880) collected bones of four individuals from a blue clay formation of Middle Pliocene age about 3 to 4 million years old. The skeletal remains show the Castenedolo individuals were anatomically modern. Some have suggested that the skeletons arrived in their positions by burial in fairly recent times, but as a professional geologist Ragazzoni was well aware of this possibility. He carefully inspected the overlying layers of sediment and found them undisturbed. A skeleton of similar age was found by other researchers at Savona, Italy, and details of its discovery were reported to the scientific world by Arthur Issel (1868).

Many influential scientists opposed such discoveries on theoretical grounds. British archeologist R. A. S. Macalister provides a good example of such scientific prejudice. In 1921 (p. 183), he wrote about the Castenedolo finds: "There must be something wrong somewhere." But had not the bones been discovered by a professional geologist in a layer of undisturbed Pliocene clay? That was not good enough for Macalister, who said: "The acceptance of a Pliocene date for the Castenedolo skeletons would create so many insoluble problems that we can hardly hesitate in choosing between the alternatives of adopting or rejecting their authenticity." Macalister, of course, rejected their authenticity and, given his prominent position, this rejection carried tremendous authority.

The Castenedolo fossils show that there were anatomically modern human beings present in Italy at the same time the Laetoli footprints were made in East Africa, about 4 million years ago. There is also some fragmentary fossil evidence from Africa itself. In 1965, anthropologists Bryan Patterson and William W. Howells found at Kanapoi, Kenya, a fragment of a humerus (upper arm bone). Upon examining it, they found it to be almost exactly like a modern human humerus (Patterson and Howells 1967). Other researchers have found it to be different from those of the australopithecines (McHenry and Corruccini 1975). The Kanapoi humerus is 4 to 5 million years old.

The French anthropologist Gabriel de Mortillet (1883), in his book *Le Préhistorique,* tells of a complete anatomically modern human skeleton found in a Miocene formation at Midi de France dated at least 5 million to 25 million years old. Another skeleton found in an Eocene formation at Delémont, Switzerland was dated at least 38 million years old. Human artifacts of similar antiquity include stone tools found by Carlo Ribeiro (1873), head of the Geological Survey of Portugal, in Miocene formations near Lisbon, about 20 million years old. They were originally displayed by Ribeiro at the Museum of Geology in Lisbon. Early in the 20th century, museum workers changed the labels to indicate younger dates within the acceptable range of human evolution. Later, the artifacts were completely removed from display and placed in storage (Cremo 2000).

Stone tools were found by Louis Bourgeois (1873) in a Miocene formation at Thenay, France, and more stone tools were found by Fritz Noetling (1894), of the Geological Survey of India, in a Miocene formation in Burma. These discoveries, made in the late 19th century, were published in scientific journals and discussed in scientific conferences. The only reason for their absence from current textbooks is that they contradict the idea of a recent human origin.

From the United States comes a human skeleton found 90 feet deep in coal in Macoupin County, Illinois. Immediately above the skeleton were two feet of unbroken slate rock. The coal in which the skeleton was found is from the Carboniferous period, making the fossil about 300 million years old. The report of this discovery was printed in the December 1862 edition of a scientific journal called *The Geologist.* The June 11, 1891 edition of the *Morrisonville Times* newspaper, of Morrisonville, Illinois carried a report of a gold chain discovered inside a solid piece of coal. The chain was found by Mrs. S. W. Culp, wife of the newspaper's publisher, when she was breaking a lump of coal. According to the Illinois State Geological Survey, the coal containing the chain is of Carboniferous age, about 300 million years old.

Also of interest is an iron pot found in a block of coal in the year 1912 by Frank J. Kenwood. The discovery occurred at the Municipal Electric Plant in Thomas, Oklahoma, where the coal was burned to generate power. Kenwood wrote in a notarized affidavit: "I came upon a solid chunk of coal which was too large to use. I broke it with a sledge hammer. This iron pot fell from the center, leaving the impression of mould of the pot in the piece of coal" (Rusch 1971, p. 201). The coal was traced by Kenwood to the Wilburton Mine. According to the Oklahoma Geological Survey the coal in that mine is about 312 million years old.

Such intriguing discoveries continue to be made. Over the past several decades, miners in South Africa have found hundreds of metallic spheres with grooves running around their equators. One specimen has three such parallel grooves encircling it. The spheres are composed of a very hard substance. Roelf Marx, curator of the museum of Klerksdorp, South Africa, wrote in a letter dated September 12, 1984: "They are found in pyrophyllite, which is mined near the little town of Ottosdal in the Western Transvaal. This pyrophyllite is a quite soft secondary mineral . . . and was formed by sedimentation about 2.8 billion years ago. On the other hand the globes . . . are very hard and cannot be scratched, even by steel" (Cremo and Thompson 1993, p. 813). No one has yet come up with a satisfactory natural explanation for the spheres, which appear to be human artifacts.

I have here mentioned only a few of the hundreds of well-documented cases showing the extreme antiquity of the human race on the earth. There is a fairly continuous chain of discoveries dating from about 100,000 years ago to over two billion years ago. Hypotheses about extraterrestrial contacts and interventions should be considered within the framework of this evidence.

References

Cremo, M. A. (1998) *Forbidden Archeology's Impact.* Los Angeles. Bhaktivedanta Book Publishing.

Cremo, M. A (1999) Puranic time and the archeological record. In Murray, T., ed., *Time and Archaeology.* London, Routledge, pp. 38-48.

Cremo, M. A. (2000) The excavations of Carlos Ribeiro. *Nexus, 8(1): 51-55.*

Cremo, M. A., and Thompson, R. L. (1993) *Forbidden Archeology.* San Diego, Bhaktivedanta Institute.

Cremo, M. A., and Thompson, R. L. (1994) *The Hidden History of the Human Race.* San Diego, Govardhan Hill.

De Mortillet, G. (1883) *Le Préhistorique.* Paris, C. Reinwald.

Holmes, W. H. (1899) Review of the evidence relating to auriferous gravel man in California. *Smithsonian Institution Annual Report 1898–1899*, pp. 419–472.

Leakey, M. D. (1979) Footprints in the ashes of time. *National Geographic, 155:* 446–457.

Macalister, R. A. S. (1921) *Textbook of European Archaeology.* Vol. 1. *Paleolithic Period.* Cambridge, Cambridge University Press.

McHenry, H. M. and Corruccini, R. S. (1975) Distal humerus in hominid evolution. *Folia Primatologica 23:* 227-244.

Noetling, F. (1894) On the occurrence of chipped flints in the Upper Miocene of Burma. *Records of the Geological Survey of India, 27:* 101–103.

Patterson, B., and Howells, W. W. (1967) Hominid humeral fragment from Early Pleistocene of northwestern Kenya. *Science, 156:* 64–66.

Rusch, Sr., W. H. (1971) Human footprints in rocks. *Creation Research Society Quarterly, 7:* 201–202.

Slemmons, D. B. (1966) Cenozoic volcanism of the central Sierra Nevada, CA. *Bulletin of the California Division of Mines and Geology, 190:*199-208.

Steen-McIntyre, V., Fryxell R., and Malde, H. E. (1981) Geologic evidence for age of deposits at Hueyatlaco, Valsequillo, Mexico. *Quaternary Research 16:* 1-17.

Tuttle, R. H. (1985) Ape footprints and Laetoli impressions: a response to the SUNY claims. *In* Tobias, P. V. ed. *Hominid Evolution: Past, Present, and Future.* New York, Alan R. Liss, pp. 129-133.

Whitney, J. D. (1880) The auriferous gravels of the Sierra Nevada of California. *Harvard University, Museum of Comparative Zoology Memoir 6*(1).

About the Author

Michael Cremo's websites are *mcremo.com, forbiddenarcheology.com* and *humandevolution.com.* He is the co-author of *Forbidden Archeology: The Hidden History of the Human Race* (1993) (also on audio cassette) and *The Hidden History of the Human Race* (Condensed Edition) (1999). He is the author of *Forbidden Archeology's Impact: How a Controversial New Book Shocked the Scientific Community and Became an Underground Classic* (1998) and *Human Devolution: A Vedic Alternative to Darwin's Theory* (2003).

Grandson of the Apollo Hoax Theory

Joan d'Arc Interviews *MoonFaker* Videographer, Jarrah White

Australian Jarrah White has carried on the Apollo moon hoax research that began in the 1970s and continued into the 1990s, taking it to video format for the modern generation of YouTubers with documentaries titled, *MoonFaker: Carrying The Liar*; *MoonFaker: Exhibit C*; *MoonFaker: Rocks & Crocks;* and *MoonFaker: Radioactive Anomaly.* In this interview, which took place in summer of 2009, White proves he's equal to the task of being "the Grandson of the Apollo Hoax Theory."

Joan d'Arc: Jarrah, thank you for your unflagging duty to carry on the moon hoax research for the next generation. It's very important that this information remains available. So, who were the grandfathers of the Apollo Hoax Theory? One of them, I presume, was Ralph René, author of the 1994 book NASA Mooned America*?*

Jarrah White: Yes, Ralph René was indeed one of those grandfathers. It is interesting to note that a lot of people assume I am the grandson of Jack White. In actuality I am known as "The Grandson" because I picked up from where Bill Kaysing left off. Kaysing was known as "The Grandfather of the Apollo Hoax Theory" because he wrote and published the first book on the subject back in 1974.

I guess you could say that I now take on after Ralph too. Ralph was still alive and kicking when I became "The Grandson." Before he died he had sent me his various research materials, such as the document that NOAA sent him during the writing of his book, and lawsuit papers from the Kaysing/Lovell trial. It was as though he knew his time was near and he had nominated me to carry on after him.

d'Arc: You do indeed look like rock singer, Jack White! When did you first meet Ralph René *and how did you two come to be such close friends?*

White: Ralph and I met over the phone many years ago when I first tried to obtain a copy of *NASA Mooned America.* As he put it, the post office had done more damage to him than any other government entity, and at first there were some troubles getting it sent. But the delivery problems were soon sorted.

After that he and I maintained communication over both telephone and email. I would often do everything in my power to help him whenever I could; be it digging up information he was in need of, sending video footage that he tried to obtain, or just generally helping introduce his book to a wider audience. I always recommended his book to others and not once did I use his research without stating where that research came from.

Before I brought my *MoonFaker* series out, the only voice Ralph ever had through YouTube was his brief appearance on the Fox special and that disgraceful *Penn & Teller* episode that tried to portray him as some crackpot. That all changed when I released the *MoonFaker* series. Ralph had granted me many hours of his time for various over-the-phone interviews, which provided great insight for my videos. I can't stress to you enough how far I would go out of my way just to make his research heard and prove that his points are indeed valid.

If you would like to see some hugely significant videos that Ralph contributed to, I recommend *MoonFaker: Carrying The Liar*, *MoonFaker: Exhibit C*, *MoonFaker: Rocks & Crocks* and *MoonFaker: Radioactive Anomaly.*

d'Arc: René died by suicide on December 10, 2008. You had spoken to him just the day before. How did he seem at that time? Did his suicide shock you?

White: I had spoken to him over the phone on November 30. He had stated over email he was dying, but really he meant he was in a lot of pain and knew his time would come sooner or later. As you might already know, Ralph spent many years of his life doing manual labor and subsequently became crippled by arthritis in both knees. He suffered from this pain for the remaining years of his life, simply because there is very poor health care in the United States. American hospitals are not run like they are in Australia, where a patient simply walks into the clinic and gets the help he needs. In the states, patients are often refused service, be it medication or surgery, and the corrupt health insurance companies do everything in their power to deny people health coverage.

Ralph was in desperate need of hip-joint surgery, but the doctors first subjected him to a pre-operation stress test. Basically, if you don't pass the test, you don't get the surgery. As Ralph described it, "It was a test that an Olympic athlete with a sprained ankle couldn't pass, let alone a man on a walker." The last thing I said to him over the phone was, "Ralph this may sound like a stupid question, but how much longer do you think you have left?" and his exact reply was, "As long as I can hold out."

He continued sending emails in the following days. The last I received from him was on December 9 (Sydney time). After that I didn't hear from him. It wasn't until a week later that I learned that Ralph had committed suicide.

From what I was told it all started on December 8. Ralph was driving with his girlfriend when there was a terrible accident and the van flipped. Both were injured but alive. Ralph was taken to the hospital but taken home the next day by a neighbour. The crash had worsened Ralph's regular hip pain to the point he became an insomniac. On the morning of December 10, he called up his neighbour to ask where his van was. Later that night he asked his girlfriend to go home early. The next day another neighbour found his body. He also found Ralph's will and a box of goodbye postcards that he had prepared in advance.

My initial reaction was shock and disbelief. Shock because Ralph was a very dear friend to me, and disbelief because he explicitly stated in his book that he was not suicidal. But I guess even the non-suicidal have their limits. I've come to learn that when one is in that much pain and there is no other option, it's no longer suicide but relief through release. At the end of the day it was ultimately the car crash that pushed him over the edge. I strongly believe that had he not had that accident he would most likely still be here today.

d'Arc: Why have you chosen to take on this work? Did you realize at first that you would be the focus of so much anger from the mainstream scientific establishment? Why do you think people get so upset at this research?

White: As a kid I wanted to be the first man on Mars. It was my dream and I spent my life studying

astronomy, collecting space books, magazines and newspaper articles, taping documentaries and news reports off the telly. Back then I believed that men had been to the moon.

Later I learned of the Apollo moon landing conspiracy theory, but I took it with a grain of salt. I looked back to everything I had already learned about astronomy, I read the conspiracy material, and of course, I came upon website after website trying to prove that the moon missions were real.

In reading through these pro-NASA websites it quickly became apparent that the webmasters in question were not trying to offer any refuting evidence at all, but rather muddy the waters, lead astray those who are without ready access to the conspiracy research or even the source material, and generally spread false rumors and incite unfounded hatred against anyone who doubts Apollo.

It's propaganda, which is why I subsequently refer to these individuals as 'propagandists.' For example, Phil Plait, one of the more popular pro-NASA webmasters, puts words in people's mouths. On multiple occasions he claimed that Bill Kaysing said, "Any kind of space travel is impossible." There is no such statement from Kaysing and in fact in his interview on Nardwaur radio, which Plait refers to at times, Kaysing said specifically that "possibly our [unmanned] Surveyor did land on the moon."

Plait clearly knows that what he says is not true. And yes, you can quote me on that! I even sent him an email asking him if he was willing to bet $100,000 that he could prove Kaysing denied the possibility of any kind of space travel, and I never heard back from Plait. I show this email in my video.

Plait's actions are typical of the level of honesty that propagandists demonstrate. So the bottom line is, if humans did set foot on the moon, why tell so many lies trying to defend these missions? It is impossible for anyone to even engage in an online discussion about the moon hoax without someone directing you to some spurious pro-NASA website. And practically all the websites one pulls up with a simple Google search are these propaganda sites.

I am outraged by the propagandists' dismissal of scientific facts that refute their claims, their misrepresentation of conspiracy arguments and outright defamation. I finally realized the time had come to debunk the debunkers, and that is what my *MoonFaker* series is about.

I began work in 2005 and continued well into 2006. It was originally going to be an essay for download off the website *www.billkaysing.com*. And so I began writing up a long essay refuting virtually every propagandist website. I spent many hours interviewing people, filming experiments, visiting the library for research material. When it was finally finished the essay was the size of a phone book! That, and it also needed to be toned down on certain less than pleasant things I had to say about the propagandists. As I stated in my very first video, "It's going to take a whole lot of one's time and effort to comment on their obnoxious defamation without getting pissed off."

So, instead of releasing it as an essay, I began adapting pieces from it to video, one after another covering a certain subject. Over the production I did more research and acquired more information, and my debunking of the debunkers continues to this day.

Naturally I get mixed responses from people with all sorts of points of view. There are those who still oppose my videos even after their heroes have been exposed. There were people who were once duped by the pro-NASA websites and praised my videos for salvation. Then of course there are fellow conspiracy theorists who already knew the missions were faked and applaud my efforts every step of the way. And interestingly there is a fourth category of people: individuals who do not doubt Apollo, but agree that the propagandists are out of line, and that there is a vast difference between believing in the moon landings and endorsing the smear campaigns these propagandists spread.

d'Arc: So let's talk about René's work, which I'm fairly familiar with since I interviewed him for PARANOIA in 1995. When René began to research the Apollo moon hoax years ago, he read Bill Kaysing's book, We Never Went to the Moon, *among other books. After Kaysing read René's* NASA Mooned America, *he said René caught a lot of points that he had missed. Do you know what a few of those points might have been?*

White: Well by far one of the most prominent things that Ralph picked up on is radiation in space. Bill Kaysing briefly scratched the surface when he pointed out that in 1963 the Russians could see no immediate way of protecting cosmonauts from the lethal effects of solar radiation. Ralph picked up on the same footnote, but also did so much more research on that subject. He has a whole chapter regarding solar radiation, and a few detailed addenda on the Van Allen radiation belts.

There are many important points that I feel need mentioning regarding radiation. First of all, during his study on the solar flares Ralph picked up on a 1963 book called *Astronautical Engineering & Science*, written by various scientists from the Marshall Space Flight Center. In this book they state that minor solar storms can deliver 25 rem/hr depending on how many centimeters of water is used as shielding [rem is the dosage in rads that will cause the same amount of biological injury as one rad of X rays or gamma rays].

The reason this is important is because propagandists claim that all the solar flares during the Apollo flights were minor and thus not lethal. They of course ignore the 25 rem/hr figure that Ralph picked up on. One such flare spurted on April 17 1972, during the Apollo 16 mission, and lasted for three days. At 25 rem/hr, a flare lasting for three days would deliver a whopping dose of 1800 rem. All it takes is 500 rem and you're dead. And that's just for one flare; NOAA's solar records show that there were over 1400 solar storms during all nine moon flights combined. Each is capable of delivering 25 rem/hr.

In addition to denying the hazard posed by minor flares, propagandists like Jay Windley and Phil Plait also claim that there were no major solar storms during the Apollo missions. This is not true. A friend of mine, Rick, managed to check NOAA's Comprehensive Flare Index for major flares. It shows that out of all the 1400 flares shared among the Apollo flights, thirty of them were major. Major flares deliver in excess of 100 rem/hr. Ralph had requested NOAA to send him this data and it took sixteen years before Rick and I finally managed to supply him with it. He received this data in the weeks before his death. At least he lived long enough to get what he was looking for.

Jay Windley, in his arrogance, claimed that the Apollo major flares were not hazardous enough to cause harm, even though some were clearly listed as being more hazardous than the major flares of August 1972—which even propagandists admit could kill an astronaut.

That brings me to another point that Ralph brought up. During his research Ralph received a document from J. A. McKinnon of NOAA. The document is titled "NOAA Technical Memorandum ERL SEL-22" and it's all about the major solar activity of August 1972. It is important to note that these major flares took NOAA totally by surprise: there were no warnings, it was not detected in any of their forecasts, and it wasn't predicted. This is important because propagandists claim that if a major flare were going to happen during an Apollo flight, NASA would have known about it in advance and postponed the mission. Clearly, NASA had no way of knowing when these eruptions would occur.

d'Arc: In my 1995 interview with Ralph he stated, "Rumor has it that once past the Van Allen shield only cockroaches were able to live past ten days." He quotes John Mauldin saying, "six feet of water or the equivalent mass of another material is needed to protect life forms from an X-ray flare."

White: James Van Allen submitted two articles about the radiation belts, one in the March 1959 issue of *Scientific American*, and the other in the December 1961 issue of *Space World*. In both articles he declared that both radiation belts were a No-Go Zone for astronauts, that adequately shielding humans from the radiation was beyond engineering feasibility, and that even a rapid transit through the belts was hazardous. Van Allen began his investigation of space radiation by sending up Rockoons (a weather balloon with a rocket attached), and later he would put Geiger counters in satellites like Explorer 1.

After detecting the radiation on the belts, these instruments would quickly become jammed because there was too much radiation for them to cope with. Even after Van Allen began shielding

these instruments with a millimeter of lead, the readings would still be 10-100 rem/hr.

According to E.E. Kovalev's article in the December 1983 issue of *Aviation Space & Environmental Medicine*, which Ralph also picked up on, without the lead shield the readings were 312.5 rem/hr to 11,666 rem/hr, depending on the spacecraft's inclination. Remember, all it takes is 500 rem and you're dead. The astronauts spent one hour each way getting through the radiation belts alone.

Ralph didn't mention this, but I will bring it up. Propagandists often claim that the Apollo's aluminum hull was sufficient shielding. In actuality aluminum is a poor shield because it increases the risk of particle fragmentation. When charged particles collide with matter, they fragment into a dangerous spray of secondary particles. In the case of colliding with aluminum, this spray of secondary particles makes the radiation hazard inside the craft worse than on the outside.

In fact, a few years ago the International Space Station used aluminum as a radiation shield. This increased the daily doses from 0.027 rem/day to 0.1 rem/day. This is about 3.7 times the normal doses encountered in low orbit. Now suppose this shield was used in fields where the radiation is normally 312.5 rem/hr at minimum.

It's for this reason that you need a lot of water to absorb all these secondary particles. Astrophysicists Eugene Parker and John H. Mauldin both proposed several meters of water shielding to protect astronauts from the radiation. As Ralph put it "anything less is suicide!" There are many, many important points that Ralph picked up on that were not related to the radiation. But this evidence alone that he dug up is overwhelming to say the least. [See René interview, page 95.]

d'Arc: In NASA Mooned America, *René stated that the "astro-nots" (as he called them) would have had a half hour outside of the water shielding to walk around on the moon. So NASA would have had to come up with another material to take the place of the water to shield radiation in the suits. What, in fact, does NASA claim to have used inside the space suits as radiation shielding material?*

White: NASA claims that during space flight to and from the moon, the hull of the spacecraft protected the astronauts. The Command Module (the mothership) had three inches of aluminum for protection. The lunar module had even less protection, it was basically equivalent to a few layers of aluminum foil on a frame. In fact, Flight Director Eugene Kranz has stated that astronauts were warned not to point any pointed objects at the walls, like a pen or pencil, because the hull was so lightweight that one could easily poke his finger through the outer hull.

Once outside the craft the only protection the astronauts had was their spacesuits. The suits were made up of layers of aluminum, neoprene rubber and Teflon. Back in the 1960s, NASA led us to believe that this would be sufficient protection from solar and cosmic radiation. But in 2003, when the major solar flare called NOAA 720 exploded, they admitted that a spacesuit would offer little resistance against that solar flare. This is discussed in one of NASA's online articles entitled, "Sickening Solar Flares."

Of course, although admitting that the spacesuit would offer little protection, they downplayed it. NASA alleged that if a suited-up astronaut were exposed to NOAA 720 the astronaut would have only absorbed about 50 rem. But they also stated that the astronaut would have showed such symptoms as vomiting, fatigue and low red blood cell count (causing anemia). To show these radiation symptoms, a dose of 100 rem must first be absorbed. Basically NASA is claiming an astronaut would have picked up 50 rem during this flare, yet showed symptoms that require a dose of 100 rem.

Another hazard posed during moonwalks is the particle fragmentation. As stated earlier the aluminum in the suits and spaceship hulls would increase the risk of fragmentation when particles collide with this material, but the moon itself would also increase the risks. According to NASA's "Radioactive Moon" article, when protons crash into the lunar surface they explode into a dangerous spray of neutrons, which fly out in all directions. Subsequently "the moon itself is radioactive"! No joke, that's what it says in NASA's article.

Of course, the propagandists want you to believe that only the 'rare' major flares can do harm. They, much like NASA, have effectively swept under the rug the fact that minor flares will do harm too. There is an interesting document by former shuttle astronaut James Van Hoften. The document was put together by his committee on radiation protection and is titled, "Managing Space Radiation Risk in the New Era of Space Exploration."

In this report Van Hoften tells us that the solar conditions on the moon are so unpredictable and so dangerous that it would considerably limit the amount of time astronauts can spend outside the protection of their spaceship, which isn't very well protected to begin with. Future moon flights will be sending up a new lunar rover with a pressurized cabin that NASA claims astronauts can live in. Van Hoften states the new rover would only offer significant protection if they park it inside a cave on the moon!

d'Arc: You mentioned earlier a NOAA document that Ralph passed on to you. What is the importance of this document?

White: The document in question is the aforementioned NOAA Technical Memorandum ERL SEL-22. This document is important because it contains NOAA's forecasts and predictions and related data for solar activity in August 1972. It also contains reprints of various newspaper and magazine clippings reporting this activity. All of NOAA's forecasts for August 1972 predicted only minor solar flares for this period. But instead, on August 2nd that year, a sunspot known as "Region 331" let loose it's first major flare without any warnings. Even the solar data NOAA released just hours before the first eruption detected that there was only going to be minor activity. And these major flares raged on for more than a week.

This document ultimately proves that NOAA failed to predict the major flares of August 1972, which are often considered the Godzillas of all solar flares. Even propagandists don't deny that these flares would have killed an astronaut. What makes the information in this document important is that it proves the propagandists wrong historically. These individuals claim that NASA could have easily been able to detect a major solar flare in advance and subsequently would postpone a moon trip to a safer date if one was going to occur. Clearly, the fact remains that NOAA couldn't detect the major flares in advance, and subsequently NASA had no way of knowing whether or not there would be a major flare during an Apollo trip. And, as stated earlier, the fact is that there were major flares during those missions.

There's another interesting piece of data worth mentioning and this relates to the Concord's flight plans for avoiding radiation encountered on a polar route. Although the Concord didn't fly into space, it crossed over the polar regions during supersonic flight. The earth is protected from solar and cosmic radiation by the magnetic field, but this field offers no protection along its axis. So the only protection you have at the north and south poles is the atmosphere. But the atmosphere gets thinner and thinner as you ascend and subsequently offers less protection at high altitudes. The Concord travels at an altitude of 65,000 ft, so naturally its occupants will be exposed to radiation during the polar route.

According to this NOAA document, if the radiation aboard the Concord exceeds 10 millirem/hr, the plane must decrease its altitude in order to lower the dose rates. If the dose rates exceed 100 millirem/hr, the Concord must avoid the poles altogether. The Royal Aircraft Establishment went through all this trouble just so that their passengers would avoid millirems of radiation, and yet NASA claims to have sent their crews in unshielded spacecraft into regions where the radiation is hundreds to thousands of rem!

d'Arc: So let's talk about William H. Kaysing, the "Grandfather of the Apollo Hoax Theory." Kaysing worked for a short time for Rocketdyne and was privy to documents from various NASA programs. He finally realized NASA did not have the technical expertise to put a man on the moon. What were his main contentions in his 1974 book, We Never Went to the Moon*?*

White: Bill Kaysing worked at Rocketdyne between the years of 1956 and 1963. During those years he worked as the Head of Technical Publications and as a Service Engineer & Analyst on the various engines the company supplied to NASA. Before I continue, I want this to be made absolutely clear. Many propagandists have tried to dismiss Bill Kaysing as incredible and say that his job at Rocketdyne was unscientific. This is profoundly untrue and quite insulting.

I contacted Rocketdyne (now owned by Pratt & Whitney) to ask about the job of a Service Engineer during the time when Kaysing worked there. According to Mr. Bryan Kidder, the job of a Service Engineer was essentially to check and evaluate the said product to make sure it was worthy of the seal of approval before it was sent out to the customer or field tested. It was Kaysing's job to offer technical support, so his job was quite clearly scientific. And yes, I have Mr. Kidder's email, which I will be more than happy to supply as proof of Kaysing's scientific background.

During his time at Rocketdyne, Kaysing became aware of a clandestine organization assembled in 1961 by NASA and the Defense Intelligence Agency. The organization was called ASP (Apollo Simulation Project). Basically this organization was assembled in order to find ways to simulate flights to the moon and then purport them to be the real thing. Bill Kaysing left Rocketdyne with this inside knowledge (which may explain why he could not generate enthusiasm to watch the famous moonwalk on TV).

The book *We Never Went To The Moon* discusses the clandestine activities of ASP and explores all the possible methods that they used or could have used to fake the moon landing. The plan was basically this. The astronauts go up the gantry for all eyes to see and board their capsule. Then they secretly come back down the elevator and remain on earth in hiding during the entire time. The Saturn V is launched and then jettisoned into the South Atlantic. During the supposed flight to the moon all the voices and telemetry data come from simulated tapes that were prepared in advance.

Quite frankly, the only people who can attest to having tracked these spaceships all the way to the moon and back are employees at the radio observatories that were either owned by or directly working with NASA. You've got stations like Goldstone in California, the Madrid Deep Space Communication Complex, and various stations such as Parkes and Honeysuckle Creek in Australia. These facilities are often cited as independent verification for the moon landings, but in actuality they are all owned by NASA and are part of their Deep Space Network. They've even got the official NASA logos sign posted all over the place. What more do you have to do to make it a NASA facility?

Bochum Observatory in Germany is also cited as having independently tracked Apollo, but guess what? Although not owned, they were directly working with NASA! I learned that straight from Thilo Elsner, director of the observatory. In other words, no independent party could verify whether the signals were actually coming from space or if all the data were coming from simulated tapes that the Deep Space Network was relaying to the world, passing them off as the real thing.

If that weren't enough, the spaceships are said to have broadcast their signals at 2GHz, a frequency not legally permitted to ham radio operators. Of course, one might argue that a ham operator could easily have tuned their antenna's to Apollo's frequency, but just for good measure the FCC (Federal Communications Commission) declared it illegal for anyone to release communications not intended for the public. In other words, if a ham operator listening in found evidence of a hoax he would be prosecuted if he tried to tell anyone about it.

It's possible that NASA had an unmanned craft already on or near the moon to either broadcast pre-recorded signals or relay signals from earth orbit. And quite frankly that's probably all that would have been necessary to make the signals appear genuine. Because none of the independent parties who claim to have tracked Apollo can attest to having tracked them all the way to the moon and back. They only claim to have picked up signals when the craft was on the moon or in lunar orbit and, if lucky, a handful of signals on the ride home. Their "return" was falsified simply by air-dropping a command module over the ocean by a cargo plane. In fact, an airline pilot once called up Bill Kaysing on a KOME radio show and stated that he saw just that on Apollo 15's alleged return.

d'Arc: What are some of the other problems Kaysing reported about NASA?

White: One of the biggest challenges that NASA faced, totally aside from the radiation problems, was getting the engines on the Saturn V to work. The Saturn V used five F-1 engines on the first stage, five J-2 engines on the second stage and one J-2 in the third stage. The F-1's were essential for lifting the Saturn off the ground, being so huge they could deliver the thrust equivalent to a cluster of smaller engines. Unfortunately during the developing stages these engines were quite prone to a problem known as combustion instability, in which the vibrations produced during combustion become too much for the engine to cope with, and so the plumes rip the whole motor apart.

Obviously you don't want an F-1 blowing up during a Saturn V launch. Fully loaded the Saturn contains over 5 million tons of fuel; enough to set Miami ablaze! In fact, there were concerns about losing a significant part of Cape Canaveral should a Saturn blow up on the pad.

Rocketdyne went through god only knows how many tests to try and overcome this problem. In fact, during Kaysing's career there was something called Project First, which was a program established specifically to try and overcome the F-1's combustion instability. But in spite of all their testing, even though the finished product was considered more reliable, Wernher von Braun could not guarantee the combustion instability problem was entirely solved.

BBC writer Deborah Cadbury wrote about this in her book *Space Race* (p. 303). She stated, "Consequently there was no actual day of celebration, just an increasing confidence that the engine was more reliable." Because no one could guarantee that the F-1 was 100% safe, this is where the ASP group comes in. There were three versions of the Saturns used on Apollo. The gigantic Saturn V that allegedly took men to the moon, and the smaller Saturn I and IB which were used for various test launches and low earth orbit shots. The Saturn I and IB both used a cluster of eight H-1 engines on their first stage. The H-1 was a smaller but more reliable engine than the F-1.

The H-1 doesn't have enough power to lift a fully-loaded Saturn V into space. But, if you strip the Saturn of all the essentials necessary for the Apollo trip, like the fuel in the upper stages, the Saturn V would only weigh about 150 tons—well within the lifting capacity of a cluster of H-1 engines.

The secret plan according to Kaysing was to substitute the F-1 motors with H-1 engines, disguised with the F-1 engine bell, and launch this virtually empty Saturn into the blue for all eyes to see. The astronauts either stayed behind on earth and the Saturn was jettisoned into the Atlantic, or they were launched with this stripped down Saturn and never got further than earth orbit.

In his book, Bill Kaysing writes about these clandestine activities of the Apollo Simulation Project, and discusses all the various technical problems leading up to the moon missions, such as engine problems, lunar module problems, and various other equipment failures. He also briefly discusses photographic anomalies, but for the most part Kaysing compiles various pieces of technical information that he and others had picked up on and goes into lengthy detail regarding ASP. His book also contains reprints of pages from the Baron and Phillips Reports, plus transcripts of the congressional testimonies of Thomas Baron and Al Holmberg.

I like to consider *We Never Went To The Moon* as more of a journal than a book. Kaysing goes into great detail about all the histories surrounding NASA and the problems encountered in the years leading up to the alleged moon missions, and ultimately why these problems would have prevented trips to the moon.

d'Arc: Was he the first to bring up the idea that there were no stars on lunar surface photos? What other anomalies did he point out in the photos?

White: Yes, Kaysing was indeed the first to point to the near total lack of star photography on Apollo. NASA had a magnificent opportunity to take pictures of the stars from the moon. And yet all we ever got back were a few blurred and fuzzy ultraviolet photos. Even the Hasselblad cameras they took on every flight could have taken great star photography simply by keeping the shot steady on a tripod, opening the aperture wider and slowing down the shutter speed. This was never done. Of course, propagandists argue that they weren't there for star photography. Well, they weren't there to play golf either!

Further, once the astronauts had completed the list of photographic tasks, there were still plenty of unused frames left over. The film magazines for the Hasselblad cameras contained 180 frames each. On Apollo 11, for example, only Magazine 40 was used to take the still pictures of the moonwalk activities; 123 frames were taken during the EVA, and an additional three were taken in orbit. That left a good 54 frames unused.

Given that they had taken all the pictures they were assigned to photograph, I'd say they had plenty of frames left over to take pictures of stars. Speaking from personal experience, under good conditions I have been able to photograph Alpha-Centuri using a daylight exposure setting. Now suppose I was outside the atmosphere, where one gets 20% more starlight, and photographing them with a longer exposure setting.

There are two photographic anomalies that I feel are worth mentioning. First and foremost, there is no blast crater under the Lunar Module (LM) where its rocket plume would surely have dug through the stone and loose dust. In fact, there are even pebbles and dust directly under the LM that should have been blasted away. The descent engine produced 10,000 lbf (pound-force) [one foot-pound force is the amount of energy expended when one pound force acts through a distance of one foot along the direction of the force] and could be throttled down to about 2500 lbf. Propagandists claim that 2500 lbf is all that is needed in order to land on the moon and that this amount of pressure is not enough to dig a hole in the ground. Wrong again, and it's easy to prove wrong too.

The company Armadillo Aerospace in Texas builds experimental rockets capable of blasting holes through concrete. Their very first LOX/alcohol powered rocket did just that and, according to the lead engineer John Carmack, it only produced 500 lbf. Now, if a 500 lbf engine can blast a hole through solid concrete, what do you suppose 2500 lbf is going to do on the moon?

The second point I'd like to mention are photographs showing the shadowed side of objects illuminated. Such photos as the portraits of Buzz Aldrin or Charlie Duke, or the photo of Aldrin stepping into the LEM shadow. Even the Al Bean photo that Ralph had on his book cover. [See page 52.] All of these show examples of astronauts lit up on the shadowed side. There was only one light source on the moon, and that was the sun, and so clearly they must have used a reflector or fill light. Either that or they were shooting this thing on a surface considerably more reflective than the moon. Propagandists have claimed that this secondary light source was simply sunlight bouncing off the moon's surface. This is extremely doubtful. The moon has an albedo of only 7%, the same albedo of an asphalt road. That's not very reflective.

There is an experiment that you can do to prove this to yourself. Take a cardboard box and a model; say, a toy astronaut or a Lego astronaut and spaceship like I used. Paint the inside of the box black. Then cut away one side of the box so that light will shine through when you turn it upside down. Cut a small circular hole in the back, just wide enough to stick your camera lens through.

Now on a bright sunny day, take your box and toy astronaut out onto an asphalt road, provided there is no traffic. Place him down on the ground and then cover him up with the box. The cardboard box is necessary because it blocks out the daylight sky. On earth the blue sky acts as a secondary light source, and for this test all you want is the sun shining into the box and the sunlight bouncing off the asphalt.

Position the box so that the sun shines through the large opening, place your camera through the circular hole at the back and take a photo. You'll clearly see that the object inside the box is virtually black. It's because the asphalt simply doesn't reflect enough light. It's a matter of straightforward physics: if you can't do it under accurately simulated conditions on earth, you can't do it on the moon. In order to make the shadowed objects appear even remotely as bright as they do in the Apollo pictures, you'd need to increase the shutter speed and or widen the aperture. And if you did that, you'd quickly overexpose the landscape and make it appear like a blinding wash of white light. Quite clearly, the Apollo photos showing objects illuminated in shade are faked.

d'Arc: Did Kaysing bring up the movement of the flags waving in the vacuum of the moon surface, as well? What was wrong with "that picture"?

White: Actually, William Brian was the first to bring up the waving flag anomaly in a book called *Moongate*. I haven't read it myself but from what I understand Brian didn't dispute the fact that men went to the moon, he instead believed that only the record was faked and there was some military cover-up with secret technologies behind this.

The fact remains that there was always some form of flag movement on the Apollo missions. A prominent example comes from Apollo 15, in which David Scott runs by the flag and causes it to wave. There was no physical contact with that flag. This video contradicted the claims of propagandists who state that the flags only moved if the astronauts were holding onto the pole and trying to plant it in the ground. When presented with this video they promptly claimed that it was static electricity that moved it! Of all the most ridiculous excuses. Even Eric Jones, editor of the *Apollo Lunar Surface Journal*, dismissed this excuse as very unlikely and if you look at the flag in the video, the flag initially moves *away* from the astronaut. If static electricity on his suit was attracting the flag, the flag would have initially moved *towards* him.

d'Arc: Bill Kaysing brought a libel suit against astronaut Jim Lovell when Lovell wrote about him, "The guy is wacky." The case was dismissed in 1999 and affirmed on First Amendment grounds. Following this, his publisher (Price Stern Sloan) decided not to publish the book after paying Kaysing an advance. What do you think happened?

White: I can't say for certain what happened about the publishing deal. But Bill Kaysing had stated in his suit for damages that getting called 'wacky' by a well known astronaut would be damaging to his ability to get published.

While on the subject of the libel suit, many propagandists have tried to obscure and cloud the events of what happened during that trial. It all started when Kaysing and a friend attended a lecture that Jim Lovell was hosting at the San Jose Convention Center. When it was done Kaysing discussed the moon landings with him. Kaysing was one of those people who would give even his worst enemies the benefit of the doubt, and even publicly apologized to the astronauts if they truly did go to the moon. Kaysing sent Lovell a polite letter basically thanking him for all his time, and in return Lovell sent Kaysing a trashy letter essentially telling him he was a kook—either he was a liar or a tragic figure who had wasted hours of his life on a futile quest.

If that wasn't enough, Lovell sent Ralph a copy of this letter and went public with this statement in the *San Jose Metro*, "The guy is wacky. His position makes me feel angry. We spent a lot of time getting ready to go to the moon. We spent a lot of money, we took great risks, and it's something everybody in this country should be proud of. His problem is, he saw that movie *Capricorn One* and now he thinks that's really the way it goes."

For the record, Kaysing's book came out before *Capricorn One* and Lovell knows it. After this article was printed, Kaysing promptly took Lovell to court on libel. Ralph signed on as a technical consultant. By far the most prominent of all the lies Lovell told was in reply to a question regarding Ralph René. Lovell denied that he knew anyone by that name, but prior to the lawsuit he had sent Ralph a copy of his letter to Kaysing.

No doubt fearing the jury's verdict, Lovell's lawyer filed for a summary judgment to get the case thrown out of court. Well, one who is guilty of perjury cannot get a summary judgment. So Ralph put together a paper proving that Lovell was guilty of such and thus cannot be allowed to get a summary. It consisted of Ralph's copy of Lovell's letter and its envelope, and Lovell's denial of knowing him.

But instead of handing in Ralph's rebuttal, Kaysing handed in a 22-page document trying to clear his name. I can't really blame him, having read the document it seems he was determined to restore his reputation as a credible writer. In his document Kaysing did briefly mention the letter Lovell sent to Ralph, but he failed to mention that Lovell denied knowing him. Had Kaysing handed in Ralph's paper, the case would not have been thrown out of court and it would have been fought to the end—with Kaysing victorious.

d'Arc: Kaysing says there's a conspiracy involving the CIA, Federal Reserve Bank, IRS and other government agencies to mind control the public. I think today we can certainly see this conspiracy unfolding in a more overt way. But why is the Apollo moon hoax central to this conspiracy? Is it because, as Rene claimed, the Apollo program actually channeled large amounts of money into black budget covert CIA operations in other countries, for instance, at the time, secret wars in Laos and Cambodia? In my mind, "black budget" is what makes it tremendously important for people to take the moon hoax seriously.

White: The Apollo program was ultimately one giant military project. Remember, this was the height of the Cold War when both the Americans and Soviets were shooting off their big mouths saying 'look what we can do.' Landing a man on the moon would certainly solidify America as the superior power in the arms race, and it would also help to draw attention away from such horrors as Vietnam.

It could be said that it is still happening today. In 2004, as his first big step towards re-election, George W. Bush proposed future flights to the moon. Remember this was during the time when Iraq and Afghanistan were the big topics of the day. And later in 2008, the U.S. government shot down their spy satellite USA-193 under the claim that it would crash to earth and spill its dangerous hydrazine fuel everywhere. This claim is profoundly ridiculous. Under the friction of reentry the satellite's fuel tank would split open in the upper atmosphere and the hydrazine would harmlessly burn up. The only reason the U.S. blew up their own satellite was to compete with the Chinese who had shot down one of their own weather satellites the year before. This was all about military supremacy.

NASA is often portrayed as an organization for the advancement of peace and science, when in fact there are many military operations and government agendas behind a lot of what they do. Unless researched thoroughly one might not realize or even know just how militaristic these space flights really are. And with so much propaganda plaguing the internet and media, it's quite difficult for the casual viewer to make sense of it all. Phil Plait and Jim Oberg, by the way, both propagated the proven lie that hydrazine from space would fall on us unless the government blew up the satellite.

d'Arc: Right, NASA continues to utilize dangerous nuclear materials in space flights even though they could use solar energy or other means.

White: Yes, space has been nuclearised over the years. Fortunately, the new Orion spacecraft that NASA will use to replace the shuttle will use solar power, but many other payloads they put in space are nuclear. A few years ago they sent the New Horizons space probe out towards Pluto, powered by nuclear fuel. There have also been proposals for nuclear-powered "manned" spaceflights to Mars. Of course, the addition of a nuclear reactor would add to the overall mass, which would already be way too heavy due to the required shielding against space radiation.

It could also be pointed out that Apollo was partially nuclear. Some of the experiments that are said to have been "left" on the moon were powered by plutonium. When Apollo 13's LEM reentered the atmosphere over Fiji, one such plutonium rod managed to survive and sink to the bottom of the ocean. NASA claims that the radiation had not been detected, but there have been unanswered demands to have this plutonium rod retrieved from the sea.

d'Arc: Did you start the website Moonmovie.com with Bill Kaysing and Ralph René? Who else is part of this enterprise and what are your plans?

White: Moonmovie.com was originally Bart Sibrel's website for his documentary *A Funny Thing Happened on the Way to the Moon*. Sibrel has long since retired from the moon hoax conspiracy movement and his website has been taken over by Wil Tracer. Tracer was originally hired as a third party consultant to investigate and evaluate Sibrel's videos. He originally believed the missions were real, but came to believe otherwise after doing his own research. He was then hired to produce short videos for advertising purposes and also to point out various anomalies with the Apollo record.

Tracer and I met via YouTube after I released my *MoonFaker* series. He and I became friends and offer each other contributions to various projects, which is how I came to be the contributing editor to Moonmovie.com and Moonhoax.us. There is a section on Moonhoax.us dedicated to my videos, including the ones that Mark Gray of Spacecraft Films tried to suppress. Tracer is currently working to release the video adaptation of Bill Kaysing's *We Never Went To The Moon* on DVD, and I am in the process of adapting Ralph Rene's book *NASA Mooned America* to video.

About the Interviewee

Jarrah White is an Australian who debunks the Apollo Hoax debunkers, both in forums and through film. He has formal training in photography and has produced over 40 documentaries discussing Apollo moon landing hoax conspiracy theories. He is the contributing editor at *moonmovie.com* and *moonhoax.us* and was a friend of the late Ralph René. He is currently in the process of adapting to video René's book, *NASA Mooned America*, and continues to produce more installments in his acclaimed *MoonFaker* series. Please see his videos at *YouTube.com*: *MoonFaker: Carrying The Liar*, *MoonFaker: Exhibit C*, *MoonFaker: Exhibit D*, *MoonFaker: Rocks & Crocks* and *MoonFaker: Radioactive Anomaly*. His videos which propagandists tried to suppress can be seen on *LiveVideo.com*: *Apollo XI: The Little Gem & Flagging The Gems*. He may be reached at jarrahw@gmail.com.

Ralph René's 1995 interview in *PARANOIA* is reprinted in this volume. The works of Ralph René are back in print at *www.ralphrene.com*. Contact srorke@mchsi.com. See also YouTube video entitled, "Ralph René: Back In Print."

ParaNotes

by Al Hidell

Scammed Again

Remember Uncle Sam's big multi-billion dollar bank bailout program (TARP), the one that was supposed to unfreeze credit markets and get banks lending again? Did it work? The answer is yes, if your standard is Wall Street profitability. On Main Street, however, things are still looking bleak. In late 2009, Federal Reserve Chairman Ben Bernanke admitted, "Access to credit remains strained for borrowers who are particularly dependent on banks, such as households and small businesses" and "bank lending has contracted sharply." In other words, the bankers took the bailout money and proceeded to lend less, not more. Way to go, Ben.

Even the much-publicized TARP "paybacks" by some of the big banks is a scam. On December 11, 2009, the IRS quietly gave government-subsidized banks a tax exemption that, for example, was worth $38 billion to Citigroup. Three days later, Citigroup trumpeted its repayment of $20 billion in TARP money. [Nomi Prins, "Wall Street's 10 Greatest Lies of 2009," *alternet.org*, 12/28/09]

The Other Bank Bailout

International criminal gangs did their part to help avert global economic collapse, according to Antonio Maria Costa, Executive Director of the United Nations Office on Drugs and Crime. He told the *Observer* (UK) he has seen evidence that some $325 billion in criminal proceeds was "the only liquid investment capital" available to some banks at the height of the crisis in 2008. Without this cash infusion, it is likely many of these banks would have collapsed. In effect, the laundering of drug money helped keep the international financial system afloat. [Rajeev Syal, "Drug money saved banks in global crisis, claims UN advisor," *observer.guardian.co.uk*, 12/13/09]

Violence in the Streets?

Imagine a country going deep into debt. Unable or unwilling to reduce its large interest payments and military spending, government leaders make drastic cuts in social services. The resulting public unrest is put down by brutal dictatorships.

This pattern has played out repeatedly in the developing world, particularly in Latin America. Is it now coming to the developed nations? Today, the United States is the world's largest debtor nation, having built up a total national debt of $12 trillion which increases by nearly $4 billion *per day*. Observers across the political spectrum believe significant cuts in social spending (as well as large tax increases) are inevitable.

A recent report by the respected credit rating agency Moody's suggests such actions could trigger social unrest in both developing and developed nations. It predicts "tumultuous" times ahead. "In those countries whose debt has increased significantly, and especially those whose debt has become unaffordable, the need to rein in deficits will test social cohesiveness," the report warns. Translation: "Get ready, because it's going to hit the fan." [Edmund Conway, "Moody's Warns of 'Social Unrest' as Sovereign Debt Spirals," *telegraph.co.uk*, 12/15/09]

"Welfare Queens" Dethroned

While the federal government can (for now) essentially print more money when it runs a budget deficit, states and municipalities don't have that luxury. The result, on the local level, is that people are already seeing big cuts in social services. In 2009, at least 43 states and hundreds of municipalities responded to their budget crises by reducing social spending. Indeed, despite talk about "big government" and people getting "too many government handouts," the exact opposite has been happening throughout America. For example, the number of welfare recipients nationally actually dropped more than 40 percent between 2001 and 2008. Louisiana, Texas and Illinois each dropped 80 percent of adult recipients during that time. Citizens of the state of Georgia saw a 90 percent drop, with fewer than

2,500 adults now receiving benefits (down from 28,000 in 2004).

According to a survey conducted by the Georgia Coalition Against Domestic Violence, the state used lies and scare tactics to reduce the welfare rolls. For example, caseworkers were reportedly telling applicants they would have to be surgically sterilized before they could apply for benefits, while others were warned that the state could take their children if they applied.

Making fiscal matters worse, many local governments are being shaken down for billions of dollars by UBS, Goldman Sachs, and other big financial institutions. As explained in *BusinessWeek* magazine, "[D]uring the credit boom, Wall Street targeted cities big and small with risky financial products that promised to save them money or boost returns. ... Many of the transactions shared a striking similarity: provisions that protected the banks from big losses and left the customers on the hook for huge payouts" if the investments went bad. [Stephanie Mencimer, "Brave New Welfare," *Mother Jones*, 1/15/09; Theo Francis, et al., "Wall Street Plays Hardball," *businessweek.com*, 11/18/09]

In Black and White

When Barack Obama was elected the first black president, commentators saw it as a capstone to decades of "racial progress." The problem is, significant inequities still exist between whites and non-whites in the economic, health, and social realms. For example, schools in the United States are more segregated in 2010 than they were in the 1960s. Furthermore, schools in low-income communities (both white and non-white) remain highly unequal in terms of funding and teacher quality. [Gary Orfield, "Reviving the Goal of an Integrated Society: A 21st Century Challenge," The Civil Rights Project, UCLA, January 2009]

Big Fat Lies

Will eating a low-fat diet prolong your life? Contrary to the prevailing wisdom, the question is far from settled. Indeed, according to science reporter Gary Taubes, the most rigorous meta-analysis to date of clinical trials of low-fat diets concluded that they had *no significant effect* on mortality. As for consumption of dietary cholesterol (e.g., the villainous dietary duo of eggs and dairy products), the evidence for increased mortality is surprisingly weak. What about increasing fiber? While there may be other health benefits, there have been no clinical studies showing that fiber consumption will help you live longer. While eating fewer calories does appear to correlate with a longer lifespan, some calories may be worse than others. He warns that sugars—sucrose and high-fructose corn syrup specifically—are particularly harmful. Always consult your doctor and do your own research before making any major dietary changes. [Gary Taubes, *Good Calories, Bad Calories*, Anchor: 2008]

Israel Harvested Organs

It sounds like something from an anti-Semitic tract: Israeli officials have harvested organs from dead Palestinians, sometimes without the permission of relatives. The admission was first made by Dr. Jehuda Hiss—then-head of Israel's Abu Kabir forensic institute—during a 2000 academic interview, but Hiss's statements were not widely publicized until a December 2009 report by Israel's Channel 2.

The Channel 2 broadcast revealed that in the 1990s specialists at Abu Kabir harvested skin, corneas, heart valves and bones from bodies, often without family permission. Palestinians were far from the only victims, who included Israeli soldiers, Israeli citizens, and foreign workers. "This activity ended a decade ago and does not happen any longer," the Israeli military said in a statement quoted by Channel 2. Israel's Health Ministry told Channel 2 that all the harvesting was done with permission, but admitted "The guidelines at that time were not clear." It added, "For the last 10 years, Abu Kabir has been working according to ethics and Jewish law." [Mark Lavie, "Israel harvested organs in 90s without permission," Associated Press, 12/20/09]

America's Toxic Exports

The Feds have been quick to criticize China when toxins are found in its exports, though such cases are a small percentage of their total exports. Meanwhile, the U.S. government has been deregulating toxic substances—such as lead in lipsticks, mercury in electronics, and endocrine disruptors in baby toys—with little notice. In contrast, the European Union (EU) has launched strict new regulations requiring businesses seeking access to their markets to eliminate toxic substances from their products. Currently, only two out of more than 100 chemicals on the EU list are regulated under U.S. law.

According to the U.S. Environmental Protection Agency, less than five percent of all chemicals used in the country have had even minimal testing for toxicity or environmental impact. All this deregulation (and non-regulation) benefits the chemicals industry, which spends an estimated $2-5 million per year lobbying Washington as well as more to lobby state governments. [Mark Schapiro, "U.S. Lags Behind Europe in Regulating Toxicity of Everyday Products," *democracynow.org*, 2/24/09]

It's Worse Than You Think

Blogger Christopher Soghoian warns that government agencies at all levels "routinely" obtain customer records of phone numbers dialed, text messages, emails, instant messages, web pages visited, queries submitted to search engines, and GPS location data. He explains that such records—stored by ISPs, Telecoms, and other third parties—are fair game because court orders and other safeguards generally apply only to the monitoring of the content of real-time communications.

Problem	Americans Killed Since 9/11	Annual U.S. Government Spending
Terrorism	**52**	**$200 billion**
Cancer	**4,000,000**	**$5 billion**
Road Accidents	**325,000**	**$851 million**

Note: All figures are rough estimates, but you get the idea. Terrorism deaths based on violent attacks by Muslims on U.S. soil, see **thereligionofpeace.com/pages/americanattacks.html**.

Although there is no legal requirement to maintain or report statistics on the disclosure of stored customer records, Soghoian has uncovered at least one disturbing fact: Sprint Nextel provided law enforcement agencies with customer GPS location information over 8 million times between September 2008 and October 2009. [Christopher Soghoian, "8 Million Reasons for Real Surveillance Oversight," *paranoia.dubfire.net*, 12/1/09]

$1 Million Per Year. Per Soldier.

In late 2009, the nonpartisan Congressional Research Office estimated the cost of the U.S. presence in Afghanistan: $3.6 billion a month. Based on troop levels at that time, it worked out to about $1 million per year, per soldier. The calculation included the significant sums paid to military support contractors—the private companies that do much of the grunt work of war, everything from mess hall duty to laundry room staffing.

One reason for the astronomical cost: over the years, despite increasing budgets, the Department of Defense (DoD) has significantly reduced its ranks of internal investigators and auditors. Even when investigators do suspect fraud, military brass generally have little stomach to bite the hands that, literally, feed them. Indeed, when the Defense Contract Audit Agency (DCAA) suspected excessive billing and tried to withhold a tiny percentage of payments to KBR—the Army's largest military support contractor—the Army bypassed the Agency and paid KBR in full. [Dina Rasor, "War Fraud Whistleblowers Under Wraps," *truthout.org*, 11/30/09]

Apocalypse Science

During his 2009 Senate confirmation hearings, President Obama's top science and technology advisor, John P. Holdren, had to assure Senators that he does not believe government should have a role in determining optimal population size. Concerns had been raised because Holdren once advocated for the creation of "a comprehensive Planetary Regime" that would enforce extreme measures of population control—including forced abortions and secret mass sterilization programs conducted through food and water supplies. In the 1977 book *Ecoscience*, Holdren and his co-authors explained that they were "firmly in the neo-Malthusian camp" on the issue of "population limitation." (In the late 18th Century, British economist Thomas Malthus defined population growth as one of the direst threats to humanity, and recommended governments act accordingly.)

Over the years, Holdren has shifted his globalist perspective from population control to global warming. In 1970, Holdren's *Ecoscience* co-author and mentor Paul Ehrlich had suggested that famines caused by overpopulation could lead to a "Great Die-Off" of some 4 billion people during the 1980s. (According to *wikipedia.org*, approximately 70 million deaths worldwide were caused by famine in the 20th Century.) Similarly, in 1986 Holdren sounded an alarmist warning that "carbon dioxide-induced famines could kill as many as a billion people before the year 2020." By 2009, he was telling Senators the scenario was possible but "not likely."

This is not to suggest climate change is not a threat, or imply that Mr. Holdren has nefarious motives. Rather, it's to point out that scientists sometimes make dire, apocalyptic predictions which do not come true. If policy changes are made based on such warnings, it makes sense to reevaluate them if the warnings are subsequently moderated or disproved. [Ben Johnson, "Obama's Biggest Radical," *frontpagemagazine.com*, 2/27/09]

Obama Staffer's Plan for Conspiracy Theorists

President Obama appointed Cass Sunstein, an old Harvard Law School friend, Administrator of the White House Office of Information and Regulatory Affairs. In 2009, Sunstein and co-author Adrian Vermeule addressed the issue of conspiracy theories in the scholarly article "Conspiracy Theories: Causes and Cures." (*J. Political Philosophy*, 7 [2009], pp. 202-227). The title likens conspiracy theories to a disease, which suggests Sunstein's dim view of this form of alternative political discourse.

The suggested "cure" is a kind of "COINTELPRO Meets Facebook" (COINTELPRO was an FBI program of covert, and often illegal, activity to neutralize political dissidents in the 1960s and 70s.) The authors "suggest a distinctive tactic for breaking up the hard core of extremists who supply conspiracy theories: cognitive infiltration of extremist groups, whereby government agents or their allies (acting either virtually or in real space, and either openly or anonymously) will undermine the crippled epistemology of believers by planting doubts about the theories and stylized facts that circulate within such groups."

By the phrase "crippled epistemology," Sunstein is suggesting people who believe in conspiracy theories only trust a small number of (faulty) information sources. Therefore, Sunstein argues, it would not work to simply refute conspiracy theories through the mainstream media. Rather, the very sources that conspiracy theorists believe would have to be infiltrated. Furthermore, these refutations must come from "independent experts" enlisted by the government. Of course, "government cannot be seen to control the independent experts," he advises.

In a smear carried over from the Bush Administration, Sunstein defines those who question and challenge official viewpoints as a "hard core of extremists." As for a "government agent" who engages in "anonymous infiltration" of activist groups, there used to be a simpler term: agent provocateur. Whether in "chat rooms, online social networks, or even real-space groups," Sunstein says the goal will be to "sow uncertainty and distrust within conspiratorial groups and among their members," and "raise the costs of organization and communication."

Leave it to an Obama Administration official to give this old-fashioned crushing of political dissent a positive-sounding (and quite Orwellian) spin. The point of these efforts, Sunstein insists, is simply to "[introduce] beneficial cognitive diversity" to the epistemologically-crippled conspiracy theorists. [Marc Estrin, "Got Fascism?: Obama Advisor Promotes 'Cognitive Infiltration,'" *theragblog.blogspot.com*, 1/11/10]

The Best Health Care System. Not.

In the debate over health care reform many Americans echo Senator Richard Shelby of Alabama, who says the U.S. has "the best health care system the world has ever known." However, this assumption is far from a truism and is itself highly debatable. In a *New York Times* Op-Ed piece, commentator Nicholas D. Kristof outlined some of the ways America lags behind. The United States ranks 31st in life expectancy (tied with Kuwait and Chile), 37th in infant mortality, and 34th in maternal mortality. A child in America is two-and-a-half times more likely to die by age 5 than in Singapore or Sweden. In a review of 10 studies comparing the American and Canadian health care systems, the U.S. did better in two areas, Canada did better in five.

Another study looked at how well 19 developed countries succeeded in avoiding "preventable deaths" among their citizens (i.e., deaths from diseases that could be cured or forestalled with proper intervention). "The best health care system the world has ever known" ranked last. There is one American health statistic that is well above the global average: life expectancy for those who have reached age 65. These happen to be the people, as Kristof notes, who for years have had universal government-controlled health care coverage: Medicare. [Nicholas D. Kristof, "Unhealthy America," *nytimes.com*, 11/4/09]

About the Author

Al Hidell is the co-founder of *PARANOIA* (*paranoiamagazine.com*), as well as an artist, photographer, and graphic designer. He may be reached at alhidell@gmail.com.

Robin Hood

The Conspiracy and Cover-up of Yorkshire's Buried Treasure

by Barbara Green

Shee laid the blood irons to Robin Hood's vaine
Alacke the more pitye!
And perct the vaine and let out the bloode
That was full red to see.
At first it bled the thicke thicke blood
And afterwards the thinne
And well then wist good Robin Hood
Treason there was within.
— Robin Hood, His Death & Burial

Deep in the heart of an ancient woodland in West Yorkshire, hidden beneath a formidable barrier of fierce thorns and dense undergrowth, there is a hidden grave. Here rests the mortal remains of Robin Hood, the Prince of Robbers, England's outlaw hero, bloodily slain by the Prioress of Kirklees Nunnery six hundred years ago and cast into an unhallowed grave.

Who was the evil nun and why did she commit so foul a murder? What was the role of Red Roger of Doncaster, the convent priest? Is it possible that he was really Will Scarlet, turned monk, also the prioress's lover? Who was the prioress? Was she Dame Mary Startin, who died of the Black Death in 1350?

All that is left of this medieval whodunit is a ruined grave, hidden in deep woodland, within the derelict priory gatehouse where Robin was so gruesomely done to death. Was the famous outlaw a victim of thwarted passion, pagan sacrifice, bad nursing, accident, natural causes or—vampirism? The entire area where this horrific drama took place is shrouded in, according to one writer, "... a mystery which local people only reluctantly tried to penetrate."

Today, Robin lies forgotten and unmourned in his lonely and desolate sepulchre, for few people know of the grave's existence or its whereabouts. Why is this so? Should not such a monument be an international place of pilgrimage, and should Yorkshire, not Nottingham, be the centre of the famous folk hero's legend? These are the mysteries this article attempts to unravel.

Lady Armytage vs. The YRHS

In 1983 I was asked to nurse Sir John Armytage, the 8th baronet of Kirklees Hall, in his last illness. I was the Brighouse district nurse at the time. Sir John passed away and the following year I asked Lady Armytage, his widow, if I could visit Robin Hood's grave. Lady Armytage had inherited the estate while Sir Martin, Sir John's son by his first wife, moved away. Shortly afterwards Lady Armytage sold the hall (which was turned into luxury flats) but kept the farm and historical sites, and went on to build a new house on the priory ruins.

In the following years I became very interested in the legend of Robin Hood, and after researching the Yorkshire connections I wrote a book called *Marian's Christmas Rose* about Maid Marian with reference to Kirklees Priory. I asked Lady Armytage if I could take the book to the Kirklees Annual Garden Party in 1985. In response, Lady A and her "organiser," Mrs. James, paid an uninvited

Illustrations by Saint John, *inkshadows.com, myspace.com/inkshadows*

visit to my home. Mrs. James waved the book around, complaining that it mentioned Kirklees. She stated that it could not be sold at Kirklees because it would interest people in Robin's grave and no one was allowed to visit it. Lady A remained silent throughout this visit.

In 1985, I formed the Yorkshire Robin Hood Society (YRHS) with a friend, Ruth Harrington. Lady Armytage was invited to become a Patron but declined, saying she was "too busy." Later, Ruth and I were filmed by the BBC programme Look North, but we had to go to Shibden Park as Lady Armytage would not let us film on site. The following year Ruth and I visited the Nottingham Medieval Market to sell my book, *Marian Christmas Rose*, which caused a ruckus. We were reported to the Sheriff of Nottingham. In 1987, Ruth and I were filmed by TV for a programme called FAX in Wakefield library because we were again refused permission at Kirklees. This film was never broadcast.

Later in the year we visited London in order to meet John Pope de Locksley of the London Robin Hood Club. We met at the Barnet Carnival, where we also made the acquaintance of Lord Sean Manchester, who offered to become Patron of the YRHS. We were very pleased about this, though we later learned that Lord Manchester was a famous "vampire hunter" who is descended from Lord Byron. The following year I was filmed again, with another member, Evelyn Friend, by the BBC for a programme called *People*. Once more, the Yorkshire Robin Hood Society was not allowed to go to the grave, though the film crew was allowed, provided they kept the location secret. When the film was broadcast, Evelyn and I were furious to find that all our comments about the grave had been edited out, and we were left talking about trivial things—Evelyn's most memorable line being, "I am Robin Hood in drag."

Up until 1990 we wrote to Lady Armytage several times, very politely asking for a date on which the YRHS could visit the grave and gatehouse. All these letters were either ignored or returned, saying she was too busy. Meanwhile, I had written a manuscript called *The Outlaw Robin Hood: His Yorkshire Legend* and had taken it to Calderdale Council with a view to promoting our local Robin Hood connection.

Jane Branton, the Tourist Officer, said it was very good but they could not publish it as they had to keep a "low profile" over Kirklees. She said that they had to respect Lady Armytage's wish to be private and they could not possibly publish it. She referred it to Paul Sheenan, the director of Calderdale Council, who had a dicky fit and said he had to protect Lady Armytage's privacy—and this, after consulting with the owner of the land! The same thing happened with other councils for the next five years, though finally Kirklees Council agreed to publish after a lot of humming and haa-ing.

During this time, Ruth and I were summoned to Kirklees for an interview with Lady Armytage and Martin Webster. Foolishly—in hindsight—we went as commanded. Lady Armytage took us into her kitchen where her farm manager, Martin Webster, was lurking around, and she stated without further ado that, "this Robin Hood business is a nuisance." She did not offer us a drink, though she was drinking herself, and then she took a phone call from one of her posh friends. When she had finished, she continued to fob us off by saying that she was too busy to bother with us, but that she would allow the YRHS to visit the following year when she was not "so busy."

The following year another letter was sent to her ladyship to arrange the promised visit, but there was no reply. However, I did receive a phone call from Martin Webster, who spoke to me in a threatening way and said no visit had been promised. Shortly afterward, I made the acquaintance of Drew Hartley, a local man who came to visit me with his cameraman with a view to making a film about the grave and other local Robin Hood connections. By now I was beginning to feel as though there was something "going on" preventing any progress, and I was not surprised to hear afterwards that Drew's plans had fallen through due to threats and other strange matters. When his investigators were visited by men in black and much more, he abandoned the project.

Meanwhile, my book *The Outlaw Robin Hood: His Yorkshire Legend* had been published by Kirklees Heritage and, although it sold well locally, I was not invited to take part in any more television programmes, despite Robin Hood being in the news with a film called *Robin Hood* (www.redmonkeyfilms.co.uk) in post production. It was the same old Robin Hood Nottingham rubbish, with no mention of Yorkshire. In fact Richard Whitely, the presenter, had made a very silly joke on Yorkshire Television about Robin Hood of Yorkshire, while presenting a Yorkshire programme.

The plot continued to thicken. John Akins, a local entrepreneur, bought a derelict Cornmill on Wakefield Road with plans to turn it into "Robin Hood Hamlet." He requested information from the YRHS, but around a year later he completely abandoned the project, telling me (although I had a fair idea) that he wanted nothing to do with Robin Hood. Apparently, in 2005, a man from the Huddersfield Collectors also said he had been "leaned on" by Calderdale Council not to publicise Robin Hood's local connections. A similar scenario also happened with Trust House Forte, who had built a new hotel nearby. They claimed they could not put anything about Robin Hood in their information pack or decor, as the grave was on private land.

From 1985 to 1995, I sent innumerable letters to English Heritage, National Trust, Save Britain's Heritage, Yorkshire Archaeological Society and other historical societies. My letters all came back with the same reply, that they could not do anything about the grave or gatehouse because it would upset Lady A's privacy, even though Kirklees Priory Gatehouse was a 'Grade 1' listed building in danger of falling down. Another person I contacted was Peter Allan, Chief Tourist Officer of the East Midlands Tourist Board. They had published a brochure about Robin Hood Country and missed out on the grave.

I wrote to Mr. Allan and asked him why the grave had not been mentioned. He said Calderdale Council had forbidden them to put it in, and that the council was acting on instructions from a "higher authority." I asked him who the "higher authority" was but he would not say, so I told him whom I thought it was, although Lady Armytage was not, in my view, a "higher authority."

Even more suspect was the behaviour of the management of a shop called Tales of Robin Hood, which had just opened in Nottingham. They had actually asked me for information about the grave, with which I had been happy to supply them. When I actually paid a visit, however, to the newly-opened shop and visitor centre, I was surprised to see a picture of the grave and three locations for it, which were not in Yorkshire and nowhere in the immediate area. I wrote to the manager Graham Black to ask him why he had made this mistake and he said it was not a mistake. I could not get a sensible answer from him and he accused me of being "paranoid."

It was around this time that the YRHS began to get many reports of paranormal activity around the grave of Robin Hood. First, a history.

The Haunting of Robin Hood's Grave

Considering the history of Robin's death—cursed by a witch on his way to the nunnery, murdered by an apostate nun, and cast into an unhallowed grave—it is hardly surprising that over the years the site is reputed to have unquiet spirits hovering around it. An elderly lady, Mrs Edith Ellis, witnessed silver arrows in the sky above Kirklees when visiting her old aunt at Hartshead in the early years of the last century. She also reported hearing a man's voice calling for 'Marian.'

A tenant farmer of Kirklees made another sighting in 1926. "One day," he recalled, " I was sitting on the grave shooting rabbits. As I was about to shoot I felt a tap on my shoulder, and my shotgun went off accidentally, removing two of my front teeth on its recoil. There was nobody to be seen at the time. On another occasion I was on my way home from the Three Nuns. As I was walking through the woods something fell out of a tree and knocked me to the ground. When I got up I could see the old gatehouse. In the window I could clearly see a man with a bow. My family always said it was the drink, but it was Robin Hood's ghost."

In 1963, guitarist Roger Williams took an unofficial stroll up to Robin's grave with a friend. About twenty yards from the grave he saw a white robed woman who suddenly seemed to glide towards the two men. What made Roger's hair stand on end was how silently she moved over the twigs and bracken. At about five yards from Roger the woman stopped and stared at him with "dark, mad eyes." Then she moved away and vanished, all on a bright, sunny day.

Mr. Williams saw the same apparition again in 1972, in full daylight, and again it stopped a few yards from him and his companion. The woman was wearing a long white dress with a square neck and long sleeves, which accords with the habit of a Cistercian nun. Again she looked at him angrily before moving off, but the eerie sequel to this experience was that Roger's house then experienced a series of strange noises and banging. After this, Roger swore, "wild horses would not drag me up there again."

Mark Gibbons, one of the founding members of Gravewatch, had a similar experience in 1998. Apparently, he and other members of the group went up to find Robin's grave one moonlit night, but got lost. Suddenly Mark saw a white figure pointing in a certain direction—which turned out to be where the grave was situated. Mark also experienced a sensation of great evil and hatred.

Shortly after this, Judith Broadbent, a reporter from the *Dewsbury Reporter*, and her photographer colleague, Sue Ellis, were allowed to visit the gravesite by the owner. While wandering around she heard heavy footsteps behind her and she was pulled to the ground by invisible forces. She shouted "get away" and her friend came rushing to help her. Her camera had jammed while trying to photograph the grave. A week later Sue was taken seriously ill and was paralysed from the neck downwards for two weeks. The two reporters later wrote an article for *Yorkshire Life* magazine, much of its content being taken from Yorkshire Robin Hood Society literature, including the next sighting, which appeared in *The Unexplained* magazine in 1992, prior to the publication of their article.

This was when vampires entered the arena, introduced to the increasingly enigmatic situation by Bishop Sean Manchester of the Holy Grail Church and patron of the Yorkshire Robin Hood Society. In 1992 Bishop Manchester and two colleagues attempted an exorcism at Kirklees. This had come about as a result of the Yorkshire Robin Hood Society asking for the site to be blessed by the local vicar. Unfortunately, permission to perform such a ceremony had been unequivocally refused to both clergymen.

Bishop Manchester, however, was made of sterner stuff than the local pastor. He was renowned for his involvement in the notorious Highgate Vampire affair in the 1970s, and it occurred to him that vampires might be behind the legend of Robin being bled to death. He felt that urgent spiritual intervention was needed, with or without official sanction. On his clandestine visit to the grave the bishop came across the body of a blood drained goat, diabolical rune signs of the priory gatehouse, finger-width holes in the ground around the grave—suggesting vampiric activity—and was confronted by a darkly clad woman who turned into a hag with red staring eyes.

A further sighting by another nocturnal visitor proved a terrifying experience when she saw two figures hovering in the trees surrounding the grave, which she took to be the evil prioress and her paramour Red Roger of Doncaster. "I felt, and saw, what I can only describe as streams of evil pouring out of the trees towards me," the witness stated. A lady from Nottingham, who visited the grave in the summer of 2000, experienced a psychic communication with Robin at the graveside, as did Robin Hood expert John de Locksley of the London Robin Hood Club, who also boldly battled through the giant ferns, murderous brambles and other lethal obstacles of the Kirklees rain forest to stand by his hero's grave one wild, wet October night of the same year.

As a result of the paranormal activities at the gravesite, the YRHS asked the Church to do a blessing. Robin Hood had, in fact, died without the last rites of the Church, and had probably been murdered. Father John Flack, the local Anglican priest, agreed to do a blessing but received an irate phone call from the Bishop of Wakefield who had, in his turn, got a flea in his ear from Kirklees.

The Right Revered Anselm Genders, the retired Bishop of Bermuda (who had exorcised the Bermuda Triangle), who lived at the House of the Resurrection in nearby Mirfield, did a blessing from his monastery, but declined to ask Lady Armytage why she was against a blessing. Evelyn, meanwhile, had crossed swords with the Bishop of Pontefract, who wrote her a very stroppy letter in reply to her concerns over the site being on a ley line, and all the bad luck, suspected witchcraft and the influence of the funny handshake brigade, whom, we were beginning to think, were behind all the obstructions.

In and among all this, we heard from Father Lionel Fanshaw from Fortean TV, who was keen to film the grave, but this was called off at the last minute with no explanation. Again, I was asked by the BBC to comment on the local Robin Hood connections on a barge trip going past the site. This was called off at the last minute by a very embarrassed presenter who said she could not tell me why, but when I guessed correctly, she confirmed my suspicions. Evelyn, meanwhile, had gone on Radio Leeds and all the instruments had gone haywire, preventing her broadcast from going out. From that time onwards she blessed anything to do with Robin Hood with holy water and advised me to do the same.

In 1991, Kirklees Cultural Heritage finally published my book *The Outlaw Robin Hood*. A German TV company, ZDF, did a Robin Hood film at Hartshead Church and included YRHS. The film crew was allowed on the gravesite but YRHS was not allowed. Perhaps it was because they were German, like Lady Armytage, who had become Sir John's second wife after the war. She had previously been the housekeeper at Kirklees.

The same year, YRHS patron, Sean Manchester, was consecrated as a bishop of the Old Catholic Church, and allegedly led a vampire hunt up to Kirklees. He had surmised that as Robin Hood died by being bled to death by the prioress, it could be a vampire causing all the current trouble. Shortly after this I became ill with a heart complaint, and my mother had a stroke, and needed nursing, so I wasn't able to do much more on the Robin Hood front for a few years.

Vampiric Message Boards

Near the end of the 1990s I acquired a computer. This opened the Robin Hood of Kirklees scene up to a much wider audience. It wasn't long before I was being attacked on an Internet Message Board, the World Wide Robin Hood Society, by John Armytage, a nephew of Lady Armytage, who accused me of all sorts of nonsense, mainly of upsetting his dear aunt. I concluded he had obtained his "facts" from certain people and got the whole story muddled up and spiced it up with malice, in order to please Lady Armytage.

As can quite clearly be seen from the previous chronology, the YRHS met a brick wall of obstruction from the word go. The same attacks were soon raining down on me by American professors and other cap-doffing knights in shining armour rushing to Lady Armytage's defence, stating what a charming lady she was and for me to leave the "poor defenceless old lady" alone. (She was in her sixties and far from defenceless.)

In 2002, a group from Bradford University approached the YRHS to assist in a film about Robin Hood of Yorkshire but, again, it wound up on the Kirklees cutting room floor. This time it was an academic named David Hepworth who had managed to get himself installed in a little cottage at Kirklees in order to write the history of Kirklees. Around this time, the "Outlaws and Nuns" walks started, but the Yorkshire Robin Hood Society was refused permission to promote their books and postcards by David Norcliffe, the head gamekeeper of Kirklees, who said we would interfere with the running of the farm.

In 2003, I took part in a Scream Team TV interview but wasn't allowed at Kirklees. However, Scream Team was, very strangely, allowed an all night vigil at Kirklees when Sean Manchester had been refused—although he said he had gone and trespassed. David Hepworth said Scream Team trespassed also, but Ronnie Buckingham their medium said they did not trespass. Probably, and more likely, a large sum of money was offered and accepted.

Message board attacks against the YRHS (and especially me) continued by people who didn't know the true facts; all these old—and some barely shaving—professors from America, cap-

doffing because they had been allowed to visit Robin Hood's Grave when a local historical group, the YRHS had always been refused—which eventually led them to trespass, as Robin would have suggested they did himself. In 2004 I attended the International Conference for Outlaws Studies in York to try and sort out the professors on the Prioress. Everyone, including David Hepworth, treated me like a long lost friend.

Catherine Fearnley, a local woman, entered the fray in 2004, when she was given permission by Lady A to visit the grave, which struck me as very odd as her ladyship usually only allowed "important" people access. Catherine's friendship with David Hepworth was also a strange part of this arrangement. Later that year Red Monkey Film Company asked to interview the YRHS for their film about Robin Hood of Yorkshire. 'Here we go again,' I thought, after I explained to their producer Andy, the problems we had had over the years. He assured me that he would not be put off by anyone at Kirklees (but he has since eaten his words).

In 2005, Tony Robinson from the Time Team television show was allowed onto Kirklees and got on TV saying he had more or less made all the discoveries about Yorkshire and Robin Hood's grave. Catherine and I were then told by Richard Rutherford Moore, a Nottinghamite, that he had been approached by Tony Robinson's research team and they had been told not to approach the YRHS as they were all "dodgy."

Later that year, David Farrant, a psychic investigator from London, came north and led a blessing ceremony at the graveside; this was filmed by Red Monkey, though we pointed out to them that they would not be able to use the footage, as we were on private land. Andy replied that the producer said not to worry, he would "fix it, and he knew how." Now five years later, the Red Monkey *Robin Hood* film is still in mothballs. There was, naturally, a problem connected with footage taken at Kirklees. Red Monkey refused to reply to any polite questions about what had happened, though it was rumoured Lady Armytage was being "difficult." As only a small bit of the film was done at the gravesite, it was hard to see what she had to do with it, or why a simple reconstruction would not have sufficed, which would have done away with any interference from Kirklees altogether.

Furthermore, Drew Hartley told me that MI5 had been involved and that the £50 million pound Heritage Fund was concerned that Yorkshire Robin Hood connections would spoil the Nottingham Tourist Industry, and everyone in Nottinghamire would lose their jobs. He had this information from the "important people" he met while filming at Baftas. Hartley became worried for his job in filmmaking. He said that "men in black" were following him and had stopped his filming of Robin Hood's grave and had threatened others. He had also been harassed by the police. He said his contacts in the film industry had told him to stay away from the Robin Hood's grave situation, that there were "bigger forces" at work in Nottingham who did not want Yorkshire to succeed.

Meanwhile, Red Monkey Film Company was still refusing to answer e-mails about why the film had not been released. Andy said he needed a troop of actors and some horses to complete a scene. In 2007, I asked the Reverend Dhoe Craig Wilde, Vicaress of Hartshead Church on the border of the Kirklees Estate, if she would stock my book in the church porch with the other local history publications. She refused. I later learned that she was a very close friend of Lady Armytage.

In April 2008, Lady Armytage passed away. Today, one year later, it is impossible to find out who has inherited the property and what the plans are for Robin Hood's grave. People meekly let whoever is in charge to get away with robbing the poor to pay for the rich. Kirklees appears to be being run by "a group" but there is no improvement in the negative response from this neck of the woods.

The Riddle of the Prioress

Most people associate Robin Hood with Nottingham and Sherwood Forest. It is a less well-known fact, particularly in our own locality of Calderdale, whose council ironically are keen to build up the tourist industry, that Robin Hood died—and was buried—two miles outside Brighouse, at Kirklees. Today the medieval nunnery where Robin was done to death by the "wicked prioress" is reduced to a ruined gatehouse with a modern mansion standing in the nunnery garden, while the historical hall, home of the Armytages for four centuries, has been turned into a condominium of luxury dwellings.

Historians have largely ignored the legend of Robin's death and little research has been done into the identity of the evil nun who bled Robin to death, or the reason for the murder. This has been partly due to the emphasis of Robin Hood tales becoming firmly attached to Nottingham, whose tourist authorities obviously have a better eye to business than those in Yorkshire. Another reason has been the difficulties encountered in gaining access to the Kirklees sites, as both Robin's grave and the gatehouse are situated on private land. Recent information, however, suggests that the landowner, Lady Armytage, was becoming more amenable to research and researchers prior to her death in 2008. Indeed, prior to this, no less a formidable academic trio than Professors Holt, Dobson and Knight embarked upon compiling a learned treatise on Kirklees, and enjoyed her ladyship's full co-operation and assistance in their undertaking. Hopefully, Robin Hood will soon be on the map of Yorkshire—a long overdue event.

Have they, one wonders, solved the riddle of the prioress? Have they been shown hitherto unseen documents, undiscovered by previous researchers? The only prioress's grave still in evidence at Kirklees is that of Elizabeth de Stainton (or Staynton) but there is no date on her tombstone. The Reverend Harold Pobjoy, author of *A History of The Ancient Parish of Hartshead Cum Clifton* in the 1990s, gives a list taken from Sir William Dugdale's *Monasticum.* He also quotes from Hopkirk's *Huddersfield: Its History and Natural History* (1846), which has a similar list, but, unfortunately, Hopkirk does not name his sources. The two lists can be slotted together without causing any discrepancy, although there are gaps. The problem of the prioress's identity is further compounded by the fact that no one knows for certain the date of Robin's death, but research suggests that it may have been 1347.

The reasons for this are discussed in my book, *The Outlaw Robin Hood: His Yorkshire Legend*. If the date of Robin's death in 1347 is correct, Dame Mary Startin was the prioress in office at the time, not Elizabeth de Stainton. According to Eileen Power in her book *Medieval English Nunneries* (Cambridge University Press) Dame Mary died of the Black Death in 1350, although in some ballads the prioress is said to have committed suicide after murdering Robin Hood. Her lover, the convent priest, Red Roger of Doncaster, is thought to have been Will Scarlet, formerly one of Robin's Merry Men.

Elizabeth de Stainton, on the other hand, could not have been prioress in 1347. She was one of four daughters of John de Stainton of Woolley, near Wakefield. Following her father's death, Elizabeth's mother married Hugh de Toothill, and Elizabeth and her sister were sent to be nuns at Kirklees for reasons of family economy. William de Notton, her uncle and their guardian, took provision to ensure that the girls had not been forced into the religious life, and a document was signed at Monk Bretton Priory in 1347 protecting the interests of Elizabeth and her sister (from a deed at Woolley Hall, in the possession of Lieut Commander Wentworth).

Graham Collins and Martin Keatman, in their book *Robin Hood: The Man Behind The Myth* (1995), have a theory about Elizabeth, which connects her with Robert and Matilda Hood of Wakefield. They suggest that when Elizabeth's mother married Hugh de Toothill, his daughter Matilda by his first wife married Robin Hood. There is mention of a woman called Matilda, in the Wakefield Court Rolls of 1314, being arrested for stealing the lord's firewood.

The authors assume that this Matilda became Robin's wife and Elizabeth's sister in law, but they do not explain why Elizabeth went on to murder him in later years. If this hypothesis is correct, however, we might consider a lethal love triangle. Did Robin perhaps fall in love with Matilda while Elizabeth was packed off to the nunnery, suffering from a medieval "fatal attraction," and exacting her revenge for her thwarted passion in later years ("hell hath no fury")?

However, as we have seen, the dates do not fit—this scenario is thirty years too early. Another mysterious clue lies in a document quoted by Wakefield historian J.W. Walker. This is also mentioned by

Pobjoy, who reports a dispute over eighteen acres of land between "the Prioress of Kirklees and Esmon, son of the noble Richard of England and Earl of Kent in 1373." The Latin text reads: "1373, Orate pro Elizabetha de Staynton quondon prioressa Kirklees quo intempere illus du carta fust adquista," which translates as: "Pray for Elizabeth de Staynton formerly prioress of Kirklees at which time the document was acquired."

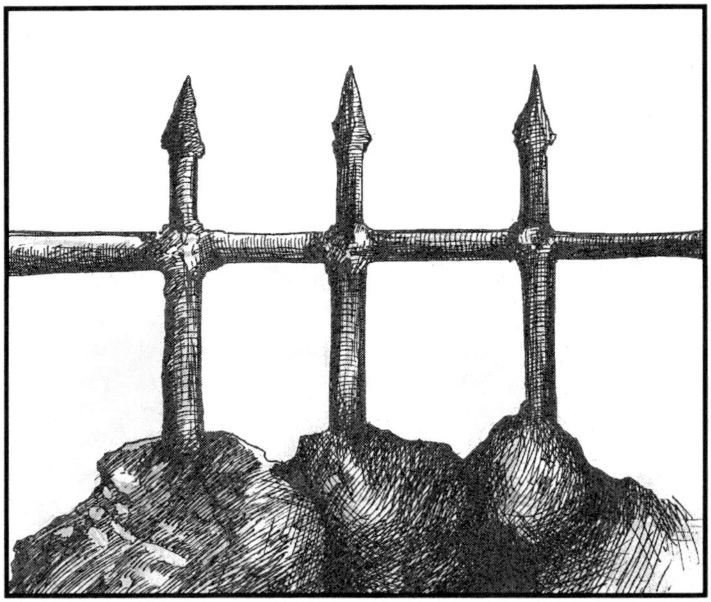

This seems to suggest that Elizabeth was prioress prior to 1373, but it can be read either way. J.W. Walker also quotes another document, which states that the prioress of Kirklees (he infers it was Elizabeth) signed a legal document in 1348, but the British Library has been unable to verify the entry, which was not under the reference quoted (Harleian 4360 Folio 517). So the riddle still remains.

Finally, why did the prioress kill Robin? Venesection ("bleeding") was common medical practise in the Middle Ages. Many people must have died as a result, but it was an ignominious end for the swashbuckling Robin, whether by accident or design. The ballads state that the prioress, and her lover "Red Roger of Doncaster," murdered Robin in revenge for his opposition to the corruption in the Church. If it was murder—for whatever reason—it was a particularly treacherous and gruesome act, and it has even been suggested that there could be links with pagan sacrifice or vampirism.

There is a fascinating mystery here, still waiting to be solved, but until all the evidence is uncovered this part of Robin's legend will stay shrouded in darkness, to remain Yorkshire's buried treasure. Is it a conspiracy or is it simply the selfish whims of the aristocracy, who wish to continue their privileged existence of blood sports and house parties undisturbed by the common hordes? Or is it something more sinister, involving the occult and certain people seeking to control the network of ley lines around Robin Hood's Grave for their own nefarious purposes?

The story of Robin Hood is well known, but that of his death and the site where it took place, and of the evil prioress, her lover, and the naughty nuns of Kirklees, is less known. Yet this bloody saga still has a strange echo with the mysterious goings on today. The final extinction of the Armytage dynasty may have finally come to pass; yet, the strongly guarded secret of Robin Hood's Grave remains jealously guarded by its newly-fledged keepers, who continue to strictly maintain their late mistress's orders. The evil influence of the prioress still casts her dark shadow over this mysterious and haunted spot.

About the Author

Barbara Green is the author of *The Outlaw Robin Hood: His Yorkshire Legend*, *Marian's Christmas Rose*, *Secrets of the Grave*, and *Spirit of the Greenwood*. She has spent almost thirty years trying to save Robin Hood's grave from destruction, and the fight still goes on. Barbara is also a retired district nurse and has co-authored *Ladies of the Night*, a novel about community night nursing. She is also involved in animal welfare, and has two cats. Her website is: *www.robinhoodyorkshire.co.uk*. She may be reached at: greenb@blueyonder.co.uk.

The Men That Don't Fit In

Joan d'Arc Interviews JFK Witness, Roderick A. MacKenzie, III

The story that is about to unwind might sound fantastic. The author of the tale is one "Roderick A. MacKenzie, III" who is now 75 years of age. I have no way to corroborate the tale, but nonetheless I feel compelled to delve into it to get the "facts." Here's how I got myself inextricably involved: In April of 2009 I received an internet link from conspiracy researcher Ron Patton to an audio interview at ConspiraZine. He suggested I listen to this man who claims to have worked for the Mob in Dallas before, during and after the JFK assassination of November 22, 1963.

Roderick A. MacKenzie, III is the author of a self-published book called *The Men That Don't Fit In: The Factual History of a Rogues Life from 1934 to 1967* (subtitle: "which includes the very interesting period of the Pre-Cuban Revolution, the Post-Cuban Revolution and Times of Intrigue and Covert Action as well as adventures around the Defense Industrial Security Command Spooks and Characters, the Outfit, the Cuban Affairs Dept., with the bonus insiders view of Circus, Carnival and Outdoor Amusements Life").

As I tuned in to the interview, I was sitting at my desk rubbing my ankle, which I have had trouble with throughout my life since spraining it when I was ten years old. The day of said mishap was a field trip to Benson's Wild Animal Farm in Hudson, New Hampshire. I didn't want to miss the field trip, so I kept the injury to myself and walked on it all day; thus making it a lifelong problem. Why am I including this seemingly trivial note? As Rod MacKenzie began his "tale of a rogue's life" from the very beginning, the hair on my neck stood up. He was born and raised in the very same small Massachusetts town where I grew up, and his uncle, John T. Benson, owned Benson's Wild Animal Farm!

MacKenzie's story started simply enough. He had a normal upbringing in a lovely rural town dotted with farms and lakes; indeed, as I can vouch, a really nice place to grow up. But he had gotten himself into a little trouble in high school, and his parents strongly suggested he join the Army. So he got out of that one horse town and traveled the world.

After service, MacKenzie eventually landed at Fort Detrick, Maryland, and trained at the Defense Intelligence Agency's "Flaps and Seals" school in the art of making false I.D.'s. It seems in his early days he had invented a suitcase I.D. system, which he describes as a "complete I.D. factory with blanks of all sorts, certificates, checks and I.D. cards, a small printing press and types, inks, seal making equipment, a compact enlarger, photo print frame, papers and chemical packs, trays and so on." In fact, according to MacKenzie, this little gift is what enabled him to escape the "Zone of the Interior" in 1964.

In his introduction to *The Men That Don't Fit In*, MacKenzie expresses relief to have made it to a good old age, "keeping secrets in my brain quiet, except for a select close few." He explains, "While most of the people that I associated with around the Cuban Affairs Groups have passed to their allotted other realms, I have been pretty much left to my own devices." Yet, MacKenzie lived in fear of a contract being put on his head by the Mob, since, he claims, he was in "elbow brushing terms" with a lot of the major and minor players involved in the events of the JFK assassination.

MacKenzie claims he was employed by Mafia boss, Sam Giancana, to run the "safe house" in Dallas, Texas when President John F. Kennedy was assassinated on November 22, 1963. MacKenzie claims he didn't know the event was going to happen; yet, as soon as it happened he realized the "precarious position" he was in. So he disappeared: "Of course," he explains, "it was a time before the mass effort to identify everyone by the social security, mom's maiden name, birth date," and so on.

So, why did MacKenzie finally write *The Men That Don't Fit In*? In his introduction, he writes, "It is not easy to answer because in revealing these facts as I know them, I open myself up to being branded everything from a nut case to a wannabe, kook, or liar. I am none of these and care little what the reader thinks. These facts have gnawed at my gut for 46 years and I do not care to head for the eternal dirt nap on the Great Midway Beyond without making an attempt at stating what I know and saw at that time."

MacKenzie describes the JFK hit as "a classic, well thought-out hit by a very large cast of characters." He explains, "They brought just about everyone who was anyone in the business of nastiness and criminality together to witness or unwittingly be part of it. I was one such person. We were all disposable, as well, and did not know that either." Following the assassination, he spent a day drinking with Malcolm "Mac" Wallace, the man who he claims "had directed the killing teams for Lyndon B. Johnson and his Texas Mafia with the help of the other Mafia." In fact, says MacKenzie, "Mac was quite talkative in a conspirator way."

In June of 2009 I began an email interview with Roderick A. MacKenzie in order to verify some of the claims in his book. As MacKenzie explained up front, "I was only on the lunatic fringe of that day in November (thankfully). However, I am the nearest thing to the actual hitters and cleaners that you're ever going to find around today, and even my educated guesses are pretty valid."

With this statement as our disclaimer, let's put Roderick MacKenzie's cards on the table and see what he's got.

* * *

Joan: You write that Mac Wallace (whom you describe as "Lyndon Baines Johnson's hit man") and Jake Miranda (your handler) were working for a government agency called "Permindex Co." which was part of the Defense Industrial Security Command (DISC). What else can you tell me about that?

MacKenzie: I know that Roselli said we were all under the "Defense Intelligence Security Command Bastards," and that was what both he and Jake Miranda called them. Later, Del Graham said that outfit caused him to have a heart attack in Tarzana, California, over the Kennedy hit while he was on the phone to Roselli at the Baylor Hospital cafeteria in Dallas. So that's one of the people Roselli talked with during the hit. Miranda and I were at Baylor cafeteria too, so all three of us were not shooters by our own alibis.

I guess it was DoD that was setting all of us into the slots where we were supposed to be. They paid for everything. I got bucks from the Permindex vouchers in Dallas and New Orleans on the road from Geno La Motta, who got it from Chicago, and at the time I ran safe houses on the carnival routes and in the Holland Avenue safe house in Dallas. Jake Miranda and Mac Wallace had me sign those vouchers for bucks, and Ruby's sister had me sign one once when Miranda was in New Orleans for money needed to do with my clients at the Holland House.

Joan: Now that you're talking about the safe house, who actually ran it? The Mob, the CIA, both? Did the cops know about it?

MacKenzie: The safe house I ran on the carnivals was for someone named "Abe." I guess he was DISC, at least that's what I was told by the mobsters. The Mob was partnered in there somehow, so was good ole Permindex; the money always goes back to that outfit. I did not ask questions. The folks that were clients were from FBI Branch Five, that Baptist front outfit in Mexico

[ACCC], the Chicago Mob and I guess the DoD. No one ever came across as CIA or other alphabet agency.

Joan: You describe Jack Rubenstein ("Ruby") as a "short fussed guy that goes off at a moment's notice over little stuff." You disliked being around him. On what occasions did you have need to be around him?

MacKenzie: The bunch at the Holland Ave safe house were from Rubenstein. The other Mob people and Jake Miranda, who was in contact daily with me, I got my orders from him. Tippit the cop was in the know and brought money and people to me. I don't think Tippit was a bad cop though. I never thought that Marcello was sending people to the safe house, but that phony preacher/missionary [Jack] Bowen [American Council of Christian Churches] sure sent a lot of "resters" there for very short times.

It all came through Miranda, though Rubenstein tried to get directly involved a time or two, but when I called Miranda he backed off. He did get a couple of signs for the Carousel out of me though The Mob, DISC, FBI-5 through Rev. Bowen, Percy [Chauncey] Holt were my contacts, plus Tippit a few times. Otherwise I can't say who ran the safe house.

Joan: Someone remarked to me that you're in the "LBJ-did-it" camp but I disagree because you bring in Permindex and the fact that these guys, yourself included, got paid by Permindex vouchers, and a lot of these guys worked not only for the CIA and FBI and ONI, but for Lockheed. It's actually closer to a military-industrial monster as described by Jim Garrison. How would you argue against the claim that you're saying it was strictly a Texas mafia hit?

MacKenzie: You are correct, Permindex was our master. That bunch ran the folks I worked with. The CIA and ONI were into it too, of course, but I feel that we were all puppets of the DoD. The other agencies were rogue type elements, but the people I knew, Banister, Sturgis, Wallace, Joe Dugan, Roselli (of course, he was Mob, and most of the others had other loyalties if one can be loyal in this business), Giancana, Rogers, Holt, Ferrie, Werbell and so on, were getting Permindex bucks. It came to New Orleans and Texas from Canada, I learned later; some sort of pipeline from Toronto. Permindex also had offices in South Africa and Hamburg, Germany, I learned through Banister's talk. Ferrie was a lot tighter lipped than that jerk Banister, even when drinking. Frank Sturgis and Felix Rodriguez never said much that did not have fifty meanings, riddles upon riddles. Compartmentalization is like that, you learn a little from the guy you deal with, but not much about the ones he deals with. Let's face it, I was there to be used. We all were. True, I was a willing person in this use, but one did not ask many questions and certainly not more than your need to know. That was a sure way of being shut out of your meal ticket, and could indeed get you killed if you got too much information. You accepted that from the get go!

You think my masters with all those phony first names were some sort of DoD guys? Agents? Who knows. I know for a fact [Joe] Dugan was I.R.A. and Defense Intelligence Security Command out of Muscle Shoals, Alabama, as was Ferrie and "Abe," and Banister as well, but one is never sure. They had I.D. cards for that outfit. But then Abe had me print up some pretty impressive cards for that outfit in Cuba on my return from Fort Detrick "Flaps and Seals" school. I also did some FBI Branch Five cards; those were FBI I.D. cards, and some white cards with multi-raised color emblem with 'Branch Five' and the agent's name in black with 'Branch V' under it. They had different phone numbers; some were in Marseilles, France, some in Canada, and some in Mexico. I never asked any questions. I kept a few but they got lost later in South Africa when I was on the Boswell Wilkey Circus.

Who knows who Branch V was, but Banister used to order those I.D.s and white FBI cards with different names on them a lot. I asked no questions. Ferrie would pick them up at the Sailor's Bar and Hotel I stayed at on Canal Street and Armory Park in New Orleans. I often wondered why a big shot FBI guy and supposedly ONI guy like Banister was using me to make FBI I.D.s, when he was formerly and maybe still with those units? Always one answer leads to more questions. My take on this is that the CIA, FBI and other alphabet agencies, plus outfits like the Birchers and the Christian right, were either knowingly part and parcel under the DoD, or unknowingly had them for masters. I can't be sure, but that was always my thinking.

Joan: A documentary called The Men Who Killed Kennedy *claims on the day of the assassination there were reportedly men behind the picket fence flashing Secret Service I.D.s to keep people out of the area. Yet, there were no Secret Service assigned anywhere that day aside from in the parade. Let me ask you, did you ever make Secret Service I.D.s? Also, did you make a fake I.D. in the name of Alek J. Hidell?*

MacKenzie: Dave Ferrie had me make a number of complete I.D. sets for the last name Hidell. I am not sure of the initials or first and middle names, DOB, etc, but the pictures on some of them were of people that could have been Oswald, I thought at the time. At the Sailor's Hotel at Armory Park on Canal Street, I had a room upstairs over the bar for that purpose; I made a lot of I.D.s and that was only one of them. It was a look-alike (for the Mexican passport) but somehow really not the Oswald I had seen around Ferrie, Banister and Martin and on Carondelet Street. This was around the time Oswald got into that New Orleans fight and made the papers and TV. We talked of it as a set-up later in the Katzenjammer Bar (next to Banister's detective shop on Camp Street, New Orleans). The I.D. kits included several types of Special Agent Cards, one for the FBI, one for DoD, one for Secret Service, one for the CIA, and one for the Houston Police Department. There was also one for the D.C. Park Police, the oldest Police Force in the U.S. that has authority to arrest anywhere in the U.S.

Then there were the passports, each of the names had different I.D.s and only three were of U.S. Passports. At that set-up I made over forty sets of I.D.s under many names. A few came up later as did the Hidell one. Percy Holt worked a deal in his I.D. set up in Los Angeles quite often on these I.D. set ups. He had access to a CIA front on the top floor of a badge making company there, and John Roselli coordinated both our duties. Nothing got done without Roselli telling me through my handlers to get it done. I assume that was the way with Percy as well.

It's interesting the parallels between Percy Holt and I; we were both trained at the Ft. Detrick I.D. School. We were both carnies. I was a trapeze artist; Percy often said he was too; however, he got up on rigging but as far as I know he never performed on any circus or show. His family did own a small circus at one time. He was a CIA Agent, not an asset like me. He was real CIA and had trained at the Farm. I was an asset of the DISC, not CIA. At least I think I was. Like I say, I was recruited in Cuba by a guy with a first name only: "Abe." He and a mobster sent me to Detrick.

Percy and I were both on the scene on the 22nd of November, and I was at Baylor with Roselli and Miranda when the hit went down. Percy was with Rogers and Harrelson in the train yard waiting [see YouTube "Spooks, Hoods & The Hidden Elite"]. I made all three of them the same I.D as I did in New Orleans months before, actually a year or more earlier, but I made the passports for four people, plus pilots' I.D. cards and flight plans from Mineral Wells (TX) Airport to the Yucatán. This was very strange to me at the time, as Percy was a fine licensed pilot in his own right, as was Rogers. Harrelson could fly and I am told did, but was not licensed. I did a lot of I.D.s of all sorts those months before Nov. 22nd for Rev. Bowen, who ran the Hit Teams. I was told to do as he ordered as far as I.D.s went. Roselli had told me that in person while I had the safe house on the carnival back-ends.

Joan: Also, what do you mean about Dugan being I.R.A.? Is that Irish Republican Army? If so, what did the I.R.A. have to do with the Kennedy assassination? Any thoughts?

MacKenzie: Yes Dugan was Irish Republican Army from way back in his teens. However he had been in the 44th Canadian Seaforth Highlander Regiment in Korea. He had been born in Ireland, he told me. He was three years my senior in age; a real tough guy. He was owner of a beer distribution company in Chicago and had the lucrative North Lincoln Ave as his own route. He could pick up full beer kegs on and off the truck all day, at 6'2" he was a massive guy. His hands were two of mine, his foot was huge. He was a killer, though never got caught, but it was well established. I

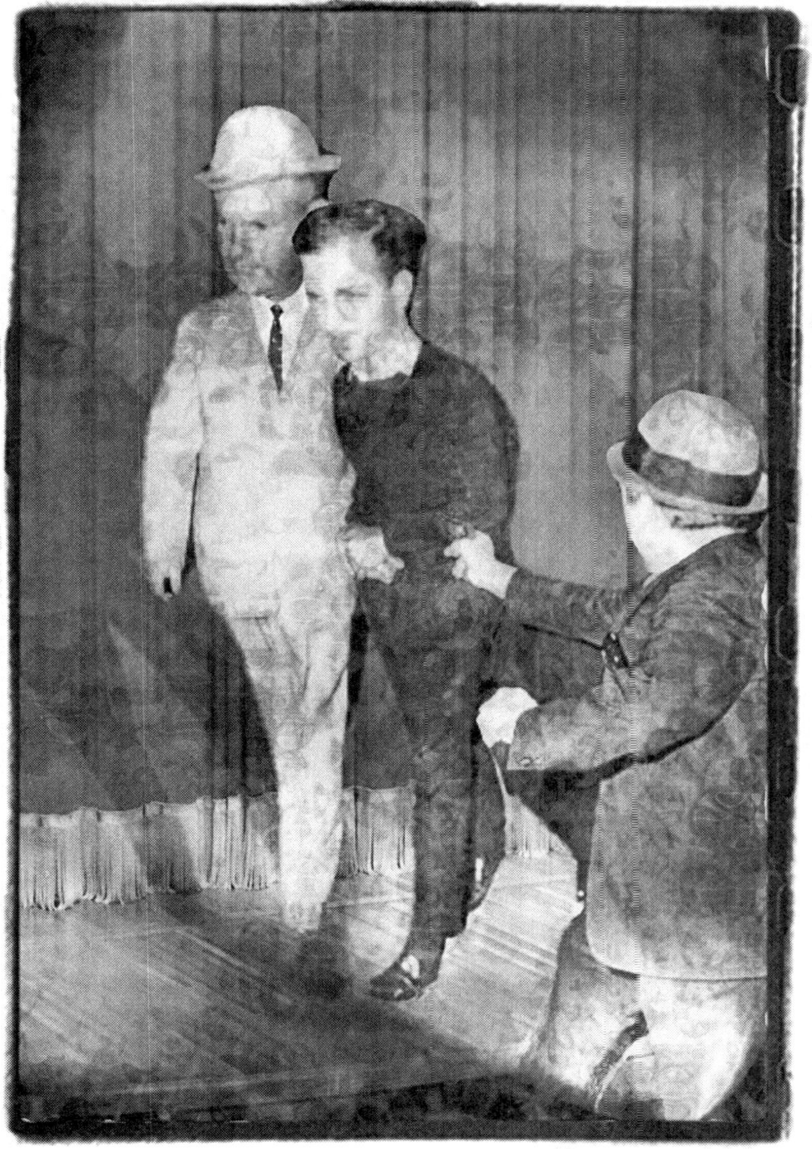

Illustration by Al Hidell, alhidell@gmail.com

walked into a floral shop that the Mob used for all sorts of stuff, and lo and beho d in back was Dugan and Paulie the Sneak with a saber saw cutting the legs, head and arms off Mickey Paluski, who they had slowly enjoyed killing. I was invited to join the merriment but declined, got my coffee and left.

Dugan contracted with the Chicago Outfit. He was sent all over but he was under either the I.R.A. or the Chicago Outfit only, unless he was doing his own stuff. He, like Rogers, enjoyed killing and torture. However, he was a good friend by me, and I tried to ignore that side of him like so many others I knew. Dugan told me any time I needed an off favor, just ask. I don't know if the I.R.A. had anything to do with Kennedy's death. Surely they were capable and oft turned on their own, and they were all mixed in with the Japanese terrorists, the Black Panthers, the Meinhof gang [West German Red Army], and the Indonesian Terrorists. I don't know. I can vouch only for the direct statements of others later that I actually knew about, like Roselli, Dugan, Graham, and others including Percy and Ferrie. Who knows about the I.R.A.

Joan: The documentary also asserts that three French hit men from the Corsican Mob were the shooters behind the fence. The documentary states that they were sent to a "safe house" afterward. Do you recall French mobsters at the safe house?

MacKenzie: I know I had about ten of those Corsican guys from Bowen's place in Mexico, who were sharpshooters worldwide, come through my safe houses both in Dallas and on the road on carnivals. I found out later they were from that outfit I made I.D.s for called FBI Branch 5. The Frenchman Mertz was the one that Mac Wallace says was in on the hit. I did know a lot of the Corsican guys later in Africa and in Veintain, Laos, as well as Marseilles, France. They are a real tough bunch, though usually pretty smooth or suave in presentation; but they make the Mafia look like Sunday School. Still I would trust them over any Alphabet Agency or the Sicilians any day or night. Their word is sacred, if you can get them to give it. The ones in Dallas were a surly lot; Mertz was a real "prick" first class and was real demanding. He wanted certain years and types of wine, and I had to go to a wine specialist in Dallas for the guy. As you can imagine, Dallas was better for the shot and beer crowd even among the millionaire bunch. I will say, I had a fine tip from the Corsicans every time they left.

By the way there's an old paperback called *Appointment in Dallas* by Hugh McDonald, and sure enough there's this guy called Saul as the hitman. McDonald gives him full credit for the hit. I don't buy him being the only hitter, but I do know that man [as Mertz]. I met him at my Holland Avenue safe house, and he was with me for about three days and nights. He had me running all over Dallas and Ft. Worth for wine and shirts to his taste. Clients at the safe house could not leave it or the small back yard facing the alley. Later, Joe Dugan, who was thick as thieves with me for many years, said this guy, who he called McGintey, was used by his Canadian (Permindex) bunch to do some hits for his I.R.A. cell. Joe also confirmed his part that day in canceling JFK's trip ticket and felt, as did I, that Wallace ran the whole shebang. Joe had practiced the hit at Sulphur, Louisiana under Wallace at Mitch Werbell's training facility. Again, it's just my word that I was told these things.

Joan: On the subject of Michel Victor Mertz, I was reading a document online (legacyofsecrecy.com) that said Mertz had a fake I.D. under the name Maurice Valentin and that he also got a passport renewal in 1963. A Frenchman named Jean Souetre says that Mertz was using his name in 1963. Do you remember any of those names? So, as you say, there were a bunch of Corsican mobsters with fake I.D.s hanging around Dallas before the hit, and you were the one making the I.D.s? Did you also make passports?

MacKenzie: Michel Victor Mertz had at least 38 names that I knew of. At present I can't recall all the identities he conned me into making, but there were a lot. He was Victor Paloski on an INTERPOL card I made for him. He paid me quite well, and not even the other Corsicans or the ones over me knew of it. Passports, yes, there were at least nine. One was Cuban under the Castro government. I had very few of these blanks. There was a Canadian, an Italian, one for R.S.S.A. (So. Africa). I had plenty of those. There was a French one, an Irish visa only, flyers papers and flight plans, a Belgian passport and others. The guy always buttonholed me for something.

I'm fairly sure that Jean Souetre and Michel Victor Mertz (in fact, I know they did this) had the chance while incarcerated with several others, both in French and Spanish prisons, and again while working with the FBI-5 bunch, to go (when their names were called) in the other's place to be printed and photographed. They did this to confuse the police, INTERPOL, etc. It's an old mercenary trick. I too have done that. We all gave our social security numbers or the equivalent to migrant workers to use. That way, no one could finger where we really were at any place in time. Yes, Maurice Valentin or Valentino was one of my clients that year. He was a real person, and Mertz, Souetre and he often posed as one another, and there were others too. Frank Sturgis, Felix Rodriguez and David Morales did this amongst themselves as well. And I made a lot of I.D.s and papers for that JMWAVE bunch, Miami station.

Oh yes, I recognize all three names [Mertz, Valentin, Souetre] as having been done by me on documents, passports included. There were 532 blank passports from different nations in my goldmine of identity change, and birth certificates from just about everywhere, and if I did not have one, I'd fake one. Just give me the dates you got out of a cemetery. All sorts of corroborating I.D.s too.

Joan: Also I read that Mertz was "deported" by the INS within 48 hours after the assassination. Isn't that a great way to get the assassins out of the country? Do you remember anything about Frenchmen getting deported after the assassination?

MacKenzie: I do not know about Mertz but do know he left Dallas with plenty of ID & passports and put a bulge in my bankroll to boot. He was a master in crossing borders and I doubt anyone would have been onto him that fast. He just did not look the part. He played a down-and-out bum a lot of times too, hiding in the open on skid rows of the cities of the world. Dugan did that too. It's an old ploy.

Joan: What was the Mob's connection to the carnival circuit? Is this how the Mob got guys out of the thick of things after hits and break-ins and so forth? Can you tell me a little more about how that worked?

MacKenzie: The carnival circuit is an invisible thread of Mob leanings, though the Mob (except for one show) has been unable to organize us and get us to bend for tribute. However, I know of a lot of times carnies worked with the Mob for one reason or another. A lot of people hid out on carnivals up to the 1970s. Today it's hard; carnies are not carnies anymore. Hell, people actually work for salaries and let the game owners do "Pick Ups." No game operator would hold still for that in my day. Hell we came into a spot, took over a hole in front of a game owner's concession with three other agents, and robbed the public blind. That was a profession in those times.

My deal with the Mob and the DoD was the only time I ever heard of that being done. However, no one on the shows knew what was going on. They thought my help was just "green" help, or "First of Mays" (amateur pick ups). We would get a "client" who would be brought to the carnival and moved into the semi-trailer. I'd lay the rules down and they went to work at the low end of percentage till they learned the ropes. As far as I know, the Mob is only on [one] show, and they run it crooked, but you can't see it just by walking the midway. My money came from that Permindex Ltd. outfit and the DISC. The Mob had their hands in there, but it was a government-funded operation.

Joan: In your book you write: "To understand the cow town attitude of Dallas in the 1950s and 1960s, one has to realize that there were a lot of power sources that were raking a lot of profit from this era. Greed was everywhere .... The politicians were very corrupt ... "organized crime was allowed to openly flourish," police looked the other way, and "no one rocked the boat." So, to understand how this hit went down and they got away with it, you have to put it in this context?

MacKenzie: Well, yes, it was all in the open in Dallas at that time. The cops knew things were all around them, if they were not on someone's payroll then they did not last on the force. Everyone was on the take except the citizens that chose to look the other way and be "marks" one way or the other. Churches, cops, judges, lawyers were pretty much on some sort of corruption. It was the way of life in Texas, Oklahoma, Arkansas and Arizona at that time, but not more so than in Dallas, Houston, Corpus Christi and New Orleans. Those were the worst, and Shreveport Alabama too. A person could be beaten up for as little as $.00 and a killing could be done as low as $20. I knew people that would kill for free if you were the "in" person.

Joan: So, as the story goes, Mac Wallace was drinking heavily. He began whispering that Jack Ruby might have to be "taken care of too." You wanted to get away from him, but instead you were sent by Jake Miranda to a quieter area. So, you headed out to drink with Wallace. Every time he gave you a few names, you went into the bathroom and scribbled the names on anything you could find. I can imagine you must have been terrified in the days following this event. So do you think the booze completely blacked out his memory of having blabbed to you?

MacKenzie: The fact that my Kennedy story is based me running as I sobered up back and forth to write the words of Mac Wallace in the bathroom, is not the best foundation for the listing of the culprits. However, I had the background with all these people for the months ahead of the "hit parade" and knew their capabilities, if not what went down on November 22. I knew Mac's murderous capabilities as well as his intelligence and his cunning ways. I also knew once saturated in the lethal doses of Wild Turkey, and on top of that his alcoholism, he was at the point of memory loss the next day. I believed him. But that's my take on it. I have no other proofs except corroboration by John Roselli, Sam Giancana and Delbert Graham of those events being as Mac said.

Joan: What was Mac Wallace's relationship to Lyndon Johnson?

MacKenzie: Mac Wallace had killed a number of people for L.B.J. That's a matter of Texas and Federal records. In fact, Mac killed a man over the fact that he was Johnson's sister's lover, as was Mac at the time. Johnson got to the courts and the Texas Rangers. Though Mac was found guilty of murder, he never spent more than a night in jail. He loved to brag on that one. After he was found guilty and given time served (which he had not served), he was given a top-secret security clearance and the job of head of all supplies to the Lockheed facilities in Texas, Arkansas and Oklahoma. He held this clearance to the day he was killed. Accident? Hardly.

Mac Wallace also took orders from Johnson's lawyer and the Texas Mafia (business types, Texas millionaires). My knowledge of all this was from the gambling games at the Adolphus Hotel and at Houston run by "Doc" Dolan. These games were where people got paid off over the tables in winnings. This was done at Cal Nueva Race Track too. I have seen J. Edgar Hoover and [his lover] Clyde Tolson take away twenty five thousand dollars. Tolson took forty thousand in so-called winnings at the Adolphus Hotel in Dallas, and a second time at Hunts retreat outside Dallas.

Joan: Carlos Marcello was a Mob boss at the time. It seems unlikely that a boss would do a hit himself. But this is what Mac Wallace told you?

MacKenzie: As far as Marcello, the tomato salesman, goes, of course he was involved, but I don't think he'd dirty his hands on Kennedy anymore than he would have on anyone else. He was old, plump, big-mouthed and ran things; he sent killers out and got results, he did not pull triggers. Dave Ferry the same way. He was a mercenary who worked for Marcello and Banister but he was not a killer. He was a smart guy and was not the "nelly fag" he has been publicized as. He was into serious cancer research with medical professionals and one of the best pilots I ever rode with. Marcello used him for investigating and transferring orders. This stuff I know personally.

* * *

Thus ended my interview with Roderick A. MacKenzie, III, although I could have chatted with the man longer and probably will. I will end this fantastic tale, with his permission, of the list of the JFK assassination "killing teams" (from page 71 of *The Men That Don't Fit In*) as told to Roderick A. MacKenzie by Malcolm "Mac" Wallace in a drunken stupor following the assassination; take it or leave it, says MacKenzie:

- Command area, 2nd floor of the Texas School Book Depository (TSBD): Cliff Carter, Carlos Marcello, Jack Rubenstein, George Reese;
- In the alley behind the fence and above the so-called Grassy Knoll: Clyde Foust, John Ernst, Jack Grimm, Joseph P. Dugan;
- Under the bridge in case the president was not shot, and above the railroad area (these people were never used): Charles Harrelson, Percy Chauncy Holt, Charles Frederick Rogers, a man called "Dimitri" from ACCC;
- Roof of the County Records Building: Harry Weatherford, Roger Craig, Richard Scalzetti, Michael Victor Mertz;
- Sixth floor of the TSBD in the nest and other setup areas: Ruth Ann Martinez, Lee Harvey Oswald (under a spell according to Mac), Mac Wallace, Lawrence Loy Factor;
- The Dal-Tex Building (the team was supposed to be on top but had problems): Eugene Hale Brading, Frank Fiorelli (Sturgis), Raphael "Chi Chi" Quintero, Richard Cain.

As MacKenzie writes in *The Men That Don't Fit In*, "When I read the misinformation about what I saw as a simple killing of an important person, I wonder at the stupidity of the general public. Perhaps it's just that they don't really care. They are just too busy scratching out a living and so on to give a shit as to what their so-called leaders are doing. I would say that it's by design, and has been from as far back as history goes. But let's never say it's a conspiracy; despite the fact that whenever two or more people plan anything it is indeed a conspiracy. Being branded a conspiracy nut ain't all that bad. Perhaps it's paid off for me to have been looking over my shoulder all these years."

About the Interviewee

Roderick A. MacKenzie is seeking a publisher for his self-published book *The Men That Don't Fit In*. He may be contacted at: MAIL BOX 209, 819 North 49th Street North, Seattle, WA, 98103-6517. ConspiraZine is on KOWA at 106.5 FM in Olympia, WA on Wednesdays from 7-9pm (PST), or *kowalp.org*. ConspiraZine is also featured on Free Radio Olympia 98.5 FM, streamed online at *www.frolympia.org*. The interview with Roderick A. MacKenzie, III is archived at: *www.radio4all.net/index.php/program/33211*.

RE-ABS, Not MILABS

How the Reverse Engineering of ET Abductees Creates a Paradigm Shift

by Melinda Leslie

Twenty years ago I came to learn of my own experiences with extraterrestrial (ET) abduction. After only two years into my discovery process, I suddenly had a new form of encounter—one that included the involvement of military personnel in my abduction experiences. This new discovery led me to research the military or covert-ops involvement in other cases besides my own, and to learn that I was not alone. In fact, many ET abductees share a similar phenomenon of covert human involvement in their lives.

I have now conducted over fifty formal interviews with abductees who have had these covert-ops encounters and I'm familiar with at least another fifty more. Over the years, these experiences became the focus of my research, but my definition of them has changed as the research grew and changed. I have come to call these experiences the "reverse engineering" of ET abductees. But in order to really grasp the greater implications of reverse engineering, a further explanation is required; one in which the correlation between ET abduction, technology and UFO cover-ups is revealed.

MILABS: An Acronym is Born

In the UFO abduction and general ufology communities the term "MILAB" (or MILABS), short for "military abductions," refers to a military presence or government agency involvement in ET abduction experiences. This abbreviation was originally coined by Dr. Helmut Lammer in a 1996 paper he wrote entitled "Preliminary Findings of Project MILAB: Evidence for Military Kidnappings of Alleged UFO Abductees," and later became the title of Helmut and Marion Lammer's book, *MILABS: Military Mind Control and ET Abduction* (1999).

While credit is due to Dr. Lammer for coining the acronym, he was not the first to introduce the notion of a possible covert military and/or intelligence community (mil/intel) involvement in the abduction phenomenon. For many years, the subject was widely spoken and written about by abductees such as Kay Wilson (1993), Leah Haley (1993), Karla Turner (1994), Debbie Jordan (1994), Kim Carlsberg (1994), and even Whitley Strieber (1995), to name but a few. As far back as 1980, military involvement in ET abduction is mentioned in books such as *The Andreasson Affair Phase Two* by Ray Fowler, in which Mr. Fowler writes about Betty Andreasson's and Bob Lucca's accounts of black helicopter incidents in connection with their own ET abduction experiences, long before the use of the acronym that has come to define it.

In the time since its inception, MILABS has become a catch-all phrase used by researchers and abductees to reference many types of experiences: from the overt presence of uniformed military personnel in ET abduction scenarios, to a litany of government mind control activities; from government-sanctioned involvement in monitoring the lives of ET abductees, to military abductions that exclude extraterrestrials altogether. Thus, the term gets tossed about, creating confusion among those whose interpretations differ.

Due to this type of confusion I started to redefine my research, replacing the acronym with a sentence: "Covert intelligence and paramilitary re-abduction, harassment, and surveillance in extraterrestrial abduction experiences."

The Research

My research shows that the covert development of extraterrestrial technologies, in combination with the military, economic, and political gains that would be derived from such a pursuit, has resulted in making ET abductions a matter of national security. I feel it also provides immense insight into why an official disclosure of the UFO reality has not been forthcoming.

I contend it would be a complete "dereliction of duty" if the national security apparatus were not monitoring the abduction phenomenon, given the sheer number of people claiming to have experiences worldwide, the totality of evidence for ET abductions, the technology to be gained, and the implications of the covert nature of abduction experiences. I suggest this targeting, monitoring, and re-abduction of abductees by covert mil/intel agencies may provide the strongest evidence for the reality of UFO abduction experiences. There is an abundance of evidence for covert involvement, such as extensive corroborating experience testimony, multiple forms of physical evidence, eyewitness testimony, accounts of military and intelligence insiders, and many forms of documented surveillance.

The variety of experiences reported by the abductees may include any of the following types of activities:

- Black helicopter harassment
- Threats made to the abductee
- Phone interruptions and phone calls
- Email and/or snail mail tampering
- In person face-to-face confrontations
- Illegal break-ins to property
- Witnessing underground bases
- Abductions by ETs with human military personnel present
- Abductions by human military with ETs present
- Abductions by human military only without ETs present
- Mind control procedures
- In-depth interrogations
- Medical and genetic procedures
- Implants removed or inserted by humans
- Testing and development of psychic abilities
- Involvement of military or intelligence insiders in the personal life of the abductee

Included in my research is evidence that such agencies are involved predominantly for the purpose of acquiring ET technology and to reverse-engineer technologies that operate on paranormal functioning (psi). The development and control of these technologies would also explain the government's suppression of the UFO subject, its policy of non-disclosure, and along with it, the suppression of our dormant human potential—a potential where psi abilities are an everyday part of human experience.

Why a Name Change?

I began to notice a great amount of confusion about the term MILAB and the scenarios it has come to represent. The confusion seems to stem from some incorrect assumptions and over time I've come to learn of possible sources. I'll attempt to shed some light on these.

There are predominately three assumptions regarding MILABS and its meaning: The first is the idea that all abductions are actually perpetrated by the military and there are no actual ET experiences. The second is that all ET abductions are mind control experiments. The third is that all MILABS are false, perpetrated by ETs or ET-hybrids in uniforms, and don't involve any actual human personnel.

I find it interesting that these three ideas are derived from opposite ends of the spectrum; either there are no true ET abductions, or abductions by ETs occur strictly without military involvement. However, both of these assumptions exclude an abundance of information found in the research of MILAB cases. I'll address each idea and where it most likely originated.

Abductions by "Military Only"

The idea that there aren't any true ET abductions, only military ones, has been proposed by multiple individuals over the years. The most notable are Helmut and Marion Lammer, authors of *MILABS: Military Mind Control and ET Abduction* (1999), and Dr. Steven Greer, Director of the Disclosure Project and author of *Disclosure* (2001).

The Lammers entertained the idea that mind control procedures played such a large part in the MILAB scenario as to suggest that many experiences could be wholly due to it. Of course, I can't rule out that mind control may be the causal factor for some experiences, but it does not appear to be the sole reason for any of the cases in my research database. The Lammers demonstrated that mind control procedures are heavily involved in some experiences, and to a degree, I agree they are. For many years, I fought with the idea that mind control played a crucial role in these experiences, but have since realized that it is simply part-and-parcel of the MILAB scenario.

Mind control methods show up in the procedures used to control the abductee during a covert-ops experience, but more so in the procedures used to suppress the abductees' memory of the experience. At this point, I can definitively say that MILAB perpetrators have honed the combined use of intimidation, fear, drugs, and hypnosis down to a science. Yet, mind control falls far short of explaining all of the evidence and it does nothing to address the reasons for covert mil/intel interest in abductees.

After a closer read of the Lammers' book it becomes clear that they are only offering mind control as a possible explanation *along with that of ET causality*. They never attempt to explain all abduction as solely mind control, and note that MILAB experiences may be present only in some cases. In their defense, in Helmut's 1996 paper titled "Preliminary Findings of Project MILAB: Evidence for Military Kidnappings of Alleged UFO Abductees," he wrote:

> I think that abduction cases involving abductee reports of being abducted by the military as well as ET beings are very important for two reasons: 1) If the UFO community has evidence that a covert military intelligence task force is involved in the abduction phenomenon, we would know that this phenomenon represents a matter of national security. 2) The alleged military involvement ... could be evidence they use abductees for mind control experiments as test-targets for microwave weapons. Moreover, the military could be monitoring and even kidnapping abductees for information gathering purposes during and after a UFO abduction.

His statement here concurs with my research and clearly demonstrates that he does not believe that all abductions are performed only by the military.

Dr. Greer has implied on several occasions that because all abductions are "negative" (in his interpretation) they are caused only by the military and there are no ET abduction experiences. I've always generally been a supporter of Dr. Greer's disclosure efforts and feel he should be commended for those efforts, but in this case, I strongly disagree with his conclusions.

I feel that Dr. Greer's view should be taken with a giant grain of salt. I once spoke with him briefly about MILABS and he contended that the claim that abduction is only being performed by the military comes from the accounts of some yet-to-be disclosed "insiders" who spoke with him regarding their personal involvement in perpetrating false ET abduction scenarios.

In an interview by Randy Peyser in 1999, Greer said that these individuals claimed to be on "abduction squads" creating scenarios using "human-built UFOs and biological matter" used "to make it look like there are extraterrestrial events going on which are, in fact, 100 percent human in origin." He also said, "People who have had real ET encounters have subsequently been targeted for this kind of faux experience to confuse the database and put a spin of fear on the subject."

I cannot help but wonder if what were actually being disclosed to Dr. Greer were accounts of MILAB re-abductions, happening because the abductees were having very real ET experiences, and that his retelling of these accounts is greatly influenced by his personal views regarding his own ET contact experiences.

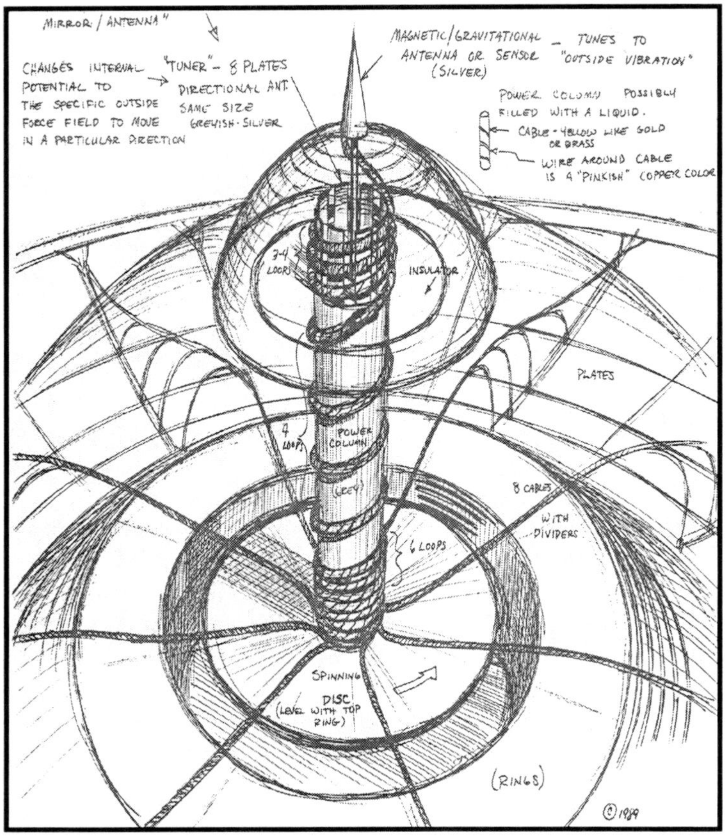

suspect the information provided might be more in line with the case evidence and not so supportive of Dr. Greer's limited view that there are "no bad ETs." Fellow MILAB researcher Joe Montaldo and I have both spoken with insiders who have claimed to be involved as perpetrators. So far those accounts have only supported MILAB abductees' accounts, and not one of these individuals has ever said they perpetrated a completely false ET abduction scenario.

ET Abductions, Government Mind Control

The idea that all abductions are mind control experiments can originally be attributed to a publication written by researcher Martin Cannon titled *The Controllers: A New Hypothesis of Alien Abduction* (1989), in which Mr. Cannon makes the argument that a government mind control program may account for some ET abductions. In a conversation I had with Mr. Cannon, he expressed anger and frustration that so many people in ufology had interpreted his paper as a claim that all ET abductions were mind control experiments, when in fact he only meant to suggest a possible explanation for *some* ET experiences. He actually thought many abductions probably were carried out by ETs and said his theory was just that; a theory. After our discussion, I asked him to provide me with a written statement clarifying this for the record, and he did. This document states clearly that he offered *The Controllers* only as a possible theory and that he always supported an alien hypothesis as well.

Dr. Greer has always related his personal contact experiences as having been only "positive" benign events, and has insisted that all "real" contact experiences are only "positive" and, therefore, any "negative" ones are not real. Thus, upon hearing these insiders' accounts of involvement, he may have heard what he wanted to hear; that is, experiences that did not conflict with his anti-abduction position. I believe he chooses to have a very one-sided view due to his own contact experiences and is conveniently able to explain away any he perceives as "negative," or as being military in origin, now that these insider folks have seemingly confirmed it for him.

When I spoke to Dr. Greer, I told him I would like to talk with his insider contacts and he vehemently refused. I wonder if given the chance to interview these individuals, I might discover their experiences are actually more consistent with what might be expected from a MILAB perpetrator. I

MILABS as Perpetrated by Hybrids

The idea that MILABS may be hybrid ETs in military uniform has been expressed by a handful of individuals, most notably Dr. David Jacobs. Dr. Jacobs is a friend of mine, and a few years back I spoke with him regarding this subject. What he generally believes was stated in his book *The Threat* (1998), wherein he says that abductees mistake human-like ET hybrids dressed in military uniform for military personnel, and these ETs bring abductees to abandoned military bases or unused areas of active bases where they examine and interrogate them. He feels there is no evidence that the military is involved in abductions.

There are a few problems with this view, the first being that in most abductee accounts, the military bases are anything but abandoned. Rather, there are many complex military activities going on. Also, how would hybrid ET beings have access to unused areas of active bases and why would they be interrogating abductees about their ET experiences? Last but not least, his view does nothing to explain all the harassment and surveillance evidence, or the presence of intelligence insiders interacting with abductees in their day-to-day lives.

I feel that Dr. Jacobs is misinterpreting some of the strongest evidence in support of his own theories. Certainly, if his theory regarding the ETs as a type of "threat" is correct, and if the number of abduction cases is anywhere near what researchers claim (the most conservative numbers indicate over 4 million abductees in the U.S. alone), wouldn't those who run the intelligence apparatus have figured this out too, and wouldn't they have had to make abductions a matter of national security? Additionally, wouldn't the intelligence apparatus, using one of its working arms such as the military, have an interest in studying such a "threat"?

If abductions are a question of national security, wouldn't abductees be a part of that question? How better to study the matter than to monitor, surveil, and interrogate those involved? If Dr. Jacobs is correct, then of course mil/intel communities are going to be interested in abductees. The evidence for MILABS actually validates his research and the ultimate reality of ET abductions overall.

Given all I've said here, it's easy to see why many abduction researchers and ufologists have a knee-jerk reaction when they hear the term MILAB. They assume the person using the acronym is claiming (1) there are no ET abductions, or (2) there is some outrageous mind control program manipulating hundreds of thousands of people into believing they are all ET abductees. Such views do not take into consideration ET abduction research data, and they ignore evidence accumulated over years of study by serious researchers, as well as the data found in MILAB accounts.

Given this insight, the view expressed in the following story is understandable. I occasionally attend abduction researcher and therapist, Yvonne Smith's, CERO (Close Encounter Resource Organization) support group. After a meeting I discussed my MILAB research with Yvonne. She stated that during public appearances and UFO conferences at which she speaks, she is often asked if she thinks all abductions are done by the military, and not ETs. The person will often use the term MILAB implying that it refers to a military cause for all abductions. This demonstrates a problem with the public's perception of the subject.

It is understandable that abduction researchers get upset when someone tries to convince them of a purely human, non-ET based explanation for abductees' experiences. This view negates years of research, overwhelming evidence, hard sought recognition, and an appreciation of abduction survivors, not to mention abduction research's hard-won respect in ufology—rather recently won and still tentative at best.

Not Military Directed

The reason for a name change is simply that the term MILAB places emphasis on a supposedly military-driven experience, which in turn causes so much derision and misunderstanding. The perception this term conjures falls short of describing all of what is going on, and also falls short of addressing why it might be going on. It is doubtful that the military is actually directing this program. It is more likely that a covert intelligence and ET information management group ("cabal") uses military personnel to conduct and carry out its operations. I would even guess that UFO crash retrievals aren't directed by the military, but performed by them. The term MILAB places an overemphasis on the military part of the equation and casts the military in a very negative light. They're probably not the ones giving the orders—the cabal is.

I want to be clear that my research data do *not* point to a military in-lieu-of ET abduction thesis, but quite the contrary; a military/intelligence community involvement *because* of ET experiences. It is because the ET experiences are absolutely real that these guys have an interest in abductees, and their interest is predominately in what the abductees know regarding ETs, their motives, and their technology. Therefore, a redefinition is needed.

I was happy with my first attempt ("covert intelligence and paramilitary re-abduction") until I was interviewed by radio host Tim Binnall on his internet show *Binnall of America.* As I was explaining a typical MILAB interrogation wherein the abductee is questioned about ET technology, Binnall said, "It's like they're reverse-engineering *via* the abductees," but I thought he said, "It's like they're reverse-engineering the abductees," and then realized that is precisely what is going on. He was right; they are reverse-engineering *via* the abductee. And I was right, they are reverse engineering the abductee.

RE-ABS: An Acronym is Reborn

I'm sure that many readers, upon seeing the title of this article, thought RE-ABS referred to "re-abductions." Well, you were half right. The obvious play on words is intentional. While it does mean re-abduction as in experiences where individuals are abducted by the military following an ET experience, or are taken again by ETs with military personnel present, it also means R.E.-ABS—as in reverse-engineering *from* abductees and/or reverse-engineered abductees.

Someone recently told me they were confused about what the term "reverse-engineering" (also referred to as "back-engineering") meant in terms of ufology. I started to realize that this widely used phrase may not be as well understood as I, or other researchers, often assume. So, for those of you who may need clarification, following are the Wikipedia and Wictionary definitions:

> *Reverse engineering* (RE) is the process of discovering the technological principles of a device, object or system through analysis of its structure, function and operation. It often involves taking something (e.g., a mechanical device, electronic component) apart and analyzing its workings in detail to try to make a new device that does the same thing without copying anything from the original. Reverse engineering has its origins in the analysis of hardware for commercial or military advantage. The purpose is to deduce design decisions from end products with little or no additional knowledge about the procedures involved in the original production.
>
> *Reverse-engineer.* To derive or duplicate the design, technical specifications, manufacturing methods, or functionality of an object by studying an existing product.

When UFO researchers use the above terms, they are generally referring to the concept that captured, crash-retrieved, shot down, given, or loaned ET technology is either taken apart or examined closely to determine how it works, in order to duplicate it, or to develop something in human technology that mimics it.

Crash Retrievals + Reverse Engineering + ET Abductions = RE-ABS: Formula for a New Paradigm

The above formula conceptualizes what my research indicates. I know that most folks would not see how such seemingly different ufology concepts could relate to one another. Yet, in my research the relationship is the key.

The targeting of abductees by covert agencies is the strongest evidence for the reality and importance of the ET abduction phenomenon. If there is no such thing as ET abduction, why would RE-AB related events be happening to people who have nothing in their lives to warrant any covert mil/intel interest other than that they claim to have experienced an ET abduction?

Harassment, surveillance, and re-abduction by these agencies suggest there must be something very important about us and our ET experiences. Why else would all this time, energy, and money be spent? To most readers, the concept of covert black budget programs existing within governmental systems is well understood. Many highly secret covert programs' financial accounting is buried in such "black budgets," seemingly overlooked by government. But make no mistake; the appropriation of monies within black budgets is still within someone's approval process. Somewhere in a chain of command the decision is being made to allocate money toward said "project." In all standard business practices, budget line items require justification.

So, given the extent of what must be involved in RE-ABS with operational task force teams—facilities in use, transportation logistics, data management, and military or intelligence personnel at every stage of the events—someone must be approving such an immense expenditure, right? My research into the experiences reported shows many common threads. One such thread is an interest in ET technology by these agencies. So, how do you justify the money that would have to be allocated for such experiences? The technology, that's how!

From UFO crash retrieval cases alone, we know the management cabal is obviously pursuing the technology. Thus, black budgets would be involved in running such operations. In his research of the subject, Ryan Wood, author of *Majic Eyes Only: Earth's Encounter with Extraterrestrial Technology* (2005), suggests there may be as many as 74 known incidents of UFO crash retrieval operations. Even if the actual number is less, obviously someone is justifying the expense for those operations. Again, the justification would be the pursuit of ET technology.

Aside from the retrieval of technology, the management cabal would also be interested in how the technology works. Now, combine that interest with the sheer number of ET abduction cases out there, and it stands to reason that the cabal would also be interested in whether or not these abductees know something, especially if those managing the ET issue are aware of the depth of abduction research and the number of individuals involved worldwide. It would be their job to know that two different Roper Polls have concluded that there are approximately four million ET abductees in the continental U.S. alone. It would be their job to know that approximately 40 abduction researchers have on the average between 500 and 1,500 documented cases each, and that ET abduction is a worldwide phenomenon. Of course, these numbers would be known to those whose job it is to know; i.e., the cabal managing ET information and technology.

No Dereliction of Duty

It would be a complete and total "dereliction of duty" for those who are managing the subject to not be involved in monitoring abductions and the abductees involved. Anything happening to that many people, especially something as covert in nature as ET abductions, would have to be a matter of national security. So, it should come as no surprise to anyone who seriously looks at the abduction subject—the numbers of cases, the nature of the scenarios in which ETs take people against their will—to hear that abductions have become a matter of national security, enough to warrant monitoring and surveillance of the participants and questioning of those involved.

To this, add the justification for a huge black budget expense, a rather convenient one consisting of military technology, and the only questions that should remain are: Why didn't the ufology community figure this out earlier? Why aren't there even more cases involved? An obvious reason that there aren't even more cases of RE-AB involvement is that the same budget that is justified to a great extent may also be limited to an equal extent. If you are an abductee with mil/intel involvement, they must really think you have information they want; after all, they're spending all that money on you. Congratulations, you are a black project!

From my research, there are four categories of information the covert-ops cabal wants from RE-AB experiences:

- ET motives and agenda
- ET and abductee genetics
- ET and abductee psi abilities
- ET technology and its operation

In the cabal's efforts to get their hands on ET technology, they gather and reverse-engineer craft, and just like they gather craft, they also gather and reverse-engineer abductees. It appears they are doing this for the exact same reasons: the development of advanced technologies, back-engineering of ET craft, information on the ETs themselves, and control over every aspect of these issues. I have deduced that their push for technology may exist for the following three reasons:

Militarism. The old military mindset may be at work here and would certainly apply if the mil/intel community thinks the ETs may be a threat. Whether preparing for a "hot war" or a "cold war" with ETs, it sure justifies a whole lot of black project spending. Even if they are only preparing for some possible future scenario, that could be justification enough for a military buildup in the form of ET-tech.

Politics. They may be attempting to level the playing field and hold their own with the ETs, or working towards eventually joining as an equal partner in a "galactic community."

Economy. The bottom line may be the bottom line. ET technology would be potentially lucrative in preparation for commerce and trade with ETs, as well as in the military-industrial complex's development and application for more mundane uses, let alone the economic potential from the advancement of military technology and any development of breakthrough ET-related technologies. Recently, I heard an insider say that "ET technology is an infinite source of wealth" for both the management cabal and their secret programs.

Reverse Engineering of ET Abductees

All of this begs the question: What specifically does the ET information management cabal want to reverse-engineer from the abductees? The following questions come directly from the abductees' accounts of what the interrogators asked during the re-abduction scenarios:

- What makes us an abductee and why are the ETs interested in us?
- What is it about our genetics that interests the ETs?
- What genetic changes or enhancements have been made to us?
- What do we know about an ET agenda?
- What mind control procedures can they learn, develop, or practice from/on us?
- What are our psi abilities and have they been enhanced? How do we do ET psi (i.e., telepathy and psychokenisis)?
- What are our mental abilities and have they been enhanced?
- What have the ETs told, shown, or taught us?
- What do we know about ET technology (i.e. propulsion or weapons)?
- How do abductees operate ET technology and can we operate a piece that a mil/intel person may hand to us?
- What types of training procedures can they develop from us?
- What medical info can they develop from us or practice on us?
- How do we process ET information and how do we adapt to the ETs or to living with ET experiences?
- What can they duplicate and apply to our technology or to our personnel?

These questions make logical sense when you follow a crash-retrieval and reverse engineering developmental curve. First, there were the retrieved ET craft, then there were the retrieved components from those craft, then there were the pilots and operators. These individuals would otherwise be known as the personnel. It is logical that when you develop the hardware, you're left with who will operate it and how they are going to do it. Logical, right?

Don't you think those involved with the management ever considered the personal accounts of those with hands-on ET tech experience? Those who may have operated it, worked its components, navigated, or flown it? Of course they would have. Let's suppose that crash retrievals are about acquiring ET technology and reverse engineering is about having human technology that does what ET technology does, or mimics it. Then reverse-engineering crashed, shot down, or retrieved alien craft is *not* about the cabal having ET hardware, but about having human technology that does what ET technology does.

Reverse engineering the abductee may also be about learning how to abduct people; hence all the practice and development of mind control procedures. Obviously, they're getting better at it, but this would more likely be secondary, a useful byproduct. Reverse engineering the abductee is more likely about having personnel that are able to do what abductees are able to do. Aside from having lots of hands-on ET tech experience, some abductees have also proved to be very resilient in dealing with the effects of interaction with ETs and adapting to their experiences.

In my research I've also come across the use of abductees in military and covert-ops training exercises. Not because they plan on using abductees in some future scenario, although they might be, but more likely to develop training procedures vis-à-vis the abductees. After all, it would be too big a risk to use abductees directly. We are too unreliable, prone to go public at any moment, too talkative, would insist on disclosure, and usually don't have the military, covert-ops, or intelligence training needed. Face it; we're just not "yes men!" But what we know can possibly be taught to these individuals, and it appears that this is what they might be trying to accomplish. To put it simply, if reverse-engineering the craft is about the technology, then reverse-engineering the abductee is about the personnel. Or, better yet, it's about the personnel and the technology. Because, when covert-ops interrogate and test abductees, they get both technical info and operational info.

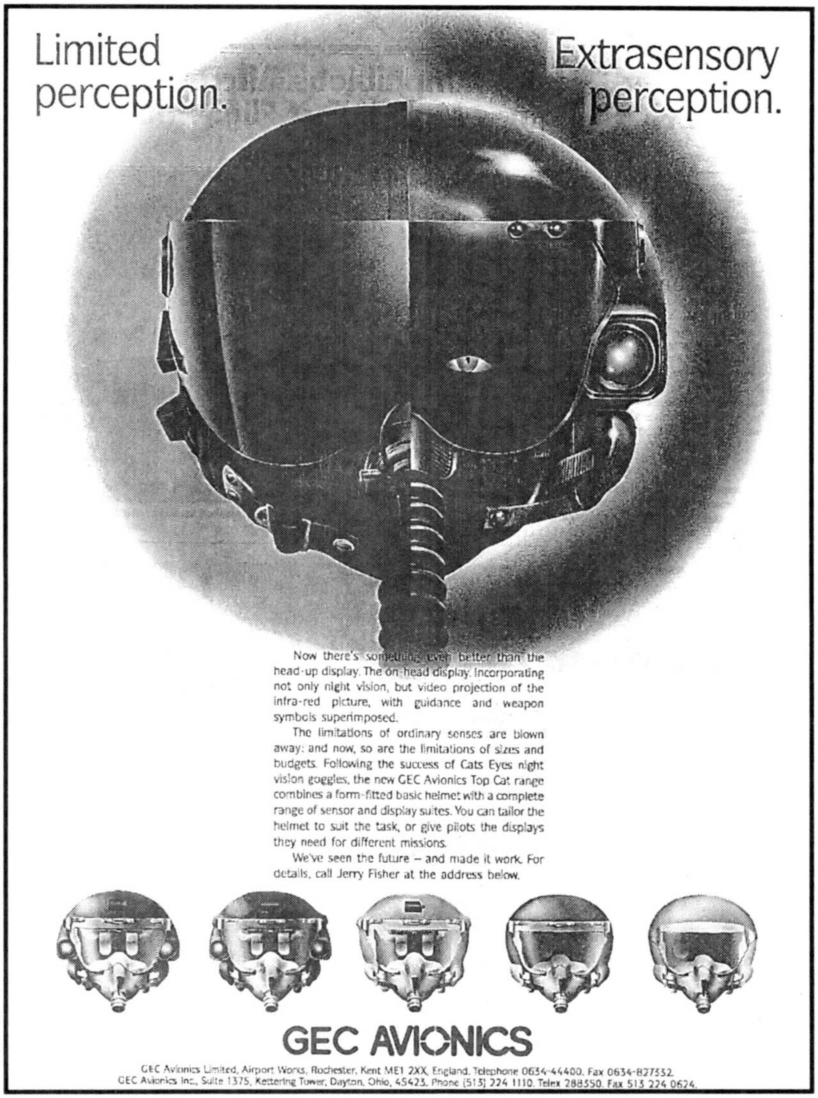

Another way to look at this is that you need a hybrid person to operate a hybrid technology. No wonder the covert-ops' also have an interest in abductee genetics. To be even more accurate, you need a hybrid functioning person to operate a hybrid functioning technology.

No RE-ABS, No Disclosure

This research ends up redefining the UFO cover-up and policy of non-disclosure as well as the abduction paradigm. There can't be a truthful official disclosure without addressing the abduction phenomenon. It is likely that ET abduction is one of the prime reasons why the policy of non-disclosure remains. If this is true, it helps one to understand why disclosure may not be forthcoming anytime soon. There certainly can't be ET disclosure without someone answering for the illegal and unconstitutional actions of those individuals involved in RE-AB scenarios.

I believe we may be able to learn a great deal about the cover-up by looking at the questions posed to RE-AB abductees by their human abductors, as outlined above. RE-AB abductees have witnessed things in their covert-ops experiences that indicate cabal involvement. Just as the cabal learns about ET tech and plans from the abductees, ufologists may be able to get a better idea of the cabal's plans by carefully examining these cases. Knowing the answers to these questions would go a long way in providing the ufology community with a roadmap for bringing about official disclosure. It is time for ufology to take the RE-AB evidence out of the closet. After all, it is some of the best evidence for the reality and importance of ET abductions.

Could it be that abductions are a central reason for the continuing existence of a non-disclosure policy? Perhaps abductions are the main reason the ETs are here and the ET information management cabal knows this; hence the reason why abductions became a matter of national security, or perhaps they always were. With RE-ABS research, ET abductions are no longer the bastard stepchild of the UFO research community, relegated to being unconnected, or at best marginally connected, to other areas of research.

Ufologists can no longer afford to separate crash retrievals, reverse engineering programs, technology development, the accounts of insiders, national security issues, UFO history, the cover-up, and disclosure efforts from the abduction phenomenon. To leave out any aspect of the UFO equation that may lead to a better understanding of a human cabal agenda, an ET agenda, or of a human-ET cabal agenda, is to have only an incomplete picture of the phenomenon. *RE-AB research builds the bridge for the inclusion of abduction in the disclosure discussion.* A partial disclosure is no disclosure at all. All you have then is a repackaged, new and improved cover-up.

Conclusion

I am not really trying to get anyone to replace one acronym with another. I may even continue to call the phenomenon "MILAB" out of sheer habit. The actual problem is not the name, but the paradigm.

I am asking that ufology expand its current paradigm to include a greater appreciation for the reality and significance of the abduction phenomenon as it relates to the overall UFO subject, and in particular, appreciation of the fact that abductees are being reverse-engineered by the military and/or intelligence ET management cabal to access many forms of ET information. Ufology must shift its paradigm to include the notion that abductees are being reverse-engineered because these experiences are an integral part of the picture, a *complete* ET presence *reality*, that abductees are reverse-engineered in experiences known as MILABS ... I mean ... RE-ABS.

About the Author

Melinda Leslie has been public with her own abduction experiences for over twenty years, has researched covert-ops involvement for eighteen years, and has interviewed over fifty abductees with this type of involvement. Melinda's research is featured in the new book, *Camouflage Through Limited Disclosure: Deconstructing a Cover-up of the Extraterrestrial Presence* by Randy Koppang. Melinda has lectured for numerous organizations and conferences, including MUFON, the X-Conference, the Bay Area UFO Expo, UFO Expo West, the International UFO Congress, the Whole Life Expo, and more. She has been a guest on numerous radio shows including *Coast-to-Coast AM*, and appeared on several television shows. For nine years Melinda was Director of a UFO lecture series hosting the most prominent names in ufology. Melinda's website is *www.alienexperiences.com/MelindaLeslie01*. Her email address is linnie@onebox.com.

Page 82: A technical rendering of the ET craft propulsion system based on RE-ABductee Melinda Leslie's drawing of how the craft operated. For more information please read interview with Melinda Leslie by Randy Koppang in PARANOIA, Issue 39.

The Gods of Eden

Al Hidell Interviews William Bramley (1994)

William Bramley is the author of *The Gods of Eden* (Avon), a work that has gained much deserved attention among UFO and conspiracy researchers. *The Gods of Eden* proposes that humankind's history of war and catastrophe is the result of a conspiracy carried out by branches of an ancient organization Bramley calls the Brotherhood of the Snake.

Al Hidell: You define the ultimate conspirators, those behind the Brotherhood, as a group called the Custodians. Could you tell me more about the Custodians?

William Bramley: I define the "Custodians" early in my book as "that specific extraterrestrial society (or succession of societies) which appears to have had ownership and custody of the Earth since prehistory." As many people are aware, there has been a consistent UFO phenomenon that is as old as recorded history. UFOs are a hidden common denominator that we have been missing in our search to understand human history.

Thousands of years ago, our ancestors claimed that Earth was owned by a humanlike extraterrestrial society. Read the ancient Mesopotamian texts and it jumps right out at you. Our ancestors also said that human beings had been created by that extraterrestrial race to serve as slaves. What many people don't realize is that this is Earth's first creation story—it was written and taught long before the Bible was written.

The idea has lingered. In 1919, after he spent years studying unusual phenomena, a man named Charles Fort wrote his conclusion that Earth is still the property of an extraterrestrial race, and that human beings still have the status of slaves or livestock in the greater scheme of things. I hypothesize the same thing.

When we look past the hype and at the actual UFO evidence from history, we discover that the behavior of the Custodians is filled with terrible violence and oppression against the human race. We also find a definite intention stated for the Custodial society to keep humanity in a condition of suffering, conflict, and fundamental ignorance. The vehicle for this appears to be a network of secret societies and associated radical religious/political factions which have arisen from an organization that existed thousands of years ago called by some people the "Brotherhood of the Snake." When you look carefully at history, you discover that these various societies and factions have been responsible for generating almost all significant strife throughout history, including today. They are also, in my opinion, responsible for generating tremendous ignorance about fundamental spiritual and scientific matters.

What it really boils down to is evidence that Earth is a textbook case of Machiavellian manipulation. Historical evidence follows the model of Machiavelli exactly. The surprise is that the source of the manipulation may not be a human source: it may be that missing link I mentioned that we have all been pooh-poohing and making fun of. It was all really a mind-blower to me. When I was a sociology major in college, I never dreamed that I would ever come up with an hypothesis like that.

Hidell: You believe the Custodians' goal to be the prevention of human unity and spiritual enlightenment. But I'm not clear as to their motivation. What interest or benefit are the Custodians (as opposed to the members of the Brotherhood) trying to maintain for themselves?

Bramley: The original motivation described in ancient texts was to maintain the human race as a slave race. The question is, why would the Custodians continue those activities when the human race is no longer being used for mining operations and other labors described in ancient creation stories?

Let me preface my answer by making an analogy. The type of research that I have done is very new and in its infancy. It is like an investigator who has just uncovered evidence of a crime, but he may not immediately understand the motive. When a homicide investigator first visits the scene of a murder, the evidence of a crime is clearly there, but it may not be immediately obvious what the motive was. I am in a similar situation. I have uncovered evidence of what appears to be an extraordinary ongoing crime. It is going to take more investigation to pinpoint what the precise ongoing motive might be. I can speculate, but that's all it is: speculation.

There are three possible ideas that people have suggested to me, and that I have considered. The first is simple force of habit. Just as the United Kingdom hangs on to some old colonies that no longer serve Britain's needs, so the Custodians may still be hanging on to Earth and managing it in the same way for no better reason than the Earth happens to belong to them, and it never occurred to them to give it up.

The second idea is reflected in old creation stories and religious teachings: people were thought of as spiritual beings which animated human bodies; it's the body-as-a-puppet-of-the-soul concept. In other words, a person's true personality resides in the soul, not the body. (We see evidence of this in near-death studies and in some of the more responsible reincarnation studies.) The Custodians reportedly understood this, and so they use Earth—which is a small planet and quite remote from everything—as a spiritual dumping ground to exile their undesirables, prisoners, etc.

The third idea may come from the UFO abduction evidence that we are seeing today. An awful lot of abductee's testimony suggests that UFO (i.e., Custodial) entities are making extensive and ongoing use of human subjects for biological engineering programs. It may be that the human race still serves as a valuable gene pool. The implication is that we still have the status of livestock or slaves, and so we are still being managed the same way.

The answer may also be a combination of all of the above. All I can say is that there is evidence that some things of a Machiavellian nature are definitely happening—and behind it all we bump into that curiosity known as the "UFO phenomenon"—but more investigation needs to be done to nail down the exact reason for why it may all be happening.

Hidell: How do you respond to people who say that conspiracy theories are too simplistic to explain a complex world?

Bramley: Conspiracy theories are much more complicated than the types of simplistic explanations that the majority of people accept. Most people believe in things happening sort of randomly or because of vague social forces that really don't make much sense when you truly analyze them down.

Another factor is that most people are basically decent themselves, and it is much more comforting for them to think that everyone else is that way except for a few isolated crooks, crazies and greedy people. Once you begin to face some of the credible conspiracy evidence, you have to begin to face the fact that there are some incredibly sleazy and ugly things going on that affect us all very deeply—things that are unthinkable to most of us, but which are perpetuated and turned a blind eye to by people to whom we have given over our trust. It is comforting to be naive; it is much more difficult to face unpleasant possibilities. Naiveté is a blessing, conspiracy research is not.

I think that many conspiracy researchers go through two phases: the initial phase is one of excitement. It is like playing detective or James Bond and uncovering exciting clues. The second phase is when it all sinks in: hey, this is all so extraordinarily ugly, and the people behind it are such unimaginable sleazy psychopaths that it just boggles the mind that such personalities can even exist—and a few of them even smile from our TVs and run for office! As a group, I believe that they are careening towards spiritual and personal oblivion, and dragging an awful lot of other people down with them.

Doing conspiracy research and having to look at what these people do becomes like diving into a cesspool of the foulest-smelling muck you can imagine. It is much easier on the psyche to say, "oh, well, that's just some lone psycho who shot that guy—gosh, what a shame—and those UFOs are such silly things, you know, and hey, it is all just some big cosmic accident that I am here anyway, so I'll just send $10.00 to the Sierra Club to do my socially-responsible thing, and tell jokes to make people laugh, and golly, I can't wait to try that new Wendy's hamburger." (Nothing against the Sierra Club, by the way. I wholeheartedly support them and encourage people to send them donations. My point is simply that we need to take more individual responsibility for the world in addition to making donations to worthy groups.)

I don't blame people for wanting to ignore or pooh-pooh conspiracy theories, but if evidence of conspiracy is there, it either has to be faced or we will remain victims. I don't think that people realize just how deeply they are affected, right into their daily lives by the widespread failure to confront and deal with the significant conspiracy evidence that exists.

There is one last point to be made about this, and that is that there is good conspiracy research and there is bad conspiracy research, just like there is good scholarship and there is bad scholarship in all fields of study. The problem with conspiracy research is that it does, by its very nature, deal with subjects that have large amounts of information hidden from view. There is a tendency to want to fill in the holes with theories, and many conspiracy researchers develop a world view early in the game that they later have trouble deviating from. Conspiracy researchers can sometimes be just as irrationally stubborn about their view of reality as debunkers can. This is not to fault such conspiracy researchers since all of us are human. Conspiracy researchers just need to be alert to not falling into the same traps and holding rigid world views in the same way as many debunkers.

Hidell: In your introduction, you say that you twice gave up on your research, but then decided to continue. Could you tell me more about what made you give up, and then what made you continue your effort?

Bramley: Regarding what made me give up, it's easy to recite the reasons: The research was extremely tough and leading into the most bizarre avenues of history that you could imagine. I initially had no intention of getting into the subject of UFOs or any spiritual questions since I did not originally perceive them as being relevant to the subject of human warfare. I was just expecting to do a comparative study on the role that outside political and monetary interests have played in warfare throughout history.

Secondly, the research was incredibly time-consuming and was robbing me of time and energy that would have been better devoted to a career. I am not a writer by profession. The only reason that I started the research was to address a problem that I was concerned about and that touched me as a human being. The trouble is, when someone takes that kind of responsibility, his or her life changes and can become much bumpier (mine certainly did). So, when the "big picture" began to emerge in my research, I was only too glad to say, "This is too strange and too exhausting. I quit. No one is going to read this anyway." I wound up throwing everything into a closet with the idea that I would never touch it again. This happened twice.

Why did I get back into it? I would see something on TV or accidentally stumble across something in a book or newspaper that completely "clicked" with my findings. It often aggravated me when this happened because it was as though fate would suddenly dangle a carrot in front of me just when I had happily put the project behind me. So, the book got completed by a series of jumpstarts.

Hidell: Most popular theories of "ancient astronauts" present the extraterrestrials as benevolent beings, helping mankind to improve their lives in some way. You might say they follow the Close Encounters model. Your theory suggests that the extraterrestrials are actually quite the opposite. Do the Custodians influence our popular culture for their own purposes?

Bramley: I have heard hypotheses of a possible Custodial (i.e., extraterrestrial) influence into our popular culture, but I did not research it specifically. One would need to trace pop culture (including the corporate side of it) in the same way as I did with political and religious groups to determine if there are similar links. There are many potentially interesting areas of research that I did not do.

Keep in mind, though, that a link is only significant if it actually influences something. Every person has many links to many things both past and present, but those links all have different degrees of influence on what we do. For example, I have a link right now to *PARANOIA* magazine by virtue of this interview, but that link is only relevant to understanding my actions to the degree that the link causes me to behave in a certain way. If the link does not affect my actions, then the link may be interesting as a bit of biographical trivia, but it is not terribly relevant to understanding me or what I do. The same holds true for every other person in this world and for groups.

I can make one general observation in response to your question. If you look at the testimony of many abductees and UFO contactees, as well as look at many ancient historical records, Custodial entities have been saying to abductees and contactees that Custodial entities are wonderful enlightened beings who have humanity's best interests at heart. These statements can then seep into our popular culture and be reflected in books and movies. However, just because someone says that they are wonderful, it does not necessarily mean that they are: one must look at their overall actions and weigh them. In light of other historical evidence surrounding UFOs, we need to consider the writings of Machiavelli who wrote that part of the formula for secretly keeping human factions at war with one another is to keep telling the people involved in the wars just how wonderful the secret perpetrator is.

To be honest with you, I too would like to think of UFO entities as benign enlightened beings who may be able to save humanity from its own foolishness—it is a comforting thought, and I can understand why it is popular. It is a lot like people believing in angels that watch over us. The grim evidence, though, suggests that the reality is quite different, and such evidence is not likely to be as popular since it does not perpetuate a "feel good" idea. On the other hand, facing up to unpleasant evidence is the first step towards dealing with the reality behind it, and once that reality is dealt with, then the world really can improve so that we can feel good on a much broader scale.

Hidell: What would you like your book to accomplish?

Bramley: A reader of my book said it to me really well, but I don't have his letter handy, so I am going to paraphrase from memory. He said that my book will have been worth it if it causes just one person to pick up a gun a little slower or if it causes someone to think again before firing up the ovens. If my book plays any kind of role, no matter how small, in bringing about a permanent resolution to the social insanity that plagues us here on Earth, then I will feel that it has accomplished its goal.

About the Interviewee

This interview with William Bramley first appeared in *PARANOIA*, Issue 6 (Fall 1994). *The Gods of Eden* was first published in 1989, and was republished as a mass-market paperback by Avon books in 1993. William Bramley was more recently interviewed by Linda Moulton Howe on Aug 22, 2008, which appears on YouTube.

The Great American Moon Hoax

Joan d'Arc Interviews Ralph René (1995)

René, author of *NASA Mooned America!*, believes that there have been no manned flights to the moon. In this exclusive interview, René asserts that the Apollo moon photos are studio creations. He also shows that NASA has lied about deadly solar radiation and the true temperature in space, and charges that NASA has instituted a policy of lying by its "astro-nots." So what did NASA really do with the money that went into its deep space pockets? Currently enjoying a wave of popularity in Russia, René believes the Apollo program helped to finance the CIA's secret war in Laos and Cambodia.

Joan: René, you claim that NASA faked the photos of Apollo moon landings, and in your book you analyze several of these photographs showing why they are hoaxes. Let's talk about the most famous official NASA photograph, from the cover of your book. The photo of Alan Bean entitled "Astronaut Collecting Lunar Samples, Apollo XII" was purportedly taken on the moon by Peter Conrad on October 20, 1969. At first glance it is an artistically contrived picture of an astronaut with the reflection of another astronaut, standing some distance away, reflected in his faceplate. Is it actually possible for astronauts to get this creative on the moon?

René: I think that the creative layout was the result of a composite picture from studio photos created by snip and paste in a photo lab.

Joan: So, in your estimation, what's wrong with this picture? [See Alan Bean photo on page 52]

René: The first thing I noticed about the photo was that the shadow side of Al Bean's suit was brightly lit. The top front of Bean's left shoulder and his whole left side is much too bright for the singularly directional sun light found in the vacuum of space.

The next thing is that the lower inside of his right arm should have been in a shadow. Then there is the fact that the Moon's actual horizon is on the same level as the horizon reflected in Bean's faceplate. Both faceplates are curved, and mirrored curves double the angle of incidence. Obviously since only two astro-nots were supposed to be on the Moon, this photo had to have been snapped by Peter Conrad. But when you take a magnifying glass to the original photo, Conrad's hand is nowhere near where the camera should be. In fact, Conrad has no camera, or if he has his hand obscured the lens. An X-ray camera perhaps!

Examination of Bean's shadow as shown in his faceplate shows that the two figures were less than 10 feet apart. Because of the faceplate's curvature, the camera that took the picture had to be at least 10 feet in the air directly between them. Since we don't see anything there, it had to have been either taken from a camera boom using a timer mechanism to trip the shutter, or there was another astro-not (stage hand) on that camera boom that we have never been told about.

We've all seen the TV travel adventures where a lone man pits his life against the wilderness and goes from hither to thither being photographed

from every angle by ... nobody! And if these explanations don't sit well, try this one. The Man in the Moon is very tall and happened to be passing, so he obligingly snapped the shot for the two tourists before he went on his way.

Another problem is found in the shiny object in Bean's hand. Again there is no shadow side even though his shadow (shown in his face plate) proves that the sun was behind him and off to his right. Since neither flash nor spotlight can compete with the light from the Sun the brightness is inexplicable.

Look at the bright circular object that is level with the top of his helmet and off to his far right side. Notice the two long structural-looking objects below it. It looks like a spotlight on scaffolding, doesn't it? Spotlights light best that which they are aimed at, hence the name. Check out Conrad (reflected in helmet)! Of all the places one can imagine, the Moon must be evenly lit because it lacks atmosphere, clouds and trees. Why should an extremely bright pool of light be centered on Conrad? Does the Sun play favorites on the Moon?

If you look at Conrad's feet you will notice the main shadow on his right going toward his rear and another one on his left coming forward. Two shadows, one Sun. Strange things were happening on the Moon.

Joan: Leading Russian space scientists have stated that they know of no way of protecting cosmonauts from deadly solar radiation beyond the Van Allen Belt. How does the Van Allen Belt protect earth from deadly space radiation?

René: In 1963, Bernard Lovell, the famous British astronomer, was allowed free access to the entire Russian space program. He was told by the leading Russian space scientists that they "could see no immediate way of protecting cosmonauts from the lethal effects of solar radiation." This is why I call most of the Apollo astronauts "Astro-nots."

The Russian space scientists made this statement to Bernard Lovell six years prior to the first Apollo landing. He dutifully reported it to NASA's chief administrator, Hugh Dryden, who just as dutifully...ignored it! The Van Allen Belt (Shield) is a natural magnetic field which diverts from the Earth much of the deadly radiation (X-rays and gamma) that the Sun routinely spits out during solar fires.

Joan: Is this why the USSR didn't bother to compete with America in its zeal to "walk on the moon?"

René: Not being a mind reader I have no idea why Russia (which lied about everything else) didn't also claim to have landed on the Moon. However, in the summer of 1972 (after the next to the last Apollo landing) the Russians were allowed to buy (at a low fixed price) one quarter of our entire year's grain crop. This raised our price over 60 percent. I believe that the deal still holds. Hey, a little blackmail never hurt a hungry nation.

Joan: How has the Van Allen Belt become one of NASA's best kept secrets?

René: It wasn't the Van Allen Belt that was played down. It was the fact that solar radiation is deadly.

Joan: How many chimpanzees have gone into orbit beyond the belt and what exactly was their fate?

René: NASA sent a number of space monkeys and apes beyond the shield but I have been singularly unsuccessful at finding any data on those shots. Rumor has it that once past the Van

Allen shield only cockroaches, which are able to withstand amazing amounts of rem (roentgen equivalent in man) were able to live past ten days.

Joan: How much shielding would be required for protection against this deadly radiation, and how much would such a vehicle weigh?

René: It took a couple of years to get the X-ray and proton solar data from NOAA [National Oceanic and Atmospheric Administration] and when the floppy came it carried a virus that wrote DOS into every one of my files that had the word NASA in it. When I finally found someone able to read the data we found that only particle energy is given. NOAA Imagineers pretend that there is no space radiation by giving only the data on the velocity of the particles. This man not only gave me the word Imagineers but also told me to ask NOAA "How many rem are there in a 20 ton meteorite moving at 20,000 mph or a car traveling at 120?

According to ex-NASA astrophysicist Bill Mauldin, six feet of water or the equivalent mass of another material is needed to protect life forms from an X-ray flare. Because these flares are always present there is no safe time to make the trip. In fact, the greatest series of flares ever recorded happened in 1972 near the low of that solar cycle. Not being a rocket scientist I cannot say how much weight a shield would add to a vessel. If I subtract the volumes of the command ship and the LEM [Lunar Landing Module] from respective spheres, each 12 feet greater in diameter, we are looking at a volume of water of about 500,000 pounds. When we add tanks and structure to support this, plus fuel and more tanks and structure to lift that fuel, we are probably looking at another 15 million pounds of mass. This would bring the total mass from 6.5 to 21 million pounds. It would also require another 13 engines for a total of 18.

Joan: What would be its chances of getting off the earth, landing on the moon, and again taking off from the moon?

René: The chance of lifting 20 million pounds using chemical fuel reaction motors ranges from none to absolutely zero.

Joan: In your book, you claim that with surface temperatures on the moon ranging from 243 degrees (F) above zero to 279 degrees below zero, tons of water would have been required to cool the space capsules in lunar orbit. Why would it have been impossible to adequately cool the capsules?

René: Lacking detailed information on the ship's structure and insulation, I can't calculate the amount of water that must be ejected into space to provide the explosive cooling that they use. It has to be considerable, though, even for the shuttle which spends half its time in orbit in the shadow of the Earth. In my book I do calculate it for the space suit, and in a half hour (even at 100% efficiency) they would have been out of water.

Joan: Oddly, Buzz Aldrin claimed they couldn't sleep because it was "too cold" in the lunar module and Cooper and Conrad, on Gemini 5, complained of shivering. Why does NASA want us to believe that space is cold?

René: NASA has always stressed the cooling systems as vital, even as the astro-nots (NASA) tell us how cold it was in the LEM on the Moon. I'm sure that this is because it is easier to heat than to chill. However, since the Moon's surface becomes so hot, a ship in space must be similarly heated.

Joan: Why do you believe this is a deliberate hoax, and that space is actually hot?

René: Space is neither cold nor hot because space contains almost zero matter and heat is a property of matter. It is the Sun that is hot and the continuous passing of infrared, ultra violet and light through space all create heat when they hit matter. This is the problem.

Joan: Why did NASA claim to need a Moon Rover on each of the last four trips to the moon?

René: The Rovers were supposed to increase the area that the astro-nots could cover.

Joan: How much did each vehicle weigh?

René: The Rovers were supposed to weigh 460 pounds each. However, I am suspicious that here the battery was not included.

Joan: How would such vehicles have been stored and carried aboard the LEM?

René: They were allegedly carried on the outside of the LEM. This made the load extremely eccentric to the LEM's center of gravity. In real life, as opposed to NASA fantasy, cargo planes and ships have loading officers to see that the load is distributed as evenly as possible. Had that mass been added to the LEM, which had a single central reaction engine, it would have [caused the LEM to] pinwheel when the engine fired and the only thing that would have stopped the rotation was the final crash onto the Moon's surface. The tiny thrusters the LEM carried would have been useless to compensate for this out-of-balance load.

Joan: Since that time, what scientific analysis has been made of the 840 pounds of moon rocks and soil purportedly collected by the Roving Moon Rover?

René: The only thing I know about the "Moon Rocks" is that they are supposed to be made out of the same materials as Earth rocks.

Joan: You allege that there has never been anything unique reported about the so-called "lunar samples." Where do you think NASA really obtained the "Moon Rocks"?

René: In 1957 a great number of meteorites were gleaned from the Antarctic ice. Later the Moon Rocks would be found to be so similar that the NASA Imagineers concluded that they were knocked off the moon by meteorites that hit the moon. How do we know? Because NASA says it's so! Here on Earth with the science of guns over 500 years old we still cannot fire a shell with a velocity of over 4,200 feet per second. To escape the Moon requires a velocity of 7,785 feet per second. Guns have long tight barrels, oblong shells, rifling and intensely strong breeches to confine the hot gasses and direct all of their pressure to propulsion of the projectile. An explosive force such as a meteor strike creates hot gasses that radiate in all directions and diminish as to the square of the distance.

How do we know? Because NASA say it's so! Meteorites are either metallic or stony. Some of the stony ones are called Carbonaceous Chondrites because of the large carbon inclusions they contain. But these same Imagineers never tell us that this proves there is life in the universe. God! I love the word Imagineers almost as much as I do the word Psychobabblers.

Joan: You claim that Apollo astro-nots never speak about the brilliance of the stars and planets in deep space, yet other astronauts who have gone into space have commented on it. Why do none of these celestial bodies ever show up in pictures of moon landings?

René: NASA apologists claim that the camera aperture is never opened wide enough nor the time set long enough to film the stars and planets.

Joan: So, since NASA was not able at the time to accurately simulate a starry background, has it told astro-nots to report stars as "dim and fuzzy"?

René: NASA has never allowed the astro-nots to call attention to the fact that the stars in space must be brilliant. The pilots of the original rocket planes reported seeing the stars in the daylight. The Russian Gagarin (first man in space) reported them to be "Astonishingly brilliant." Since neither the Apollo astro-nots nor the shuttle crew ever report about the stars and planets, I believe that NASA's standing orders are to evade all discussion and refer to them as dim and fuzzy.

The Apollo missions happened before the age of computer enhancement and at the time it would have been impossible to fake the star fields onto photos taken in a studio. Millions of star buffs worldwide would have instantly detected the hoax. When they "take" us to Mars in a couple of years, we will not be able to dissect the new pictures because of computer graphics. They will be able to tell any lie they wish and we will believe.

Joan: How does NASA control the astro-nots' disclosure of the space hoax?

René: I believe that the early astronauts (most of whom were genuine heroes) were slowly dragged into the mud by small lies and sexual indiscretions. Then via direct threats to either their fellow astronauts and possibly even their families, they were turned into astro-nots! I do not even rule out drugs or hypnosis...

Joan: Since the Apollo space capsules did not have the necessary two meters of shielding mass for protection against space radiation, you believe that most of the Apollo astro-nots would be dying of cancers and blood disorders if they had really gone to the moon. Why have American astro-nots not suffered ill effects from space radiation?

René: Consider the fact that the Concord jet will change its polar route course and drop altitude if it detects 10 millirem of radiation. I believe I got more radiation from my CRT while writing *Nasa Mooned America!* than they ever did because it is hard to get severely radiated without actually penetrating the Van Allen shield.

Joan: How did NASA solve the problem that the Russians were unable to solve?

René: The old saying "if you can't make it—fake it" was applied and the problem was "solved."

Joan: You state that you cannot find a picture of a "space-walking astro-not" demonstrating the ballooning effect of a pressurized suit, but rather all of the pictures show wrinkles in the suits. What's wrong with that picture?

René: To maintain the ability to breathe and move about we need a minimum pressure of over 5 psi (pounds per square inch) even when on pure oxygen. A boxer's punching bag has a warning label on it to limit pressure to 4 psi. Ever try to bend a speed bag? A young man's erection (referred to as a diamond cutter) is sustained with about 2 psi of blood. Need I say more?

I made a vacuum chamber that holds a glove whose skin is just strong enough to take 5.2 psi of pressure. When the glove is tested it balloons so badly that it inhibits most hand and wrist functions. No matter what you add to any material it gets stiffer. No matter how much money you have to spend, it will not change that fact.

In addition, I recently detached the space glove and inserted my bare arm into the vacuum chamber. I threw the switch and the pump began to extract the air. By the time it reached 3 psi my arm had been sucked into the metal sleeve a few more inches. It got to be 4 psi and my hand felt very bloated and started to feel "pins and needles." Then I became light headed. I flipped the switch and, since I always maintain a bypass valve slightly open to the air, I knew that the vacuum would zero out in less than 10 seconds.

What I had forgotten is that time is relative. When there is no trouble a second goes by in the blink of an eye. When you are in trouble a second can seem like an hour. It is possible that the normal pressure on the rest of me caused that feeling, but I don't know. I do know that NASA is supposed to have made similar tests over thirty years ago. If I am so wrong they can prove it real quick. Just suit up a man and blow the suit pressure up to 19.9 psi during a big TV show. Then let him prance around like they did on the Moon for the duration of the show. But I want to use my own brand new gauges to be sure that they aren't using a half pound of pressure.

Examine the Collins photos, one taken in an airplane and the other allegedly taken in space and see if you can find any ballooning.

Joan: On the subject of aliens, you state that the "new wave of NASA apologists," mainly generated since the first draft of your book, claim that "we went to the moon as hitchhikers using either ships or technology provided by aliens." What is your feeling about the belief that "somebody else is on the moon" and that is why we were not allowed to land there?

René: The Winter 1995 edition of *PARANOIA* carried an article entitled "The Dark Side of the Moon" by Scott Corrales. The theme was that strange things were happening on the Moon. And these, the author reported, were believe to be caused by ETs. Although I believe that our infinite universe must have other intelligences, I do not believe the recent conjecture that aliens are in charge, have been captured, or are cooperating with us. I think these stories are all government-based New World Order propaganda. I expect any day now to be told we must give up our guns, our property, our children and our sovereignty or else the aliens will get mad.

NASA apologists then claim that spacesuits are radiation shields. If this were true, then they would have sent men into the partially melted down Three Mile Island reactor to remove all the fuel rods. To the best of my knowledge, fuel rods become ever more radioactive through use. The term "spent" fuel rods is a deliberate government misnomer. Because of the speed of fission, controlling atomic reactors is always a hairy job. With ever more reactive material in the pit, the atomic beast must become increasingly unstable.

Furthermore, if "beams of light" from moving vehicles on the moon can be seen by astronomers, as the *PARANOIA* article claims, why didn't NASA include a few magnesium flares in the six missions that allegedly landed men on the Moon? The whole world would have held its breath each mission just before they lit the flares. Why weren't the exhaust gasses of the LEM's landing and take-off visible? That much burning fuel must have generated an incredible splash of light.

As far as there being gigantic shadows from immense spires, the Empire State Building is pretty tall and it doesn't cast a shadow across the Hudson River first thing each morning. Airliners are also pretty big and they go over the New York area continuously and once they are 1,000 feet in the air they have no more pronounced shadow. And during an eclipse, the Moon doesn't cast night upon us. Dusk, yes, Night, no.

I believe that the same forces that faked the landing are now about to finish the destruction of both Christianity and our country by "proving" that powerful aliens are demanding both our weapons and our last bits of national sovereignty.

If we ever, in any way, landed men on the Moon, why would NASA have to fake the photos? I can understand them faking the equipment and the capsules, but why did they fake the landscape? Why didn't they take real pictures? And even then, how did the astro-nots live after hours of exposure under the naked sun? Please bear in mind that all Moon photos originate with NASA. When do you trust a known liar? I don't believe there is anything on the Moon. Why are all the alleged remains on the backside that we can never see with our telescopes? Were those ancient alien builders (or modern ones) so afraid of us that they hid their works?

Joan: Do you believe the three Sky Lab missions were at least partially faked, as were the Apollo missions?

René: The Skylab rescue had to have been faked. The Sun heated the ship hot enough to disassociate the plastics, which stopped NASA from pressurizing the ship to prevent an oxygen fire from breaking out. It had been supplied on launch with food which would have been destroyed from such heat. Set your oven at 175 and put a bag of flour in there and see if it remains usable.

Joan: What are the reasons for hoaxing the American public, and the world?

René: There are many possible reasons for the lie. American revolution was in the air because of Vietnam and we needed to be distracted from the CIA drug war.

Joan: Was the Apollo program a way to preoccupy us during the war?

René: Yes, but the Apollo program also helped to cover up and finance the CIA's secret war in Laos and Cambodia. It also demonstrated how gullible we were when they waved the flag, and this show of patriotism probably set back the timetable for our destruction by a few years.

Joan: The NASA moon hoax swindled an incredible amount of money from the American taxpayers over the course of many years. What happened to all of this money? Did it go to the Black Budget?

René: I can answer this in another way. In May 1994, Congress reduced NASA's budget to its 1961 level. This information made headlines. I celebrated because from the very first printing of my book whenever I heard of a Congressman or national political leader who was the least bit rebellious I sent them a free copy. Every copy was accompanied by a prepaid and addressed postcard to enable them to verify receipt. During the past three years I sent out almost thirty books but only David Duke acknowledged receipt.

Suppose you were working for nickels and dimes back in 1961 and then you began to rake in the money hand over fist. However, your employer stipulated that you couldn't keep any of it year to year. When he fired you, how long would it be before you had to let the servants go and sell the Rolls? What about the big parties you used to throw? Could you still afford them?

Even before I knew the truth about the Federal Reserve I had always suspected that they bypassed Congress and directly funded the CIA. Well, by the end of the summer, when NASA's lifestyle changed not a bit, I finally knew the truth. The private corporations known as the FED do anything they damn well please. The only thing this dispensation costs them is that these funds do not show up on the federal debt tab. Big Deal!

Joan: Has NASA now found a way to get a ship into deep space with the necessary two meters of radiation shielding?

René: Not only couldn't it be done with the technology available in the late 1960s, it can't be done even today. The greatest reason is that men cannot survive a trip past the Van Allen Shield to the Moon without six feet (two meters) of radiation shielding. The shield must completely surround the crew to block the powerful x-rays and protons emitted from solar flares. According to NASA, we were barely able to send a ship that was 13 feet in diameter with a paper thin hull, let alone the 30 ft. diameter required if the shielding is added. For shielding we can either use a layer of thin lead or 6 feet of water. It is equivalent mass that counts more than the material that is used. Where would we get the engines necessary to lift this mass from the Earth, then lower it onto the Moon's surface and then take it home again?

The original Apollo ships purportedly lifted a mass equal to that of a destroyer (6,400,000 pounds) because of the fuel needed to land the tiny LEM on the Moon and lift the top half of it off again. However, since this much shielding would be required on both the orbiting command capsule and the LEM, there would be no great fuel saving in having two separate craft. Then, even though the Moon has only one-sixth the gravity [of the Earth], it would still require a vehicle at least one third as big as the original to lift it from the Moon and back to Earth. That's two million pounds!

Joan: Do you believe that any future space rides by NASA would constitute further swindling of American taxpayers?

René: It took 6.5 million pounds of vessel to launch about 75 tons (150,000 pounds) of command capsule and LEM. This ratio is about 43 to 1. To launch the new 2 million pound vessel that weighs about 43,000 tons (86 million pounds). This is 14 times larger than the monsters that we saw launched all those years ago. Until and unless we develop anti-gravity or unlock a new power source that we don't even know about today, the simple ejection of mass (hot gasses) to drive ever larger space ships on ever longer trips will not happen except in NASA's computer graphics department.

Joan: Will NASA continue to "moon" America until we wake up and smell the hoax?

René: A while ago NASA released word that they had found possible ancient life forms in a rock from Mars. The NASA Imagineers claim that this rock was blown off of Mars 16 million years ago by an asteroid collision. It is further claimed that after 16,870,000 years (13,000 years ago) it plunked down in Antarctica. Since it must have been red hot and traveling like hell when it hit, it must have buried itself deeply in the ice.

Add to that the known fact that about two feet of ice a year accumulates there. If it doesn't, then how did a light density object like an airplane come to be buried under thirty feet of ice after being parked there for fifteen years. Let's see, 13,000 years x 2 feet per year equals ... really deep. In fact, deeper than the deepest ice known. How do they know that it wasn't a piece of the asteroid instead of a piece of Mars? Don't these same Imagineers claim that gravity breaks up meteors as they approach a planet? Wouldn't a glancing approach leave some pieces of a meteor traveling even faster from NASA's famed slingshot effect?

For it to have finally hit Earth it must have had an unstable orbit. In this whirling solar system, before you can tell where it came from you must know orbit, trajectory, direction, velocity, date and time! Did they ask that dumb chunk of rock its personal history? I am unaware that we ever lifted anything from Mars let alone another piece of rock. That kind of an accomplishment would have been loudly touted. Therefore, how do they know this rock is Martian? In their dreams!

About the Interviewee

This interview first appeared in *PARANOIA*, Issue 15 (1996). Mr. René passed away in December 2008. He was the author of the self-published work, *NASA Mooned America*. Please read the interview with Jarrah White in this volume for more information about the work of Ralph René, *www.ralphrene.com*. Contact srorke@mchsi.com for all purchases. Also search YouTube for "Ralph René: Back In Print."

True History of Man in Space

Can Lucian's *True History* Explain Legends of Missing Warriors?

by Steve Ahlquist

> *"... for this one thing I confidently pronounce for a truth, that I lie... for I write of matters which I neither saw nor suffered... Let no man therefore in any case give any credit to them."*
>
> – Lucian, *True History*, translated from the Greek by Francis Hicks (1902)

The history of mankind has been one of continual warfare. As a species we have mastered many arts, magics and sciences, and turned them all towards the destruction of each other. We are so warlike that many authors have imagined that the purpose of the world is to breed warriors like ourselves. Perhaps powerful aliens with great minds but puny stature occasionally harvest our greatest warriors to fight distant wars on strange planets and in other dimensions.

It would certainly explain the disappearance of soldiers and battalions gone missing in action. These men and women might vanish from the killing fields of Earth only to reappear on board a starship or in the trenches of some alien world, armed with unthinkably advanced weaponry. According to this concept, throughout the galaxies the race of man is feared as the fiercest, most powerful warrior, the perfect mix of strength and mind, and adaptable to any circumstance.

Sometimes whole crops of warriors may be harvested. Consider the disappearance of the Amazons, warrior women lost to history. Consider Atlantis, or the mound builders of ancient North America. Did mankind truly exterminate the Neanderthals, or have our human-like cousins simply been harvested and shipped off to war in some hellish conflict?

If a soldier taken from Earth were to survive his distant service, how could he hope to be treated by his alien masters? Would they return him to Earth, where he would live out his days being considered a man driven insane by his experiences in war? Today we would say such a person has post-traumatic stress syndrome, and discount his story. Perhaps the soldier would be disposed of in the same way we might ship a race horse past its prime to a glue factory.

Is it possible that a soldier, or a group of them, might return to Earth either through escape or through the benevolence of their captors? Perhaps a clever human could master enough of the alien science and technology to return to Earth. Weapons do have a tendency to be turned against those who wield them. Humanity, armed with advanced weaponry far away on a distant world, might be more than our creators could handle.

This brings us to Lucian's *True History*, the oldest surviving account of a man voyaging to the moon. As the opening quote amply demonstrates, Lucian prefaced his work with his admonition that nothing he writes should be taken the least bit credulously. In fact, the quote is only a tiny sampling of his pages of denials as to the veracity of his tales, but are denials enough to completely dismiss his assertions? As Shakespeare might say, he "doth protest too much."

We might be inclined to believe Lucian, and take him as the liar he claims to be, but there are details in his history, details that would make no sense to his contemporaries and translators until relatively recently. Before we get too deeply into that, however, let's give some background on Lucian and his *True History*.

Lucian lived from approximately 125 AD to 180 AD. He was an Assyrian Greek who has had over eighty works ascribed to him, but most modern experts agree he did not write all of them. He worked as a rhetorician, which is sort of like our modern lawyer, and traveled widely, collecting considerable fame and wealth as a storyteller. He was a self-described "barbarian."

True History, admits the author in his roundabout style, was written as a travelogue to parody the stories of Homer and Herodotus. He wanted to pile one outlandish tale upon another, adding as much exaggeration as possible. Modern commentators, taken with its story of space travel and interstellar war, are sometimes interested in approaching the story as proto-science fiction.

The story starts with Lucian having outfitted a ship with fifty crew and setting out past the Straits of Gibraltar and into the Atlantic Ocean. After many days of travel the boat arrives at an island where they find a tablet written in Greek that says, "Thus far traveled Hercules and Bacchus." On this island Lucian discovers rivers of wine and seductive tree women. Two of his crew attempt to copulate with these nymphs, but unfortunately, "were knit fast together at their nether parts, from whence they grew together and took root together."

This part of the story is no more or less strange than anything in Homer's *Odyssey*. It is because of the many fantastic elements present in the works of Homer that it was so long viewed as mythology. It was only when the *Iliad* was viewed as history by Heinrich Schliemann that the ancient city of Troy was rediscovered and the works of Homer were verified as historical. The works of Herodotus, the so-called "father of history," are filled with similarly weird events; yet, vast parts of Herodotus have been verified as factual. Lucian's description of an island inhabited by strange creatures should in no way be taken as an indication that the whole of the work is untrue.

Leaving the island and two of his crew behind, Lucian re-provisioned his ship and set off once again toward lands unknown. "...but about noon, when we had lost sight of the island, upon a sudden a whirlwind caught us, which turned our ship round about, and lifted us up some three thousand furlongs (375 miles) into the air..." Lucian and his crew became suspended, their sails filled with air, and they sailed for seven days and nights.

Notwithstanding the similarities between Lucian's means of travel and that of Dorothy's from *The Wizard of Oz*, the description of a whirlwind that transports someone through space bears some resemblance to the modern physics concept of the wormhole. According to Wikipedia;

> "In physics, a wormhole is a hypothetical topological feature of spacetime that is fundamentally a 'shortcut' through space and time. Spacetime can be viewed as a 2D surface, and when 'folded' over, a wormhole bridge can be formed. A wormhole has at least two mouths that are connected to a single throat or tube. If the wormhole is traversable, matter can 'travel' from one mouth to the other by passing through the throat."

Theoretically, a wormhole could be created by a very advanced race of aliens, and it may be the only possible means by which to travel the vast distances of space in anything like a human lifetime. Wormholes can connect distant points in space, bridge one universe to another, or even allow for the possibility of time travel. Were a boatload of Greek explorers suddenly swept up into a "whirlwind," suspended in the air, and then transported interstellar distances from the Earth, they might be forgiven for not realizing that they had actually crossed an Einstein-Rosen Bridge.

The detail of the sails being suddenly filled with air is also telling. From our position here in Lucian's distant future, we know that there is no air in space, and that all sailors aboard the wooden Greek sailing ship would have instantly perished in the extremes of space. But the sails filling with

Illustration by Lee Harvey Roswell, *www.leeharveyroswell com*

air indicates that whatever alien race snatched our Greek sailors also supplied them with air (and presumably warmth) for their journey. According to Lucian, "...on the eighth day we came in view of a great island, of a round proportion, gloriously glittering with light, and approaching to it, we there arrived, and took land."

Once landed, our travelers found the land to be inhabited. When night came, Lucian could see other "islands," one of which he took to be the Earth due to his ability to see the cities and seas. Of course, we know this to be impossible. The only manmade structure visible from near Earth orbit would have been the Great Wall of China, a structure with which Lucian would not have been familiar. Also, after seven days' travel through a wormhole, the crew could be thousands of light-years from near-Earth orbit.

It is much more likely that Lucian and his crew were brought aboard a large spaceship or star-ship. From here they could observe moons, stars and planets, and in their naïveté come to believe that one of the planets spied was the Earth. Here the band of Greeks meet their first aliens, the Hippogypians, men riding on three-headed "horse-vultures." These horse-vultures are described as gigantic, with every feather longer than the mast of a ship. This kind of exaggeration is typical of Lucian. He describes men riding mounts similar in size and form to King Ghidorah, enemy of Godzilla. The actual creatures would have been slightly larger than horses, at best.

The Hippogypians bring Lucian and his men to a human of Greek descent named Endymion, who describes himself as the "King of the Moon." Here Lucian writes, "...rapt up long since from the Earth as he was asleep, and brought hither, where he was made king of the country..." The use of the word "rapt" is interesting. One definition is "to be carried off spiritually to another place, sphere of existence, etc." Here we learn of a human who falls asleep one night and is transported to another world. This corresponds nicely with modern UFO abductions. The fact that Endymion was made a "king" more likely indicates that he has been put in charge of the war to come. It seems that the beings responsible for harvesting warriors from Earth might have little capacity for war: They perhaps need the warrior mind of a human to guide their battles.

Lucian begins to explain that he and his crew have been brought to the moon, which is at war with the Sun, also populated and led by a king named Phaethon. This is by our knowledge today plainly impossible, but looked at from Lucian's point of view, he is describing to an audience in 160 AD an interstellar war. He has carefully introduced the concept that the planets above us are like islands, inhabited by strange beings.

In the days before Copernicus, the Earth was still at the center of the world. The audience of the time would not have understood Lucian unless he phrased his celestial adventures as taking place within the architecture of heavens as understood at that time. So instead of some distant alien planet being at war with another, the armies of the moon are at war with the armies of the Sun.

The cause of the war is one we have seen time and again in our own history. The people of the "moon" attempted to colonize another planet (a planet Lucian refers to as the morning star, what we would call Venus, but of course we can read this as a distant world). Phaethon's armies prevented this colonization with a mind to colonize the world himself. Lucian and his band of Greeks are invited to participate in the coming battle.

After a great feast and a night's rest, Lucian and his men are each given Hippogypian mounts. Lucian describes the army amassed as numbering about 100,000 troops. In addition to the mighty three-headed horse-vultures, the army consists of many other fantastic alien beings. There are "mighty great fowl" with leaves instead of feathers, called Lachanopters. There are the Cenchrobolians and Scorodomachians, which Lucian declines to describe.

Allies called Psyllotoxotans arrive from the "Bear Star"[1] riding great flea-like insects as large as ten elephants. The Anemodromians are the army's footmen, with special adaptations in their legs that allow them to fly. Additional allies are expected, but Lucian describes them by name only: Struthobalanians (ostrich-acorns) and Hippogeranians (crane-cavalry). Finally, mighty spiders are employed to spin vast webs through space in order to constrain and ensnare the enemy.

Another way of viewing this monstrous army is as different types of spaceships. The various ships could be described as being like insects, birds of prey, or even one-man battle suits. The spiders might be specialized ships built to dispense "webs of energy." Lucian and his crew of Greek warriors would find that these ships have advanced computers on board that merge with the nervous systems of the pilots. No training would be needed; the ships are designed to work seamlessly with humans.

Arrayed against Endymion and his Greek allies (or conscripts) are the armies of Phaethon, every bit as fantastic. In addition to his armies, Phaethon has allies from Sirius[2] and "the Milky Way." Lucian says that when the armies of the Milky Way failed him, Phaethon "in displeasure over-ran their country."

The battle is as grand as one might expect, and things go well initially for Endymion and Lucian. But the war is lost upon the arrival of Phaethon's allies, the Nephelocentaurs, gigantic flying beings, half-man and half-horse, each as large as the Colossus of Rhodes. They are led, says Lucian, by Sagittarius himself. The war lost, Lucian and two of his men are taken captive. Phaethon orders the construction of a gigantic wall that blocks Endymion's planet from the rays of his Sun. Defeated, Endymion sues for peace, and Lucian is returned to his men.

The war over, Lucian declines the offer to stay forever in the Kingdom of Endymion and re-provisions his ship for a return home. Once the ship returns to Earth it is promptly swallowed by a gigantic whale. Once again I invite you to rethink the traditional reading. The adventures that ensue are so outlandish, and so unlikely to have occurred on Earth, that it becomes obvious that these are adventures occurring in the deep reaches of outer space.

Literal reading of ancient manuscripts flies in the face of conventional literary analysis, with its emphasis on metaphor and meaning. However, if the locusts of the Bible's Revelations can now be seen as black helicopters, and the fires of Sodom and Gomorrah as nuclear holocausts, is it necessarily wrong to interpret the fantastic creatures of Lucian's interstellar war as spaceships?

Perhaps one day a future astronaut will utilize Lucian's *True History* in the same way Heinrich Schliemann used Homer's *Iliad* to find the lost city of Troy. This future astronaut will travel to Sirius or Polaris, and might find the fossilized remains of gigantic insect creatures or the descendents of mighty alien raptors.

It is said that T. E. Lawrence, the famed Lawrence of Arabia, always kept a copy of Herodotus close at hand. Perhaps some future exobiologist or exosociologist will feel the need to keep Lucian's *True History* equally close.

Endnotes

1. Polaris is also known as the North Star or the Pole Star. It is 430 light years away. According to the Church of Scientology it is the home planet of the Thetans. In DC Comics it is the star orbited by Thanagar, planet of the Hawkmen.

2. Sirius is also known as the Dog Star. It is one of Earth's closest neighbors, being a mere 8.6 light years away. The ancient Dogon people of Africa are said to have a special relationship and unique knowledge about the star and its inhabitants.

About the Author

Steve Ahlquist is a longtime writer of comics and maker of short films. He is the creator of the cult hit *Oz Squad*, the *Peeny-Boy* mini comic, and co-creator of *Strange Eggs*. His graphic novel, *The Weirdly World of Strange Eggs*, is available on amazon.com. He has been nominated for the prestigious Harvey Award. He lives in Providence, Rhode Island. His website is *www.mythographical.com*.

Inside Job

All the Questions You Were Afraid to Ask About 9/11 and Osama bin Laden

Joan d'Arc Interviews David Ray Griffin

David Ray Griffin is a leading proponent of alternative theories questioning the 9/11 "official conspiracy theory." He is the author of several books on 9/11, including *The 9/11 Commission Report: Omissions and Distortions*, *Debunking 9/11 Debunking*, *The New Pearl Harbor Revisited*, *Osama bin Laden: Dead or Alive* and *The Mysterious Collapse of WTC7*. He is a member of the group, Scholars for 9/11 Truth & Justice, and is a frequent contributor to the *Journal of 9/11 Studies*. He is a retired professor of philosophy of religion and theology. He is co-director of the Center for Process Studies at the Claremont School of Theology.

Joan d'Arc: David, the day after 9/11 you began writing a history of American imperialism. You write that at that time you had accepted the government's "official conspiracy theory" of 9/11 and the "liberal" interpretation that 9/11 was "blowback for U.S. foreign policy." What made you initially begin instead looking at the attacks as a "false flag operation"?

David Ray Griffin: When I first heard the theory that 9/11 was an inside job, I dismissed it, thinking even the Bush administration wouldn't do something this heinous. But then a colleague sent information about a website (*WantToKnow.info*) that contained an abbreviated version of Paul Thompson's "Complete 9/11 Timeline." I found in it hundreds of stories from the mainstream press that contradicted some aspect of the official account of 9/11. It took only a few hours to see that something was seriously wrong.

Joan: What are the essential differences between the false flag view and the government's official conspiracy theory?

David: The most obvious difference between the two conspiracy theories is the identity of the conspirators. The government says they were Osama bin Laden and various members of al-Qaeda. The alternative theory says that they were central members of the Bush administration and the military. A less obvious difference, which it takes a little study to see, is that, although each theory has its supporting evidence, all the evidence supporting the government's theory crumbles upon examination.

Joan: So in the government's conspiracy theory, we wake up the very next morning and see the mug shots of 19 Muslim hijackers on the front page of the newspaper and learn the now familiar term Al Qaeda. But you claim that all of this evidence—passports, luggage, phone calls, security videos, bin Laden confession videos, etc.—is suspect. Do you believe this evidence was planted?

David: Yes. My evidence to support this claim, which is contained in *The New Pearl Harbor Revisited*, is summarized in an online essay, "Was America Attacked by Muslims on 9/11?" (*davidraygriffin.com*) The fact that some of the evidence was planted is obvious. For example, does anyone really believe that when Flight 11 hit the North Tower, creating a giant fireball, a passport could have flown out of Satam al-Suqami's pocket, escaped from the cabin of the plane and from the building unsinged by the fire, and floated to the ground where it would be found by a passerby?

But with some of the purported evidence, one must do some research to see that it was planted. For example, I learned only while writing my 2008 book *9/11 Contradictions* that the most important story about the discovery of evidence implicating al-Qaeda had been invented several days after 9/11. This was the story that officials in Boston had found Mohamed Atta's luggage, which contained many pieces of incriminating evidence, including Atta's will. The story was that he and another member of al-Qaeda had on September 10 driven a Nissan rental car up to Portland, Maine, stayed overnight and then caught a commuter flight back to Boston the next morning. Although they made the transfer, Atta's luggage did not.

This story first appeared on September 16. The first story had been that this evidence had been found in a Mitsubishi Atta had rented and left in the Boston airport, and that the Muslims who had taken the commuter flight to Boston after staying overnight in Portland were two brothers named Bukhari. On September 13, however, the FBI discovered that neither of the Bukharis had died on 9/11 (one had died the year before, the other was still alive). So the authorities simply changed the story, saying that it was Atta and another man who drove the Nissan to Portland and took the commuter flight to Boston the next morning. The incriminating evidence, instead of being found in a Mitsubishi, was found in Atta's luggage. The new story resulted in the absurdity that Atta had planned to take his will on a flight he was going to crash into the World Trade Center.

Joan: Was Islamophobia planted in the American mind by this racist propaganda?

David: Yes, there's an excellent essay on this by Diana Ralph ("Islamophobia and the 'War on Terror': The Continuing Pretext for U.S. Imperial Conquest") in *The Hidden History of 9-11*, edited by Paul Zarembka (the Seven Stories updated paperback).

Joan: Were any other alleged hijackers found to be alive and well?

David: Yes. The clearest case is that of Waleed al-Shehri, who showed up alive in Morocco ten days after 9/11, explaining to journalists and U.S. authorities that he could not possibly have been on Flight 11, as the FBI had alleged. His story was reported in the British press, including the BBC. And yet when the 9/11 Commission issued its report in 2004, it suggested that al-Shehri had stabbed one of the flight attendants shortly before American 11 crashed into the North Tower.

Joan: Regarding the bin Laden "confession" I have read that the FBI has admitted it has no evidence of bin Laden's involvement in 9/11 and that he's actually wanted for the bombing of U.S. Embassies in 1998. How can the U.S. be involved in two wars—Iraq and Afghanistan—on the pretext of searching for a terrorist who is not wanted at all for the events of 9/11?

David: Yes, this admission (which I discuss in *New Pearl Harbor Revisited* and "Was America Attacked by Muslims on 9/11?") is simply one of the dozens of damning facts that our "free press" refuses to publish. Another one—about which I've just completed a small book—is that Osama bin Laden has probably been dead since December 15, 2001 (the day his funeral was reported). This means, of course, that all the bin Laden audiotapes and videotapes that have appeared since then have been fabricated, as former CIA operative Robert Baer has suggested. (Baer told me: "I believe there's a vast industry of contractors, corporations, and pundits who need bin Laden alive, all of them eating at the trough.")

Joan: You point out over 100 instances of deception in the 9/11 Commission Report, which have led you to confirm your suspicions about government complicity and/or involvement. I read that the 9/11 Commission Report has "more lies per square inch than the Warren Commission Report."

David: Trying to determine which of those documents contained more lies per page would be like trying to determine who had told more lies per week, George Bush or Dick Cheney.

Joan: OK, first let's start with what these two documents have in common . . .

David: After I completed my critique, The *9/11 Commission Report: Omissions and Distortions*

(2005), I went back and studied the major critique of the Warren Commission Report, namely, Sylvia Meagher's magnificent *Accessories after the Fact: The Warren Commission, the Authorities & the Report* (1967). The major thing the two documents have in common is indicated by the two words in my subtitle: omissions and distortions. They both dealt with evidence that contradicted their preordained conclusions by either distorting it or simply omitting any mention of it whatsoever.

The major thing the two commissions had in common was people dedicated to covering up the truth. Perhaps the most important such person on the Warren Commission was Allen Dulles, who had been fired from his position as CIA Director by Kennedy and who was, according to many students of the assassination, probably one of its architects. The most important such person on the 9/11 Commission was its executive director, Philip Zelikow, who was virtually a member of the Bush administration (see the final chapter of *New Pearl Harbor Revisited* or my online essay, "The Bush Doctrine & The *9/11 Commission Report*: Both Authored by Philip Zelikow").

The major difference between the two reports is that, whereas the Warren Commission published the evidence it had gathered (or at least most of it), including all (or at least most) of the interviews it conducted, the 9/11 Commission published next to nothing, aside from the transcripts of the public hearings it held (which were already in the public domain). This difference accounts for the fact that, whereas I was able to write my critique in about six months, it took Silvia Meagher three years to write her study, because her main method was to compare the Warren Commission Report itself with the evidence on which it was supposedly based (26 non-indexed volumes). Her resulting critique was devastating, as she was able to show that, on point after point, the Commission had contradicted the evidence that it itself had gathered.

It appears that the 9/11 Commission learned from this that it should simply keep its interviews and other evidence secret, so that no such comparisons could be made until many years later. I was able to show that the Commission had contradicted various kinds of evidence, such as news reports of still-living "hijackers," facts about the collapses of the World Trade Center buildings, photographs of and testimonies about the Pentagon damage, and the reports by a few people, such as Sibel Edmonds, of what they had told the Commission behind closed doors. But there was no way to compare the Commission's report about an interview with the transcript of that interview itself.

This fact is most crucial with respect to the reported testimony of Khalid Sheikh Mohammad (KSM), the supposed "mastermind" of the 9/11 attacks. Almost everything the Commission says about Osama bin Laden's responsibility for the attacks is supported in the notes by a three-word phrase, "interrogation of KSM." This means that KSM was effectively a blank slate, on which the Commission or the CIA behind it could write anything they wished. We have no way of knowing whether KSM said any of these things (or, if he did, whether he was tortured until he said what his interrogators wanted).

Joan: And secondly, what do the two events these reports cover up have in common?

David: Both were major subversions of democracy, insofar as democratic decision-making is impossible if lies are used to get support for various matters of public policy. And in both cases the lies were for the sake of war (and hence war-profits). JFK had been resisting calls from the Pentagon and most of his foreign policy advisors to initiate a full-scale war in Vietnam (as shown in various studies, such as David Kaiser's *American Tragedy: Kennedy, Johnson, and the Origins of the Vietnam War*.) The escalation was ordered immediately after Kennedy was assassinated. And the 9/11 attacks have, of course, been the pretext for the already planned wars in Afghanistan and Iraq. The Bush administration and its Pentagon had planned, moreover, to attack several other Muslim countries (as I document in *New Pearl Harbor Revisited*).

Joan: Did both events have the total cooperation of secret government and military/industrial players? Let's get down to it, who are the players in this 21st century terror ruse as compared to the JFK assassination? Can you offer any ideas on that?

David: I don't try to answer the question of "what really happened" in any detail, which would include naming the masterminds. Getting answers to those questions would be the task of a true investigation. Even apart from such an investigation, however, it is clear the main people at the operational level included Dick Cheney, Donald Rumsfeld, and General Richard Myers. Part of the reason for this clarity is that they and the 9/11 Commission lied about their whereabouts that morning, as I show in *9/11 Contradictions*.

Joan: OK, down to the events of 9/11, over a third of Americans believe the government participated in some way in the 9/11 attacks—that works out to millions of Americans—and an even higher percentage of New Yorkers who suspect foul play. Describe what you mean by "total building collapse." Essentially 110 stories were reduced to a pile of rubble about seven stories high sitting in its own basement?

David: Each of the twin towers had 287 steel columns running from their sub-basements to their roofs: 240 peripheral columns and 47 massive core columns. For the towers to end up as relatively small piles of rubble, all of the columns had to break into quite small sections (most of them were evidently 30 to 50 feet long). And for the towers to come down as they did—straight down at almost free-fall speed—all 287 columns had to fail simultaneously on successive floors. If the failure had not been simultaneous, the buildings would have fallen over sideways.

Prior to 9/11, no steel-frame building had ever suffered total collapse for any cause other than having their steel columns sliced with explosives. Anyone who has studied the destruction of the Twin Towers—and also WTC7—knows that these buildings also did not collapse without explosives. (See comments by physicists, engineers, and architects at *patriotsquestion911.com*.)

Joan: Is this also an accurate description of a successful building implosion?

David: Yes, in an implosion, the building folds inward, so that it comes down (roughly) into its own footprint. Implosion is the most difficult kind of controlled demolition. The easiest kind is simply to cause the building to fall over sideways, but this would have created enormous destruction in lower Manhattan—which would have led insurance companies to demand a real investigation. Actually, only the collapse of WTC7 was a classic implosion in which the collapse begins from the bottom. The destruction of the Twin Towers began with massive explosions near the top, which hurled sections of steel columns out as far as 600 feet horizontally. But after that, they came straight down, largely into their own footprints.

Joan: Can you explain, what are "squibs" and how are they indicative of building implosion?

David: Squibs are puffs of smoke and debris that are ejected out of the building when the explosives go off. They can be seen running down the WTC buildings just prior to the collapse front. Defenders of the official account claim that they were simply puffs of air and smoke being forced out of the floors as they collapsed. One can see, however, that the squibs were produced prior to the collapse of the various floors. These squibs are just one of about a dozen signs that the buildings were deliberately imploded. I have already mentioned three others: the horizontal ejection of pieces of steel, the straight-down nature of the collapses, and their virtually free-fall speed. Another decisive sign was the melting of steel—which fires could not have caused.

Joan: You write that the NIST (the National Institute of Standards and Technology) created a phenomenon called "total top-down progressive collapse" to describe what has essentially only happened once in history—on September 11, 2001—to three buildings. The official theory depends almost entirely on the "fire" explanation—that the intense heat of jet fuel caused the steel to melt, not the weight or impact of the jets. Is that correct? But is jet fuel any hotter or more flammable than other types of fuel?

David: This characterization, "top-down progressive collapse," was used by NIST only for the Twin Towers (WTC7 collapse clearly started from the bottom). The idea was that after the airliners created a hole in each building, the section of the building above the hole fell down on the rest of the building, causing it to collapse at virtually free-fall speed.

This theory massively violates some basic principles of classical physics, such as the conservation of momentum and energy. For an analogy, imagine that you are driving a little sports car down the freeway at 80 miles an hour. Not seeing a huge, fully-loaded truck that is stopped in front of you, your sports car runs into the back of it and starts pushing it down the highway at 80 mph. That's close to what the authors of the NIST report suggest happened to the towers—with or without a straight face.

Much of the public evidently still believes that the jet-fuel fires caused the steel to melt, because some "experts" on early TV specials said this. But it is ridiculous. Jet-fuel has no magical properties. It is essentially kerosene. The fires in the building were fueled only by it and other hydrocarbons, and diffuse hydrocarbon fires can under the most ideal conditions get only to 1,800 degrees Fahrenheit. All the evidence indicates that the fires in the towers did not get much hotter than 1,300 degrees (if that). Steel does not begin to melt until about 2,800 degrees.

NIST itself points out that the fires did not melt any steel. This acknowledgment meant, however, that they had no way to explain the existence of melted steel—including a couple of pieces of steel that had been partially evaporated, so that they had holes in them, producing a Swiss-cheese look. The *New York Times* called this phenomenon "the deepest mystery uncovered in the investigation." It was described by three Worcester Polytechnic Institute professors in the appendix to the 2002 FEMA report on the WTC. But the NIST reports on the Twin Towers and WTC7 simply ignored this phenomenon, as well as the pools of molten steel that were reported by many reliable sources.

My book on NIST's WTC7 report, titled: *The Mysterious Collapse of WTC7: Why NIST's Final 9/11 Report is Unscientific and False*, quotes a former NIST employee who reports that NIST had become a political, not a scientific, organization, and that the scientists working on the WTC report, in particular, had completely lost their scientific independence, having become little more than "hired guns."

Joan: The WTC buildings were actually built to withstand a crash of a 707. Is this why the official theory depends on immense heat bringing the buildings down?

David: Actually, NIST tried to undermine that report, pointing out that Boeing 767s, which hit the towers, are larger than 707s. But this was a bogus argument, because that early report to which you refer envisaged a tower being hit by a 707 going 600 mph, whereas the 767s were said to have been going only 440 and 540 mph, so they would have had less momentum and hence caused less damage than the envisaged strike by a 707.

NIST claims, nevertheless, that the towers collapsed because they were so greatly weakened by the combined effect of the impacts and the fires that gravity brought them down. Although NIST granted that fire could not have melted the steel, it claimed, or at least implied, that the steel columns got so hot that they lost 90 percent of their strength. One problem with this claim is that NIST's own empirical studies provide no evidence that any of the steel got hot enough to lose even 1 percent—let alone 90 percent—of its strength. Another problem is that even if steel in the upper parts of the towers had become weakened by the fires, the steel in the lower 70 or so floors would have been virtually unaffected; and yet the core columns—which were extremely massive in the lower parts of the buildings—collapsed as if they were not there. In sum, NIST relied on intense fires that didn't exist to produce effects that would have been impossible even if they had existed.

Joan: I see. Now with regard to heat, just how hot would the fire have to be to cause fires to burn for months afterward?

David: One type of evidence that explosives of some sort were used was the fact that extremely hot, inextinguishable fires continued to burn in the rubble for several months. No amount of water and chemical fire suppressant fazed them. If the official account is accepted, there is no explanation for the twofold fact that these fires were burning underground, where oxygen would have been scarce to nonexistent, and could not be put out. But as chemist Kevin Ryan, physicist Steven Jones, and chemical engineer James Gourley have shown in a peer-reviewed paper published in *The Environmentalist* (August 4, 2008), a quite simple explanation is available for this and other anomalies: the presence of "energetic nanocomposites"—which provide their own energy and oxygen—such as nanothermite (also called superthermite).

Joan: So, let's talk about thermite and the evidence for it being used.

David: Ordinary thermite is an incendiary. It is made of aluminum plus an oxidizer. Iron oxide is evidently the most common, but other metals, such as barium, copper, molybdenum, nickel, titanium, vanadium, or zinc, can be used instead of iron. Thermite can be used to slice steel. If sulfur is added, it is called thermate, which can melt steel at a much lower temperature. Ultra-fine-grain metals are called nanometals. If nanometals, such as nanoaluminum, are used, the substance is known as nanothermite. Being far more powerful than ordinary thermite, it is classified not merely as an incendiary but also as a "high explosive."

The hypothesis that nanothermite was used to bring down the WTC buildings can, besides explaining the fires, also explain the fact, shown by EPA monitoring, that during the period when Ground Zero remained so hot, violent fires occasionally flared up, releasing various toxic substances into the atmosphere. The hypothesis that nanothermite—specifically nanothermate—was used can also account for the otherwise inexplicable levels of iron, aluminum, barium, silicon, and sulfur discovered in the WTC dust.

Joan: How does the official 9/11 Commission Report explain the total collapse of WTC7, which came down several hours later and was not even hit by a plane?

David: When I published *The New Pearl Harbor Revisited* (2008), I assumed, based on NIST's previous statements, that it would argue that WTC7 came down because of damage caused by debris from the collapse of the North Tower as well as the fires produced by (burning) debris. But NIST ended up saying that, for the first time in history, fire alone caused a steel-frame building to collapse. Its theory is that fire heated up some (horizontal) steel beams sufficiently to cause significant thermal expansion in them. These beams, by becoming longer, displaced a girder so that it lost its connection with one of the building's 81 steel columns. This column, having lost lateral support, buckled, and this buckling caused two other columns to fail, and their failure led the rest of the building to fail. The only problem with this theory is that every part of it is absurd—as I will show in my book, *The Mysterious Collapse of WTC7*.

Joan: The new owner of the WTC complex, Larry Silverstein, admitted in 2002 that they decided to "pull the building" because the fire was going to bring it down. The official whitewash report says Silverstein was talking about "pulling the firefighters out." Would firefighters and building officials agree that to "pull the building" means to implode it for the safety of the public? If it was ostensibly for the safety of the public, why then can't they admit they pulled it?

David: Silverstein didn't actually say that they made the decision to "pull the building." Rather he said, in talking about WTC7: "I said, 'We've had such terrible loss of life, maybe the smartest thing to do is pull it.' And they made that decision to pull and we watched the building collapse." The fact that he merely said "pull it" allowed a spokesman for Silverstein Properties to claim that he was talking about pulling the contingent of firefighters out of the building. This explanation was even endorsed on the State Department's website while Condoleezza Rice was still secretary of state.

However, besides the fact that this interpretation is implausible, given Silverstein's following sentence ("they made that decision to pull and we watched the building collapse"), Silverstein himself, perhaps not being the brightest bulb on the string, undermined it. It is widely agreed, even by NIST, that all firefighters had been pulled out of the building by 2:00 PM. And yet Silverstein, when asked about his comment by a "We Are Change" group, said that the decision to pull was made "around 3:30 or 4:00 PM." Accordingly, if he made that statement, it could not have referred to pulling the firefighters out of the building.

Joan: Several people in Building 7 have reported hearing large explosions while trapped in the building. Do architects and builders generally design buildings with implosion materials in place, like they do in Las Vegas? Is this completely out of the ordinary? There are also reports that tenants heard a lot of loud noises coming from empty floors in the weeks before 9/11, indicating that someone was using these floors to install explosives. What can you tell me about that?

David: I cannot address either of these questions. I can say, however, that NIST certainly did not appeal to any pre-set explosives to explain the testimonies about explosions—which were given by at least 150 people with regard to the Twin Towers and at least ten people in relation to WTC7. Rather, they simply wrote their reports as if such testimonies were nonexistent or mistaken, including the testimonies of two city officials—Barry Jennings and Michael Hess (Mayor Giuliani's corporate counsel)—about a massive explosion that occurred in WTC at about 9:15 that morning. NIST, followed by the BBC in a 2008 documentary about WTC7—changed the Hess-Jennings timeline, pretending that the event they called an "explosion" had occurred at 10:28, and was simply effects caused in WTC7 by debris from the North Tower's collapse. The BBC even got Michael Hess to endorse this view in a second version of its program on WTC7, which they produced after Jennings, who had appeared alone in the first version, had conveniently died—just before NIST released the first draft of its report in August 2008.

Joan: Another point you make is there was media foreknowledge of the Building 7 implosion because BBC reporters were standing in front of the building announcing its collapse thirty minutes before it fell. Why do you think Building 7 was taken down? What was in that building?

David: There certainly was a widespread *belief* within the fire department, of which some members of the media would have known, that WTC7 was going to collapse. This expectation started spreading by 2:00 or even earlier. The real question is: Why did anyone in authority start saying that this building was going to come down, given the fact that nothing other than explosives had ever brought down a steel-frame building? WTC7 had not been hit by a plane and had only small fires on a few floors. There would have been no reason whatsoever for anyone with knowledge about fires and steel-frame buildings to think that the building would collapse. The only reasonable explanation for the widespread belief that WTC7 was going to collapse is that this belief was spread by people with knowledge that explosives had been placed in it.

It is good to close this interview with a discussion of WTC7. President Obama has promised that science will again count in determining public policy, so that policies will no longer be based on reports in which science has been distorted for the sake of political ends. There is no more extreme case of such distortion than NIST's reports on the World Trade Centers, and it is NIST's report on WTC7 in which the violation of scientific method and principles is most obvious.

*****

The following questions were added to this interview following publication of David's book, *Osama bin Laden: Dead or Alive?* and *Mysterious Collapse of WTC7 (summer 2009).*

Joan: David, according to a December 26, 2001, report in the Pakistan Observer, bin Laden had died in Tora Bora ten days earlier. Was there a specific cause of death given? Was bin Laden's death also reported widely in the U.S. media?

David: The *Observer* story, which was entitled "Osama Has Died a Natural Death," said that, according to a Taliban leader who claimed to have attended the funeral, Osama bin Laden (OBL) had died "in mid-December in the vicinity of famous Tora Bora mountains." According to this man, OBL had been "suffering from some serious lung complication" and had "succumbed to the disease for lack of proper treatment."

In attributing the death to complications in the lungs, this report seems to differ from the cause of death that would have been expected, namely, kidney disease. Several reports indicate that OBL had been suffering from this problem for some time. According to the Paris newspaper *Le Figaro*, he had been treated in the urology department of the American Hospital in Dubai in July 2001, at which time he also ordered a mobile dialysis machine to be delivered to Afghanistan. This *Le Figaro* story was reported by the *Guardian* and *Times of London* and by UPI, and President Musharraf of Pakistan was quoted by CNN as saying that OBL had taken two dialysis machines into Afghanistan. Moreover (something that I did not know when I wrote the book) CBS News reported that, on the night before 9/11, OBL was in a "military hospital in Rawalpindi [Pakistan] for kidney dialysis treatment."

Finally, in January 2002, Dr. Sanjay Gupta was interviewed on CNN by Paula Zahn about the last of the undoubtedly authentic OBL videos, which had been aired by Al Jazeera on December 27, 2001, having been made sometime after November 16 (the date of an event mentioned on the videotape). On the basis of various features of OBL's appearance—including "frosting" and the fact that his left arm was immobile, suggesting that he had had a stroke—plus the report that he needed renal dialysis, Gupta suggested that OBL had been in "end-stage renal failure."

Although the idea that OBL died from kidney failure, which Musharraf came to believe, might seem to be refuted by the report that he died of complications in the lungs, this is not necessarily the case. It is possible that his followers, not wanting to admit that he had died from kidney failure, invented another cause of death. Or perhaps OBL's kidney disease led to other physical problems, including problems in his lungs, so that the two explanations would not be contradictory. The Taliban leader's report that OBL "succumbed to the disease for lack of proper treatment" could well have applied to the problem of getting proper kidney dialysis in the Tora Bora mountains. Sanjay Gupta had spoken about this, saying that unless OBL had, in addition to a functioning dialysis machine, also electricity, water, and a sterile setting, he probably would not have survived very long.

Joan: When did the first bin Laden video appear? Did any of them appear while he was still alive or was December 27 the first one?

David: I'm not sure when the first authentic OBL video appeared. After 9/11, however, he started issuing messages immediately, denying on September 12, 16, 17, and 28—in some case by means of audiotapes—that he had had anything to do with the attack. As for videotapes, ones that were issued on October 7 and November 3 are relevant to the question of whether any fake OBL messages appeared while he was still alive. If one traces his physical appearance, as revealed in these two tapes, with the post-November 16 tape released on December 27 (analyzed by Sanjay Gupta), one sees that his health appears to get progressively worse. London's *Telegraph* said that in the final video, OBL had a "gaunt, frail appearance," with a beard that was "much whiter than on November 3."

But then on December 13, the Pentagon released a video that had supposedly been made on November 9 and found in a house in Jalalabad later that month. If this were true, one would expect bin Laden's appearance in this "Jalalabad video" to be somewhere between that of the November 3 and post-November 16 videos. But it is not. Rather than being a little more "frail" and "gaunt" than the bin Laden of November 3 and having a whiter beard, the bin Laden figure on this tape is rather well filled out and has a dark beard. Also whereas bin Laden was left-handed, this man writes with his right hand—and not because his left arm is immobile: he easily lifts it above his head. Also his nose seems broader and his hands are stubbier. Finally, as I point out, he says several things that Osama bin Laden himself would not have said.

Joan: What did "bin Laden" say in this "Jalalabad video," and what was the response of the White House?

David: This videotape appeared after both the Bush and the Blair governments had promised to provide proof of bin Laden's responsibility for 9/11 but had then failed to do so. The BBC had pointed out the absence of "direct evidence in the public domain linking Osama Bin Laden to the 11 September attacks." Very conveniently, then, the OBL figure in this Jalalabad video boasted about the success of the attacks, which he said he had planned. As I said, however, this man said things that OBL himself would not have said. For example, he said that, on the basis of his experience as a building contractor, he had expected that "the fire from the gas in the plane would melt the iron structure of the building and collapse the area where the plane hit and all the floors above it only." (He didn't expect the whole building to come down.) But the real bin Laden, given his experience, would have known that the buildings were supported by steel, not iron, and he would have known that fires, which themselves could not have been hotter than 1800 degrees Fahrenheit, could not have brought the steel up anywhere close to its melting point, which is about 2,700 Fahrenheit.

This video was, nevertheless, taken to be authentic by the US and British governments. President Bush said: "For those who see this tape, they'll realize that not only is [OBL] guilty of incredible murder, he has no conscience and no soul." Jack Straw, the British foreign secretary, said: "By boasting about his involvement in the evil attacks, Bin Laden confirms his guilt."

Joan: What about the FBI? Does it accept the authenticity of this "confession video?"

David: Evidently not. If you look up "Usama bin Laden" on its website for "Most Wanted Terrorists," you will find that it does not list 9/11 as one of the terrorist attacks for which he is wanted. When asked why not, Rex Tomb, who was then the head of investigative publicity, replied, "because the FBI has no hard evidence connecting Bin Laden to 9/11." If it considered that video, with its confession, authentic, it would surely consider this hard evidence. The same would be true of all the other tapes on which "Osama bin Laden" confesses, such as the "October Surprise" video of November 29, 2004, which helped Bush get re-elected.

Joan: On December 27, 2001, just who weeks after the Jalalabad video appeared, the video with the frail, gaunt, white-bearded bin Laden was released. What did the Bush administration say about it?

David: Surprisingly, at least from our present standpoint, after dozens of "messages from bin Laden" have been pronounced authentic by our government's intelligence agencies, the White House back then suggested that the release of this video might mean that OBL was dead. A White House aide speculated that OBL, after making the tape, may have ordered that it be released after he died. And Bush himself, according to a *Telegraph* story, had hinted, on the basis of this video plus the fact that no more messages between OBL and his followers had been intercepted, that he might be dead.

Joan: Who else came forward to state that bin Laden is, or might be, dead?

David: Quite an impressive group of people. Besides President Musharraf of Pakistan, also President Karzai of Afghanistan, Secretary of Defense Donald Rumsfeld, Iran-Contra criminal Oliver North, FBI counter-terrorism chief Dale Watson; members of the Pakistani and Israeli intelligence agencies; Professor Bruce Lawrence, generally considered the leading authority on OBL in the academy; former CIA operative Robert Baer, who said "Of course he's dead"; and Boston University professor Angelo Codevilla, formerly of the Foreign Service, who wrote an essay entitled "Osama bin Elvis." At one time or another, moreover, CNN, CBS News, Fox News, the *New York Times*, the *Telegraph*, and *Time* magazine all put out stories saying that OBL is, or may be, dead. These stories largely came to an end in the latter part of 2002, when the Bush administration started getting the American people ready to accept its planned attack on Iraq. It appears that they decided that a still-living OBL would be useful; as, in fact, he turned out to be, when, for example, military intelligence produced evidence, now widely accepted to have been fabricated, of connections between al-Qaeda leaders in Afghanistan and "al-Qaeda in Iraq."

Joan: Didn't Pakistani Prime Minister Benazir Bhutto also state publicly that bin Laden had been killed?

David: Yes, but this was simply a misstatement on her part. While being interviewed by David Frost not long before her own death, she referred in passing to Omar Sheikh as "the man who murdered Osama bin Laden." Omar Sheikh, however, is widely known as "the man who murdered Daniel Pearl," and she surely meant to say this but said "Osama bin Laden" instead, because she had just mentioned one of his sons. That she did not mean to say "Osama bin Laden" is shown by the fact that, while speaking to CNN the very next day, she said she didn't think that Musharaf knew the whereabouts of OBL. Ten days later, moreover, she told NPR that she had said to a policeman assigned to guard her house: "Shouldn't you be looking for Osama bin Laden?" All of this is documented in a YouTube video entitled "Bhutto Didn't Mean to Say 'Osama bin Laden.'"

Joan: Do you think the CIA believes largely that bin Laden is dead?

David: I do not know. The CIA is, of course, a very large and diverse organization, so there are likely many points of view within the agency. I do report, however, that Robert Baer said that he took a poll, in the latter part of 2008, of CIA officers who have been on OBL's trail, and found that not a single one of them reported being certain that he was still alive. On the other hand, I was recently interviewed about this issue by the BBC, which plans to air a show about it early in 2010. The interviewer told me he had found several people, including members (or former members) of the CIA who said that they were certain that he is still alive. And it is quite possible that they believe this. As I said, CIA is a large and diverse organization.

But whether the BBC will provide convincing evidence that OBL is still alive—which it seems intent on doing—remains to be seen. If it does, that's fine. That will not contradict my book, because I did not claim to have provided proof that he's dead. I merely showed that, at the time I wrote the book, the publicly available evidence suggested that he was most likely dead. Publicly available evidence can, of course, always change. And if the controversy created by my book stimulated the BBC or someone else to make this evidence available, then it will have performed an important service.

The fact will remain, however, that neither the BBC nor any other news organization had done its job. There were various types of evidence provided in 2001 that OBL had died; many mainstream figures and news organizations had stated that OBL was probably dead; then these stories virtually disappeared after the US government started preparing to attack Iraq. In September 2002, tapes purported to be from OBL started appearing. In spite of all the reasons to be suspicious of these tapes, the mainstream media simply repeated the assurances from US intelligence agencies that they were authentic, which meant that OBL was still alive. There was no serious examination of the contradiction between these assurances and all the previous evidence that OBL had died. The news media simply allowed these tapes to have their full propaganda value for ginning up support for the "war on terror."

This continues until this day, as the news media simply report, without critical comment, the assurances by intelligence agencies that OBL is almost certainly hiding in Pakistan, near the Afghan border—a claim that is used to justify US military incursions into Pakistan (which regularly result in Pakistani deaths, including the deaths of women and children attending weddings or funerals). So even if OBL has been alive all this time, the use of him as pretext for the Western military efforts in Afghanistan and Pakistan was not justified, because neither the intelligence agencies nor the news organizations had provided evidence that he was still alive (and had provided no evidence of his responsibility for 9/11).

About the Interviewee

This interview first appeared in *PARANOIA*, issue 50 (Spring 2009), and was expanded after publication of David Ray Griffin's books, *Osama bin Laden: Dead or Alive* and *The Mysterious Collapse of WTC7*. David Ray Griffin is also the author of the following books on 9/11, available at *www.interlinkpress.com*, *amazon.com*, or your local book shop: *The New Pearl Harbor* (2004); *The 9/11 Commission Report: Omissions and Distortions* (2005); *Christian Faith and the Truth Behind 9/11* (2006); *9/11 and American Empire: Intellectuals Speak Out* (2006); *Debunking 9/11 Debunking: An Answer to Popular Mechanics and Other Defenders of the Official Conspiracy Theory* (2007); *9/11 Contradictions: An Open Letter to Congress and the Press* (2008); *The New Pearl Harbor Revisited: 9/11, the Cover-Up, and the Exposé* (2008).

As Above, So Below

My Adventures in Valhalla

by Mark Elliott

All the world's a stage, and all the men and women merely players: they have their exits and their entrances; and one man in his time plays many parts, his acts being seven ages.

~ William Shakespeare

First Incident

I'm lying on my stomach in the back of my family's Conestoga wagon. For hours I have been fighting the boredom of the almost featureless horizon of waving grass plains, a monotony of light brown grass and cyan sky.

I've spent the day lazily watching the earth move beneath the squeaky wooden wheels, their spokes casting stuttering shadows on the sandy trail below.

I hate the Conestoga. It represents every bad decision my father ever made. In my boyish heart, I have a hard time understanding why we couldn't stay in town where everyone we knew lived. So what if we were poor? Wouldn't we still be poor when we finally settled in California or wherever my father decides to plant us?

This wagon just reinforced the image of poverty. I hated the squeaky wheel with its thick, black grease. I was embarrassed every time the family entered a new town with this wagon's weathered pine sideboards. Grey and dry as a bone, one even had a knot hole the size of a silver dollar. I couldn't wait for us to finally quit the trail and sell off this symbol of my misery.

But wait! Now we're entering a treed glade where the road dips a bit. I can smell the stream before the horse's hooves even get wet. I sit up to see the water. It's a small stream, about the width of two tall men laying end to end, its depth only to my father's knees.

As we pause mid-stream to water the horses, I resume my previous posture, staring down at the trail below. Now, in sharp contrast to brown dust, I see a multitude of colorful stones under the fast flowing stream. Reds and whites and copper ripples of the most enticing variety greet my tired gaze. Each stone appears as a precious gem, a treasure ready for the picking.

I want to call out to my father and ask if we might stay just a little longer in this paradisiacal oasis, but we're on the move once again. I know that he will never stop now. He always says that easy water draws Indians, and Mother is deathly afraid.

***

My reverie is suddenly interrupted by the familiar sound of my second grade teacher. She is holding a book on American history as she explains the advantages of the Conestoga wagon, and why it was the choice of the early settlers of the western frontier.

I am suddenly shocked to realize that I'm not really that "me" in the wagon, but "me" in 1958. For a while, I'm actually confused and a bit worried that *this* scene is the dream. Am I *that* boy dreaming about a future me?

The "reality" of the here-and-now eventually wins out as surely and suddenly as a dream forgotten. It dawns on me that as soon as my teacher mentioned the word "Conestoga," I was off on this other life. I say "other life" because that's exactly what it was like.

Known as a bit of a daydreamer as a kid, I was very familiar with getting lost in my thoughts. This incident was entirely something of a different order of things, however, for rather than merely dreaming of a place, I was truly there. I wasn't asleep either, as I remained upright in my seat the whole time. I hadn't needed to awaken, as I already was wide awake. This was something entirely new. I simply was another person for a while.

I never told anyone about this, of course, as I didn't want to be laughed at.

***

As the years went by, I pretty much forgot about my strange experience that day in second grade. I grew up without other such strangeness, as far as I can recall, until I was nineteen years old. It was then that the floodgates holding back my akashic memory let loose, setting me on a lifelong review of my past lives. This tale of mine is not about those akashic memories, however. Not directly, anyhow. What I want to tell you here is the true account of how it all began.

All of the tales in this journal are true, no matter how outlandish they may sound. They have shown me that I, and others around me, have all been here before. If you are amongst those peoples who believe in reincarnation, you will quickly understand. Others (like yours truly) who were raised in a more Western (Catholic) tradition, may be tempted to cast aside my tales as either the ravings of a madman or an idiot. I can't blame them, as my tales are tough to grasp as "reality." In my travels, however, I have found the concept of "reality" tenuous, at best.

The Death Match

I'm standing in a grassy field, watching tiny hoppers bound through the tall weeds at my sandaled feet. Leather straps form a helical pattern around my ankles. My skin is a light bronze. On my right bicep I wear a wide copper band, a prize and symbol of my stature as champion.

I am thinking about how these grasshoppers are living their lives without the fear of their own kind, unlike men, who seem to hold violence as a part of themselves, loving it as they love life. I'm thinking about the uncaring whims of the gods.

I raise my head to look at the platform twenty long paces away. Made from split logs, it's about eight feet in length and again as wide. It stands about four feet off the ground on thick wooden columns.

On my right, opposite this platform, are seated a royal entourage. They sit on a raised Dias, in three connected booths entirely surrounded by colorful brocades and silks. The center booth contains the Royals, themselves. This booth is marked with purple bunting. I can't see them behind the richly colored side panels, but I know just by the way the crowd speaks in hushed whispers that "They" have been seated. The two booths on either side are occupied with all the ministers, royal secretaries and ladies in waiting, who coyly peek over the front rail towards me, their Hero.

Across from the Royal entourage stand the plebes and serfs, straining at the barricades, excitedly wagering on blood. I can tell by their actions that the bet weighs heavily in my favor, as it should. Haven't I made many a pocket jingle already? Since being captured by these people who made me kill in order not to be killed, I have proven tougher than even they. True, I kill for their entertainment. True, I am naught more than a slave. Yet, I have earned their respect. Their women all want me as surely as their men all wish they *were* me, their "savage" champion.

This thought helps me swell with the confidence I'll need on this day, for directly across from me, twenty more paces away from the platform, stands a new prisoner. I size him up. He's from some unknown tribe. I feel sorry for him, not only because he is looking upon his last sights on Earth, but because he's being forced to do so against his will, in a foreign land where he doesn't even understand the curses being hurled his way. That was once me, before I proved myself.

I notice my opponent shaves his head, but for the very top, where he sports a tail of hair that falls to his left shoulder. Mine is the color of wheat, cut short, but for one tight braid on the right, reaching to my waist. His skin is the color of red dust.

Now the crowd raises a shout as the order to attention is signaled. Then they are silent, as the anticipation grows.

Now I focus on the short ramp leading to the top of the wooden platform halfway between me and this human sacrifice. I know he's counting in his mind how far away the ramp is on his side. In the center of the platform stands a spear, its razor sharp blade stuck firmly into one of the split logs. I glance at my opponent to find him now mouthing what I can only assume is his death song.

Now the signal is given. Now all I've trained for comes into play. Tonight I will dine so well and fuck so many women that I'll need to be careful not to make my liege jealous!

My strong calves spring into action as I lean into a run. Within a few strides I have my right foot on the ramp. Two more steps and I'm grasping the shaft of the spear. I'm yanking the spear from the wood with all my might as I notice my opponent just reaching the top of his ramp. As soon as his foot touches the platform he leaps at me in a desperate attempt to save the day.

His fear of me has not served him well, as it causes him to land at arm's length. This is his fatal mistake, as I take the opportunity to slash out with the blade. Being too close for a full swing, I choke up on the shaft and, holding it firmly with both hands, I throw all my weight at him, slashing from right to left at gut level. I feel the blade slice into him, then suddenly stop as the head buries itself deeply into his mid-section. He jerks as he realizes what has just happened. He reaches out to put his arms around the back of my neck for support. This only causes him to pull in closer.

The pressure on the wooden shaft at this point is too much, and it breaks in two. I quickly get a grip on what's left of my spear, which is now but a foot long, its leaf-shaped blade the size of a hand now firmly buried. He has me in a bear hug now. I worry that the double-edged blade will slice into me also. My opponent's eyes tell me this is his plan. He knows he's about to die and figures he'll take me along.

This makes me angry, and serves to give me the extra strength necessary to finish the job. Pushing away with all my might, I yank the spear-head from his belly. I have no idea if in doing so I've also sliced my own gut open, as he still has me in the bear hug and I can't move my head to look down. Anyway, I haven't the luxury of time to find the truth just now.

At this point, we can both feel his intestines falling to the platform. I can feel his warm blood on my sticky hands. The look in his eyes now has changed. Where before I saw only rage, I now see surrender. His grip loosens as I draw the blade to my side, raise it and slash down and across his left temple, slicing into the cheekbone. The blood flows, but not nearly fast enough. I don't want to make my worthy opponent suffer unduly, but I'm very fatigued.

My next move brings my forearm across his face. I hit his chin with my elbow. In this position, I pull the blade's edge from the left, across the right side of his neck. This leaves a wide gash from just behind his right ear, down and across his jugular.

Now does the blood gush out and his face turn pale. In my fatigue, his dying form collapses onto me, sending me crashing to the platform on my back. My opponent's lifeless body now lies on top of me, wet and warm.

I push his body off me and slide to the edge of the platform. Jumping down, I notice the blood and gore dripping through the wooden slats, staining the shaded grass below.

For the first time since the action started, I notice the cheering of the crowd. They are going wild. I guess everyone made money on their bets. I stand before the royal pavilion to receive their praises as I check my belly for wounds, happily finding none. I can't even hear the royal proclamation, the crowd cheers so loudly. I walk back to my quarters with a sense of loathing for myself as well as my masters. I'm in need of good wine and a hot bath full of young women to wash it all away.

***

I come back to this world suddenly, discovering to my surprise that I'm already sitting up in bed. "What the hell was that?," is the question that greets my confused mind.

I've always been a pacifist. This was especially so at nineteen. (We're talking 1970, after all.) Where did this vision come from?

Now, at this point, I can't blame the reader for pointing out that I was asleep during this "vision." What makes me think this wasn't merely a dream? To these doubters, all I can say is that, having had many dreams in my life, I know the difference. For, unlike dreams (or even "lucid" dreams), there is a sense of reality unknown here. Whereas in lucid dreaming everything appears real, the unreality of it all comes to the fore as the experienced lucid dreamer gains control of his or her dream environment. In the case of these visions, however, there is no control. It is a scripted event with me as mere actor. The director is hidden behind the scenes somewhere.

What are these little scenarios I'm forced to relive? Although the reader may have doubts, I declare that they are showing me events that took place in past bodily existences.

I can't blame the reader for being cynical of my claims, as they sound ludicrous to the Western mind. Believe it or not, I don't care. I write this down because I feel in my heart that I'm not alone in this.

The Red Bridge

I'm standing on a sandy beach, looking out at the ocean. I'm startled by the light, as it comes not from the clear, blue sky. Instead, everything emits its own light. Each grain of sand, every molecule of water, even the air itself shines. This chiaroscuro makes the scene brighter than the brightest day ever remembered.

I examine the water before me, noticing that the surf is very light. I can see the water is only a couple of feet deep close to shore, but then gets much deeper toward the horizon. While I'm gazing at this wonderful sight, I suddenly get a strange feeling that I'm being stared at.

I turn to my right and see a man standing about fifty yards down the beach. His sudden appearance is enough to frighten me, but it is the odd way he looks that sends an electric shock through my spine. I say this because, although I've already called him a "man," this appellation may not be correct. What I saw standing there on the glowing sand was only the silhouette of a huge man. Standing a good seven feet tall, the form stood there, its right hand waving in a gesture of greeting. He shone as brightly as if he were made of chrome reflecting the August sun. This caused me to cover my eyes against the reflection and only added to my distress. Who was this? What was this?

Then, just as suddenly as my fear had struck, it ended with such a wave of trust and love as I have never before experienced. I understood that this creature, in some way, had sent this pleasant wave my way as a means of introduction. Realizing I was in the presence of pure love, I instantly surrendered to it and started making my way toward him. He started toward me also, meeting me half way.

As I stood there, averting my eyes against his brilliance, he introduced himself to me. I learned that he'd known me through many lives, and I recognized him as a "guardian angel." We then walked down the beach, the water on my left, him at my right. I remember having a long discussion, where he let me know why certain events in my past had to happen according to a plan. I also learned of things that would occur in the future, which I found exciting. I also remember my disappointment upon learning that I was to forget the details of this future gazing so I couldn't interfere with said plan.

I say we had a "discussion," but the word doesn't do justice to what took place. It was more like this entity sent images into my mind, bypassing the filtering process of language. Simply wondering about something was enough to draw answers from "him," whom I attribute as "male" solely on the mental image I received of a strong, male presence to the entity/angel.

After strolling for awhile and experiencing the thrill of learning from my guide, I was told to turn to my left. Doing so, I saw a very large, black fish swim up to us in the shallows. It looked like a ray, or skate, with sting ray-like wings, about four feet wide. Its body resembled that of a large snake, about eight inches at its widest and narrowing at the tail, which was a good five feet from the head.

The fish hovered in the shallow water, its fleshy wings and reptilian body undulating to keep it stationary. Its huge, lidless eyes stared up at us as it opened its mouth, displaying double rows of needle sharp teeth. It then spoke to me, in my father's voice.

"Come into the calm waters of the past with me," said my father, "You will live in comfort and forgetting."

Once again I was startled. At this time in my life, I hadn't had any contact with my father for years. I immediately understood why this beast had used my Dad's voice. Dad certainly did represent a more comfortable past. Yet, past it was and that's all it was.

At this point I was asked by my angelic friend which path I would choose. Would I join my father and swim away into that sea of forgetfulness, or would I choose a new life and the unknown, no matter the pain? Without hesitation I told my guide that I chose his path, at which point the fish swam back into the depths and disappeared for good. The angel then told me to turn again to my left, looking back to where we'd come from.

There, on the shore, was one end of the most impossible foot bridge ever seen. Made of what looked like red brick, it sprung from the ground at such a steep angle that one would need climbing gear to scale it. At about a dozen feet wide, with four foot high side-walls, it more resembled a man-made rainbow than it did a bridge.

I approached it with curiosity as well as a bit of trepidation. By sending the fish away, had I volunteered for some impossible spiritual quest? I also wondered why I hadn't noticed it earlier when I was standing in the very same spot. I asked my guide what its purpose might be as I stared into the sky, vainly trying to find the bridge's apex which had disappeared into the clouds.

"You don't need to climb this bridge," my guide silently informed me, "merely put one foot on it."

So I did. Within the blink of an eye, I found myself standing at the bridge's dizzying apex. Before me, at the very top of the bridge, stood a stone arch. Crossing beneath this arch, I noticed, on the right-side wall, a very large book. Lying next to this book was a silver ankh, that Egyptian cross with its typical loop at the top. The length of the shaft below the loop and arms of the ankh extended about a foot, ending in an angle cut nub like that on an old fountain pen.

Lifting it from the top of the wall where it rested next to the large book, I noticed it was indeed a pen. Studying the book, I noticed it was a list of names. Each page listed dozens of unreadable names, and the book contained thousands of pages. The open page contained half a dozen names, starting from the top. The rest of both pages remained blank.

Taking up the ankh/stylus, I confidently wrote my name in the next available space in the book. My hand moved deftly, inscribing a name I couldn't read, in glyphs unrecognizable. Although surprised at my confidence in writing whatever it was I was writing, I realized that my hand was moving correctly. This is because there was a small voice somewhere telling me that this name was my real one. We sometimes take familial names with us upon reincarnation and we sometimes take on new names. Our real names never change, however. This is the name I signed in that big register, the name of my soul, a name unknown to my mortal heart.

After "signing in," I stood at the wall for a while, watching the beautiful cloud formations far below and listening to the high wind's hypnotic whisper. I then turned and proceeded over the bridge's crest, wondering how I was ever going to descend. I hadn't needed to worry, it seems.

On a Distant Shore

As soon as I stepped toward the dizzying downward arch of the bridge, I found myself at the base, my feet in the warm sand of a different beach. Here the sand appeared more dull and earthlike. The water, now at my back, rolled in the same small swells as on the other shore, but without the glow.

The sky, though bright blue, shone only as brightly as the sun in the sky provided. Things seemed more real here.

Before me was a grassy rise. Its long and verdant blades arched over the sand below, creating shadows that danced in the light sea breeze. A few yards beyond stood a small beach house, painted white, with red trim and shutters. A few feet from the house's front door stood a pair of poles painted in the same white, with clothes lines strung between them. There were four lines and they were all occupied by white bed sheets in the process of drying. They moved with the wind like sails, their whiteness intense, pure, inviting as vanilla ice cream.

I approached the house, hoping to find someone who could help me understand where I was. I did know that I wasn't in the "real world" anymore, but I had no fear. I found this lack of concern quite odd, but after what I'd just been through with the glowing "angel" and the "guest book," I figured I was supposed to be "here," wherever that was.

Walking to the door, I heard a woman's voice coming from the far end of the last line of sheets. Turning to look, I was surprised to find a young woman softly humming a tune as she held a wooden clothes pin between her lips. She was arranging one of the sheets, carefully smoothing it down before taking the pin from her mouth to secure it to the line.

She then bent over and lifted a large wicker basket to her right hip as she turned toward me. I was about to introduce myself when she jumped with fright, dropping her laundry basket to the grass below, a look of shock on her face.

"What are you doing here?," she asked demandingly.

"Umm. I'm not quite sure," said I, suddenly concerned.

"You shouldn't be here. At least not at this time!"

"This...*this* time?," I stuttered.

I could see her trying to formulate a way to tell me something I might not grasp as she pursed her lips, her eyes focusing upwards and to the left. Now focusing back on me, she spoke in arcane phrases.

"We have...a season. Yes, that's it. There's a season for such as you, and this is not it!"

Seeing that I was still as clueless as I was harmless, her demeanor softened. I felt that, despite my continuing confusion, I could at least trust this woman's intentions.

"I'm afraid I still don't quite understand," I replied. "What is this 'season' you mention?"

"It's a holiday, you understand?"

I was about to ask her more when she suddenly stiffened with fear. Taking me forcefully by the arm, she dragged and pushed me through and between the rows of white sheeting until we reached the beach. I looked for the bridge, but it was nowhere to be seen on the strand that stretched into the distance in both directions.

There where the grass met the sand was a row boat turned over to allow for drainage. Its rough planking was painted in a light green, its oars resting on the lawn. She directed me to crawl under this boat to hide.

"You want me to hide? Why?"

"Don't ask why, just do it!," she fearfully whispered, "I'll explain later."

So I crawled under the boat as requested, wondering just what I'd gotten myself into this time.

"And whatever you do," my mysterious lady then demanded, "do not give in to the temptation to peek out. I mean it. Keep concealed! It will be very dangerous to us both if you don't. Do you understand me?"

"Yes, I understand. I'll hide under here until you tell me everything is alright."

"Good. Be patient."

She then returned to her laundry hanging a few feet away. I could see her slender ankles, her white leather flats, and the hem on her flowered sun dress. I could hear her humming, a bit nervously it seemed, or was that just my imagination?

It was then I heard the dulcet tones of a distinctly male voice. It was a clinically polite voice, friendly yet slightly menacing. Then my heart pounded as a pair of shiny black shoes stepped into view. Resting precisely on the third lace from the top was the hem of a very well tailored pair of black, pin-striped pants. The owner of the fancy suit was having a rather animated conversation with the lady. Although I still couldn't hear the man's side of the conversation for some strange reason, it was obvious from her side that she was being questioned by some form of authority. I wondered what kind of cop it could be. The suit was too expensive for an ordinary police detective, I figured.

After a minute or so of this kind of questioning, they both walked away, back toward the house. I wondered if it was safe to peek out of my hole yet, but the force of the woman's admonition to keep out of sight held me there for the seemingly interminable minutes it took her to return. I watched her feet approach and stop at the boat. Then her smiling face was peering into my hiding spot.

"It's safe now. You can come out."

The Twins

I am once again in the strange land. I stand before a fine, if modest house. My heart jumps as I suddenly realize I'm being observed by two people peering at me from behind a corner of the house. As they laughingly approach, I can see they are twins, brother and sister look-alikes. Twenty something and attractive, they both share the same carrot-colored hair and spray of freckles across the bridge of their pugnacious noses. They ooze wealth, not so much in the downscale sweats they both wear, but in the way they seem to glide over the ground as though they haven't a care in the world.

"Uh oh!," says the young woman with a tone of mock conspiracy, "someone shouldn't be here." They both laugh at her joke, leaving me more confused.

"Why am I not supposed to be here?," I ask sheepishly.

"He really has no clue," says the male of the pair. He's finding all this very amusing.

"Come inside with us and we'll explain everything," says the young woman. "Don't worry, we're safe."

We enter the well-appointed house with its thick wood paneling and gold trim everywhere. All the furnishings are top shelf. It's obvious that these twins are quite spoiled and, I suspect, quite decadent.

Then the explaining starts, and I'm out of my league again. They tell me that this place, where I am at this minute, is another "reality." The word rolls off their lips with some effort, as though it is the only word they can find that might explain the true situation to this poor ignorant savage.

The story they tell is that this version of "reality" I presently find myself in is what the Vikings of old called Valhalla. They tell me that everyone in this land is between lives in that plane I call "the real world." I am informed then that this place is where all the violence in "the real world" comes from.

They then tell me the most outrageous thing; that no one really "dies" in Valhalla. In Valhalla, I'm told, death only comes about through murder, and that even then, death depended upon surprise. When I ask for clarification, I am told that, for instance, a gunfight might result in someone's death for ten seconds or so. This is simply because both parties expect it. A surprise assassination, however, might cause the victim to be out of commission for hours.

At this point, they could clearly see by the look on my face that I didn't believe a word of what they were telling me.

"You mean death isn't permanent here?," I asked, trying to form words that didn't sound too ridiculous.

"Well, not for us. For you, it's a different story."

"A different story?" I asked weakly.

"Yeah. You get hit, you're out of here. Back to the plane where you came from."

"But what about an explosion? What happens if someone's head gets blown away?" A gruesome thought, but I needed answers.

"Why would anyone do that? Yuk!," said she.

"That's just not sporting!," said he.

"But... let me see if I get this right. You two can't die?"

"Correct!," said the young man as his sister shook her head in happy agreement. "Allow us to demonstrate."

He produced a gun from under his brown corduroy jacket. It was a small, semi-automatic pistol with a long silencer attached to the barrel. The pistol was small, maybe a .22 caliber. Its color was olive drab. The silencer was polished brass.

He pointed it at his twin sister's chest as she smilingly stood a few feet away, facing him with outstretched arms. He pulled the trigger, causing the gun to kick back with a sharp cough. His sister reacted to the shot, her face now blank as she sank to the floor.

I could clearly see the red hole in her shirt made by the bullet, just above her heart.

"Holy shit!," I exclaimed, stuck to my chair. I was nervously wondering if I was next.

After a few seconds, the young woman opened her eyes and smilingly arose. She approached me, unbuttoning her blouse to display the area just drilled by her brother's bullet. The skin there was soft and warm, with no sign of injury.

"We enjoy doing this here," she said with a smile.

I was dumbfounded, but figured I'd play along at this point. I was here for some unknown reason and I needed to get to the bottom of things. To that end, I decided to go along with anything these two said.

They then asked me to do something that I considered totally against everything I believed in. Yet, after my dream of killing a fellow slave earlier, I had to wonder just where my boundaries were drawn. What they told me was essentially that they wanted me to kill their parents.

"Oh, it will be such a surprise!" they both said. "They have no idea someone from the "outside" is among us. That hardly ever happens. What a treat!"

So, against my better judgment, I said I would.

They took me through the house to the basement, where their parents were watching a movie in their private theater. I was led to a pair of swinging doors with port hole windows, as in a restaurant. These doors were covered in red tufted leather.

I peered through one of the round windows to see a pair of silhouettes in the front row. I don't recall what they were watching, as I was too intent upon my bizarre mission. I lifted the gun and released the trigger safety as the twins stood with backs against the wall, giggling like children playing a naughty trick on mom and dad. I quietly pushed the door aside and stood there for a few seconds. I wondered if they'd notice me standing there, but they never turned their heads. I lifted the pistol and aimed first at what I figured as the father's outline. I pulled the trigger twice. The gun kicked back only slightly as the bullets left the silencer. Then without skipping a beat, I fired a pair of rounds into the back of Mom's head. They both slumped to the floor as I turned to hurriedly leave. Back out in the hallway, I found the twins in a state of hysterical laughter.

"Oh man, we got them good this time!," exclaimed the male.

"Thanks again," said the girl, smiling broadly.

I handed the pistol to her then, wondering what to do next. One part of me wanted to stick around to see if the parents would really come back to life. The other half just wanted to leave. This caused me some consternation as I wondered why I could perform such an act on just the word of this odd pair. Deciding that I couldn't bear to know the truth if they were lying, I turned and left without further word.

I rose from these "events" with the usual sense of wonder. What the hell was going on here? It was not a dream, after all. The gun, for instance, had a balanced weight that surprised me. When I fired it, I was at first alarmed by the kickback from the sliding chamber when the shell ejected.

Mind you, at this point in my life I had never fired a pistol. Thus, I had no clue about these things. Many years later, I attended a shooting class where I discovered that those little details were exactly as experienced in... where? Where, and what, was that distant shore? The twins had called it Valhalla, that grand hall of the Vikings, the heavenly reward of those who died bravely in battle. If the place truly was occupied by those who enjoyed killing and being killed, then maybe these twins were right.

Valhalla

Over the course of the following year and a half I visited Valhalla often. I soon discovered that Valhalla truly was what it was called, though it was far from the gargantuan wooden hall described in writings of old. It may have begun as such, but time in this "alternate" reality seems to have been affected by culture just as it has in "this" reality. Both cultures overlapped in numerous ways.

I decided to keep my eyes open in this place of nasty surprises. I also determined that I would be careful in my "real" world to avoid any situation where I might cause another's death. I figured that maybe if I could get through my life without killing anyone I'd be achieving something. As for Valhalla, I figured that I had been sent there for a purpose. I decided that purpose was to find its base of power in the golden towers and destroy it. I figured if all the violence on Earth came from there, then stopping it there would free the Earth.

During my adventures there, I eventually met up with compatriots. These dozen or so men and women were, like me, a bit confused as to this world, for, like me, they usually resided in the "real" world. Those who had been there the longest taught the newcomers. We had a kind of "rebel alliance," as it were.

Here is what I learned of Valhalla: The entire land is located upon an isthmus that juts out into a sea. There is a city bordered by suburbs which eventually turns to farmland and thick woods. Different peoples inhabit these different areas.

If you were to enter the city from Valhalla's outskirts, you'd find the forest very lightly inhabited. When in the forest, one does not want to run into any of the residents. The deep forest is home to those who, when on earth, create evil magic. Any evil poisoner or kidnapper/torturer who ever dwelt on earth resides here. Some declare them wizards capable of the black arts, but they are mostly just vicious and clever charlatans.

The next zone would be the farmland. This area is occupied by stupidly violent and brutally idiotic farm boys who enjoy slaughter and revel in their own animalism.

Then you enter the suburbs. Here the architecture is Mediterranean. The streets are narrow and confusing. It doesn't take long to realize this confusing layout is purposeful. It's done to trap the unwary. None of the houses have windows on the ground floor, just a heavy wooden door. Any windows are on the upper floors, with a small porch overlooking the door. If you knock on one of these thick doors, the homeowner will appear on this porch so he can see who's there. In short, everything here is designed with defense in mind.

These suburbs are occupied by those who spent life on earth in isolated tribes. Paranoid of any not their kin, they make the streets dangerous for those caught out after dark. Getting through this zone on your way into the city is fraught with danger for the outsider.

A small group of us had managed to find proper disguises that would allow us to safely walk the streets. Our mission was to create a map. Dressed in the same kind of Moroccan robes common there, we managed to blend well enough not to raise suspicion. We followed some twisting alleys until we found ourselves on the edge of a large, open air market. Sticking to the edge of the crowd with our hooded heads low, we were making our way to a street opposite.

Suddenly, the background roar of the market stopped as though someone had given an order to be quiet. We all looked toward the center of the market, as everyone else did. There, in the middle of the teeming crowd stood a tall "man," wearing a very well tailored black, pin-striped suit. I couldn't see his feet, but I just knew they were shod with those same, shiny cop shoes I'd glanced from under that skiff during my first visit.

His black suit and tie and his crisp white shirt gave him a look of noblesse authority. Yet, something was entirely wrong because, you see, he had no head. Not that there was nothing at all above his shoulders, for instead of a head, there was a large white egg. It was a little larger than a man's head, but featureless and blank. We all shivered at the sight.

This being was making some kind of official proclamation to the effect that there were outsiders in the land and all citizens were expected to be vigilant. We knew that meant us. The beings voice was as hypnotic as it was authoritative. I marveled at the obedience displayed by the citizenry toward the egg head man and had the impression that he was the very last person you'd want to cross in this crowd.

The being's words rang in my ears as though the being were standing right next to me. It gave me the creeps. I noticed my compatriots were all suffering the same effects.

"It appears he can broadcast three hundred sixty degrees around his head!," whispered one of my older compatriots.

Then we witnessed another marvel. The egg head directed his voice to a member of the crowd who stood a good hundred feet away. The man received the message and shook his head in agreement with the egg head. Those at the recipient's shoulder reacted only to their neighbor's sudden attention toward the egg head, but not to the

Illustration by James Quigley ("Gunsho"), *http://scuzzdemon.blogspot.com* or gunshojames@gmail.com

voice. This was because, like us, they couldn't hear a thing. We suddenly realized with a start that the being was speaking directly into the recipient's ear, and his ear only! Those who were just inches away couldn't hear what the egg head whispered across the distance.

"So he can not only broadcast to everyone, he can also whisper in your ear from a hundred feet!," I said as quietly as I could.

We then observed the egg head break off his silent conversation and stand at attention for a few seconds. He spun on his heels to face a woman in the crowd at his back, performing the whispering trick on her this time. She shook her head in a way that told me she was receiving instruction of some sort.

What was informative in his sudden pirouette was that it clearly displayed to us that, not only could he speak in all directions, he could also see in all directions! He had been scanning the crowd when he appeared to merely have been standing still. No wonder that lady I met on my first visit told me not to peek out from under the boat.

"These guys are just too powerful," said my older compatriot,

"We better skeedaddle!"

It was then we noticed the egg head wasn't alone. Another, looking just like him, was snooping near the corner we needed to get to. We decided on another route which led us into a dead end. We eventually backtracked, using our map drawn to that point to get back to our hideout in the farmlands. During that eighteen month period there were many misadventures and numerous harrowing failures at trying to get through the "burbs", until we discovered a railroad bridge that allowed us to sneak into the city above the heads of the tribals.

We had to get into the city, you see, to destroy whatever "it" was controlling things in this place. It had to be destroyed because it was also responsible for all the violence on the Earth plane, this present "reality." The denizens of Valhalla weren't happy just staying put, you see, but were continually being reborn onto this planet for the purpose of keeping the pot boiling. We were determined to enter the city and possibly bring about heaven on earth.

The city itself occupied that aforementioned isthmus. It resembled New York in many ways, not the least of which were a pair of twin towers. Mind you, "our" twin towers of 9/11 fame were not even finished when I was experiencing these visions. True, they had been in the news, but as a nineteen year old I had much better things to concern me.

What makes me doubt that these visions of mine weren't merely dreams is not only the clarity of being one experienced there, but also the continuity of the scenery. The steel railroad bridge always had the same dark green paint job. The riveted girders were always the same. There were always the same four sets of tracks spanning it.

As to the twin towers of Valhalla, any similarity to "our" former landmarks ends at them being twins. These towers were not only much taller and wider, they were entirely made of some sort of golden material. No one knew whether or not they were truly made of gold, only that gold was their color. You couldn't even glance their way when the sun bounced off their massive walls without risking temporary blindness.

No one knew which tower contained the "beast" we were after. All we knew was that we somehow had to enter these towers and destroy whatever ran the place. To this end we attempted many times to infiltrate the city. It was a learning process whereby we first suffered in the forest, until we learned how to protect ourselves there. Then we learned to avoid the idiot yokel farm boys. Then we were constantly "murdered" and forced out of phase with the Valhalla plane by the guardians of the suburbs.

When we finally did discover the bridge, it looked too simple. We suspected a trap. The bridge is long, a good half mile to the train yard on the other end downtown. It is constructed of open steel beams mounted on huge stone pillars about sixty feet up. It's quite a frightening prospect attempting to sneak, out in the open air, two stories above the teeming mad masses below. If one of them looked up, we'd be sunk once again.

So it was in small steps that we, one at a time, crawled across the train trestle, peering through the railroad ties to the crazies below, praying they wouldn't see us and hoping an unscheduled train didn't come by. This was a major reason for the holdup, in fact, as we were forced to waste a lot of time just hiding away while copying the trains' schedules.

The strange thing about this railroad is that it was the only form of transport in the land. From the hilly suburbs that overlooked the city on the shore below, not one other form of transportation was to be seen. The streets were designed for pedestrians only. No boats graced the harbor. Whatever was on that far shore remains a mystery.

Even the trains had no passenger service. They only carried freight. They'd take off toward the forest region to return later loaded down with goods. We determined to someday sneak on board to find out what might be on the other end of the line, but for the present we had our hands full.

When we finally managed to sneak into the city successfully, we found ourselves stymied once again by confusing territory. We never made it out of the train yard before we were overwhelmed by the well-armed citizenry. I saw my compatriots get chopped to bits before getting hit in the back myself and fading away.

The Eight Planets

After this, I stopped having these visions for a few months. My sleep was now either dreamless, or else my dreams were as usual—a hodge-podge of non-fitting puzzle pieces. I wondered what it had all been for, but had no answers. Then it happened again, but with a difference.

I find myself standing in an open market. I don't recognize anything here. Looking up, I am amazed to find I'm standing directly at the base of one of the golden towers.

"This is different," I think as I look around, trying not to look suspicious. It's then I notice other compatriots whom I recognize from past adventures. A man here, a woman there—they all appear as confused as I feel. We eventually manage to gather together at the edge of the crowd, which seems especially loud and festive for some reason. We exchange furtive glances at each other, constantly keeping an eye peeled for the egg heads.

"Well. If it isn't our outsiders!," bellows a large man a few feet away. My heart is pounding in my chest as I expect to hear a gunshot or feel a blade in the base of my spine. A good portion of his face is occupied by a red handlebar mustache. He wears some kind of overcoat with epaulettes and gold braid. I can't tell if he's a general of some sort or a bandleader. Beside him stands an egg head, his featureless blankness frightening me to my very core. My blood runs cold as I think, "it's over."

"Ha ha ha!," laughs the bandleader general, "you folks have it all wrong!"

It's at this point we notice the gathering crowd. They're smiling, but not in their usual mean-spirited way. The large, laughing man then tells us the following tale.

He tells us that, once every seven years, all eight planets in their system come close enough together to allow for a grand festival. He tells us we're on the largest of the eight planets and that Valhalla is where the celebration is always held.

"Didn't you notice the sky?," he asks, poking an index finger heavenward.

It's only then that I notice that, sure enough, seven planets are visible in the day lit sky. They spread out in an uneven line across the dome of the heavens like multiple full moons.

"During this festival," he tells us, "no one can commit any form of violence. For five whole days, our brothers and sisters come from the far reaches of space in order to party here. So enjoy yourselves while you may, you are completely safe here!"

As they left, the egg head quietly whispered to us all, "Don't let us find you here afterwards."

As soon as they departed, the crowd moved in on us, wanting to shake the hands of these strange outsiders. We were quite the oddity, it seems.

"Can you answer a question for me?," I asked a man who had earlier demonstrated a small flying device as thin as a credit card.

"What, or who, is in the towers?"

He looked away, pausing as though searching for the correct words.

"I can't explain it to you. Actually, I could, quite easily, it's just that..," again, he paused, "Mind you, I don't mean any insult when I say this, but... I'm not sure you could understand my explanation."

"Just answer this, then...," I said, "is whatever resides there evil?"

"Ahh, now there's the big question. Let me ask you, what *is* evil? Is it something you disagree with? Something most or all of society disagrees with? When a baby dies, is that *evil*? Is nature, in her daily rounds then, evil?"

"Well," I stammered, "there's 'nature' and then there's 'evil'. The theological arguments on this subject go back and forth..."

"The old, 'why doesn't God prevent this sorrow and pain' argument?"

"Exactly!," said I.

"Well, think of this...if not for pain, how would you know the opposites of joy and ease and comfort?

"But this doesn't really answer my question. Why can't we exist without pain?"

"For the reason I just gave! If there was no pain in the physical universe, you'd never learn."

"Learn what?," I demanded.

"Whatever it is you are supposed to learn."

I sat there considering what a clunky universe I found myself in. I still couldn't fathom why all this pain was necessary.

"I see you're still confused," he said with a bit of exasperation. "Well then, let me tell you this, then I won't say another word on the subject of exactly why the world you know is the way it is.

"Imagine being the first cause, or whatever 'it' was at the very beginning. Imagine the scene; there's nothing but...what? "You" don't exist yet because "you" have no way to recognize your own individuality. Floating in space, a sudden curiosity grows as it's seen that there is some "out there" separate from...."I"!

With this "I" realization comes a realization that "I" am alone. The outside is not like the inside.

Now imagine a baby born on the Earth plane. This baby is born with the most awful handicaps. The poor thing is blind, deaf and missing vocal cords or any other means of making a sound. This poor baby has an undeveloped nervous system. It has no way to experience the outside world.

In other words, this poor being, born with a conscious mind, has no way of knowing where, what or when, *it* is. In short, there is no reality, as we experience, for this poor creature.

This being, with no idea of language, still manages to create a world of thought images. It creates a world occupied by creations that itself would consider right for this creation. Can you understand this concept?"

"Sure, I guess so, though it does take some mental calisthenics. It's hard to imagine so much nothing."

"Good. Then you understand the nature of what you call 'God'."

I sat there, stunned. I'd never considered such an idea. I tried to parse it all out in an attempt to find a hole in his logic, but I couldn't. This explained every spiritual question I'd ever had. It all made such wonderful sense. Of course such a creature would invent pain if it needed experience. I still had a question though.

"If, as you say, this god-creature is using us as mere actors in some great passion play, then what is the expected result?"

"To wake up, what else?"

"Wake up?"

"Of course. Think of the creature described. It controls what we lovingly call the 'universe'. Your world. My world. They are all in 'Its' head! So, what we have here is the equivalent of someone in your plane, trapped in a coma. Our creator knows all the worlds are mere substitutes for what 'It' is missing."

The shock of this idea hit me. "You mean... we're all just a dream? If the godhead ever comes out of its comatose state..?"

"Yep," he said. "If 'It' ever awakens, all worlds end. But this is a good thing because then we'll all be integrated into the godhead, you see? There will be no more pain then.

"When do you expect this to come about," I asked.

"When we all have experienced everything there is to experience, or when 'It' has had enough to awaken."

"So, in the meantime, we're all just actors on some stage? Puppets?"

"No. You are one spark of a greater flame."

"And this is why we have evil?"

"Yes. Without 'evil' there is no adventure. It appears that the godhead is hooked on adventure," he said, smiling broadly.

"We here in this plane bring violence to your plane in a measure decided by the godhead, you see. All of the so-called evil people in your plane cycle through here. Some, like those denizens of our suburban zone, are as mere children in your plane. These 'people' are all fairly new creations of the godhead. After a number of lifetimes, they eventually sicken of violence, but until then, their actions can be very informative to the godhead. You see?"

"This is why, when you inquire as to the inhabitants of the towers, I can't truly answer, for we know not. We, on this plane, are as in the dark on this subject as you."

"I see," I replied, "Sorry for trying to destroy your towers."

"That's alright. There's no way that ever could have happened anyhow. Not unless 'It' wanted it that way, that is. These towers will exist as long as evil is needed in your world."

Istanbul

After this "holiday" visitation, the visions stopped. No longer did I visit Valhalla. After what I'd learned about the nature of evil in that plane, I figured going back was redundant. Once knowledge is gained in this school, you are sent out into the "real" world, ready for new mysteries.

Thirty years later I found myself in the unique position of having both the money and the time for travel. Whereas most might use the opportunity to go to Paris or Rome, I had an itch to visit Turkey. This is because I kept seeing scenery from the country in movies that thrilled me. The snow white pools of Pamukkale. The "Fairy Castles" and tunnel systems of Cappadoccia. I just had to see these things myself.

Thus it was that I found myself booking a flight to Istanbul. In doing research, I discovered that September is the best time to visit, so I made reservations at a small hotel called the Sultan's Inn for September 11th, 2001. This choice was completely random. (Or was it?)

I left New York on the evening of the tenth, landing in Istanbul around eleven in the morning, Istanbul time. A driver was there to take me to the hotel, where I showered, shaved and took a walk around the beautiful neighborhoods of that ancient city.

After a few hours I returned to my hotel for a nap, planning to go out again later that night to check out Istanbul's vaunted night scene. This was around 1 p.m.

While I slept the sleep of happy innocence abroad, terrible jets were crashing into the Twin Towers of the World Trade Center. As I slept off my jet lag, thousands of people who showed up for work that beautiful blue morning back in New York were launching themselves skyward.

I woke at 10 p.m. and set out onto the street. I walked a few blocks up the hill toward the Blue Mosque when I was accosted by a local tout, employed to drag tourists like me into the restaurants and carpet shops along the boulevard.

"Excuse me sir," called out the Ringo Starr look-alike.

"What country are you from?"

"America," I answered.

At the mention of "America," Ringo slapped both palms over his heart, saying, "Ahh... America! My heart goes out to you!"

He could tell by the perplexed look on my face that I had no clue as to what he just said.

"You don't know?," he asked, incredulously.

He held a closed fist before his face, and with the other, smacked it, saying, "Your huge towers! Planes! Bombs!"

He then spread his hands, palm down, at his waist. "Your place of generals! More Planes! More bombs!"

Then he pointed a finger into the air, making a circular motion.

"Your president Boosh! In the air! No one knows!"

I stood there for a second in stunned silence. What was this guy trying to tell me? I'd heard these touts could be tough, but this was beyond the pale! He couldn't be saying this in order to get me to buy something? Could he?

At this point his boss came out of the restaurant to talk to me. Fortunately, he spoke English very well.

"It's true," he said. "The Twin Towers were attacked by planes, as was the Pentagon. Not so much damage there, but New York is bad."

I returned to my hotel later that night, where I climbed the stairs to the rooftop restaurant. I knew it was closed and dark, and that's how I wanted it. As I stood there at the rail, observing the majestic beauty of the nearby Blue Mosque, I recalled the words of my guide on that Valhallic holiday all those years ago. "These towers will exist as long as evil is needed in your world," is what he'd said.

I cried there on the rooftop in Istanbul that night. I cried for all those poor people who should have called in sick that day. I also wondered if those towers of gold still stood on that other shore, if 'It' "wanted it that way," as my guide had said.

About the Author

Mark Elliott is a writer, traveler, assistant editor for *PARANOIA*, and a cancer survivor. When existing on this plane, he resides in the wilds of Rhode Island, playing his hand drum for the local belly dancers. He also plays the Turkish drum in the Providence band, Alec K. Redfearn and the Eyesores.

Lady of Fatima in Alabama

Is the Virgin Mary Appearing in Caritas?

by Dail Cantrell

On July 1-5, 2009, tens of thousands of people from all over the world gathered just outside of Birmingham, Alabama at a small evangelical commune called Caritas in the hopes of seeing an apparition of the Virgin Mary. Her appearance had been predicted by a witness to the ongoing visions reportedly occurring at Medjugorje, a small town in Bosnia-Hercegovina now famous for such sightings.

Along with the increase in reports of a "mysterious hitchhiker" being seen on the Natchez Trace Parkway between Mississippi and Tennessee, and the crosses of light that have reportedly been seen in the windows of Copper Ridge Baptist Church in Knoxville, Tennessee, Caritas is quickly gaining worldwide attention as it relates to claims that the Virgin Mary is regularly appearing in conjuncture with the "seers" of Medjugorje.

Marian groups and associations exist in all fifty of the United States and in countries throughout the world. Marian conferences take place frequently, supporting people who have an ongoing interest in the occurrences in Fatima, Guadalupe and Lourdes. More recently however, discussion has focused on Medjugorje.

The story is relatively well known; on June 25, 1981, five teenagers and a ten year old began telling others that they were seeing the Virgin Mary, who was holding the infant Christ in her arms, on a local mountain. These events occurred in Medjugorje, which is located in what was then Soviet-controlled Yugoslavia, now known as Bosnia-Herzegovina.

Three of the witnesses, Vicka, Marija, and Yvonne, still claim to have daily apparitions. Two of the young seers, Ivanka and Jackof, claim to have visions once per year; Ivanka on June 25, and Jackof on Christmas. The sixth alleged prophet, Mirajana, claims to witness an apparition on the 2nd of each month and annually on March 18th, the date of her birth.

Since the sightings occurred in 1981, millions have traveled from all over the world in pilgrimage to Medjugorje. Among them is a young American named Terry Colafrancesco, who allegedly was so inspired after his visit that he founded Caritas of Birmingham in 1986. Mr. Colafrancesco has written multiple books under the pseudonym "Friend of Medjugorje" and supervises a multi-million dollar enterprise whereby he organizes pilgrimages from Alabama to Medjugorje, and regularly hosts events at Caritas.

Mr. Colafrancesco's real work began in 1989 after he befriended Marija Pavlovic Lunetti, one of the original seers, and paid for her brother's trip to Birmingham for a kidney transplant. Colafrancesco subsequently built the "Tabernacle of our Lady's Messages," a thirty thousand plus square-foot building, and is responsible for operating the multi-million dollar business that Caritas has become. Mr. Colafrancesco claims that "Our Lady" speaks directly to his community through her daily messages.

Colafrancesco originally purchased the Alabama property for $400,000 and then solicited approximately two million in contributions to build the center. His "ministry" exploded after Marija conveniently claimed to have had a vision on Thanksgiving Day in a field located on the property. She is now a regular visitor to Alabama, and apparitions are announced well in advance, and Colafrancesco benefits from the influx of hundreds of thousands of dollars to the community each time an apparition occurs.

Unlike Fatima or Lourdes, the Catholic Church, through the Congregation for the Doctrine of the Faith (CDF), does not recognize what is allegedly occurring at either Medjugorje or Caritas as being an apparition of the Virgin Mary.

On January 25th, 1991, a report contained in the *Catholic Herald* written by Vivian E. Heweit in Rome, reported that the CDF was imposing a ban on further information on the issue of Medjugorje. The report coincided with a campaign led by several Italian Bishops who were against pilgrimages to Medjugorje.

In a letter to Father Hugh Thwaites, dated August 2, 1987, the late Pavao Zanic, the local bishop in Medjugorje at the time, stated bluntly that Our Lady does not appear at Medjugorje, that there are no miracles, and that the "messages" cannot possibly come from Our Lady. "They are the fruit of a fabrication, fraud, and disobedience to the Church. It is about big money and personal interest too."

Despite this, the Medjugorje industry grew rapidly in the United States and the Caritas community began hosting events which they call "miracles." Today, millions regularly visit and monetarily support both Medjugorje and Caritas. According to Colafrancesco's website, "supernatural signs are a method God has used throughout history to know Him and to bring His children to conversion. It is a way God speaks to us or to insight our hearts to believe in coming to Him."

When church leaders counter with scripture taken from the Holy Bible, and offer that Jesus once said: Matthew 12:39 "An evil and unfaithful generation seeks a sign, but no sign will be given except the sign of Jonah the prophet," Colafrancesco contradicts the Bible by stating that on March 25, 1990, Our Lady revealed through the visions that "God wants to save you and send you messages through men, nature, and so many things which can only help you understand that you must change the direction of your life."

In the weeks preceding the July 2009 so-called apparitions, Colafrancesco and the Caritas community spent hundreds of thousands of dollars promoting the event. Billboards and advertisements were purchased in the United States and elsewhere, urging people to make the pilgrimage to Caritas in order to be a witness to the apparitions. I, along with my friend Joe Weaver, decided to make the pilgrimage and arrived in Birmingham, Alabama on the evening of June 30, 2009. We stayed approximately 25 miles outside of Caritas, and found that the Virgin Mary apparitions were being marketed in the style of a rock concert or a political rally, with flyers and Mapquest-generated directions left at area hotels and restaurants.

We arrived at Caritas on the morning of July 1, shortly after 7:00 a.m., as morning activities and announcements were scheduled to occur at 8:00 a.m. By the time we arrived, several thousand people were already on the property. Once we walked onto the grounds we were directed toward the Tabernacle, an impressive structure with state of the art equipment. We were told that the morning events had been pushed back an hour, and we were invited to visit the various gift shops and vendors located on the property, and to take a tour of the facilities.

Once inside the main Tabernacle, a member of the Caritas community greeted us and immediately began soliciting donations for the mission's current fund drive. The Caritas community publishes several books and documents that can be purchased through their website, and this particular fund drive (which just happened to coincide with the scheduled apparitions) was designed to raise 1.4 million dollars to "retool" the printing facilities. A pleasant young man, along with other Caritas community members, explained to us how our donations could help further the ministry.

We were then shepherded toward a several thousand square-foot gift store that sold Mr. Colafrancesco's books, as well as items that were made and embroidered on the property. Here, several pleasant Caritas community members told us that these items were for sale, and that the Virgin mother would bless them during the apparition. We were advised that they would make for a beautiful heirloom or keepsake for our families.

Later in the morning another young lady, who appeared to be the spokesman for the Caritas community group, led a morning prayer and made what she called the first "pitch" that we would hear during the next five days. The pitch related to what was available to be purchased and what sort of contribution plans might be arranged during the event. She explained the cost of hosting an event such as this one, and assured us it was only through our donations that the message could be spread.

By now there were several thousand people gathered at the Tabernacle awaiting the announcement of the time of the apparition and when we would be able to speak with Marija Pavlovic Lunetti. We were informed that instead of appearing at the "field of apparitions" located on the property as advertised, the Virgin had informed Marija and Mr. Colafrancesco that she would be appearing in the personal bedroom of Mr. Colafrancesco. Unfortunately, those of us assembled would not be allowed into the bedroom to witness the apparition, but were told to assemble in the field across the street from the property. We were assured that although we would not be able to witness the apparition, the Virgin Mother would be able to see us and would bless the items that we were purchasing. We were then told to come back the next day, and perhaps the apparition would appear in the field at that time.

As one might expect, the July 2 apparition also appeared in Mr. Colafrancesco's bedroom and the pilgrims were again led to believe that if they returned the following day the Virgin Mary would appear in the field. At this point Joe and I lost interest and decided to head back to Tennessee.

However, before we left we were able to hear an hour-long speech from Mr. Colafrancesco who is an intense and gifted orator. The first fifteen minutes of his message were focused on the evil of cellular telephones. He told multiple anecdotes about how he had recently struck a lady that was text messaging someone during one of the apparitions, and had poked another lady with his umbrella. He explained that if any cellular telephones were caught on his property at Caritas they would be confiscated.

In addition to cell phones, Mr. Colafrancesco did not allow any photographic devices, recording devices, cameras, or video of any kind. This rule was strictly enforced. His staff, however, took multiple photos that were posted on his web site.

I spent my time at Caritas talking to the other pilgrims and the members of the Caritas community. I found all of the members to be extremely friendly and accessible. I did not see anything that I would describe as "cult-like" behavior, and left feeling like the community members shared an extremely positive living environment and were honestly dedicated to their mission. Based upon my experiences, the criticism of this community as being a "cult" is unfair. Caritas appears to be an extremely productive and peaceful place to live.

I am basing my assessment on the definition of a cult as being a religious collective, few in number, held together by a forceful leader. I view a "cult" as having poorly defined beliefs that are often viewed as bizarre or sinister. Devotion to the Virgin Mother and to "her" message is too widely accepted to be considered cult-like behavior. Similar occurrences at Lourdes and Fatima have followings in the tens of millions. Likewise, the devotion to these events is neither strange nor malevolent.

With that being said, this enterprise is obviously making millions of dollars not only on the property, but also on the high volume of pilgrimages that Mr. Colafrancesco is organizing back and forth to Medjugorje. There are direct non-stop flights that regularly leave from Birmingham to Medjugorje, and travelers often pay a fee for members of the Caritas community, including Mr. Colafrancesco, to take them back and forth.

The most disturbing thing I witnessed during my time at Caritas was the devotion from said pilgrims to Mr. Colafrancesco and to the messages. During the time I was there, I never once heard a reference to the Holy Bible or to any Church doctrine. The Caritas community has adopted the daily messages that are allegedly received from the Virgin Mary as their scripture. They are referred to in much the same manner as Bible verses, as though a religion has been developed based upon what the apparitions are telling a select few. I think that this alone is dangerous.

It is easy to see why the Catholic Church is distancing itself from what is occurring at Medjugorje and not from, say, Fatima or Lourdes. I saw nothing that I would describe as supernatural or prophetic. What I witnessed were several thousand people hoping to see something that never appeared. If the purpose of a retreat at Caritas is to experience four or five days of prayer and self-reflection, then the beautiful property offers just that. But pilgrims hoping to be enlightened by an apparition of the Virgin Mary should not hold their breath.

I unequivocally accept the idea that supernatural events beyond scientific explanation occur. I also believe that there are a great number of people trying to make money off of those who desperately want a "sign" to substantiate their faith.

If something is appearing to the six original seers at Medjugorje, I am not convinced that it is the Virgin Mary. Could it be an "evil spirit?" Perhaps. What I know for sure is that a lot of money is flowing into Birmingham, Alabama. And when this much money is at stake, an institution should be able to withstand a reasonable amount of scrutiny. Caritas cannot.

About the Author

Dail R. Cantrell is the managing partner of Cantrell, Cantrell & Fisher and a retired professor from the University of Tennessee. He has written several books and articles on a wide range of subjects. His latest book, *Equal to the Task*, was a national Book of the Year nominee. Joseph Weaver is employed by the Oak Ridge National Laboratories.

Eustace Mullins at 86

Blacklisted Historian's Works Reveal the Deception of Mainstream History

by John Kaminski

On February 2, 2010, Eustace Mullins passed on to the higher realms where he will join his good friend, poet Ezra Pound. This profile was written prior to his passing.

Lots of fine folks around the world have been worried lately about the welfare of legendary anti-establishment historian Eustace Mullins. Actually, half-baked reports and calculated rumors have had him killed, kidnapped, missing or otherwise under siege for decades. Some of these items have been true, others only near misses.

I'm here to tell you that Eustace is fine. One is tempted to describe him as "never better," but for a writer as young as myself, describing an old codger of 86 years filled with intrigue and tragedy, whose legs don't work very well anymore and who is prone to nodding off after a good meal, that would be a subjective judgment I would not care to make.

I've been hearing stories about the persecution and exploitation of Eustace Mullins by shadowy people with ulterior motives since the late 1980s, when they'd already been happening for thirty years. To make a long story short, Eustace would be dead today—murdered, actually—if not for the miraculous intervention of a guardian angel. Yes, it does happen.

The thing that first strikes me as remarkable about Eustace is his face, especially when he laughs, which is often. Good humor amidst adversity is perhaps the finest human trait, which this battler for objective human truth possesses in abundance.

Even though the subject at hand may be tragic and portend dire consequences for the entire human race, when the point is made, and Eustace laughs wryly, all the wrinkles on his face disappear, except for two little crow's feet. His eyes sparkle as he glances upward, as if to say, "I tell them what I've found, Lord, that's about all I can do." The best way I can put it is that he is infused with a kind of light I've seen in very few others.

Eustace Mullins is the most blacklisted, suppressed and harassed writer in American history. In the introduction to his *A writ for martyrs*, which is a report on the files the FBI compiled on him for decades, Mullins writes, "In a single day, my life changed from one of peaceful artistic endeavor to one of constant struggle for survival. One dark winter day in 1948, some friends persuaded me to visit the poet Ezra Pound in his cell at St. Elizabeth's Hospital, Washington, D.C. That day was to cast a pall over my life, and to bring great suffering to my innocent family."

After 25 books, including such pertinent titles as *The Secrets of the Federal Reserve*, *Murder by Injection*, and *The World Order: Our Secret Rulers*, Mullins is now living the good life, sort of, thanks to his rescue from oblivion by a lone man who takes life very seriously. Mullins and his steadfast caretaker Jesse Lee are essentially homeless, but touring the country, going from friend to friend, selling the same books Mullins has been peddling for sixty years. (You can acquire these precious, museum quality books—and possibly get a visit from Eustace and Jesse in the bargain—simply by writing to me and I'll pass the info on.)

But in their happy travels, they do something a lot more than that. With Jesse's thoughtful guidance, they raise eyebrows and elicit love wherever and with whomever they meet. The minute Eustace's message reaches the unenlightened, they seem to universally respond, "I need to hear this information, because it relates to what is happening now more than anything I've ever heard on TV."

Sitting comfortably in an easy chair, Mullins dismisses the physical problems that have plagued him in recent years with a wave of his hand, and says matter-of-factly, chuckling with that twinkle again, "I still have 25 more books to write!"

Savor the titles of some of Mullins' pamphlets: "The plagues of pharaoh," "Jewish TV: Sick sick sick," and "Why General Patton Was Murdered." But more importantly, understand the content of all these publications and simply marvel at the profound enormity of the output.

Among his major works:

The Secrets of the Federal Reserve may just be the single book that can save the American republic, if that's possible, because it objectively examines how the international bankers have reshaped reality throughout the 20th century and turned our freedom into slavery.

Murder by Injection: The Story of the Medical Conspiracy Against America reveals the American Medical Association's sordid history of killer quackery and heartless profiteering that continues today with the ubiquitous use of poison medicines to cure fictional diagnoses.

The World Order: Our Secret Rulers names the five men who rule the world.

In *The Rape of Justice: America's Tribunals Exposed*, Mullins writes: " . . . the cause of our legal dilemma, that our Constitutional courts, as authorized in the Constitution, have stealthily been replaced by equity courts, operating on the stern military principles of admiralty punishment."

So now you have some idea why the notorious FBI director J. Edgar Hoover put a tail on Mullins for decades; in fact, probably, the agent is still posted.

Eustace's guardian Jesse says *The Curse of Canaan* is the key to all of Mullins' works, because it explains the demonic plot that has plagued civilization for five thousand years. Back in the late 1980s, when I first encountered *Curse of Canaan*, I was put off by religious terminology I didn't understand, and I thought all evangelical types were the same—hypocrites.

Since then I've learned differently. Like the debate about good Jews and bad Jews, there is no debate that there are good Christians and bad Christians. Israel-poisoned shills like John Hagee, Billy Graham and Jerry Falwell are the bad Christians; but the good ones like Jesse Lee and Eustace leave no doubt in anyone's mind that they are driven by the light of truth, and overjoyed at the prospects of the trip they're on.

As stimulating as reading Eustace Mullins can be, conversing with him can be even more startling, not to mention educational. "People don't realize the United States didn't win the Revolutionary War," Eustace casually says. "They let us think we won, but it never really happened."

Jaws usually drop considerably at that line. Summoning my meager knowledge of America's war for independence, I began to babble on about Alexander Hamilton, the guy on the $10 bill, as being one of the key figures preventing America's independence from Britain and the international bankers. I brought up a name familiar to Eustace, the respected Jewish economic historian Emanuel Josephson, who was Mullins' close friend when they both lived in the same New York City neighborhood a half century ago.

Josephson wrote that Hamilton was half black and half Jewish, went to Hebrew school in London, and later prevented the fledgling colonies from financial freedom by reserving the printing of paper money to the banks, rather than the government, despite what the Fourth Amendment of the Constitution appears to say.

"That kind of reminds me of Abraham Lincoln," Eustace retorted. "Lincoln's mother was a slave and his father was a Jew. Did you know that Lincoln's wife went mad and spent the later part of her life in an insane asylum, and that both of Lincoln's sons committed suicide?" He continued. "Lincoln was put in place by the bankers, too. That whole greenbacks thing was just a smokescreen."

After a pause, Eustace went on. "Did you know that for two whole years, Averill Harriman was the leader of Russia?"

Harriman, member of an infamously rich American family comparable and in league with the Bushes, was sent to Russia by the Rockefellers right after Hitler invaded in 1941, because when that happened Stalin had a nervous breakdown which lasted two years. Harriman later returned to the U.S. and ran for vice president in 1948.

Perhaps with Eustace Mullins rather than any other author, you can really get a feel for how deep the rabbit hole goes. Among Mullins' more astounding publications are among books of commentary on the Jewish question, including a mammoth tome titled *Mullins' New History of the Jews*, and small booklets containing the riveting essays "Jewish War Against the Western World," "Sigmund Freud: Anti-Christ Devil," "There's a Gulag in Your Future," and "The Biological Jew," plus scores of other essays and short works with similar titles and subject matter.

So it seemed natural to suggest my own observations for his scrutiny, and when I did, was I surprised.

"So, Eustace," I queried, "who really runs the world?"

"The Queen," he answered quickly.

"You mean it's not the Sanhedrin!?" I exclaimed, flabbergasted. "Are you sure it's not the Sanhedrin that runs the Queen?"

"No, it's Queen Elizabeth who runs the Sanhedrin and everything else—most definitely."

As I said, with Eustace Mullins, both with reading his works and listening to him, prepare to be astounded. Prepare to learn the real history that has been concealed from us by the people who own the media, who just happen to be the same people who own the banks and the government.

Since 1988 I'd been hearing secondhand stories about Eustace and about how numerous charlatans would make their way to his modest Staunton, Virginia home to try to steal the rights to Eustace's books. Many times I pondered how the only thing that could really save Eustace from the ravages of time and inattention was a guardian angel.

For decades, said angel never appeared, and Eustace's health rapidly went down the tubes. Then suddenly, right after filmmaker Randy Atkins made the video *The Neo-Zionist World Order*, which consisted of an extensive interview with Mullins, the latest team of these charlatans spirited Eustace out of the Virginia nursing home where he had been living to another nursing home in Texas.

Two criminals named Blackburn and Spencer were all set to commit Mullins to a Texas state institution, where it would have been all but impossible to get him out. During this dangerous episode, Spencer actually reprinted one of Mullins' works, carefully removing all instances of the word "Jew," and pocketing all the profits for himself.

As Eustace recalls it, "Spencer told me that if I took the word out of all my books, we could make a million dollars." That, Eustace recalls, is what G. Edward Griffin did. "He totally plagiarized my *Secrets of the Federal Reserve* and made two million dollars."

Just as Mullins was to be committed to a Texas state institution, along comes Jesse Lee, son of a Baptist preacher, who perceived the unjust horror of the situation. Jesse snatched Eustace from the clutches of money-grubbing opportunists and the poisoned nursing home, and drove him off to Maine for a 40-day raw vegetable fast.

And that's what saved Eustace's life. Since then Eustace and Jesse have lived a nomadic life, going from friend to friend, all over the U.S., spreading the real history of the United States and waking people up in the friendliest of ways.

Jesse Lee, you may know, looks just like Santa Claus (well, much thinner). While on a previous fast in the mountains of Colorado, Jesse took a Nazarite vow to never again cut his hair as a sign he was a servant of the Lord, and the task he adopted as his life's work was to resuscitate and renourish Eustace. So far this mission, a tremendous amount of work since Mullins is essentially not able to sustain himself without significant care, has been a complete success. And a great gift to those they choose to visit.

Jesse's goal for the future, suggested by Atkins, is to reacquire the old Mullins homestead in Staunton, also buy the house next door, and turn them both into the Eustace Mullins Ezra Pound Institute for Civilization, sell books and protect the works of Mullins, Pound and other authors who have been blacklisted by the authorities who control people's thoughts. That plan at this point is only a dream.

"We're not out to sell books," Jesse stresses. "We just want to spread the word."

Lately I've noticed something that I've never noticed before. I guess it's one of the perks of getting older. I've noticed that a lot of the best people—not the ones who are trying to make lots of money or assume positions of power after they steal them from whomever possesses them at the moment—exude a certain kind of light about them.

Jesse has asked me if I was a Christian, and I said no, but added that Jesus was a close personal friend of mine. Jesse didn't know that I am one of the most trenchant and persistent critics of organized religion in the world. Or at least that's what I like to think.

But lately I've noticed that the people who say and do the best things are all driven by a certain faith in God, and are made happy by it, regardless of whatever historical anomalies that I might hold in such high and incriminating regard, and regardless of whichever creed—except for that horrible one we've been talking about—that espouses veneration of a highest power with an emphasis on love, charity and service . . . you know, that highest power that has given us our lives. I've seen it just as strongly in Catholics, Muslims, Baptists and Buddhists. Sorry to say I don't know any Hindus, but I'm sure they have it, too.

It's the light of faith that shows through in good works for the highest purposes, and it is the most beautiful thing in the world. Lately I feel this light rising in myself, the light of safety, and I don't know what do about it, trenchant critic of psyops religions that I pretend to be.

A thought crosses my mind: What if all the believers in the world united against the nonbelievers? I'm not talking lockstep Hageeism here. I'm talking about understanding we all have shared goals and shared beliefs, but some agency in the world somehow exacerbates our differences instead of emphasizing our commonalities. They foment conflict for the purpose of exploiting both sides. As a direct result, society is in chaos while the mind-locked government works to mass murder as many people as possible so the rich can have less crowded playgrounds.

What if all the believers in the world found their commonality and exposed and neutralized the one group of nonbelievers that controls everything for a purpose that can only be described as selfish and evil? Well, it's just a dream. A dream that could be made possible if everyone understood everything that Eustace Mullins has ever said, and put those thoughts into action.

The phone rings. It's Randy, supposedly the next stop for Eustace and Jesse. "They're not here yet." I get on the phone. "Jesse, where are you?" "Oh, we stopped at Mia's. Don't know how long we'll be here, but we're having a great time."

Join in if you like. You'll never regret it.

***

For videos and information on Eustace Mullins, check this website: *www.whale.to/b/mullins_h.html*, where you will read the following statement by Bill Meridian: "In the late 1980s, the "Morton Downey, Jr. Show" invited Eustace Mullins, author of *Secrets of the Federal Reserve* and myself to speak about the Fed on the air. I declined and Eustace accepted. About a month later, major sponsors pulled their backing and the show was cancelled. I recall reading an article in which Downey lamented that he could not understand why his life had suddenly taken such a downturn."

About the Author

John Kaminski is a writer who lives on the Gulf Coast of Florida and was recently graced by a visit from the two above-mentioned angels. He may be reached at: skylax@comcast.net. His website is: *http://johnkaminski.info/.*

Books by Eustace Mullins

A Writ for Martyrs
Mullins' New History of the Jews
Murder by Injection: The Medical Conspiracy Against America
My Life in Christ
Secrets of the Federal Reserve
The Curse of Canaan: A Demonology of History
The Federal Reserve Conspiracy
The Rape of Justice: America's Tribunals Exposed
The Sedition Case
The World Order, A Study in the Hegemony of Parasitism
This Difficult Individual:Ezra Pound
War! War! War!
The Secret History of the Atomic Bomb

Pamphlets and Other Works

Murder by Injection the great swine flu massacre
27 Billion Dollar Rip Off; The Power Brokers
Boycott: The Jewish Weapon
Canada: A Financial Report For 1992
Criminals On Capitol Hill
Death To The Peacemakers
Education For Death
Education for Slavery
Every Man A King
FDR
Federal Reserve Notes: Shackles Of Slavery
General MacArthur The Man Who Refused to Lose
Genocide In America
How The Media Is Manipulated
How To Become A United States Senator
Is There A New World Order?
Jewish TV: Sick, Sick, Sick
New Israel
Our Identity
Sigmund Freud: Anti-Christ Devil
Supreme Court Burns Us Again
The Hidden Hand Behind Televangelism
The Holocaust Explained
The Lindbergh Murders: Hauptman Was Innocent
The New World Order
The Plagues Of Pharaoh
The Power Brokers Of Canada
The Scandal Unveiled
The Trilaterals Are Back In The White House
The Vietnam Wall
The War Against Christianity
The War Against Vietnam Veterans
There's A Gulag In Your Future
Trotsky: Where Are You Now?
War Is The Only Way Out
Warning: The Department Of Justice Is Dangerous To Americans
Washington DC: City Of Fear
What Are We Fighting To Preserve?
Who Owns the TV Networks ?
American Patriotism Means Loyalty to Israel
America's New Robber Barons: Exclusive Report

Note: This is not an exhaustive list.

NEW JERSEY
A
GREAT
PLACE
Tiny Tim

Where is Irving Thalberg Now?

An Interview with Tiny Tim (1994)

by Joan d'Arc and Mark Westion

We met with Tiny Tim one Sunday afternoon at the bar in the Howard Johnson's Motor Lodge in Warwick, Rhode Island for a chat and a few beers. Mister Tim is a sweet man who is polite to everyone he meets, always placing a Miss or Mister before their first name. He drinks Molson Ice with a straw and wears really cool sequined sneakers. And Mister Tim obviously had a good upbringing; apparently the women in his life did not. His first wife, Miss Vickie, whom he married on the Johnny Carson show in 1969, has now seen fit to sell the perverted version of her story for big bucks to a tabloid, *The Star*. Miss Vickie should get a life. His present wife, Miss Jan, should quit being a cheat and hand over her little black book to her lawfully wedded husband. And Mister Tim's Eternal Princess, Miss Stephanie, should stop opening the door to everyone but him, and prepare to fly through the portals of Heaven and the New Earth with Tim and Tim alone.

Mr. Tim: Praise the Good Lord for giving me a sliver of the future; I believe everything comes from him, thank his blessings. This is an unbelievable world...the more I think of it, the more mysterious it gets! Last night—(and I'll answer any questions you've got, if you've got all day so do I, because we may never have this time again. Everything that goes out is a document, whether it's the *Times*, or college kids or high school juniors. Keep the word going. Years ago I went into the New York Public Library on 42nd Street and I was amazed at how many articles you could find, day by day, that nobody knows about, it would take a lifetime to read).

So anyway, last night on Channel 2, I saw a program called The MGM Years, all about the early film "talkies" and there was Irving Thalberg, director of *Mutiny of the Bounty*, a genius, taken away at the young age of 37, way before his time. I was in bed in the early morning, wondering where he was. You can't talk to him any more! It's like the old scripture "Dust thou art and to dust you shall return." Now he's gone! All the people—my parents, everyone—all floating specks of dust! There must be a great silence among the dead. I wonder about all these things; where is Irving Thalberg now? All I can do, all any of us can do, is to have blind faith. I can only go by the documents of history. I didn't see Lincoln here, but the facts say he was here. I didn't see Washington, I didn't see Jesus Christ, but I believe he was here and he arose from the dead. I believe in the great Yahweh, God, Creator of Israel. Perhaps the Good Lord called him [Irving Thalberg] because he wanted some movies made up in heaven. We never know what's going on.

Miss Joan: Have you ever seen a flying saucer?

Mr. Tim: No, I've never seen a flying saucer, although I wish I could, and perhaps only a few have been fortunate to see them. There are people who believe in reincarnation, and certainly everyone can have their opinion until proven right or wrong. However, there was one instance only that I talked with a woman in Florida in 1990, whose husband was a sheriff. She claimed she was abducted by a flying saucer at a shopping mall. I asked her how these beings looked and what she could remember about it and right away she blanked out. Her husband came in from outside about five minutes later and during that time she said nothing. People who actually have these experiences most of the time will be able to name names, places, times, facts and give some proof. But mostly it's not possible (Miss Peggy, could you bring another round?)

Here's another interesting story: In 1968, when I started to get "hot," Shelly Winters invited me to her house. When I walked into her house, she started ranting and raving that she was responsible for President Kennedy's death! Bobby Kennedy had just been shot, John Kennedy's death had been years before, but she blamed herself. And I asked her, "When did you have this premonition that the President would die? Did you see the date, did you see who would do it, did you see the time and place?" I told her that if she didn't see all these things, then she can't blame herself.

Miss Joan: The President may not have listened to her warning anyway.

Mr. Tim: That's a very good point. At least if she had the time and place down, they would have listened to her. When I left the house, she never spoke to me again. In all these phenomena—like the flying saucer mystery at Roswell, New Mexico—if the military is hiding things, these people all have dates, times, and it's all been written down how everything at the crash site looked. So if it's true that the Air Force is hiding things, these are exceptions to the rule.

Miss Joan: So you believe that there is a government cover-up of alien beings and flying saucers?

Mr. Tim: I would say yes. There is a government cover-up of something unusual, something that would shock mankind.

Miss Joan: Meaning it would affect our religions?

Mr. Tim: Now Miss Joan, that's a great question! Not only would it affect all our religions, Catholics, Protestants, even Jews, but that opens up a can of worms, because the questions now are, "Did the Garden of Eden apply only to the Earth beings or to beings in the entire Universe? Does the banishment from the Garden of Eden apply only to Earth beings? How does this affect Mars, or Venus, or planets in another galaxy?"

Miss Joan: Yes, and do we share heaven with beings from other planets?

Mr. Tim: Or if they have a Hell, have they sinned, or does this only apply to the banishment from the Garden of Eden? Remember God's command: "Thou shalt have no other gods before me." We don't know what outer space holds and who is dominant. There might be some beings who have never heard of this particular great god Yahweh. They might have their own god in another galaxy, or it very well may be that Yahweh is the Creator of all of the galaxies. So yes, this would certainly change aspects of religious beliefs. In the last days, there will be many things that will befuddle everyone. Where is our God, where is He? The last days could be today, or centuries from now.

Miss Joan: And if Jesus showed up in a spaceship would people be shocked?

Mr. Tim: They would be shocked, but does he have to walk on air? He may have chosen to ride. The great God Yahweh always keeps something from man; he surprises him all the time! There really is no religion that knows it all. But we'd like to think that we know it all.

Take for example, the film *The Last Temptation of Christ*. It's 1988, a hot summer in New York City. I was barely paying the rent after my mother left. *The Last Temptation of Christ* was opening up to penalties of error and sin, at the Ziegfield Theater on 54th Street. I had nothing to do, it was hot in my hotel room. I did not, I repeat, I did not go down there for publicity! Something beckoned me to go to this opening. I took a cab and got off at Broadway and saw lines all the way down on both sides; on one side protestors against and on one side lined up to see the movie. I had to walk down the middle of the street, and everyone was pointing and saying there's Tiny Tim! I did not want this publicity. The protestors were shouting that it was a sin to see this picture because it proclaims that Jesus Christ sinned.

Then the cameraman from ABC comes up and asks me if I believe it was a sin to see this picture.

I said "that's why I want to see the picture." If Jesus Christ sinned with Mary Magdalene, that makes me believe more in him, because then he realizes that since he came from God and became as a man, he would truly realize the pain, the suffering, the loneliness and sexual desire, which is needed here in the heat of the day, in the afternoons of time. Would that make me believe less in him? On the contrary! And then I got in line to see the movie and I was booed by the other side.

When I saw the picture, it had made allowances for that before it started. It said that the picture is only the opinion of the writer. But here's where I was shocked with the picture: it showed that Mary Magdalene was very beautiful, and that Jesus was in love with her and she didn't want him to die, but as he was going on the cross, a beautiful little girl told him to come down, she said, "you've suffered enough." So he came down from the cross and lived many years with Mary Magdalene. Judas, who had betrayed him, later said to him, 'you know I betrayed you, who knows if it was meant to be or not, but look what you did, you sold yourself, you came down from the cross!' Then he tells Jesus that the little girl was Satan; the devil appearing as an angel, a beautiful little girl!

I pray that Satan and his demon angels repent. Let's say Satan is tired of this warfare and the great God gave him the ability to enter the Garden of Eden to take the challenge. Instead of being his robot, he lets him roam the world as a prince of evil; and let's face it, he won the battle! Today we have a world gone wild. Who can stay together? Who can get to heaven? But Satan himself will be bound up by the Almighty. Suppose he said: "Jesus Christ says to forgive the enemy ten times over, I'm asking you to forgive me. Me and my demon angels were wrong to rebel against you; we were mighty but you were Almighty. I was jealous when you created man as lower than the angels, so deliver us, show us your example and deliver us from our insanity and schizophrenia, bring us back to sanity and home to heaven."

So, you can see, instead of the second coming, it would be the second going, back to heaven! If the great Artist of the Universe allows this to happen, then no one goes to Hell and the Garden of Eden can be recreated, because of his mercy, with one exception: those who are born again will have the knowledge of good and evil and what happened before! Not saying that Satan will not try again. I thank God for giving me life, for giving me breath, and the ability to think.

Miss Joan: What about all the earthquakes and calamities going on right now. Is the end near?

Mr. Tim: It might be near, I believe, but we've thought this throughout the centuries. I feel something is coming, from inner space perhaps, or from outer space, we will see them coming.

Mr. Mark: Do you think we'll see this during our lifetime?

Mr. Tim: Yes. It's no great wisdom, but I think about inner space and outer space. I had a strange dream one time: there were many different types of people. (I think there will be aliens who come to our rescue and aliens who do not). I saw a time when the Earth was captured by beings from another universe. These beings had taken over and were ruling the Earth. They looked like polar bears. They needed to eat human meat, and so in captivity they were feeding the earthlings enough to get fat and they were carting them off in cattle cars to go to slaughter. They would start out being secretive about it. Also I saw the young ones. I saw stores that were selling human legs, all shaved, and little kids were taken like young calves.

Miss Joan: You're not alone in that theory, others believe we are being "farmed" by an alien species; first as slaves, now as a food source.

Mr. Mark: There are thousands who disappear every year, nobody knows where they go.

Mr. Tim: You can never stop thinking about how high the sky is. All these news items in the *Sun*, the *Enquirer*, the *Examiner*, could very well be subconscious revelations, like the early robots in comics who are now our computers, all subconscious revelations. The Good Lord gave to man to create for the future, but everything came with a struggle, the light bulb, the telephone...

(Miss Joan gives Tiny Tim a gift: A Schwa alien pin and an alien necklace made in Providence.)

Miss Joan: These will keep you safe from alien abductions.

Mr. Tim: Thank you. How beautiful. But I wouldn't mind being abducted as long as they bring me back safe.

Miss Joan: Well, some of the things they do aren't very nice.

Mr. Tim: Oh? What do they do?

Miss Joan: Well, sometimes they force you to have sex, maybe because they need our DNA.

Mr. Tim: Oh, that would be wonderful! (Oh, Miss Peggy, we'll have another round). Now take President Clinton. Here is a man who, take a look at him now, a great guy with a charitable heart, a compassionate man, he loves fame, glamour...

Miss Joan: He loves women too...

Mr. Tim: Yes, he does. Well, he has the care of the country, health care, the crime bill, and of making things better for people and yet he has the same things in common with John Kennedy, both loved women and both have to face the consequences of the Great Yahweh God who hates fornication and wants marriage to remain sacred. I pray for mercy for myself, that the God of Sexuality and Sensuality, who is prevalent in this world, no matter how good his intentions (thank you so much Miss Peggy, you're wonderful); he committed adultery on his wife! If he gave her "the world," the stain of deception is always there. He would have to repent for her to forgive him.

Miss Joan: She forgave him on television. I saw her. She said "when you're married ten minutes you'll be forgiving someone."

Mr. Tim: Well, who knows what went on with her and Vince Foster! If such is the case, if she remained faithful (I heard, well, some assumptions were made) and after he and Jennifer Flowers, well you know, she's not a bad looking girl! If I had met her in the sixties, but that's a one-sided affair, it usually is anyway. But marriage is a sacred vow and it's hard to live with someone who has broken that vow, believe me I know with Miss Vickie. And Miss Jan, boy this one takes the cake!

Mr. Mark: Is that your second wife?

Mr. Tim: Yeah. I haven't seen her more than three times this year [October, 1994].

Miss Joan: A woman of the world?

Mr. Tim: She sure is. I'm trying to find that black address book she's got! There's something about being faithful. Now Miss Stephanie, did I tell you about her? I praise the Good Lord. Now, I had good parents, and great success at one time, you know the ups and downs. I praise the Good Lord for good health and to be able to see what I have, but with all that I pray to find the Eternal Princess. If I ever get to heaven, I pray that He will make me another Miss Stephanie, and this time give her the grace to love me as she can't do now. I want to continually flow through the portals of Heaven or the New Earth with her alone.

Mr. Mark: Who is Miss Stephanie?

Mr. Tim: Stephanie Bohn (B-O-H-N). I met her in Texas in 1988; she was twenty years old then. I met her at the Club Donna through a booker who used to go with her, Big Bucks Brunette. I told her what I'm telling you now. She opens the door to everyone but me. But she is my eternal love. When I die I want to have on my tombstone: Here Lies Tiny Tim "God Grant Me in Death the Love You Denied Me in Life: Miss Stephanie." Did you ever read the *Unauthorized Biography of Tiny Tim*?

Miss Joan: No, who wrote that?

Mr. Tim: It was out in 1976, written by Howard Stern. No, I mean Howard Stine. (Miss Peggy, another round!) In that book he writes something about me that's very strange. Now, I don't really like guys, but I'm sensual, or at least I was. But one time I had, not a homosexual affair, but I massaged this guy, he was 16 and I was about 22. There was a great attraction. I tried to get out of it for a long time. I can't explain it to this day. I don't like guys. If I did I'd let you know, but there was a strange sensuality there, and finally he got married in 1960 and I related this story in the book for this reason: you know, in this life you can be as straight as an arrow, but you never know who you are going to meet, man or woman, who is going to knock you off your feet! It can't be explained. So many things just can't be explained.

Miss Joan: Thank you, Tiny Tim.

All: Oh, Miss Peggy, another round!

This interview with Tiny Tim first appeared in *Newspeak KataZzzine*, Issue 1 (1994). Tiny Tim passed away in 1996. His official website *www.tinytim.org* contains discography, memorabilia, pictures, books and more.

The Uninvited States of America

The Tavistock Agenda Revealed

by Iona Miller

"In 1941 a group of psychiatrists at the Tavistock Clinic saw that the right questions were asked in Parliament in order to secure the means to try new measures. As a result they were asked to join the Directorate of Army Psychiatry, and did so as a group."
– Tavistock Institute

Deep Cover: From Think Tanks to Army Tanks

They wind you up because they know what makes you tick. The "Tavistock Clinic," one of Britain's leading psychiatric research establishments, studied shellshock (post-traumatic stress) in World War I, but switched to developing psychological warfare in 1922. Rather than helping traumatized soldiers, it calculated their breaking points. Tavistock shock doctrine now permeates global life. Their social engineers are a Who's Who: Sigmund Freud, Carl Jung, Alfred Adler, Melanie Klein, Wilfred Bion, Edward Bernays, Eric Trist, A.K. Rice, Eric Miller, Aldous Huxley, and more.

Tavistock sent German-born psychologist, Kurt Lewin, to the Massachusetts Institute of Technology in 1945 to establish the Research Center for Group Dynamics in the U.S. Lewin is the founder of "social psychology." The Center moved to the University of Michigan in 1948 where it became the Institute for Social Research, and continued to co-opt legitimate psychosocial research and exploit mass psychology. By then, the original Clinic became part of Britain's National Health Service.

In 1946, the Tavistock Institute of Human Relations split off a policy-making "mother of all think tanks," publicly claiming to research and direct groups and organizations while it continued massive covert operations in social engineering. The think tank registered as a charity in September 1947, in London, England. It devised and spread interdisciplinary models of Group Relations and training in management, administration and sociopolitics. Promoting creativity and organizational policy, it remains an influential intelligence organization tied to MI6, CIA, Project Paperclip German scientists, Rockefeller Foundation, and cryptocracy.

Founder, John Rawlings Rees, claimed:

> Public life, politics and industry should all . . . be within our sphere of influence . . . If we are to infiltrate the professional and social activities of other people I think we must imitate the Totalitarians and organize some kind of fifth column activity! We must aim to make it permeate every educational activity in our national life . . . We have made a useful attack upon a number of professions. The two easiest of them naturally are the teaching profession and the Church: the two most difficult are law and medicine.

Former MI6 Intelligence officer John Coleman first exposed their covert activities with his insider knowledge in his 2005 book, *The Tavistock Institute of Human Relations: Shaping the Moral, Spiritual, Cultural, Political, and Economic Decline of the United States of America*: "The enemy is clearly identifiable as the Committee of 300, the Club of Rome, NATO, the Black Nobility, CFR and all of its affiliate organizations, the think tanks, and research institutes controlled by Stanford and ... last, but certainly not least, the military establishment."

Coleman includes the Eastern Liberal Establishment "aristocracy," its banks, insurance companies, giant corporations, petroleum cartels, foundations, communications networks, publishing houses, radio and television networks and the movie industry. Mission creep has penetrated organizations far beyond "the Tavi," and they are scripting our wars, our lives and our future. As the power behind the think tank thrones, instead of "doctoring the soul" the clone organizations systematically attack it. The consensual goals of mental health and group relations parted company. The promise became a curse.

World's Most Influential Think Tank

"By Names and Images are powers awakened and re-awakened." – Golden Dawn

What if everything you were brought up to think about society, every layer of cultural meaning about healing and freedom, was wrong? What if someone was subverting your beliefs, ideas and values with behavioral tricks to use them against you? In "the world according to Tavistock," social drivers are disguised as their exact opposites to create a worldview that is illusory, reinventing the world in distorted form.

Tavistock invented what you *should* believe. It is no accident that we have become victims of future shock in the Long Crisis. It's a battle for your soul. Ego is mental structure, not a separate entity from soul. Whether you view it psychologically or spiritually, soul is structured through ego development with mental forms, i.e. words and images. It can also be fragmented with them. We lose our soul when we lose our dreams.

What appears progressive, nurturing or good can have exactly the reverse effect. But seeing the world as it is, not as we are told or wish it to be, brings us closer to real solutions. Turning away from or denying the darkness doesn't make it go away. Embodying our collective shadow, Tavistock is a hydra-headed Secret Agent that runs rampant, aggravating the interconnecting set of global problems.

How is the mind bent and toward what ends? The masses are bent through control of resources and the environment, mind control, massive manipulation, crisis and social turbulence. Nonprofit foundations have teamed with corporate, military and governmental entities to form a covert control force. The art of war became a management problem. Unintended consequences result. Under the guise of prevention they create oppression.

Cultural psychology was used to assess the enemy mentality. The original "Tavi-stalkers" didn't stop with creating the enemy and rewriting history. They spread their "Tavistock Method" theory and practice of mass mind control into all strategic institutions. Their psystrat—turning reality inside out—had multiple vectors, unifying levels of strategy to produce fractal control effects.

Once you learn how to organize behavior—"joint optimization"—you know how to disorganize it with value-dilemmas in groups and international networks. Chaos Theory describes increases in complexity. The contemporary environment is a turbulent field in which the amount of disorder is increasing to the limit of a "vortical" state in which healthy adaptation is impossible.

The "talking cure" became the signature of the "Tavistock Method," and a blanket solution (with psychotropic drugs) to mental distress. The character-building method is self questioning and psychiatric investigation. While therapy gives empathy a mirroring face, it also substitutes a surrogate parent with sanctimonious certitude for self-care and self-regulation.

When Tavistock pioneers began exploring the psyche, it was *terra incognita*. Now that once unknown ground is riddled with the twisted roots of Tavistock's insidious penetration and experimentation, which has permeated the collective psyche. Modulating someone's internal state is a powerful form of control using the power of narrative, imagery and frequency. Conditioning replaces external constraint with internal compulsions on both essence and substance.

Tavistock's goal is a subtle sinister control agenda that no one engaging in therapeutic activities could imagine from surface appearances. Have we been unwittingly "sleeping with the enemy," inducing trauma even as we try to heal it? The cure is a poison. Rather than healing the sick, Tavistock deliberately makes the healthy ill.

Untrustable "Brain Trust"

"What we traditionally have meant by human perception (vision, insight, ethical judgment, discriminating between reality and illusion) has been effectively shut down, almost surgically replaced by the virtual vision machine of the militarized imagination. We are suddenly rendered vulnerable to the new virtual myths about the supposedly hygienic character of post-human warfare." – Arthur Kroker

Tavistock's tentacles are holographic feedback loops of physical, emotional, mental and spiritual control. The lies are different in each dimension of experience. Their back doors and wormhole shortcuts among cultural institutions have created a stranglehold on global culture.

Unpacking each association reveals widespread effects encompassing Intelligence, Military, Government, NGOs, Economics, InfoTech, Mass Media, Philosophy, Occult, Religion, Science, Academia, Psychology, Psychiatry, Medicine and Zeitgeist (Worldview). Co-opting ancient occult principles, Tavistock took the healing genius of Freud and Jung and aimed it at mass psychology in a controlling way.

The means mirror the early relationship of Freud and Jung, who wound up with a six-year nervous breakdown when Freud essentially brainwashed him. Freud displays a pattern of turning his "heretical" followers into mental cases, even suicides—Jung in 1913, Victor Tausk in 1919, Herbert Silberer in 1923, and Wilhelm Reich in 1927. Freud broke their personalities down providing a model his 'magical child' Tavistock used as a *modus operandi* on many social fronts. Tavistock began with research on "shellshock" or post-traumatic stress, propaganda and applied mind control. They have broken down our whole country with collective ego death. They have used Jung's metaphysics to remythologize and "spiritualize" society, using the memes of "hope" and "change" as dope for the New Age.

Civilizations need a myth to live by. Irrespective of national sovereignty, Tavistock's foundation ideology orchestrates archetypal battles of good and evil by futuring in all cultural domains toward totalitarian ends. Arguably in doing so, they have distorted civilization, morals, psychology, history and religion. They have seized a monopoly on human judgment. Futuring includes six synergetic aspects: 1) mapping acceleration, 2) anticipating, 3) timing and 4) deepening the future, 5) creating alternatives to the present and 6) transformation. Aspirational futuring and analysis includes environmental scanning, forecasts, scenarios, visions, audacious goals and understanding change and strategic issues. The equivalent Russian program is "Psychoecology" from the Psychotechnology Research Institute.

Dreams & Memes

"Without Tavistock, there would have been no WWI and WWII, no Bolshevik Revolution, Korea, Vietnam, Serbia and Iraq wars. But for Tavistock, the United States would not be rushing down the road to dissolution and collapse." – John Coleman

The geopolitical and psychosocial Game of Life is rigged. To understand mass psychology, you need to know the real rules of engagement. Their world is governed by appearances, not reality. There are so many global extinction stories on television now because life as we have known it for mankind is under grave threat of extinction.

The energy shortage, rise of food prices, scandals in government, and unwinnable wars against ideas like ideologies and "terrorism" are the first harbingers of the approaching mega-crisis. There are two routes from here: that of stagnation and eventual total collapse, and that of flexibility and growth leading to a golden age. Chaos Theory reveals both catastrophe (bifurcation) and renewal are likely inevitable.

Rather than the obsolete paradigm of a "world machine," we need to think in more organic terms of holistic self-organization—reorganization at a higher level—as revealed in Chaos Theory, which demonstrates nature's own creative way of evolutionary assembly. All things are simply connected.

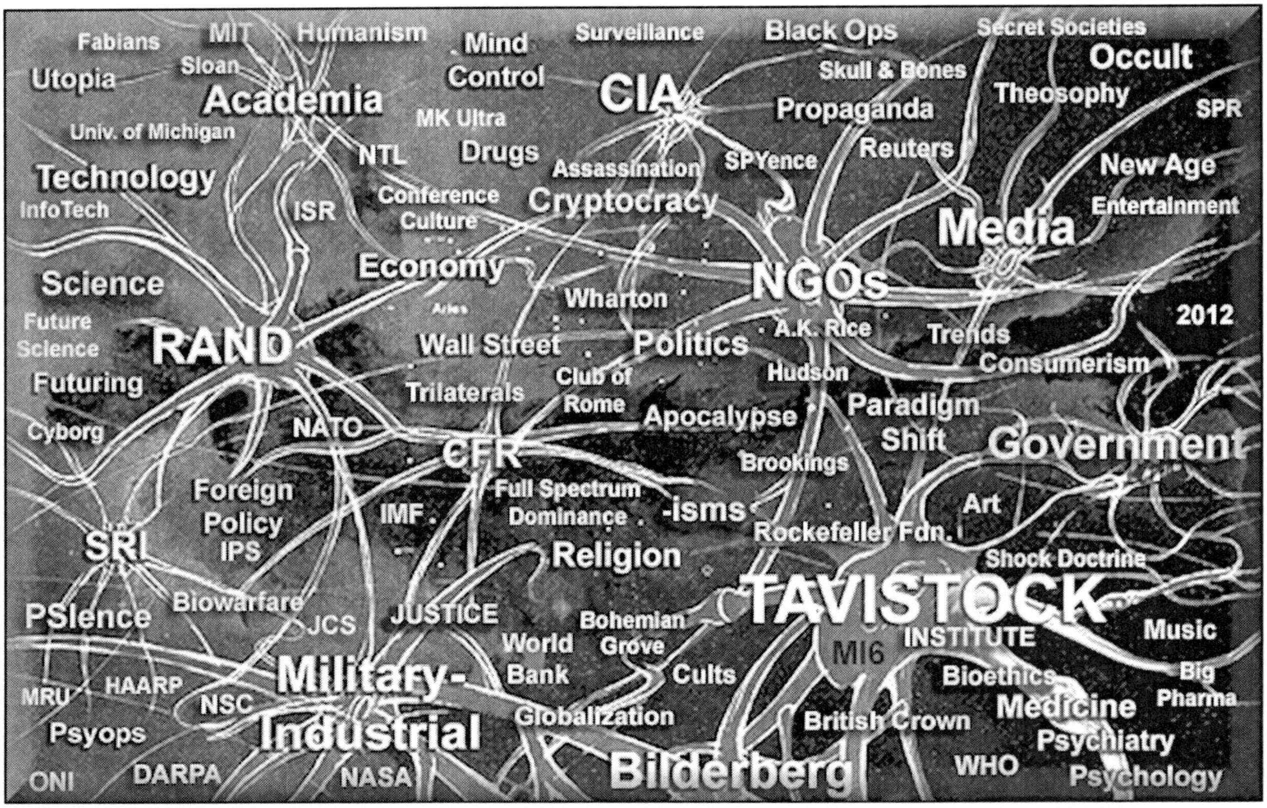

"Tavistock Nerves" by Iona Miller

The real crisis is this war conducted inside your head by those who do not have your best interests at heart, by those who program you for exploitation while robbing you of rights and freedoms. Events take place along a utopian/dystopian spectrum that ranges in the individual from euphoria to dysphoria.

Underlying forces are playing your underlying forces, modulating your moods like an emotional organ. Conflict, fear and trauma are used to manipulate and control individuals and whole populations. Drugs are ever more readily available, legally and illegally. Transnational drug trade supports even more black ops "social engineering" in other areas.

The depth psychology models of Freud and Jung, the inherent nature of the psyche and human response to trauma, have been played against our dreams of a better tomorrow. Tavistock created protocols to deliberately initiate and manipulate breakdown and programming, in both individuals and the masses. Reinforcing this with media manipulation has created a conformist society. Framing the narrative of world events, it has manufactured history according to its own agenda.

It has done so with a mystique of authority, through a compartmentalized global network of think tanks and non-profit organizations, which promote the same agenda of social engineering, population control and exploitation. Spanning the entire sociopolitical spectrum, they have spread their shadow over the globe as an uninvited trance. Another Tavistock alumni, "father of public relations" Edward Louis Bernays (1891 – 1995), who was the double nephew of Sigmund Freud, turned his understanding of mass psychology into the shameless PR and advertising juggernaut of consumerism.

Silent War

"[I]n almost every act of our daily lives, whether in the sphere of politics or business, in our social conduct or our ethical thinking, we are dominated by the relatively small number of persons who understand the mental processes and social patterns of the

masses. It is they who pull the wires which control the public mind, who harness old social forces and contrive new ways to bind and guide the world."
– Edward Bernays

Covert forces are playing on your unconscious mind. With global hypnosis, they have made themselves the rudder on the ship of state, setting policy, advising and dominating governments, corporations, and the educational structure. The shortlist of Tavistock's fellow globalist institutions includes Rockefeller Foundation, CIA, MI6, Stanford Research Institute, Brookings, RAND, Club of Rome, Council on Foreign Relations, International Monetary Fund, Project for a New American Century, Pilgrim's Society, Wharton School, NASA, and World Bank.

Probably the easiest way to understand the convoluted history and absorb the complex psychoecology of Tavistock's penetration of culture and the cryptocracy is to watch some of the classic videos that can be found while searching the subject online. Relationships of certain individuals and groups are matters of public record. Tavistock tailors programs to specific situations as well as setting standards in psychiatry, psychology and organizational management. It declared itself the ultimate authority on mental health and human relations. Divergent thought is declared crazy or antisocial.

Programs with proven historical contexts originating or rooted in Tavistock "brain trust" include: "War on Terror," "War on Drugs," "Total Information Awareness," "Full Spectrum Dominance," Joint Vision 2020, "Shock & Awe," "New Left," "Basic English," propaganda, narco-capitalism, social engineering, psystrat, "Open Government" or "transparency in government," and "Infowar." You can't really wage war against an idea, but you can campaign for and against them.

In their endless bag of tricks we also find behavioral modification, mass brainwashing, "buzzwords," suppressed science, manufactured wars, counterculture, LSD, New Age, cults, -isms, disinformation, false-flag ops, crisis creation, postmodern apocalypse theory, presence-in-absence, manufactured psychological shocks and stress, encounter groups, Aquarian Conspiracy, corporate feudalism and more.

There is a psychosocial war for your mind, your body, and even your soul. By making their mental health guidelines and human relations practice the standard, Tavistock became the de-centralized arbiter of what is considered sane and what is deemed crazy. But they have employed the devices of toxic interaction and deployed them against the populace. By framing reality, naming the issues and producing iconic imagery, they have sold us a media gloss that simulates and substitutes the "Big Lie" for truth. "Too big to fail" and Wall Street "bailouts" are recent examples.

Dirty tricks include the double-bind, "crazy-making behavior," forced choice and dual reality, to name a few. Since WWII, this psyops strategy has allowed them to achieve "full-spectrum dominance" of the cultural landscape. They are inside your head from the cradle to the grave, using every control mechanism known to behavioral science, creating and fulfilling your desires with programming and emotional manipulation. Everyone senses it at some level, but who does anything about it?

"Bourne Again" Mindbenders

"We shall have World Government, whether or not we like it. The only question is whether World Government will be achieved by conquest or consent." – James Paul Warburg

In the 2002-2007 film series, a take-off on the Tavistock-inspired CIA's MKULTRA program, hypno-patsy Jason Bourne learns how intelligence eats its own. As the series unfolds, we see how mind control and programmed assassins are used to steer sociopolitical "reality," while concealing and erasing memory of the mind-bending puppet masters. Only the biggest lies are "too big to fail."

The irony is, in this sense, "we the people" are all "Bourne Again." Not surprisingly, the fourth film of the franchise is on the way, and a first-person shooter video game is already here. The seduction/murder perps who pull the magic trigger on the smoking gun have perfected the art of hiding in plain sight in their Magic Kingdom. Tavistock is the rudder on the pirate ship of state.

They don't even care if we know how it works because "plausible deniability" has become irrelevant in the Theatre of Cruelty that molds minds with metaphysics while shattering our perceptions. "The Secret" of reality creation is that it's beyond your control, far out of reach of your wishful thinking. The new Holy Trinity of our warring instincts is money/sex/power. The GOD we learned to worship is GoldOilDrugs.

Riding the coattails of *The Manchurian Candidate* (1962), a B horror movie called *The Mindbenders* (1963) depicted Dirk Bogarde as the victim of British brainwashers who isolated, water-tanked him and destroyed his marriage. Mindbender scientists discover that eight nightmarish hours of water-tank isolation equates with eight months of intense brainwashing.

Apparently someone in Britain knew what was going on at the Tavi. The 'Mindbenders' break both the volunteers and their relationships, inducing dissociation. Freud proved that broken relationships and imposed sexual repression can be used as a weapon, spreading emotional contagion and arousing primitive emotions in targeted populations. Emotions can simultaneously be used to build entire mythic systems.

Tavistock's "Time Machine"

"All news is lies and all propaganda is disguised as news." – Willi Muzenberg

Just outside London, Tavistock Institute is the sloganeering nerve center of a global psywar apparatus that attacks our collective conscious and unconscious relentlessly. Established after World War I, the original Tavistock Clinic developed psychological warfare for British intelligence.

More than an international institution, Tavistock became a nonlocal community of practice—a dark "invisible college," the Castaglia of the cryptocracy. Tavistock's grandmother is the drug empire of the British East India Company and Theosophical esoterics. Its grandfather is "The Open Conspiracy" of Utopian H.G. Wells, Bertrand Russell, Cecil Rhodes and Fabian socialists. The Society for Psychical Research (SPR) helped create the Fabian Society.

Tavistock is the paranoid child of the Liepzig and Frankfurt Schools of critical thinking and behaviorism. The psychodynamics of Freud and Jung are its godparents. But Tavistock's birth mother was a whore—a propaganda front called Wellington House, known as "The Lie Factory."

One of Plato's tricks was "forbidding the question." His *Republic* is a blueprint for tyrannical systemic philosophical control. The Big Lie, a hypnotic propaganda technique, is rooted in Plato's Noble Lie, the myth knowingly told by the elite to maintain social control.

Using time as their fulcrum, Tavistock explorations in crafting reality became exploitations; selling Utopian idealism to the New Left and patriotic Homeland Security to the born-again Right. Pitting them eternally against one another is a neocon racket that molds all political party themes. The game is collapsing the traditional world. They employ both religious and secular currents in the same way, playing both sides against the middle.

Grinding the Gears of Paradigm Shift

"A society of sheep must in time beget a government of wolves." – Bertrand de Jouvenel

Turning "Great Game" strategies on the public, Tavistock's agenda transcends institutional boundaries, hoodwinking us about the nature of reality with stealth psystrat, media and cultural tactics while imposing and maintaining control through the collective psyche. The seat of power has switched from a pyramidal to a holographic power structure.

Intelligence tricks are deployed from the heart of the machinery of state to engineer the consistent illusions of our psychosocial culture—an interactive fiction. The social glue of trust has dried and cracked, leaving less than enlightened self-interest in an "I'll get mine first" mentality.

Tavistock is now selling downshifting income, aging lean and collective ego death through the razzle-dazzle of apocalyptic archetypes. Modulating someone's internal state is a powerful form of control using the power of imagery. Conditioning replaces external constraint with internal compulsions on both essence and substance. The destiny of individual freedom depends on maintaining critical ethical judgment and a clarity that can filter out propaganda and rebel against it. Too bad even our rebellions are controlled. The story must be continually upgraded to keep the audience engaged.

Tavistock is a "strange attractor" in the global psychodynamic field. It has brought us all to the self-organizing state of criticality—the precipitous boundary of chaos and order. We need to develop filters against such psychic infiltration. In such radical crisis the individual must courageously refuse to assent to totalitarian power.

Cultural Hegemony

"The core of the belief in progress is that human values and goals converge in parallel with our increasing knowledge. The twentieth century shows the contrary. Human beings use the power of scientific knowledge to assert and defend the values and goals they already have. New technologies can be used to alleviate suffering and enhance freedom. They can, and will, also be used to wage war and strengthen tyranny. In the twentieth century, these technologies were used to implement state terror and genocide on an unprecedented scale. Ethics and politics do not advance in line with the growth of knowledge—not even in the long run."

– John Gray, *Heresies*

Forms of cultural hegemony include psychological, spiritual, emotional, political, social, military, economic, medical and intellectual oppression and domination. Certain research projects are suppressed by dogmatic science. Like any ideology, Tavistock asks us to believe its deceptive promises and refrain from questions about what they don't tell. "Lies of omission" control the highs and lows of our expectations and the controlled demolition of the boom and bust economy. To think otherwise may be painfully naive.

Most of us don't expect them to manufacture ideologies and phony enemies to mobilize the masses. We don't expect them to engage in covert dirty tricks, secretly foment revolutions or use deceptive diplomacy to execute a secret social and esoteric agenda. We can hardly believe anyone would actively work against our health and welfare, destroying the food chain, good air, water and earth, not to mention developing biological weapons.

We don't expect them to engineer arrested development and family breakdown. We don't expect them to use "planning theory" and pop culture to foster alienation and dysfunction. We don't expect them to poison the well of global society in their undeclared war on humanity. We must learn to see through what they do as coercion, using their esoteric techniques of crisis creation and management. Their initial project—*Operation Research* on military management techniques—was turned on civilians.

Authority for Authority

Tavistock is an immersive process, a transnational inter-agency collaboration, whose "research" is best evaluated by its real-world phenomena—the cumulative effects of machinations, trendspotting, memes, and propaganda. They look at effects, then find the causes to produce them. They begin with solutions and find the problems they solve. They create media and products to satisfy needs that don't yet exist. They shape the world by shaping opinion.

Even "sanitized," their programs have global repercussions. In quantum information theory, if all records of an event are de-correlated from it, then by definition there is no way to know whether this event has ever happened. This situation is indistinguishable from its not having happened.

Our only defense is awareness and DIY mind control. But the torrent of information is manipulated to guide our motivations while engineering consensus by repackaging myths, memes and metaphors. In the 1960s, the Milgram Experiment demonstrated the draconian perils inherent in authority overriding personal conscience to compliantly "follow orders" to inflict psychophysical harm on others. The sun shines alike on torture and compassion.

Multimedia quietly changes our thoughts and opinions, creating a mash-up of fiction and reality—a friction that rubs everyone the wrong way. The magic circle of the hypnotic primetime television schedule holds all in its restrictive spell of dominion with celebrity ringmasters. We stare blankly, enthralled with the train wreck of intelligence and common sense.

While it captures the appearance of things, mimesis holds up an illusory mirror. Catharsis creates communal emotional discharge that orchestrates identification with group feelings. To Freud, catharsis was the traumatic transfer of a memory ["meme-ory", collectively] from the unconscious to the conscious. Though it effectively empties us of our own potentially meaningful creative content, the culture is addicted to it.

Rather than purging our pathologies, emotional ventilation voyeuristically facilitates them. It evokes them with daily rituals. Simulation becomes second nature like breathing—we are The Sims. First-person shooter games are Transmodern scapegoating. What we 'Discover' on one channel becomes 'History' on another. As one commentator put it, "Armageddon is the new black."

Prisoner's Dilemma: Crisis Creation & Human Bondage

"The technetronic era involves the gradual appearance of a more controlled society. Such a society would be dominated by an elite, unrestrained by traditional values."

– Zbigniew Brzezinsky, *Between Two Ages: America's Role in the Technetronic Era*, 1970

Everywhere is Ground Zero. Not reserving their techniques for the enemy, Tavistock spread their contagious theory and practice of mass mind control into all strategic institutions. Tavistock wrote the blueprint for global domination, a triumph of image over substance. The hydraulic model of tensions has given way to the Field Theory of full-spectrum domination. The holographic structure is everywhere contained in its fractal satellites, each of which contains the entire program and can take over where others fail.

They wrote the book on propaganda, prognostication and profiling—the staples of the full-spectrum surveillance society. They have contrived history. Fractured facts mixed with fiction produces "Pulp Friction." The simulation substitutes for reality. A ritual is just a play with audience participation, but it changes you in the alchemical process.

Funded by British royalty, Rothchilds, Rockefellers, the Federal Government and Wall Street they invoked "the secret" of transmuting infinite symbols of transformation into infinite power. Without wielding overt control, the Tavistock blitz influences the direction and effects of virtually every human endeavor with political and psychological warfare through its web of interlinking institutions. Following the lead of the British East India Company, transnational drug money flows like the mother's milk of black ops politics.

Through a twist of fate, the shaping of Tavistock became synonymous with the shaping of global culture by forcing unwelcome changes and seizing psychological control of the human race. The brainwashing institute has twisted our beliefs into their very opposites by collapsing our psychic boundaries. Now, we are permanently "shellshocked." When we lose our story we lose our history.

Holographic Power Structure

"Political language is designed to make lies sound truthful and murder respectable and to give the appearance of solidity to pure wind."

– George Orwell

The Tavistock agenda creates macro-trends, such as the "New Left" and militant activism as counter point to Neocon manipulation through radical religious policies and bunkered militia-mentality. It is a primary polarizing entity at work throughout all levels of society, playing both sides against the middle. It creates outside Adversaries through propaganda and projection, such as distracting terror, drugs and media wars. Viable solutions simply aren't allowed and are actively suppressed.

A Rockefeller grant gave birth to the Tavistock Institute of Human Relations in London in 1947. Tavistock joined with Kurt Lewin's Research Center for Group Dynamics (RCGD) at the University of Michigan the next year and begin disseminating human relations literature, relating theory to practice, including promotion of change, engineering consensus, mass persuasion, breakdown of cognitive structure, and overcoming resistance.

Tavistock sets national agendas for the global shadow government. It used covert techniques to sell the war with Germany, the state of Israel, the Domino Theory and the Cold War for financial gain. Deliberate creation of crisis is psychic Cold War, a global psychodrama. Other networked think tanks are its dissemination organ. They create peer pressure throughout all strata of society designed to break people down into consensus conformity.

Globalist Change Agents

"Countless people... will hate the new world order... and will die protesting against it... When we attempt to evaluate its promise, we have to bear in mind the distress of a generation or so of malcontents."
– H.G. Wells, *The New World Order*, 1939

The Cryptocracy is involved in "alchemical processing" of mass consciousness by psychological manipulation. With the help of foundations and secret societies, experiments in world shaping continue multimedia and military campaigns. The goal of social engineering is seeding and controlling mega trends so the masses live as controlled puppets and wage slaves of the ruling elite.

Tavistock's agenda is used to create and topple governments. Entire populations are controlled through drugs and sophisticated psychological techniques, including group dynamics. Disciplines include anthropology, economics, organizational behavior, political science, psychoanalysis, psychology and sociology.

They are selling collective ego death with apocalyptic visions. Any technique which breaks down the family unit, and inculcated principles of religion, honor, patriotism and sexual behavior, is used by Tavistock scientists as a weapon of control. Now a war of extermination is waged on the small American farmer through high-interest loans and bankruptcy. Corpoglomerate land trusts gain while our diet suffers.

Futurist programs identify discontinuities and emerging dilemmas. Discontinuities challenge business as usual and dilemmas demand new ways of thinking about complex problems. Together, discontinuities and dilemmas provide a vista of new practices and points of view that shape tomorrow's organizations and today's choices. Over the years Tavistock's healing emphasis changed, and by the mid-1930's there was a sinister slant to the research in eugenics, political and cultural engineering. There are rumors of an earlier version of Tavistock, which trained Lenin, and later after WWI, Adolph Hitler (Hallet).

With the outbreak of World War II, Tavistock operatives took effective control of the Psychological Warfare Directorate of the British Army, while its allied network in the United States embedded itself in the American psychological warfare apparatus, including the Committee on National Morale and the Strategic Bombing Survey.

By war's end, the combined influence of Tavistock (which became the Tavistock Institute in 1947) and of the former Frankfurt School operatives, had created what Director Rees called a cadre of several thousand "psychological shock troops," and "cultural warriors." Today that network numbers several million around the world, and is the single most important factor in determining the design and content of mass media product.

By World War II, Tavistock was a real MI6 Agency and its stress-related techniques were well advanced. They knew how to relieve mental and emotional pain, as well as how to amplify it, physically and psychologically. In fact, Tavistock's recommendations for excessive use of force were used tragically by Winston Churchill in the terrifying fire bombing of Dresden and Hamburg.

Sigmund Freud was Tavistock's "prophet" and first director, followed by his daughter, Anna. Tavistock programs were used to program the postwar leaders of Germany's government, churches, schools, corporations, etc.

Research into the use of microwave weapons and their use for mind control (psychotronics) began at the Tavistock Institute in the 1950s, when researchers explored various ways of mind-controlling the British population without their knowledge. Its main U.S. branch is located at the University of Michigan. The same principles were used to create pop culture and counterculture, so even societal rebellion is a programmed trend to channel and discredit opposing energy.

Popular culture is engineered to brainwash each of us from cradle to grave. Trends and mega trends are manufactured, engineered by corporations. Nothing happens in politics or society by accident.

Games, Scripts & Rackets

Freud's nephew, Edward Bernays, a principle at Tavistock Institute, is the godfather of propaganda and the "engineered consent" of Madison Avenue. He took Freud's principles of mass psychology and applied them to social exploitation, numbing and manipulation of the masses. He created consumerism.

The Nazis employed techniques outlined by Bernays in his 1928 book *PROPAGANDA*, and later brought them to the U.S. under Operation Paperclip, where they were picked up by the CIA and subsequently morphed into mind control programs such as cyborg assassins and MKULTRA. Similar programs were instituted in the USSR around the same time. The CIA also spreads propaganda across the entire political spectrum through founding and funding front organizations.

In the wake of the Enlightenment, the notion of an intellectual elite arose. A distinguished social stratum can be traced far back into classical history. Elite classes of intellectuals or well-educated people emerged in most European countries.

The intelligentsia (e.g., artists, mystics, psychologists, psychiatrists, scientists and teachers) engages in complex mental and creative labor directed into the development and dissemination of culture Bohemians. They were the forerunner of what we can call the "psychedelic intelligentsia" and today's New Age spiritual fusion.

Utopian socialism is the philosophical root of modern socialist thought. Anyone can be a utopian socialist, but the trend emerged in the 19th century. From the mid-19th century onwards, other branches of socialism overtook utopianism in popularity. But groups such as the Fabians continued working their strategic agendas behind the scenes of perpetual class struggle.

Societies are cyclic, always in a continual process of constructing themselves and destructing from within. Utopian socialists are forerunners of communal hippie life, intentional communities and cooperatives. Utopian nostalgia is exemplified in the Star Trek and Star Wars philosophy. Its dystopian reflection is The Matrix, the postmodern Brave New World where nothing is believable or trustable.

Quasi-socialist intellectuals created hypothetical visions of perfect egalitarian and communal societies without actually concerning themselves with the manner in which these societies could be sustained. Yet, they shared a dream, which for the world at large has become a mind control nightmare.

Name Your Poison

"There will be, in the next generation or so, a pharmacological method of making people love their servitude, and producing dictatorship without tears, so to speak, producing a kind of painless concentration camp for entire societies, so that people will in fact have their liberties taken away from them, but will rather enjoy it, because they will be distracted from any desire to rebel by propaganda or brainwashing, or brainwashing enhanced by pharmacological methods. And this seems to be the final revolution."

– Aldous Huxley, Tavistock Group, California Medical School, 1961

Tavistock is married to Big Pharma by psychiatry. The paradoxical Greek word "*pharmakon*" can be translated as "drug," which means both remedy and poison. In *Plato's Pharmacy*, Derrida traces its meanings in Plato's dialogues: remedy, poison (either the cure or the illness or its cause), philter, drug, recipe, charm, medicine, substance, spell, artificial color, and paint.

The alchemists also call their elixir or panacea both a cure and a poison, describing the dangers of the interactive field experience, including failure to recognize trance states. Derrida notes, "This *pharmakon*, this medicine, this philter, which acts as both remedy and poison, already introduces itself into the body of the discourse with all its ambivalence." Tavistock paints a picture of the world (simulacrum; textual trance) and we must embrace it.

Because the *pharmakon* is artificial and comes from outside rather than from within, it always has side effects. When not treating a disease, a psychotropic becomes dope. The *pharmakon* is the paradoxical medium in which opposites are opposed and contradictory meanings play out. It is a war of opposites Freud saw as a life/death struggle and Jung saw as a death/rebirth mystery of cyclic passages and renewal. Rebirth is the mythic enactment of "the one story" whose pattern is found in every narrative.

Culture takes place in between the war of life and death. Those caught between two stages of development without clearly defined social identities, feel marginal, excluded, without identity or influence. "Outsiders" occupy an edge realm of creative potential for new ideas and concepts and so pose a threat to the establishment.

Relationships and social status are negotiated at the threshold. We are either rejected from or welcomed to the other side, submitting to the rules of that place. At the threshold, one can also enter new territory. Outsiders live beyond roles assigned by law, custom, convention, and ceremony. As visionaries, they question, expose, critique and redefine the central values of culture.

Pharmakos, "human scapegoat" or "sacrificial slave" derives from the same root, but changing the scapegoat doesn't change anything real. We are all victims. In Latin, *victima* is a beast of sacrifice, a consecrated animal. Psychotherapy replaces the scapegoat with mind-numbing catharsis, a form of self-sacrifice, for purification and emotional purgation. Transmodern scapegoating takes place in the virtuality, first-person shooter games.

Pharmakeus means druggist, poisoner and by extension, wizard, magician, trickster or sorcerer, initiator—the spellbinding shaman/healer. Shamanism is medicine for the imagination using tricks or techniques to alter perception. Whether transformation is induced through drugs, collective dreams, behavior modification, or emotive talk therapies, the purpose is to change perception of reality. Defense mechanisms include denial, acting out, fantasy, dissociation, idealization, intellectualization, isolation, projection, rationalization, repression, and somatization. All can be corrected by creative self-help and self-regulation—becoming your own shaman or alchemist.

Culture Hero-Trickster

The psychotherapeutic approach to healing essentially represents order (through chaos). The shamanic approach represents chaos, often including trance, drugs, adventure and spiritual power plays. These worldviews seem divided but the true nature of reality is dynamic interplay of chaos and order. The healer is also an eternal Trickster. And the Trickster entraps by controlling perceptions, guiding the collective vision of emergent worldviews.

Soft-core brainwashing is so subliminal most people don't recognize it. Nor do they recognize covert pressures hiding in plain sight. You can't really fight this hydra-headed monster and you can't flee the mind-bending No Exit game with a geographic or mental escape. They want you to escape into virtuality and leave the "real" world to them. If you withdraw into virtuality you are no longer a protagonist in the social setting.

A state of criticality (SOC) is the governing dynamical mechanism. Various kinds of systems can be engineered into a *critical state* by fine-tuning the parameters. Kindling changes can lead to cascades of morphing dynamics, avalanches of consequences. Though the edge can be a horizon of creativity, chain reactions and catastrophic collapse are also possible.

Instead of inhabiting the United States, we are plunged into the bizarro world of imposed trance-states—the Uninvited States of America. Whether on the Left or the Right, we are played against one another in the social construction of reality (totalitarian environment) with indirect suggestion, political and religious clichés and milieu control.

We fear the results of forced choices. Loss of biometric identifiers like self-reliance, house, job, credit cards, bank account, driver's license, spouse and family is equated with death—or worse—irrelevance. You must obey the doctrine or lose the personal identity that was created for you and will be stripped away. So don't question too much; just follow along.

Self-care and self-regulation are your frontlines of defense in the fight for your liberty and human rights. In the culture at large, therapeutic authority has transformed personal and group relations in family, work, school, hospital, office, media, government and military. While it has taught us "better" communication, it has undermined traditional roles. Stories we consistently tell ourselves determine our reality. But culture is articulated by subversive innovation.

Do-It-Yourself mind control helps you create a reality from your experience, made of symbols weighted by metaphors. All communication is hypnotic. Neuro-Linguistic Programming demonstrates how even casual conversation can be loaded with sleight of mouth, cues, "embedded commands," and suggestive language patterns. Parallel realities, triggers and anchors, time binds, illusory choice, submodalities, persuasion and psychological drivers can be manipulated. You can recalibrate your own mind, instead of succumbing to collective programming.

The collective will of the people has been undercut with "shock and awe," frustration and demoralization. Tavistock first fed us illusions as stepping-stones before weaning us on disillusion, exemplified in lowered expectations, healthcare debates and a failing greenback. Positive and negative reinforcement include "the takeaway," turning dreams into pipe dreams and mystical manipulation. But we can always create new dreams for a new era.

Even though its agenda has jumped the boundaries of its parent organization, Tavistock has seeded chaos leading to the death of an outworn post-industrial mindset, clearing the stage for a transmodern information society with a distinctly fascist tone. Or, perhaps, as chaos theory suggests, something entirely new and wonderful will emerge from the most creative sector of society. That future is still in our hands.

References

Coleman, John, 2005, *Tavistock Institute of Human Relations: Shaping the Moral, Spiritual, Cultural, Political, and Economic Decline of the United States of America*

Coleman, J., 2006, *A Conspirator's Hierarchy: The Committee of 300*, 4th Edition, Global Review Publications, Inc., Las Vegas, NV.

Cooke, Ben "The Tavistock's Everday Use of Benzedrine." *Management and Organizational History*, Vol. 4(2), 2009. http://moh.sagepub.com/cgi/pdf_extract/4/2/203

Corbett, Sara, "The Hoy Grail of the Unconscious," in *New York Times*. http://www.nytimes.com/2009/09/20/magazine/20jung-t.html?pagewanted=1&_r=2

Gray, John, *Black Mass: Apocalyptic Religion and the Death of Utopia*, Doubleday, 2007.

Gray, John, *Heresies: Against Progress and Other Illusions*, Granta (UK), 2004.

Hallet, Greg, 2005, *Hitler Was A British Agent*, Progressive Press, 2005.

King, Chris, "The Prisoner's Dilemma." http://www.dhushara.com/paradoxhtm/prisoners.htm

Klein, N., *The Shock Doctrine: The Rise of Disaster Capitalism*, Metropolitan Books, New York, 2007.

Miller, Iona (2009) "Tavistock Agenda Revealed" http://tavistockagenda.iwarp.com

Schneck, Jerome, "Countertransference in Freud's Rejection of Hypnosis," http://ajp.psychiatryonline.org/cgi/pdf_extract/110/12/928

Szafranki, Colonel Richard (1995) "A Theory of Information Warfare" http://www.airpower.au.af.mil/airchronicles/apj/apj95/spr95_files/szfran.htm

Tavistock Timeline: http://tavistockagenda.iwarp.com/whats_new_25.html

Trist, Eric, "The Social Engagement of Social Science: A Tavistock Anthology" http://www.moderntimesworkplace.com/archives/ericsess/tavis1/tavis1.html

Wolfe, L., "Brainwashing: How the British Use the Media for Mass Psychological Warfare," in *The American Almanac*, May 5, 1997. http://american_almanac.tripod.com/warfare.html

Wolfe, L. "For Whom the Polls Toll" in *The American Almanac*, May 5, 1997, http://american_almanac.tripod.com/polls.htm

About the Author

Hypnotherapist Iona Miller writes on future science, intelligence and esoterics. She analyzes the collective psyche and cultural effects of geopolitics, religion, science, art and psychology. This "Meta Hari" covers social engineering, pop culture, physics and psychology, media, psi research, esoteric espionage, cults, psyops countermeasures, creativity, and extraordinary human capacities. Where it is impossible to unravel "the truth," rather than being interested in the unproven and untraceable, she analyzes general trends visible to all with a startling viewpoint. Her websites are: *http://tavistockagenda.iwarp.com* and *http://ionamiller.iwarp.com.*

The Sons of the Sun of God

Joan d'Arc Interviews Acharya S.

Acharya S is the author of several books on the subject of "astrotheology" and the mythical nature of the pantheon of gods that people the sky. She was classically educated and is a member of the American School of Classical Studies at Athens, Greece. She has served as a trench master on archaeological excavations in Corinth, Greece, and Connecticut, USA, as well as a teacher's assistant on the island of Crete. She has traveled extensively around Europe and speaks, reads and/or writes English, Greek, French, Spanish, Italian, German and Portuguese. She has cross-referenced the Bible in the original Hebrew and ancient Greek. And she has written some of my favorite books, including *The Christ Conspiracy: The Greatest Story Ever Sold*, *Suns of God: Krishna, Buddha and Christ Unveiled* and her latest bombshell, *Christ in Egypt: The Horus-Jesus Connection.*

Joan: A "mythicist" is someone who perceives biblical characters as being mythical and the origin of myths as being based in nature worship and "astrotheology." How did you come to be a mythicist and astrotheologist? Does this necessarily mean you're an atheist?

Acharya: I began reading about myths—especially the Greek myths—when I was a small child. After that time, I had a growing curiosity about mythology and religion, which has evolved into a longstanding passion. By young adulthood, I knew a significant amount about the religions and myths of many cultures around the world. But I myself did not really have a religion.

I was born into a mild Protestant sect and attended a Congregational Church, but I rejected it all as boring from about the age of seven onward, and I emancipated myself at 12. I went to Greece when I was 14, and the rest, as they say, is history... and archaeology... and mythology.

With all that strong background in mythology for so many years, I was prepared for when I had the epiphany of the mythical nature of Jesus. I don't mean the vague sense of rejection of the miracles that many people likely experience, leading them to become "evemerists," or those who believe Christ was a real man to whose mundane biography his ardent followers attached many fables and fairy-tales. A mythicist is someone who perceives the gospel as a whole to be mythical, with no historical core to the onion when the mythological layers have been peeled. This contention is not to say, however, that there are no historical characters in the New Testament. Herod and Pilate appear firmly rooted in the historical record, for example. But the gospel story itself is like *Gulliver's Travels*, a historical novel that is placed in England but that nonetheless remains fictional.

When it comes to the Greek and Roman gods, practically everyone is a mythicist, believing these characters, such as Zeus and Hercules, not ever to have been "real people" but to represent in large part natural phenomena, such as storms, thunderbolts, wind, the sea, the sun and so on. All told, the religion and mythology of old were very concerned with not only the afterlife and underworld but also the here and now of *this* world, which they likewise perceived as sacred.

The cosmic part of this nature worship is called "astrotheology," specifically the reverence for and worship of the sun, moon, planets, stars, constellations and so on.

Being convinced of the mythical nature of many gods, godmen and heroes of old, and being fascinated by the astrotheological origin of many myths and traditions, does not necessarily make or require one to become an atheist. I have no interest in being categorized in either the theist or atheist camp, and I have no desire to create either theists or atheists with my writing. What you do with your own mind is up to you, so long as it doesn't spill out onto others in a negative fashion. If you wish to sit and daydream about a beautiful, heavenly place where there is a radiant being of bliss you call "God," not only is it none of my business, but I would actually encourage you to do so, if it brings some joy to your life.

If, however, something tragic happens—and it always does—and you wish to think there could not possibly be any good god in charge of everything, your thoughts too would be none of my business, except that I would say they are entirely appropriate for the situation.

Frankly, the archaeoastronomical, astrotheological and cosmological knowledge expressed by the ancients—one of the planks of mythicism—is so exciting to me that it fills me with the wonder and awe often deemed a religious experience. Yet, I neither believe nor dismiss it. I simply enjoy it.

The Talisman of Orpheus: A third century amulet. (Public Domain)

Joan: According to your website (StellarHousePublishing.com), mythicism began in France and Germany at the end of the 18th century. Can you tell me a little bit about this tradition and whether your work is based, in part, on this European tradition?

Acharya: To my knowledge, the most extensive effort in Europe in this subject of Jesus being a myth began at the end of the 18th century with the publication of the French scholar Charles Dupuis' multi-volume masterpiece, *Origines de tous les cultes*. I have been scrutinizing the English abridgement of his work, *The Origin of All Religious Worship*, as well as some of the original French edition, for over 15 years, and I have found it to be scholarly and solid. Not only did Dupuis highlight numerous mythical motifs from pre-Christian deities, godmen and heroes, but he also evinced that Jesus was as mythical as Hercules. Dupuis further showed numerous of these mythical motifs to be solar in nature, theorizing that Jesus was originally a sun god. Dupuis's writings were so powerful they caused much excitement among the European elite, including the French scholar's most famous pupil, Napoleon Bonaparte.

Another of Dupuis's students was Count Volney, author of *Ruins of Empires*, which followed the same theme. Volney likewise became one of Napoleon's teachers. Indeed, it is claimed Napoleon once remarked that the question of Christ's existence was a "good one." It is also asserted that Dupuis and Volney's work was so convincing as concerns the Egyptian origins of much Christian myth and ritual, one of Napoleon's main motives in exploring Egypt was to find evidence in this regard. The one discovery of the Rosetta Stone alone by his troops was enough to make Napoleon's expedition successful, as this granite monument allowed for the accurate translation of Egyptian hieroglyphs, which eventually did reveal significant potential influence of Egypt on the Christian effort, as I demonstrate quite thoroughly in my book *Christ in Egypt*.

Obviously, I am influenced by some of these individuals, as well as others. However, their inspiration has come in the form of digging down into the evidence for their contentions and theses, which means I've spent the last many years unearthing the primary sources and testimonies of ancient writers. These individuals of the past eras were intelligent and highly educated. They were multilingual, including being able to do research in Greek and Latin—I studied these languages too, as well as others, and I do research in them.

In other words, I read the ancient testimonies in their "original" form. One problem is that these ancient writings have come down to us through the copying efforts of many people, who both made mistakes, and put their own spin on things at times. Therefore, ancient writings need to be disentangled from these alterations and interpolations in order to be called "original."

Joan: Do you also argue from the Greek "evemerist" position, that the "gods of old" were kings and heroes who were later deified? According to your research, does this argument have some basis in reality?

Acharya: Despite the commonality of euhemerism or evemerism, only a relative handful of gods and goddesses could be said to represent evemerized individuals, i.e., human beings deified at some point during their lives or afterwards. Alexander the Great is one of these figures, as are various other rulers to whose biographies fantastic motifs have been added. The Egyptian god Imhotep appears to be an evemerized physician of ancient times. Other gods, however, were clearly never "real people," and this conclusion needs to be determined on a case-by-case basis.

My work largely serves to demonstrate that those commonly believed to have been evemerized "real people," such as Jesus, Buddha and Krishna, cannot be said to have truly "walked this earth," as they are obviously compilations of characters, and a composite of twenty people is no one.

Joan: Right! So this leads nicely to the subject of your latest book, Christ in Egypt. *Let's talk about Horus, the Egyptian god who was known as the "Sun of God," or "Son of God" as well as "Lord of lords" and "Lord of the sky." His dad was Osiris, who was also a Sun god. What are some of the many epithets and motifs commonly shared between Horus and Jesus?*

Acharya: Phew! There were so many, I had to pluck them out of *Christ in Egypt*. In the Pyramid texts appear the following epithets of Horus, among others:

> God, Great God, Great one, Son of a Great One, Heir of the father, Hereditary Prince, First-born god, King of the gods, Lord of the sky, Lord of men, Lord of men and gods, Presider over spirits, Presider of the living, Presider over the imperishable ones, Presider over the mighty, Morning star, God of dawnings, the Gleaming One, Lord of the two lands, Lord of the horizon, Master of the sustenance of truth, Master of his people, Mighty over gods.

You can see the similarities there, as well as in the many epithets of other gods in the various texts of ancient Egypt. If you factor in these other gods, which include Osiris, Isis, Horus, Re, Anubis, Thoth and Seb, you will come up with a list like this:

> Lord of Lords, King of Kings, Lord of the Universe, Lord of Eternity, Lord of Truth, Savior, the Divine, All-Powerful, the Unknowable, Great God, Lord of All, Inviolate God, God of Justice, Lord of Justice, Lord of Right, Lord of Power, Lord of Might, God of Authority, the Sole and Only One, the Eternal One, Most Glorious One, His Majesty, Mighty One, God of Mighty Names, Mighty Enlightener, Wise One, Potent One, Holy Soul, Good Being, the Great, the Mighty, the Ancient One, Sovereign, Protector, Universal Lord, Author of Eternity, Eternal Lord, Ruler of Eternity, Ruler of Everlasting, Lord of Everlasting, King of Eternity, the Eternal King, King of Everlasting, Prince of Eternity, Prince of the divine Powers, Hereditary Prince of the gods, the Peaceful One, Lord of Resurrections, Lord of Righteousness, Lord of Life, Living Lord, Lord of Time, Lord of Life for All Eternity, Giver of Life from the Beginning, Master of masters, Supreme among gods, Father of the gods, Lord of the Gods, Leader of the gods, King of the gods, Everlasting King, King of Heaven, Lord of Persons, Lord of the Law, Leader of the Host, Primeval One, Great One, Son of a Great One, United of Good, Lord of mysteries, Lord of the Age, Lord of the Soul, Lord of Strength, Lord of Offerings,

Defender in the Netherworld, Lord of the Unseen, and so on.

The title "KRST" as concerns Osiris is also an important one, for its obvious resemblance to "Christ," a subject I discuss in detail in *Christ in Egypt*. Ditto with the apparent epithet of Horus as "Iusa," the "ever becoming son," which resembles "Jesus," or "Iesous," as it is in the original Greek of the New Testament.

Joan: What other solar deities also share some of these common names, motifs or attributes? What is it essentially that makes them all Sun gods?

Acharya: The list is long indeed. The most obvious of these are Buddha and Krishna, who share many important similarities with Jesus. Most people would not think of these two as "sun gods," but I've made that case pretty thoroughly in my book *Suns of God: Krishna, Buddha and Christ Unveiled*. Other gods and goddesses from the ancient world who possess solar attributes and have been deemed sun gods, among other epithets, and who possess parallels in common with Christ, include the following, from a list in my calendar, *The 2010 Astrotheology Calendar*:

> Asclepius, Adonis, Amaterasu, Amun, Apollo, Ares/Mars, Arinna, Attis, Baal/Bel, Bacchus/Dionysus, Balder, Brahma, Buddha, Dumuzi, Hades, Hathor, Helios, Hephaistos/Vulcan, Hercules, Hermes, Horus, Hu, Iao/Yahweh, Indra, Inti, Isis, Janus, Jason, Jesus, Krishna, Mithra, Molech, Moses, Neith, Odin, Orion, Orpheus, Osiris, Pan, Perseus, Quetzalcoatl, Ra, Samson, Saturn, Serapis, Shamash, Shiva, Sol, Surya, Tammuz, Thor, Thoth, Viracocha, Vishnu, Zeus/Jupiter, Zoroaster and many more.

The solar attributes vary from god to god, of course, but some of those in this list are depicted as born miraculously—including of a "virgin"—in a cave or other dark place, a classic solar motif. They may also do miracles and be deemed "savior," again characteristics of the sun god. Raising the dead, healing, walking on water—these are all solar attributes.

Being put on a cross represents the sun at the equinoxes, while the birth at the winter solstice is an obvious mythical motif concerning the lengthening of the day. Fire, heat, light—these attributes of various gods are obviously solar in nature. Some, like Helios, Apollo, Krishna—and Jesus in a famous mosaic—are depicted as riding in chariots pulled by white horses, another common solar motif. Then there's the motif of "the Twelve," which you personally enjoy. Hercules, Buddha, Horus and Jesus, among others, are associated with this number because it reflects the months and signs of the zodiac.

Joan: Another fascinating subject you get into in Christ in Egypt *is the common motif of the Virgin Mother of these gods, as well as their common birth stories. Which gods were born of a Virgin Mother and what are some of these shared attributes concerning the mother of god?*

Acharya: The debate rages on whether or not the mothers of so many gods, godmen, heroes and other figures were "virgins," or merely mortal women who may or may not have been "chaste." Examples of this debate can be found concerning Buddha and Krishna, and I have written extensively on whether or not their mothers could be deemed "virginal." One thing to keep in mind here is that we are discussing *myths*, and myths do not have human body parts, so they can be attributed with all sorts of characteristics that may contradict each other. For example, while Isis is depicted as impregnating herself using Osiris's "phallus," that object is not necessarily what people think it is, as it is portrayed in the ancient texts as the "sharp star" of Sothis or Sirius, not a man's penis.

In this particular myth, Osiris is the water of the Nile, received by the river banks of Isis, to produce Horus. Regardless of the manner of impregnation, Isis was likewise styled in ancient, pre-Christian texts as the "Great Virgin." The "virgin mother" motif is common enough that academia uses the term "parthenogenesis" to discuss this subject, in a manner that may float above the heads of the masses, who are thereby kept in the dark about all these parallels to the Christ *myth*.

One famous virgin in Greek myth is the goddess Athena, whose virginity was so highly prized that her main temple at Athens was named the "Parthenon," which is the Greek word for "virgin." Yet, we discover that even she is portrayed in the myths as having given birth to the

gods Hephaistos and Apollo. The randy Zeus himself—whose myth is abundant with romantic dalliances—is deemed "parthenos." So it goes with myths. This theme often revolves around the constellation of Virgo, as well as the goddess of the Dawn, who arrives every morning fresh and virginal, to give birth to the golden sun. In its proper context, this motif, along with many others, is entirely comprehensible. And quite beautiful and inspiring, I might add.

Joan: Which gods were crucified on a cross, and did they rise from the dead in three days? What does this motif astrotheologically represent?

Acharya: This motif is also complicated, because we first must define what it means to be "crucified." Because of the gospel story, we immediately think of tough leather-clad Roman soldiers throwing the effeminate, robed Jesus to the ground and pounding nails through his hands and feet into a huge wooden cross. In reality, to be "crucified" could mean simply to be in a cross-shape or in *cruciform*. If we understand that gods, goddesses and other figures in cruciform were a common theme in pre-Christian times, we will see why this motif was picked up by the creators of Christianity, who subsequently changed it by fleshing it out as we find in the gospel story. I have written extensively on this subject, so I would direct the reader to my books for more information.

The long history of human sacrifice on this planet is also involved in this theme of "the crucified." In ancient times, a "sacred king" or a criminal proxy for him were frequently sacrificed in order to ensure fertility for the people, their animals and their lands. Hence, we find an old human-sacrifice ritual line in the New Testament when the Jewish people represented at Jesus's crucifixion make the strange remark, "Let his blood be upon us and our children." They are asking for fecundity and fertility, because being sprinkled in the sacrifice's blood was a ritual specifically for that purpose. We find this theme repeated in the Old Testament, where the priests slaughter hundreds of animals and throw the blood all over the congregation.

The three-day period or *triduum* is indeed another common motif in mythology, representing in significant part the time it perceivably took for the sun to change its course at the solstices, as well as the equinoxes. Hence, at the vernal equinox we find the *sun* of God hanging on a cross-the equal night and day—to rise again in three days, meaning that at the end of the equinoctial period our hero is beginning to gain strength towards full adulthood, which he achieves at the summer solstice. After that three-day period, he proceeds to the autumnal equinox, after which he starts to lose strength or "die," to be resurrected or reborn at the winter solstice.

The winter solstice in particular was viewed as a three-day period, because the ancients noticed that on the sun dial the shadow no longer moved southerly but stood in the same place for three days, after which it began to move north again. If you sunbathe over a period of several months at the same time of day, you will notice that you have to keep turning your body in order to face the sun, to the south if you live in the northern hemisphere. After the winter solstice, you will have to start turning your body north again to face the sun.

Joan: You have lately begun using your real name, D.M. Murdock, in your various online writings, blog and books, and your articles posted at examiner.com. Where does your pseudonym Acharya S or Acharya Sanning, come from?

Acharya: When I first went online I decided to use the pseudonym for purposes of privacy and safety. I was a *Christian apostate* writing scientifically about Christianity, and the reaction was fierce, to say the least. It continues to be, with all manner of invective and calumny tossed at me. My real name was unceremoniously outed by someone who apparently believed I was a "competitor," a nasty move that scared the bejesus out of me, because I was pregnant at the time, and my home address and phone number began to be circulated on the internet. Needless to say, I wasn't too pleased with this individual, although we have since become friends.

In any event, the name "Acharya" is actually an Indian title meaning "teacher," "master" and "priest of the sun," the latter of which I did not know about until relatively recently—it's quite an appropriate meaning, in consideration of what I do for a living, which largely revolves around solar mythology. "Acharya" is also a common Indian last name, so it's no big deal, although people like to make it into one. A group of Hindu fanatics, for example, ended up getting my Wikipedia page deleted, evidently because they did not like the fact that when someone searched for "Acharya" they landed on my page. That's religion for you.

The "Sanning" came because someone told me he couldn't publish one of my articles without a last name, and "S" wouldn't suffice. "Sanning" means "truth" in Swedish, which is one of my principal genetic heritages, so my full pen name means "teacher of truth." I like the combination of ethnicities there, the Indian and the Swedish, both of whom represent old and wise cultures.

Joan: Let me ask you the million-dollar question, Acharya S—who created Jesus and why did they do it?

Acharya: The creators of the Christ myth constituted a multinational group working over a period of decades who were more or less connected through various brotherhoods that abundantly ringed the Mediterranean and beyond. This group of religionists was continuing the long tradition of the priesthood in many countries in creating gods and goddesses out of natural phenomena or other, older deities and so on.

One prime example of this priestcraft occurred in the creation of the Greco-Egyptian god Serapis, who was specifically devised a few centuries before the common era by a similar group for the purposes of uniting the warring Greek and Egyptian factions of Alexandria. Also tossed into this mix, it was hoped, would be the Jews, who were likewise rabblerousing and who, like the Greeks, insisted on performing animal sacrifices.

Serapis was a god to whom the Greeks and Jews could sacrifice animals, and since he possessed many attributes in common with Osiris —he was, in fact, a combination of Osiris and his Apis bull—it was hoped the Egyptians would become devoted to him as well. This Serapis effort lasted until well into the common era, when the Christ figure began to replace him. In fact, the Jesus character adopted many of Serapis's features, including his long-haired, bearded appearance. Serapis, however, apparently wasn't strong enough in his Jewish characteristics, so a new creation, Jesus Christ, was needed.

The main reason for the creation of the mythical figure of Jesus Christ was in order to unify the Roman Empire under one state religion. We see the germ of this effort in the creation of Serapis, but we also find in the first century a well-funded movement to merge Paganism and Judaism, at the hands of the very powerful and wealthy elite headed by the emperor Vespasian. More information concerning this fascinating development can be found in my books, especially *The Christ Conspiracy*, *Suns of God* and *Christ in Egypt*.

About the Interviewee

Acharya S a.k.a. D.M. Murdock is a scholar of comparative religion, mythology and astrotheology. She is the author of the controversial bestselling book *The Christ Conspiracy: The Greatest Story Ever Sold*; as well as *Suns of God: Krishna, Buddha and Christ Unveiled*; *Who Was Jesus? Fingerprints of The Christ*; and *Christ in Egypt: The Horus-Jesus Connection*. More of her work can be found at *TruthBeKnown.com*, *StellarHousePublishing.com* and *TBKNews.blogspot.com*.

Programmed to Kill

David McGowan on the Politics of Serial Murder

Interview by Al Hidell

A deluge of news reports, books, and movies has shaped the public perception of serial killers and mass murderers. They are generally assumed to be solitary, deranged loners whose killings always fit a certain pattern. It is perhaps the ultimate "Lone Nut Theory." In his book *Programmed to Kill*, author David McGowan explodes these common assumptions, revealing largely hidden facts that suggest there's more to the serial killer phenomenon than meets the eye.

Al Hidell: Your book Programmed to Kill *suggests that some serial killers have connections to political figures, the FBI and CIA, and Satanic cults. Let's start with the political figures. Two examples you cite are George W. Bush's unusually lenient treatment of notorious serial killer Henry Lee Lucas, and his brother Jeb Bush's similar compassion towards Lucas' partner in crime. While this isn't proof of the killers' high-level political connections, it's certainly odd. Can you describe what happened, and what made it unusual?*

David McGowan: Henry Lee Lucas was convicted of numerous counts of first-degree murder, and was credited with scores, maybe even hundreds, of additional uncharged murders, many of them involving such depravities as torture, mutilation, cannibalism and necrophilia. Nevertheless, he had the unique distinction of being the only man to have his death sentence commuted during George W. Bush's tenure as governor of the state of Texas. Governor Bush personally, and quite uncharacteristically, requested that the Texas State Board of Pardons and Paroles (whose members were his own appointees) review Lucas' case. Strangely enough, that board uncharacteristically issued a recommendation that Lucas' sentence be commuted, and Bush then quietly signed the order sparing his life.

This all happened in June of 1998, but the media never really bothered to report the story, most likely because Bush's efforts on behalf of Lucas defy any reasonable explanation. This is, after all, the same governor who eagerly, sometimes even gleefully, signed off on every other execution order that crossed his desk, even in cases where there had been clear irregularities in the condemned inmate's conviction, and even in cases where the inmate was a woman, a juvenile, or was mentally impaired.

Lucas' partner, Ottis Toole, also managed to get his death sentence set aside, even though he was convicted and sentenced in Florida, a state that is not known for shying away from enforcing the death penalty, and even though his crimes were every bit as heinous as those of his partner. I believe, though, that the commutation of Toole's sentence predated the reign of Governor Jeb Bush.

Hidell: OK, so Jeb gets a pass on this one. Do Texas and Florida have anything else in common besides being controlled by the Bush Boys?

McGowan: As I discuss in the book, Texas and Florida have several things in common: they are two of the three states that provide a point-of-entry into the country for the vast majority of the illicit drugs trafficked through South and Central America; they are both rife with cult activity; and they have both been home to an inordinate number of serial killers. As you noted, at the time I began writing my book, Texas and Florida were both controlled by members of the Bush family. Interestingly enough, the third point of entry for illegal drugs, the state of California, which is also rife with cult activity, and which has also spawned an extraordinary number of serial killers, has now fallen under the control of someone who appears to be a close confidant of the Bush clan, Arnold Schwarzenegger.

Hidell: You suggest serial killers Jeffrey Dahmer and Ted Bundy had political connections. What led you to that conclusion?

McGowan: First, let me say that I am not necessarily arguing that any hard and fast conclusions can be drawn about any specific killer from the evidence presented in my book. From my perspective, the key to understanding the world that we live in is pattern recognition. I approached this book in much the same way that I approached my last book, *Understanding the F-Word: American Fascism and the Politics of Illusion*—by combing the published literature for all the inconvenient facts that are generally just sort of brushed over because they don't fit the official story. Just as my previous effort was an alternative political history of 20th century America, created from largely hidden threads, this book is an alternative history of violent, sensational crime in 20th century America. And what I found was that many of the threads that ran through my last book also run through this book.

Since this book is ultimately about fleshing out the hidden patterns that connect the life stories of the various notorious figures profiled therein, the case that the book attempts to make is necessarily a cumulative one. In other words, it is very easy to dismiss bits and pieces of evidence that tend to indicate, for example, that a particular serial killer had political and/or intelligence connections as simply an anomaly, a coincidence, an insignificant detail, etc. It is much more difficult to dismiss such evidence when it can be seen repeating in so many seemingly unrelated cases.

With that disclaimer out of the way, let me add that the most intriguing indication of Dahmer's political connections was his ability, while on a senior class field trip to Washington, D.C., to spontaneously arrange, with an impromptu call

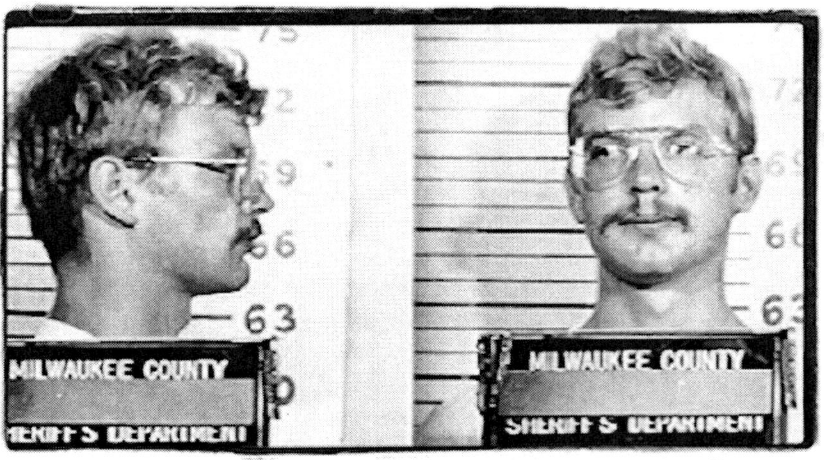

Jeffrey Dahmer (Milwaukee County Sheriffs Dept)

from a payphone, a private tour of both the Vice President's office and the office of prominent political columnist Art Buchwald. Needless to say, that's not something that the average 17-year old kid can pull off.

As for Ted Bundy, he was considered a rising star in the Republican Party who some say could have had a brilliant career as a lawyer or politician, or both. And it could probably be argued, in the world we live in, that Bundy was indeed ideally suited for either profession. In any event, Bundy had connections to a number of key Republican figures in the state of Washington. He worked as a driver and bodyguard for Lieutenant Governor-candidate Art Fletcher, then later as a key organizer of Governor Dan Evans' reelection campaign, and still later as a special assistant to Washington's Republican Party Chairman, Ross Davis. Bundy also had connections to various law enforcement entities, which is another common thread that runs through many serial killer stories.

I should add here that unusual treatment by the law enforcement and/or criminal justice systems can be an indirect indication of political connections, and there were serious irregularities in the investigations and prosecutions of virtually all the serial killer cases that I looked into while researching the book. Some segments of the criminal justice system seem to function as facilitators of violent killers, and persecutors of apparent patsies. That frequently recurring pattern is one of the clearest indications that there is a political dimension to the crimes of many so-called serial killers.

Hidell: What about serial killer Bob Berdella's alleged connection to Lt. Col. Oliver North? Is there any evidence to back this claim?

McGowan: Certainly no "smoking gun" evidence, but much of the evidence in the case was suppressed. Berdella was a Dahmeresque cannibal killer who kept numerous souvenirs of his exploits. Like Dahmer, he kept a photographic record of his victims. Berdella also kept very detailed written logs to document, among other things, the duration and intensity of the various forms of sadistic torture that he inflicted on his victims. Among the notations in those logs were specific references to a certain Lt. Col. Oliver North.

Hidell: What was the nature of the references? Did they suggest that Berdella may have known North, or were they more the form of general rantings?

McGowan: I don't know that it can be determined with any certainty what the exact nature of the references was, but when that information leaked out, the entries created quite a stir, enough so that they were specifically addressed and explained away in Berdella's supposed 'confession'—which was obtained under very unusual and carefully controlled conditions. Interestingly, the police detective who led the investigation obtained Berdella's confession, and then coauthored a book on the case—in other words, the man who shaped the public's perception of the Berdella case—had previously been employed by the Central Intelligence Agency.

As for Berdella, he took all his secrets to the grave not long into serving his prison sentence. That is yet another common thread that runs through the stories of many serial killers, including Jeffrey Dahmer, Albert "The Boston Strangler" DeSalvo, and Richard Chase.

Hidell: When it comes to serial killers and links to social elites, Belgium's Marc Dutroux is a particularly shocking case in point. Can you summarize the Dutroux case and cover-up?

McGowan: How best to summarize the Dutroux case? I can start by saying that it differs from most of the other cases discussed in my book in two important respects: Dutroux operated in Belgium, rather than in the United States; and many of the threads that were unreported by the American media were reported by at least some outraged and incredulous European media outlets.

Dutroux was a man with no real visible means of support, and yet he lived quite well, with several homes and several large bank accounts. In at least one of his homes, he had a custom-built, soundproof torture chamber/dungeon, in which he imprisoned young girls whom he repeatedly raped and tortured. Some of the young victims were eventually killed and buried on Dutroux's various properties. The fate of the others remains a matter of speculation.

As the Dutroux case unfolded, it became increasingly obvious that he had not acted alone, and that his operations had not only been protected by corrupt and powerful elements in the police, the judiciary, and in the highest reaches of the federal government, but that some of those powerful actors may even have been complicit in some of Dutroux's crimes. Far from being a "lone nut," the evidence strongly suggests that Dutroux was essentially a procurer of victims for a ring of powerful figures in the Belgian establishment.

As the details emerged, and the cover-up ensued, the Belgian people grew increasingly outraged, ultimately staging a general strike that all but shut the country down while about 300,000 enraged citizens took to the streets. The entire sitting government appeared to be at risk of being ousted, but ultimately the people were handed only a couple of sacrificial lambs, and the cover-up, sadly, continues to this day. That cover-up has resulted in a trail of dead bodies.

Hidell: In addition to the Dutroux case, you cite similar events in Portugal, Italy, Mexico, and Latvia.

In all these places, seemingly isolated cases of child rape, abuse, and murder were actually being conducted by organized pedophile rings. Most disturbing is the fact that these rings consisted of wealthy politicians, business leaders, and celebrities. Is there any indication that such rings have been or are operating in the United States as well?

McGowan: The unfortunate reality is that there are indeed indications that such rings are operating in the United States. There is also a wealth of evidence indicating that staggeringly large rings are operating globally, trafficking in child pornography, child prostitution and various other forms of organized child abuse and exploitation including documented cases of the production and distribution of videos featuring children (and sometimes adults) being brutally tortured and even, in some cases, killed.

In the U.S., the three most compelling cases to surface have been the Larry King Franklin case, the Craig Spence case, and the "Finders" case. All are discussed in detail in the early chapters of my book, as are various other related cases.

Hidell: Can you tell me more about these cases?

McGowan: The Franklin case was inadvertently exposed during what began as an investigation of a failed S&L in Omaha, Nebraska, and quickly mushroomed into an investigation of an alleged pedophile ring run by politician Larry King [not the talk-show host], considered a rising star in the Republican Party. The ring apparently catered to a very elite clientele that included powerful political, media and business figures, both locally and in Washington, D.C. As in the Dutroux case, the cover-up of the Franklin case included a trail of dead witnesses, including a private investigator and his young son who were killed in a very suspicious plane crash.

Closely tied to the Franklin case was the case of Spence, a behind-the-scenes powerbroker in the nation's capitol. Spence ran a call-boy ring that catered to some of the same rich and powerful patrons who were connected to the Franklin case. The Spence case did receive some coverage by the Washington media, although that coverage was largely in the form of a "limited hang-out." Many of the details of the case, and most of the prominent names implicated in the scandal, have been suppressed. Spence conveniently opted to commit suicide and the media quickly moved to other things.

The "Finders" case involved a Washington, D.C.-based group with ties to the CIA that evidence strongly suggests was involved in, among other things, the international trafficking of children. The "Finders" case was almost entirely ignored by the American press, but it did result in the issuance of a U.S. Customs Service document detailing the results of officers' searches of two of the group's properties—searches that yielded a considerable amount of incriminating evidence. For that reason, many consider the "Finders" case to be something of a smoking gun. That notorious Customs document is reproduced in its entirety in my book.

Hidell: To return to the subject of cults, most people think David Berkowitz, New York's infamous "Son of Sam," acted alone. Tell me why you believe the killings were related to a Satanic cult.

McGowan: I'm not really the best person to ask about the Son of Sam case. Maury Terry has done a fantastic job of documenting the real story behind the crimes attributed to David Berkowitz, in his seminal book, *The Ultimate Evil*. Terry's research on the Son of Sam case was so thorough that it took him over 500 pages to tell the story that unfolded. I couldn't begin to do justice to the body of evidence that he has compiled.

Terry's book was largely my inspiration for writing *Programmed to Kill*. I had read countless serial killer chronologies before reading Terry's book, beginning when I was still in school and was assigned a few of the "classics" in the genre to read, including Truman Capote's *In Cold Blood* and Norman Mailer's *The Executioner's Song*. In the years that followed, I read many more such titles, and, until I read Terry's book, I pretty much accepted the stories that I read at face value. That all changed after *The Ultimate Evil*, which reveals that there wasn't one Son of Sam, but actually many Sons of Sam, that there were specific motives for some of the murders, and that the killings were tied to other high-profile crimes, including the Manson murders and the Cotton Club murder.

After digesting all of that, the wheels in my head started spinning and I began to realize that there were parallels to other cases that I had read about in the past. Then, about that same time, and purely by chance, I stumbled across the curious fact that Governor George Bush had chosen to exercise a little "compassionate conservatism" on behalf of Henry Lee Lucas. With my curiosity aroused, I did a little digging into the Lucas story and discovered that the Henry Lee Lucas story, as told by Henry himself, had uncanny parallels to the David Berkowitz story.

At that point, I knew there was a story here that needed to be told. So, I pulled all the serial killer books off my bookshelf and began rereading then, searching for all the incongruous bits and pieces of information that escaped my attention the first time around. And then I went out and bought a couple dozen more books and read them. And I kept on reading and gathering information until I had enough to at least sketch out the broad outlines of an alternative theory of what the serial killer phenomenon is really all about.

Terry provided an in-depth study of one notorious serial killer case—the Son of Sam case—and the evidence that he brings to the table strongly suggests that the truth about those murders is something much different than what was sold to the public. My goal was to survey a few dozen notorious cases to demonstrate that, as bizarre as Terry's version of the Son of Sam case may at first appear to be, it may not be at all unique.

Hidell: Let's discuss some other famous serial killers. Tell me about child killer John Wayne Gacy, the so-called "Killer Clown." What was his connection to the FBI, and how on earth did he get a White House security clearance?

McGowan: I'm glad you asked about Gacy since that gives me a chance to give equal time, so to speak, to the Democrats. Since we have already discussed a few men (Ted Bundy, Larry King and Craig Spence) with deep ties to the Republican Party, it seems only fair to note that Gacy seems to have been equally well connected to the Democratic Party. Well enough to get a face-to-face meeting with then-First Lady Rosalynn Carter, commemorated by an autographed photo of the two of them together in which Gacy can be seen sporting a lapel pin denoting that he had been given a very high-level security clearance—in spite of the fact that Gacy already had, at that time, a rather checkered criminal history. How checkered? That's hard to say, since parts of Gacy's criminal record were blacked out by the FBI (as one of the attorneys on the case noted).

Unfortunately, I cannot tell you the exact nature of his connection to the FBI, nor can I tell you how he got that security clearance from the Secret Service. For better or worse, there are countless tantalizing leads in *Programmed to Kill* that I was unable to follow up on. As you probably know, no one earns a living as a serious political researcher and writer. Like many others in this field, I have to hold down a day job and am only able to do this in whatever free time I have available. Unlike Terry, I don't have the luxury of being able to travel about the country visiting crime scenes and interviewing witnesses and law enforcement personnel. In fact, I didn't do any primary research at all for this book. Everything in it has been previously published, in almost all cases in mainstream avenues of the media.

That brings up an interesting point, by the way: While this book is decidedly controversial (to the extent that it has, to date, been completely ignored even by the "alternative" media, with the exception of this interview), that controversy is created only by the way that the information has been organized and presented.

Hidell: How so?

McGowan: As they used to say on *The X-Files*, "the truth is out there"—but with the caveat that it won't be delivered to your doorstep in the morning newspaper, or broadcast into your living room on the evening news. And you won't find it in any of the books topping the *New York Times* nonfiction bestseller list, or in any of the documentaries airing on cable TV. What you will find in all of those sources of information are disembodied bits and pieces of the truth, generally either tossed out as insignificant, throwaway pieces of evidence, or surrounded by heavy doses of spin.

Getting to the truth of any conspiracy (for lack of a better word) is a matter of properly assembling a puzzle. To do that, you need to first track down all the right pieces, which requires wallowing through a lot of muck to find the nuggets hidden within. And you have to be very discerning, because there are a lot of red-herring pieces that look very much like real pieces, but actually are not. Once you've found enough of the real pieces, you must then properly assemble them. Only then does a coherent picture begin to emerge, and only then is a threat posed to conventional wisdom. The individual pieces pose no threat at all, even though many of them are hiding in plain sight.

The point that I want to make is that *Programmed to Kill* raises a number of questions that have yet to be answered. It is my hope that, just as Maury Terry's research inspired my own, my book will in turn inspire others to take an in-depth look at the cases that I have presented, and others as well. I believe that, with enough digging, an entire book could be written about each and every one of the notorious figures profiled in *Programmed to Kill*—and each of those books would tell a much different story than the 'true-crime' books that currently fill bookstore shelves. Of course, that would require that a lot of people spend a good many years doing a whole lot of digging.

Hidell: What evidence do you have that serial killer Gary Heidnik was the subject of CIA MK-ULTRA mind control experiments? Also, can you speak in general terms about the CIA's links to serial killers and mind control cults? What is the Agency's motivation?

McGowan: The Gary Heidnik case is rather unique in that it isn't necessary to connect various dots and then speculate about what picture it is that those dots combine to create, because Heidnik's military records reveal explicitly that he was an unwitting participant in medical experiments while in the U.S. Army stationed at a military hospital in West Germany. Of course, those records do not specifically refer to the MK-ULTRA program, but they do reveal that he was, without his knowledge, administered powerful hallucinogenic drugs. And any mind control researcher worth his salt knows that that is a classic MK-ULTRA scenario.

To understand the Agency's motivation for creating and cultivating the serial killer mythos, one need look no further than the current obsession with creating phantom terrorists. "Serial killers" and "terrorists" serve largely the same purpose: namely, scaring the hell out of people—to such an extent that those people will willingly surrender some of their most cherished civil, due process and privacy rights so that the government will be better able to protect them from largely phantom threats. It is all about control through fear, and prior to the arrival center-stage of the threat of "terrorism," nothing instilled fear in people like serial and spree killers—precisely because, according to the prevailing wisdom, serial killers can strike anytime, anywhere, for any reason. And according to conventional wisdom, anyone can be a serial killer—a friend, a neighbor, a co-worker, even a family member. So, with serial killers on the prowl, no one is safe and no one is above suspicion. It is not hard to see then how the specter of the marauding serial killer serves to both instill fear in the populace, and to shatter social and community bonds. Before the arrival of the "terrorists," nothing better served to advance an authoritarian, police-state agenda than the notion of serial and spree killers.

The modern serial killer phenomenon has clear parallels to, and clear ties to, the CIA's notorious Vietnam-era Phoenix Program—which, for the uninitiated, was a program designed to terrify the Vietnamese people into acceding to the demands of U.S. occupiers. This was accomplished through the wholesale use of kidnapping, rape, torture, and murder. The crime scenes of Phoenix operatives in Vietnam were often indistinguishable from the crime scenes of serial killers here in the states, with the bodies of victims often horrifically mutilated and left in gruesome displays, for maximum shock value. Just as the goal of the Phoenix Program was control of the Vietnamese people through fear and demoralization, one of the primary goals of serial killings appears to be control of the American people through fear and demoralization.

Hidell: The "Boston Strangler" murders and the "Atlanta Child Killings" are two examples of this sort of control through fear and demoralization. However, contrary to popular belief, alleged "Boston Stranger" Albert DeSalvo and alleged "Atlanta Child Killer" Wayne Williams were never convicted of those killings. Do you think they had any role in the murders? Who else may have been involved?

McGowan: Let's take a look at the Boston Strangler case first, which is somewhat unique in that it has now been semi-officially acknowledged that Albert DeSalvo was not responsible for at least some of the killings that he was publicly, though never legally, convicted of. In fact. DeSalvo was never even charged with a single count of murder, let alone tried and convicted. Many of the detectives involved in the investigation have never believed that DeSalvo committed the notorious Boston-area murders. Neither have the family members of DeSalvo and some of his alleged victims. No witnesses or physical evidence ever tied DeSalvo to any of the victims or to any of the crime scenes. The sole piece of evidence allegedly tying DeSalvo to the crimes was an extremely dubious, and inaccurate, series of supposed confessions.

It was already pretty clear from the circumstances of his pseudo-conviction, and the circumstances of his murder while incarcerated, that DeSalvo was railroaded for crimes that he did not commit and then was conveniently silenced. In recent years, exhumations and forensic and DNA analysis have lent considerable weight to that conclusion.

Based on all the available evidence, I do not believe that DeSalvo had any role at all in the murders, other than as a patsy. As for who was involved, the best research into that mystery has been done by Susan Kelly, who penned the book *The Boston Stranglers*. And, no, that is not a typo; Kelly's research suggests that there were several individuals involved in the murders, most from prominent families with intriguing connections. Kelly's book is another fairly good example of the type of book that I believe should replace the traditional 'true crime' bestsellers.

As for Wayne Williams, he also was never charged with, nor convicted of, any of the crimes that he has been publicly declared guilty of. Williams was charged with two counts of murder, but both counts involved adult victims. No charges were ever filed against Williams in connection with the death of a single child, and his convictions on the other murder charges were a travesty of justice. As with the Boston Strangler case, many of the families of the victims of the Atlanta Child Killer believe that Williams was railroaded, as do I.

However, evidence does suggest that Williams may have been involved in at least some of the killings, albeit not as the actual killer. Indications are that the killings were connected to a group of male pedophiles/child pornographers, quite possibly with cult involvement, and with possible overtones of medical experimentation. In other words, there was no shortage of weirdness surrounding the Atlanta Child Murders (some researchers have also pointed the finger at the FBI and White Supremacist groups).

It appears that Williams may have functioned as something of a photographer for the cult. He and his father destroyed and/or disposed of a considerable amount of photographic evidence after Williams fell under suspicion. But while Williams may well have documented the killings, and possibly helped troll for victims as well, the evidence does not suggest, and the irregularities in his trial do not suggest, that Williams actually committed the murders.

Hidell: How might the 1975 murder of Karen Grammer, sister of Frasier star Kelsey Grammer, fit into this? Why do you think we haven't heard more about it?

McGowan: Karen Grammer's murder was briefly mentioned in my book because of the indirect connection to the JonBenet Ramsey case (which obviously wasn't a serial killer case, but which is covered because of the parallels to other cases). Lou Smit, the private investigator brought in to work on the Ramsey case—first for the DA, and then later for the Ramseys—was previously best known for purportedly solving Grammer's murder. I found this to be an intriguing connection, primarily because Smit seems to be far better at providing spin than solving crimes.

The Karen Grammer murder is yet another one of those tantalizing factoids that you find sprinkled here and there in the mainstream media coverage of high-profile crimes, and then never hear another word about. As it turns out, the Grammer case is, perhaps not surprisingly, a bizarre one. She was purportedly killed by a gang of current and former GIs stationed at the Fort Carson Army base near Colorado Springs. Grammer was supposedly one of seven victims killed as part of a murder spree—except that her murder was markedly different than the other six murders. All the other victims were men and most of them, if not all, had some connection to Fort Carson. At least three were soldiers who were currently or formerly stationed there, and another was a cabdriver killed on the base. At least one victim was himself a member of the gang. Most were shot, execution style. Grammer, on the other hand, had her throat slashed after being brutally raped.

Most of the murders were undoubtedly part of some kind of clean-up operation going on at Fort Carson at the time. It is unclear how or if Grammer's murder was connected to whatever was going on at the Army base. Smit just lumped her murder in with the others and wrote them all off as just another senseless, largely motiveless, murder spree.

As an interesting side note, Kelsey and Karen Grammer's father was murdered as well, in a separate incident in 1968. And as another interesting side note, the prosecutor on the Karen Grammer case was later a prosecutor on the Ted Bundy case.

Hidell: You believe another killing, of the Otero family in 1974, may have also had military connections. You suggest the so-called "BTK" serial killer was a legend created after the fact to cover up the true motive for the slaughter of the family, right?

McGowan: Yes, that does appear to be the case—and it is far from being an unusual situation. Yet another motivation for the CIA/FBI's creation of the serial killer mythos is to provide a handy way for the state to disguise politically motivated assassinations as random, motiveless killings.

Until the so-called "BTK" case was recently resurrected by the police and media (for reasons that are unclear at this time), it was a relatively obscure case. I didn't come across a single reference to it in all the reading that I did while researching my book. But with the case now being flogged by the national media, I was inspired to take a closer look. And as it turns out, some new facts have only recently emerged, courtesy of a surviving family member of the first purported victims.

On January 15, 1974, four members of the Otero family of Wichita, Kansas were brutally slaughtered in their home (not unlike the Ohta family, which was slaughtered in Santa Cruz, California just a few years earlier). All indications are that this was not a random act of violence, but rather a targeted assassination likely carried out by a commando team very likely known by the primary victim, Joseph Otero, a 20-year Air Force veteran. There are indications that the house was being watched prior to the murders, and Joseph Otero's actions in the days leading up to the slaughter suggest that he was convinced that he and his family had been targeted.

Charlie Otero, who discovered the bodies of his parents and siblings, is convinced to this day that his father was killed because of something that occurred during what he describes as his dad's sometimes secretive life in the military, which kept him away from home for months at a time. Joseph Otero was involved with the Inter-American Air Forces Academy, which is essentially an Air Force branch of the U.S. Army's notorious School of the Americas, which has long been associated with death-squad training and drug trafficking in Central and South America. Charlie is also convinced, for good reason, that there is no possibility that a sole assailant was responsible for the carnage in the Otero home. Joseph Otero was a trained commando and a former champion boxer. In other words, he was very well equipped to defend himself, and since he had been anticipating an attack, he was not likely caught off-guard. His wife, Julie, had had self-defense training, as had the two Otero kids killed that day.

Hidell: Earlier, you spoke of the social role of serial killers and terrorists. In this regard, do you have any thoughts about the D.C. "Beltway Snipers"? According to a family friend, Lee Malvo's mother said John Muhammad was "brainwashing" the boy into being his slave, and she suspects they had a sexual relationship. What do you make of that?

McGowan: The "DC Sniper" case—the first post-9/11 "serial killer" case to receive national media exposure—is of particular interest because the authorities and media talking heads quite deliberately attempted to blur the line between serial murder and "terrorism"—or, to phrase it more accurately, to blur the line between "terrorism" and domestic crime in general, thus furthering the agenda of converting the country into an overt police state where "anti-terrorist" legislation can be enforced indiscriminately against American citizens.

Although I followed the Sniper case quite closely, it didn't make it into the book. Instead, I opted to cover the story on my website [www.davesweb.cnchost.com] with a series of posts that went up as the first Sniper trial played out. Anyone interested in the Beltway case can read the Center for an Informed America Newsletters #20, and #45 through 48, which trace some of the parallels to other serial killer cases, and which also highlight the fraudulence and corruption of the criminal "justice" system. That series of posts serves as a sneak preview of the type of stories that can be found in *Programmed to Kill*.

About the Interviewee

This interview appeared in *PARANOIA*, Issue 38 (Spring 2005). David McGowan is the author of *Programmed to Kill: The Politics of Serial Murder* (iUniverse.com, 2004), *Understanding the F-Word: American Fascism and the Politics of Illusion* (Writers Club Press, 2001), and *Derailing Democracy: The America the Media Don't Want You to See* (Common Courage Press, 2000). He is the host and webmaster for the Center for an Informed America, *www.davesweb.cnchost.com*.

Illustration by John David Moore, *www.noir33.com*

Six-Legged Cattle

The Future of Entomophagy

by David Gracer

I run an unusual business, and many folks think I'm crazy for doing it. But maybe when I explain my reasoning, you (as an intelligent reader) will be forced to acknowledge that there's some sense to what others have chosen to call 'madness.' My company advocates for and seeks the development of entomophagy: the consumption of insects as a food source for humanity. Sure, there are a few problems with the concept, but there are always problems. Unfortunately, the main problem with entomophagy is the unreasoning and ignorant stubbornness of Western societies in general, and American society, in particular, even though there are a couple of good role models for the subject.

One example is Aristotle. The famous Greek thinker (it's often said that all of Philosophy is merely footnotes of his work) was particularly fond of cicadas. The higher-class Romans—meaning, the ones who could afford it—similarly indulged, pampering themselves with large beetle grubs made fat on wheat flour dampened with wine. Then there is the spectacular example of Dracula's insane assistant. Renfield, who makes a hobby of seizing bugs (and sometimes rodents) around the laboratory for snacks. Renfield was convinced that if he ate them live he would capture their 'life essence,' and this was one of the main proofs of his 'insanity.'

We can also find representations of entomophagy in modern televised media, but most of them focus on the sensationalized aspects. On *Man vs. Wild*, for examp'e, Bear Grylls generally scrunches up his face in repulsion before sampling insects. Of course, this pales in comparison to *Fear Factor*, where contestants scream and cry for mercy as they're "forced" (by nothing other than their lust for cash prizes) to eat bugs. Granted, those bugs are alive, whereas I suggest cooking them before serving, although that's not as entertaining. I prefer a more rational approach to the subject.

Insects would be a fantastic food for humanity because of the relationship between the amount of resources required to produce a unit of edible material and the amount of nutrition inherent in the food. While it would be ridiculous to compare the production requirements of a cow to that of a cricket, we can break down the increments of resources required to produce a quarter-pound of processed product for each kind of animal. When we do this, we'll find out just how much better insects are for the planet. This requires that we table the fact that most people in North America and Europe cringe and shriek at the mention of eating insects, and are, therefore, unwilling to consider engaging in the practice.

The Ectotherm Difference

Since insects are so much more efficient than vertebrates in their conversion of energy inputs, they're an attractive choice for an overcrowded planet. Let's look at several reasons why insects are far superior to the mammals and birds that we're more accustomed to eating:

Energy. The most crucial aspect concerns the percentage of energy-from-food-source that a given type of animal can retain from the feed that it's given. Mammals and birds are endotherms, meaning that they maintain relatively high body temperatures and, therefore, a lot of the energy they get from their food is devoted to keeping themselves alive. This makes them physiologically inefficient; neither the animals nor the farmers can change this basic physical reality, so it doesn't matter whether the animals are raised in feedlots or alone in a field. Bugs are ectotherms. When kept at relatively high ambient temperatures, they will retain the energy from their food sources, allowing us to capture that energy when we consume them.

Some readers might ask, 'well, wait just a minute. If the farmer has to provide warm conditions for the bugs, then he or she will be spending a lot of energy and money on that and where's the environmental benefit?' There are several solutions, the most obvious of which would be to locate insect farms in warmer areas of the country (such as abandoned "big box stores" in the southern and southwestern states). But any clever architect or civil engineer could find economical ways to achieve the same results in northern cities, thereby reducing transportation costs for the final product.

Water. Insects require the smallest fraction of water that our standard food animals do. This is most obvious when we look at the requirements of large mammals. Few Americans have taken the time to understand the extremely tenuous situation regarding the global supply of fresh water. In fact, bugs are superior not only to food animals but also to crops. They require far less: water, space, land, time, labor, electricity, human training, dubious chemistry (including antibiotics and pesticides), petroleum-driven machinery, etc.

Nutrition. In addition to the advantages outlined above, it also turns out that bugs are better for the human body. Regarding nutrients like protein, vitamins, and minerals, various insect species (unsurprisingly, there is a good deal of variation from one to the next) are equal or superior to the usual suspects: beef/pork/chicken/fish. For example, cricket has roughly half the protein that beef does, but it far outstrips beef in terms of fat, carbohydrates, calcium, and B vitamins. We see this frequently: insects are not better than other foods in every category, but in most of them.

For instance, the Insect Nutrition Table found at the Entomology Department at Iowa State University (www.ent.iastate.edu/Misc/insectnutrition.html) details the comparative nutrition of insects vs. beef and fish. Cricket contains 12.9 g protein, 75.8 mg. calcium and 9.5 mg iron; relative to beef, which contains 27.4 g protein, but 3.5 mg iron and no calcium to speak of. The simple household termite offers 14.2 g protein and 35.5 mg iron. The grasshopper is a high-hitter at 20.6 g protein, 35.2 mg calcium and 5.0 mg iron; while broiled fish contains 28.5 g protein and 1 mg. iron. "Hands-down," insects offer higher iron and calcium levels, with the caterpillar offering a whopping 35.5 mg of iron.

Recognizing all of the above puts me in a somewhat unhappy position: I can see a better way of producing food, but the solution is blocked by arbitrary stubbornness born out of cultural conditioning. At educational events, I talk about the subject, show various kinds of media, and then serve the cooked insects. At such events I'm a nice guy who doesn't abuse the audience. I remind myself that it's really not their fault that our species is in the mess it is; yet, it's also true that every single one of us bears some responsibility for the collective situation. This is far more the case for Americans, since we individually consume a much larger amount of resources than, for instance, the average French, Indian or Botswanan. I use humor and common sense to convince people to try their first insect, which is usually a cricket. It's a bit like a sales job, though I'm not a salesman because I don't rely on a commission. I enjoy addressing the public, but it's the production aspect of the industry that I want to be involved in.

Production. Production can take a variety of forms. Professor Robert Kok of McGill University has drawn up blueprints for a production facility that could easily feed the population of a large city, and a Dutchman has proposed a factory producing insect biscuits that could supply African communities with much-needed sustenance. Of course, small-scale projects are also possible and anyone with rudimentary equipment and simple conditions can raise their own animal protein supply in their basement or spare room. Although numerous books and websites (cited at the end of this article) describe more specific procedures involved, the basic elements to produce crickets or mealworms include:

- ambient heat (85 degrees Fahrenheit is frequently cited)
- plastic bins
- cardboard shelter
- substrate (several types are suggested; wet sand is popular)
- chicken feed or dry vegetables (damaged goods not a problem, of course)
- damp paper towels

There's very little smell to insect production, and harvest time (roughly every two months) involves a minimum of mess, since you don't have to butcher these 'farm animals.' Not only that, but a little more processing will yield insect flour to make breads, pasta, muffins, etc. Processing allows you and your guests to enjoy all the nutritional and environmental benefits of entomophagy without having to consume entire and intact bugs.

Some species of insects are not suitable for mass rearing, including dragonflies, ants, and most caterpillars. Some species are unsafe to consume, including stinging wasps and several kinds of beetles. However, this leaves a goodly list of candidates, such as: crickets, mealworms, cockroaches, and sowbugs (technically not an insect, but rather a terrestrial isopod.) These could be raised in a single bin—though probably not in mixed populations—in one's basement, or in vast grids of bins each running on its schedule. In that scenario, one could easily harvest every day and achieve a self-sufficient protein supply.

Preparation. I freeze my insects to kill them, give them a quick parboil, then rinse and freeze. There's no complicated cleaning, and every part is edible. Most insects can be made toothsome by baking, roasting, or sautéing. Some are a little more or less "chitinous" than others; chitin being their exoskeleton. That's what makes them crunchy. Some folks ask me about chocolate. It's a wonderful food, but I don't put it on insects because I want the latter to be taken seriously as entrée material. No one puts chocolate on hamburgers; same concept. There are several good insect cookbooks out there (listed at the end of this article); someday I'll contribute my own, but that's not at the top of my list at the moment.

Environmental Impact

I pursue this line of work because I'm entranced by the idea that humanity could live within its means. Historically, humanity had managed to do that for a long time, but agricultural advances led the way to industrialization. Now most of us act as though we're "addicted" to the very foods that pose the greatest harm to our collective future. The more damaging the food is (to our bodies or our planet), the likelier we are to demand it on our plates.

In 2006, the Food and Agriculture Office of the UN (FAO) released "Livestock's Long Shadow," a major report that details the diverse impacts of cattle production on various ecological resources and systems. The news is not pretty: among its assertions is that "livestock are responsible for 18 percent of greenhouse gas emissions, a bigger share than that of transport." In addition, livestock land use is a major driver of deforestation and land degradation, and contributes to water pollution by animal wastes, antibiotics, hormones, chemicals from tanneries, fertilizers and pesticides. The report suggests, "The environmental costs per unit of livestock production must be cut by one half, just to avoid the level of damage worsening beyond its present level" (*www.fao.org*).

Yet, most people fail to see, or perhaps refuse to see, the link between what they eat and the environmental impact. This is because these are "normal foods," and normality is based on what we grow up with and what others tell us. Therefore, cultural norms are slow to develop and slow to change, and this explains the vast diversity of foods around the world. For instance, I once tried Balut, a Philippine specialty consisting of a fertilized chicken or duck egg. When the boiled egg is opened, the diner consumes the partially-formed embryo. One can choose an egg at varying stages of development. If we find this distasteful, it's because it wasn't popular in our home environment when we were growing up. Who are you to judge?

Cultural Conditioning

At educational programs, I remind the audience that Americans eat foods that those from other nations might find weird or questionable, like cheese or hotdogs. I ask the audience how many of them enjoy eating crustaceans, which are the marine equivalent of insects. Of course, many raise their hands. I tell them that other than their marine versus terrestrial lifestyles, the main difference between crustaceans and insects (which I refer to as "land shrimp") is that while the former eat feces and carrion, many insects eat only vegetation. One might expect that this would make them a more logical food choice than lobster and crab, but clearly that's not the case. That's because *we* have already *decided* that lobster and crab taste good; therefore, little inconvenient realities like their shit-eating habits don't matter. (Warning: anyone allergic to crustaceans will also be allergic to insects, since they're all arthropods. Something to keep in mind when serving.)

Food preferences are never objective. And the funny thing is that those Americans who won't try insects are eating them anyway. The FDA knows—as does similar regulatory machinery operating in countries throughout the developed world—that food manufacturers can't possibly keep bugs out of the food supply chain, so limits have been set for particular generic foods. All I want to do is to raise that limit, admittedly by quite a lot.

More could be said about food preferences; for example, there might be objective evidence that the human brain prefers fattier animal flesh, and it could be hardwired into us as a legacy of the lean hunter-gatherer times. A truly comprehensive explanation about why we eschew insects would include many other subjects, but most of all anthropology and the Judeo-Christian urge to show our domination of Nature through the management of large animals. Nonetheless, as our large-scale food production methods fall apart, none of these academic explanations will matter.

I make such dire predictions because, well, look what we're doing. We've made our chosen foods all inbred for maximum efficiency, such that people going to work in a pig farm have to scrub as though they're going into surgery. Seriously. The animals are vulnerable to the common cold. The same appears to be the case in the plant world. As for the introduction of genes from other forms of life into plants and animals, the possible consequences of that manipulation are unknown. Maybe everything will be okay forever, but given how we've altered every corner and aspect of the natural world this seems unlikely.

Another consideration regarding cultural conditioning is that the great majority of ethnic groups that practice entomophagy have a range of other foods to choose from: insects are rarely a starvation food. In various marketplaces around the world, insects fetch higher prices than other foods do; this indicates that they're valued. We could learn to perceive these foods in the same way.

The Future

From what I've seen, the main criterion we use to determine which foods are "the good ones" is taste. In this, we adults are fairly similar to the average three-year-old that wants cake and ice cream at least three times a day. That's why parents are needed, to remind the very young that there are other considerations. Too bad there are no such sources of guidance for adults, since diets high in mass-produced beef and pork have analogous effects on our planet that large amounts of cake and ice cream have on the bodies of individual people. The problem is that we can't see the long-term effects of that food production. Technology has given us the ability to pretend that the forces of Nature do not apply to us. But they do apply, and our food production systems put us in conflict with those forces. Ultimately, our food preferences will become completely unimportant as fresh water and other resources become increasingly scarce.

Our future as a species is pretty bleak. And that's because we're self-destructive. Even though we're different in so many ways from other animals, we're still pulled around by our biological imperatives, such as the urge to breed excessively. While other species are held in check by competitors in their environments, humans have done a pretty good job of removing those obstacles to our growth. Unlike a school of fish or a flock of birds, humans get dumber when they're put in groups. Whereas animals act so as to protect as many individuals as possible, humanity is made up of individuals primarily interested in their own pleasure and convenience rather than the smooth functionality of the group. This kind of behavior could be lethal to all of us.

My work tries to show how we could wise up. I sometimes ask people to imagine that they have a friend who's very intelligent, and starting to go blind. The friend had received the diagnosis some time before, and now his sight is starting to go. If he's intelligent, I remind my audience, he'll recognize reality and start practicing with the cane and the dog before he absolutely needs them. That would be the smart thing to do: recognize the reality coming toward you, and act in anticipation so as to be ready for it. That's just what I'm talking about regarding food supply.

I could claim that producing a hundred pounds of edible insect protein would require a ten-thousandth of the fresh water needed to produce the same amount of beef or pork, but without citations I'm just a crazy guy on a street corner. If past history is any judge, and it certainly is, humanity will be compelled to learn from the consequences of its ways rather than manage to correct its errors ahead of time. Our society has data on the consequences of uncontrolled resource consumption, and of the finite nature of those resources; yet, it hasn't made any difference. Various films and other media have made the argument that all of us have to change our ways if we want a livable future, but those arguments haven't made much difference in our daily lives.

In the final analysis, 'crazy' and 'insane' are words that identify whatever is in conflict with dominant ideas about what's normal. These are convenient labels. But if the standard ways of doing things (like producing and consuming food, for example) are manifestly destructive to the entire society—and it's not hard to prove that this is the case regarding the production and consumption of large mammals—then that's what's crazy. Just as suicide is considered a sign of mental abnormality, stubborn adherence to a self-destructive food preference is just not healthy, mentally speaking.

Please re-read the second sentence of this article. In your mind, I have either sufficiently explained my reasoning for the serious contemplation of the future of entomophagy, or you consider me 'mad.' Can you yet acknowledge that the consumption of insects as a food source for humanity makes a lot of sense, or are you still—even now—held firmly in the grip of the standard and predictable group-think mentality that afflicts so many Americans? Perhaps this article has urged you to consider a more responsible way to live, such that you're finally ready to count yourself among the slowly increasing number of visionaries who are willing to consume in a way that would create a better world for all of us.

Suggested Reading on Entomophagy

Bodenheimer, F.S. 1951. *Insects as Human Food*. The Hague: W. Junk.

Gordon, David George. May 1998. *Eat-A-Bug Cookbook.*

Holt, Vincent M. 1885. *Why Not Eat Insects?* London: E.W. Classey, Ltd.

Menzel, Peter; D'Aluisio, Faith. 1998. *Man Eating Bugs: The art and science of eating insects.* Berkeley, Calif.: Ten Speed Press.

Ramos-Elorduy, Julieta. 1998. *Creepy Crawly Cuisine: The Gourmet Guide to Edible Insects.* Rochester, Vermont: Park St. Press.

Taylor, Ronald L. 1975. *Butterflies in My Stomach. Or: Insects in Human Nutrition.* Santa Barbara, Calif.: Woodbridge Press Publ. Co.

Websites on general entomophagy:

www.food-insects.com
www.smallstockfoods.com
www.insectsarefood.com

Websites for rearing food-insects:

http://crawford.tardigrade.net/bugs/cricketsuppl.html
www.hollowtop.com/finl_html/mealworms.htm

About the Author

David Gracer advocates insect husbandry on his blog, Bugs For Dinner, at *http://bugsfordinner.blogspot.com*, and on his website Small Stock Foods, at *www.smallstockfoods.com* (previously known as Sunrise Land Shrimp). He has been interviewed on *The Steven Colbert Show* and has been written up in *New York Times Magazine* ("Man Bites Insect," Feb, 2008). He may be contacted through his website, Small Stock Foods.

PARANOIA Library

The following back issues of *PARANOIA* Magazine are still available at $7 each (includes shipping) while supplies last. Please send check, money order or cash to PARANOIA, P.O. Box 1041, Providence, RI 02901. Or you may order by Paypal at *www.paranoiamagazine.com*., where you can also see free PDFs of several sold out issues and other free reading materials.

Issue 5: Virgin Mary and UFOs; Satanic Child Abuse: The McMartin Scandal; Tibetan Yetis & the CIA; Psychic Warfare and Non-lethal Weapons; Cattle Mutilations; Trevor Constable Interview; The Lindbergh Kidnapping Hoax; CIA Connections to Leary and Manson; The Watergate Plane Crash.

Issue 6: Masonic Symbolism in the JFK Assassination; UFOs and the Black Death; Who is Alek J. Hidell?; The Clinton Body Count; The Death of River Phoenix; Medical Mayhem; William Bramley Interview; Constitution in Trouble with William Cooper and Linda Thompson; Paranotes by Al Hidell.

Issue 11: Cult Awareness Network; CIA Connections to Mind Control Cults; The Fatal Vision Murders; Asset Forfeiture Update; UFOs: Chariots of the Damned?; The Dark Side of the Moon; Colin Powell Exposed; Adventures in Psychedelics with Thomas Lyttle; The Numerology of Oppression: Speech by Louis Farrakhan; Al's Paranotes.

Issue 12: Subliminal Sex in Advertising; The Goatsucker; Human Mutilations in South America; Kennedy Family Control over JFK Autopsy; The State of the World Forum and Shirley MacLaine; Holocaust Revisionism Overview.

Issue 14: Dead Ringers: JFK and Officer Tippit by Robert Morningstar; Project Monarch Mind Control by Ron Patton; How Mainstream Media Obscure a Cancer Cure by Barry Lynes; Star Trek: Sci-Fi or Psy-War by Jerry E. Smith; Liberation Theology, Ecumenicism and the NWO by D. Guide; Diet for a Zombified Planet by Mark Westion; plus Rants; reviews and Al's scary Paranotes.

Issue 15: Special Hoax Issue! Joan d'Arc interviews Rene on the Great American Moon Hoax; The Paul is Dead Hoax by Joyce Rodgers; Alternative 3: The Great Brain Drain by Joan d'Arc; Demons In Alien Clothing by Ron Patton; Nazi UFOs: Interview with Henry Stevens of the German Research Project; Crop Circle Hoaxes by Joan d'Arc; Crying Wolf: Hate Crime Hoaxes by Gargoyle; No Aliens: Just Assholes by William Lyne; Paranotes by Al Hidell.

Issue 16: Where the Hell is Madalyn Murray O'Hair? by Fred Woodworth; Larry Flynt and the Gemstone Thesis by Joan d'Arc; TWA800: No Single Missile Theory by Al Hidell; The Assassination of Yitzhak Rabin by Barry Chamish; EMF Weapons the New Arms Race by Cheryl Welsh; OJ, DNA and Conspiracy on Trial by D. Guide; Gulf War Syndrome and AIDS by Alan Cantwell; Satanism, the Illuminati and the Andromedans by R. Roy Blake; The Real Evita Peron: To Dallas from Argentina by Mae Brussell; Mystery of the Knights Templar by Scott Corrales; Al's Paranotes.

Issue 17: Honey Did You Leave Your Brain at Langley Again? (A Brief History of Modern Mind Control) by Robert Guffey; Psy-Ops and UFOs by Alex Cox; Spooking of UFO Researcher Paul Bennewitz by Bruce Rux; AIDS is Man-Made by Alan Cantwell; Asset Forfeiture Exposed by Joan d'Arc; UFOs at the Edge of Reality Lecture by Jim Keith; Hale-Bop, the Green Horse and the Fourth Seal by Wendy Wallace; AT&T and the Phone Number of the Beast by Texe Marrs; The Mental Status Quo (MSQ) by Frank Berube; plus wicked good Paranotes.

Issue 27: Science Fiction as Manipulation by Robert Guffey; Blaming Gays, Blacks and Chimps for AIDS by Alan Cantwell; Wendy Wallace on the Hidden Agenda of Darwinism; Scott Corrales on the Chupacabras; The Endgame of ET Exposure by Randy Koppang; Victor Hugos' Conversations With Eternity by John Chambers; The Control of Candy Jones; Paranotes by Al Hidell.

Issue 28: Richard Nixon and the Kent State Conspiracy by Katie Klemenchich; Conspiracy: A Matter of Generations by Scott Corrales; Real Strategies Behind the War on Terrorism by Al Hidell; The 9/11 Media Spectacle by Joan d'Arc and Frank Berube; Troll Cams: The All Seeing Eyes of GOG by John Paul Jones; Bush-Cheney Drug Empire by Mike Ruppert; Symbolism of Nibiru (Planet X!) by Andy Lloyd; Maitrya: World Teacher by Paul Cronin; plus wicked good Paranotes.

Issue 30: Special 10-Year Anniversary Issue! Did Nostradamus Predict Bin Laden? by Eric W. Taylor;

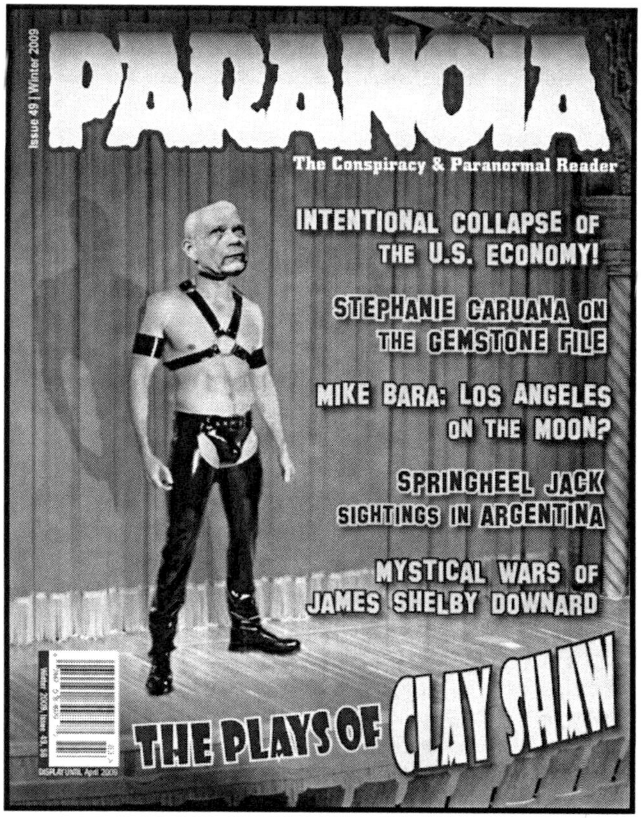

UFOs and Bodily Harm by Scott Corrales; Gaudi's Grand Hotel on the Hudson: A WTC Architect Speaks Out by Paul Laffoley; Pagan Origins of Christian Mysteries by Acharya S; Richard Nixon and Kent State Part II by Katie Klemenchich; Disney and American Futurism by Randy Koppang; The Stronghold and the Shrine: ET Origins of the City-State by David Pearson; Cruisin with the Spooks on a Spy Cruise by Kathy Kasten; The Rockefellers: An Intuitive Perspective by Jaye Beldo; plus shocking Paranotes.

Issue 31: Concentration Campus: Thought Control in American Education by Robert Guffey; What Carl Jung Knew About Flying Saucers He Got from Freud by Joan d'Arc; I-Spies, Israeli Espionage and 9/11 by Al Hidell; The New West Nile Virus by Alan Cantwell; Short History of the Illuminati Agenda by Frank Berube; Animal Mutilation Wave in Argentina by Scott Corrales; Psychiatry and Psychology: Re-Examining a Sacred Cow by Steven Ferry; Al's wicked Paranotes.

Issue 32: Decoding the D.C. Sniper by Michael A. Hoffman II; The State Terror Thesis: 9/11 "Coordination" Problems; Did NASA Really Go to the Moon? by Mary Bennett and David Percy; Masonic Conspiracies in Spain and Latin America by Scott Corrales; That Which Has Fallen: Gods and Water by Boyd Rice; Myth of the Lost Years of Jesus by Acharya S; Planet X and the Dead Sea Scrolls by Andy Lloyd; Homeland Security More Than Meets the "Eye" by James John Bell; Chinese Guest Star of 1054 (Planet X?); and Al's scary Paranotes.

Issue 33: The Manson Family and the Beatles by Adam Gorightly; JFK and the Manchurian Candidate by John McLoughlin; The Reptilian Agenda for the New World Order: Interview with David Icke; Darwin and the Scientific Dictatorship by Phillip Darrell Collins; The Dragons of Eden by R. Boulay; The Hidden Face of Terrorism by Paul David Collins; Disney Influence in the Age of Knowledge Part II by Randy Koppang; A Funny Thing Happened on the Way to the Moon by Bart Winfield Sibrel; Silent Weapons for Quiet Wars; What Evil Is by John Paul Jones; Al Hidell's scary Paranotes.

Issue 34: Tolkien's Seven Stars: Planet X Symbology in the Tarot & The Lord of the Rings by Andy Lloyd; The SARS Virus: Bioterrorism and the Media by Dr. Alan Cantwell; Messages from Space: A Chronology of Anomalous Radio Signals by Joan d'Arc; The Supressed Teachings of Gnosticism: Robert Guffey Interviews Dr. Stephen Hoeller; Dead But Dreaming: Lovecraft's Cthulhu Reinterpreted as Sumerian/Atlantean Kings by Tracy Twyman; The Mormon Masonic Connection by Peter Farley; Saucers & Soldiers: The Amazon Scenerio Examined by Scott Corrales; The Montauk Project & Physics Run Amok by Alexandra Bruce; and Paranotes by Al Hidell.

Issue 36: Drugging America: Fast Tracking the Smallpox Plague by Lynne Born; Marian Apparitions: Between Religion and the Paranormal by Scott Corrales; The Mass Psychology of Fascism in the United States by Robert Guffey; The Propaganda Preparation for 9/11 by Chaim Kupferberg; The Van Dyke Letters II by Hartford Van Dyke; Lost in Translation: A Field Report on the 9/11 Commission Hearings by Len Bracken; Darwin and the Scientific Dictatorship: The War Against the Black Race by Phillip and Paul Collins; book reviews; Paranotes run amok.

Issue 39: Special All Girl Issue! Beef Without Borders by Ann N. Martin; The Illuminati and the

Auric Field by Beth Goobie; The Invisible Hand: Is the Price of Gold Being Suppressed? by Marilyn A. Guinnane; Travis Walton UFO Abduction by Joan d'Arc; The Minders: Interview with Melinda Leslie by Randy Koppang; The Chrononauts: An Interview w/ Jenny Randles by Joan d'Arc; The Magic and Mystery of America's Money by Tracy R. Twyman; book reviews!

Issue 40: China's Plan to Destroy America by Al Hidell; Wandering Planets by Scott Corrales; Psychologizing by Andrea Runyan; NASA Cover-up in Space by Joseph Gutheinz; The Four Horsemen of Oil by Dean Henderson; Hartford Van Dyke and the Pearl Harbor Story by Joan d'Arc; The Alien is Under Construction by Colin Bennett; A Neo-Con Counter-Conspiracy by Will Banyan; The Underground Mystery of the Dero by Jack Grimes; Alien Medical Interview by Dr. Roger Leir; Paranotes.

Issue 41: Secret History of NASA's Close Encounters by David Wolin; The Threat of Fundamentalism by Andy Lloyd; Myths and Truths of the Knights Templar by Chevalier William Vandry; The Intelligent Design Revolution by Joan d'Arc; The Lady of Fatima by Dail R. Cantrell; U.S. Babylon by Mark Westion; NASA's Plutonium Gamble by Joseph R. Gutheinz; Jr.; Kabbalah of the Cryptocracy by Craig Heimbichner; Baphomet and the Temple Fortune by Tracy R. Twyman; Taxes and the Crown by Mark Owen; wicked good Paranotes and book reviews.

Issue 42: Secret of Subliminal Advertising by August Bullock; Meteorite Mythos and Esoteric Knowledge by Lisa Agnew; Big Oil and the Wall Street-Russian Mafia Connexion by Dean Henderson; Man-Made Origin of AIDS by Alan Cantwell M.D.; Interview with Texe Marrs by Devin LaRue; The Pharmacratic Inquisition by Jan Irvin and Andrew Rutajit; Are We Conspiracy Geeks? Interview by Joan d'Arc; Wayne Madsen: The Man and the New Media by Len Bracken; Strawman and the Commerce Game by Mary Croft; Animals, the Oversoul and Predicting Catastrophes by Barry Warmkessel; Paranotes of course!

Issue 43: Your Life as an Atom: the Codex Alimentarius by Steven Ferry; America's Disinformation Factory by Wayne Madsen; Sinister Forces and Political Witchcraft: Jaye Beldo interviews Peter Levenda; Manson Family Secrets by Adam Gorightly; Decoding the Zodiac Killer by Curt Rowlett; The Idiot's Guide to the Cryptocracy by Craig Heimbichner; The Queen's Death Star: Depleted Uranium in the Atmosphere by Leuren Moret; Planting the Seeds of Hatred in the Arab-Israeli Conflict by Joel Bainerman; The Politics of Consciousness by Kathy Kasten; Paranotes!

Issue 44: The Invisible Residents of Ivan Sanderson by David Hatcher Childress; The Israel Lobby by Will Banyan; Terror at Thames House by Tracy Twyman; Blinded by the DMT Light by Iona Miller; Agent Orange in New Orleans by Jane Crown; Finnegans Wake!: Joan d'Arc Interviews Bob Dobbs; Magical Mystery Tour by James Shelby Downard; Paranoids: Alchemists at Armageddon by Aeolus Kephas; Devin LaRue Interviews Jim Marrs; America Attacks Itself by Don Grabau; Toxic Brain on Aspartame: Jaye Beldo Interviews Cori Brackett; get yer Paranotes!

Issue 45: Lee Harvey Oswald: Fortean Man by Colin Bennett; The Kennedy Assassination and the Current Political Moment by Joan Mellen; Cancer, Sex and the HPV Vaccine by Alan Cantwell M.D.; The Poe Conspiracy by Steve Ahlquist; Geophysical Weapons of the Secret Government by Jerry E. Smith; Directed Energy Weapons and the World Trade Center by Len Bracken; A Semi-Detached Ayatollah: The (Rather Odd) Face of Radical Islam in the Pre-9/11 World by Jon Ronson; NASA's Astronuts by Joseph Richard Gutheinz; Jr.; The Gilgamesh Project: Forbidden Science and the Secret of Eternal Life by Andrew Sokar; The Poussin Code: Tale of Trigonometry and Treasure by Mary Alice Bennett; Ray Santilli's Alien Autopsy Video: Interview by Philip Mantle; Paranotes!

Issue 46: The Demons of Eden: Lydia Cacho Human Rights Activist by Scott Corrales; Covert Bio-Warfare Research and the JFK Assassination: Dr. Alan Cantwell Interviews Ed Haslam; Adam Gorightly's Pilgrimage to Conspiracy Con 7; A Cast of Characters: The Assassination of President Kennedy: Joan d'Arc Interviews Joan Mellen; Tom Bearden: Wizard of Zero Point by Iona Miller; The Cryptocracy's Greatest Hits by Craig Heimbichner; The Tangled Web Icke Weaves: Who is Behind David Icke's Freedom Foundation? by Will Banyan; The Revelation Will Not Be Televised: An ET Cover-up and its Mistaken Identity by Randy Koppang; The Kabbalah Unmasked: The Eschatology of Solomon's Seal by John Paul Jones; Persian Gulf Rent-A-Sheik by Dean Henderson; Strawman and

the False Concept of Authority by Mary Croft; Ghostly Pioneer Lady of Constable Jacks; Paranotes by Al Hidell!

Issue 47: The Janus Program by Beth Goobie; A Cast of Characters Part II Joan d'Arc Interviews Joan Mellen; Proof in the Stars - Betty and Barney Hill by Stanton T. Friedman; Tuesday Weld's Psychedelic Illuminati Conspiracy by Douglas Hawes and Adam Gorightly; Five Real Monsters You Should Be Afraid Of by Matthew J. Pellowski; Mothman: The Angel of Conspiracy by Andrew Colvin; The Power of Paranoid Awareness: Mark Westion Interviews Aeolus Kephas; Christianity: Turning Jesus into a Prude by Robert R. Arthur; The Cryptocracy's Greatest Hits Part II: Death on the Installment Plan by Craig Heimbichner; Top Secret Tourism: Area 51 by Harry Helms; The Star of the Magi: Science; Religion and Other Strange Bedfellows by Courtney Roberts; scary Paranotes!

Issue 48: Invisible Denizens of the Borderland by Trevor James Constable; Interview with Dr. Jesse Marcel Jr. by Phillip Mantle; The Russian "Woodpecker" Beam by Philip Coppens; Planet X and 2012 by Andy Lloyd; Nixon, Kissinger and the New World Order by Will Banyan; Rev. Wright Was Right about AIDS by Alan Cantwell; Return of the Empire by Jack Grimes; Whitley Strieber and Mind Control by Aeolus Kephas; Wall Street Mafia by Paul Collins; Nine Stages of American Autogenocide by Martha Rose Crow; Interview with Wayne Madsen by Len Bracken; Interview with David Worcester Channeler of Cosmic Awareness by Bob Dobbs; Eros Magic and the Renaissance by Jaye Beldo; wicked good Paranotes!

Issue 49: The Protocols of Zion: Fact or Fiction? by Jack Grimes; The End of History and the Clash of Civilizations by Robert Guffey; The Ugly Truth About Petroleum Politics, Alternative Energy and Islamic Terror by David Grossack; WWII "New World Order" Plan Revealed by Al Hidell; Just Say Know to Your Neo-Controllers by Iona Miller; What Clay Shaw's Literary Life Reveals by Michael Snyder; The Lie is Different at Every Level: Joan d'Arc Interviews Mike Bara; Intentional Collapse and Takedown of the U.S.A. by Richard C. Cook; James Shelby Downard's Mystical War by Adam Gorightly; Memoirs of Stephanie Caruana on the Gemstone File - Interview by Joan d'Arc; Jumping Jack Flash: Springheel Jack's Latin Cousin by Scott Corrales; get your Paranotes here!

Issue 50: Gloucester Sorcery: Strange Swamp Tales of Cotton Mather by Steve Ahlquist; Black Sun Rising: Satanism and Exorcism in the Americas by Scott Corrales; Demystifying the Myth Called "Roswell" by Kathy Kasten; When the Truth is Found to be Lies by Frank Berube; Yes, We're Matricidal: Murdering Mother Earth by Jason Miller; The Code Killers: An Exposé of the Nuclear Industry by Ace Hoffman; Is Earth Becoming a Dune Planet? by Iona Miller; A Monetary Reformer's Interpretation of The Lord of the Rings by Richard C. Cook; Obama-Neptune Trance Formation in America by Francis D. Grabau; Inside Job: Everything you were never allowed to ask about 9/11: Interview with David Ray Griffin by Joan d'Arc; Sleepwalkers Awake! Steps to Creating a New Paradigm by Paul Tice; Al's excellent Paranotes.

Issue 51: King Horus and His Twelve Followers by D.M. Murdock (Acharya S.); The Choosing Ones: Joan d'Arc Interviews Canadian mind control survivor Beth Goobie; Sinkhole de Mayo: Mystery of a Famous Texas Sinkhole by Joe Gutheinz; Interview with a Capitalist Vampire by Jason Miller; The Mystery Man Behind the Docu-

mentary Evidence of Revision by Victor Thorn; Dracula in Britain by Philip Coppens; Two Guns-No Justice: Who Killed Bobby Kennedy? by Shane O'Sullivan; Constantine and the Spear of Destiny by Jerry Smith; The Invisible Currency of Fascism by Len Bracken; Paranotes by Al Hidell.

Special Issues

Paranoid Women Collect Their Thoughts, A special issue of *PARANOIA* (150 pages, 1996). Featuring: Judy Wall, Leah Haley, Eugenia Macer-Story, Jean Erhardt, Judy Bari, Mae Brussell, Cheryl Welsh, Joan d'Arc, and more anonymous paranoid women and fabulous artwork by Beam! $10.

HunterGatheress Journal, A Collection of Fiction and Non-Fiction from the Middle Stoned Age, Volume 1, edited by Joan d'Arc (144 pages, 2008). Featuring the women of The Paranoid Women Institute: Joan d'Arc, Iona Miller, Joan Mellen, Jane Crown, Tracy Twyman, Cori Brackett, Cheryl Welsh, Beth Goobie, Eugenia Macer-Story, Dr. Carolyn Dean. Also featuring Robert Guffey, Paul Laffoley, Phill Weber, Len Bracken, Alek K. Redfearn, James Quigley, and more. Available from PARANOIA for $10.

HunterGatheress Journal, A Collection of Fiction and Non-Fiction from the Middle Stoned Age, Volume 2, edited by Joan d'Arc (144 pages, 2009). Featuring: Joan d'Arc, Acharya S, Courtney Roberts, Bob Dobbs, Remy C, Randy Koppang, Scott Corrales, Ken Ratcliffe, Paul Laffoley, Guy Benoit, Iona Miller, Beth Goobie, Doug Crill, Jonathan Thomas, David Morrow, Phill Weber, James Quigley, Mark Elliott, and artwork by various artists. Available from PARANOIA for $10.

PARANOIA: The Conspiracy Reader, Volume 1 (April 2010). The book you are now holding in your hands. Order one for a friend! Philip Coppens on 2012, Iona Miller on Tavistock, Astrotheology according to Acharya S, Lovecraft and the Necronomicon, Craig Heimbichner on the OTO, Robert Guffey on Albert Pike, Michael Cremo on Forbidden Archeology, The Reabductions of Melinda Leslie, Eustace Mullins at 86, RAND and UFOs, Who Murdered Robin Hood?, Is the Virgin Mary appearing in Alabama?, New JFK Witness Revealed, David Ray Griffin Interview, Round II, The Apollo Hoax!, and Paranotes by Al Hidell! Available from PARANOIA for $17 ($14 + $3 shipping).

Breinigsville, PA USA
03 March 2010
233301BV00003B/2/P

9 780615 299952